JOHN SPELLMAN

Politics Never Broke His Heart

JOHN C. HUGHES

THE WASHINGTON STATE
HERITAGE CENTER

LEGACY PROJECT

This is one in a series of biographies and oral histories published by the Washington State Legacy Project. Other history-makers profiled by the project include former Governor Booth Gardner; former U.S. Senator Slade Gorton; Northwest Indian Fisheries leader Billy Frank Jr; former State Senate Majority Leader Sid Snyder; former Congresswoman Jennifer Dunn; former first lady Nancy Evans; astronaut Bonnie Dunbar; Bremerton civil rights activist Lillian Walker; former Chief Justice Robert F. Utter; former Justice Charles Z. Smith; trailblazing political reporter Adele Ferguson; federal Judge Carolyn Dimmick; and Nirvana co-founder Krist Novoselic. For more information on the Legacy Project go to www.sos.wa.gov/legacyproject/

Also by John C. Hughes
Nancy Evans, First-Rate First Lady
The Inimitable Adele Ferguson
Lillian Walker, Washington State Civil Rights Pioneer
Booth Who? A Biography of Booth Gardner
Slade Gorton, a Half Century in Politics

For Sam Reed, who gave me the job of my life,
and Drs. Ken Hunt, Juris Macs and Jim Lechner, who saved it

Paula —

Those were the days my friend. Thanks for being an important part of them.

[signature]

The governor-elect leads the family in a chorus of "When Irish Eyes Are Smiling."

CONTENTS

CONTENTS

A Paradoxical Politician

"Who was Washington's last Republican governor?"

John D. Spellman is tired of being the answer to a trivia question. It's as if he hasn't done anything since 1984 when he lost to the charismatic Booth Gardner after one bumpy term. Or, for that matter, it's as if he didn't do anything before he was elected governor in 1980. When I told a long-time Democratic campaign consultant I was writing Spellman's biography, he said, *"Why?"*

Consider this: But for John Spellman, an oil pipeline with a capacity of a million barrels a day could be snaking along the bottom of Puget Sound. Rejecting Northern Tier's pipeline application in 1982 in the face of a full court press by the Reagan Administration was "monumental," says Tom Bancroft, executive director of People for Puget Sound. "An oil spill in Puget Sound from a pipeline could be absolutely devastating. It could mean the demise of the killer whale, of salmon stocks, of recreation and the livelihoods of hundreds of thousands."[1]

Moreover, during 14 eventful years at the King County Courthouse, Spellman swept out a rat's nest of patronage and palm-greasing to create a modern government. "John was the George Washington of King County" after the voters approved a home-rule charter in 1968, says Dow Constantine, who was elected county executive in 2009.[2]

Spellman promoted racial equality, criminal justice reforms, land-use planning and farmlands preservation. He persevered at every turn to build a landmark domed stadium, the Kingdome, and helped secure the sports franchises that made Seattle a big-league town. Former state treasurer Dan Grimm, a Democrat who sparred with Spellman when he was in the Legislature, disagrees with using public funds to finance sports stadiums. "But the ones we have now and those yet to be built in generations to come" owe their existence to Spellman. "The Kingdome was nothing more than the initial incarnation of what he achieved," says Grimm. "Justice dictates every major stadium in King County should have 'Spellman' in its name. There oughta be a law." [3]

These things are important to remember, not just for the sake of history and fairness but because there are lessons to be learned from opportunities missed and mistakes made. "A lot of the challenges haven't changed all that much," Constantine says. [4] And in Olympia, nearly 30 years on, the governor and Legislature are still struggling with cutting and taxing and their "paramount" constitutional duty to amply fund the public schools.

I THOUGHT, going in, that this would be an easier story to tell because I had already written Booth Gardner's biography. I soon discovered that Spellman's life story—86 years at this writing—is also the story of King County's bumpy road to maturity, if that's the right word. He was born in the last week of 1926, the grandson of Northwest pioneers. He has fleeting memories of the halcyon days before the Depression when Seattle spit in the eye of Prohibition, thrilled to college football and built grand hotels. Spellman saw the "Hooverville" down by the tracks where the homeless huddled during the darkest days of the Depression. He watched sleek, silver B-17s leaving the Boeing factory and dropped out of high school to join first the Merchant Marines, then the Navy. He went to college on the GI Bill; studied for the priesthood and became a national moot court champion during law school. As a young Seattle attorney in the 1950s, he took up civil rights and union cases; joined the clean-government progressives and campaigned for "Forward Thrust" programs to clean up Lake Washington, build parks and improve transportation. He served on the Municipal Civil Service Commission and became one of the nation's most influential Roman Catholic laymen.

While Seattle put its best face forward during the 1962 World's Fair, its police force was rife with corruption. The prevailing attitude toward minorities owed more to Century 19 than Century 21. As a dark horse candidate for mayor, Spellman stood for open housing and an end to the "tolerance" policy that sanctioned vice. Elected county commissioner in 1966, he promoted a progressive new charter and became the first county executive in the state. He faced down 3,000 angry white construction workers who marched on the Courthouse to protest his push to give minorities access to apprenticeship programs.

Spellman led the county through the "Boeing Bust" of the 1970s when a famous billboard urged the last person leaving Seattle to turn out the lights. His tireless lobbying—and friendship with Senator Warren Magnuson—secured federal aid for the state. He and his wife spearheaded food banks and fundraisers. He played a key role in securing a half-cent local-option

Governor Spellman listens to a reporter's question in 1983. He said his administration "relies more on love than fear."

sales tax for hard-pressed counties and cities. As the only Washington governor to have served as a county commissioner, Spellman had a special understanding of local government problems.

He lost his first bid for governor to the inimitable Dixy Lee Ray in 1976, the year of the political outsider, and inherited a fiscal mess four years later when she was summarily rejected and he was elected. With the state facing what was then the worst downturn since the Depression, Spellman abandoned an expedient no-new-taxes pledge, went to war with diehard conservatives—he called them "Troglodytes"—and raised taxes by a billion dollars to avoid deeper cuts to education and social services. Read on and you can draw your own conclusions whether that was reckless or prudent. The conservatives called him a pseudo-Republican. The cartoonists portrayed him as "The Amazing Waffleman."

Congressman Denny Heck, who in 1982 was the Democrats' 31-year-old House majority leader, says this about the task Spellman faced right off the bat as governor: "Degree of difficulty off the charts."[5]

"BLANDNESS IN POLITICS can be a formidable political weapon," David Brewster, the perceptive Seattle journalist who covered Spellman's rise in

King County, observed optimistically in 1981 just before Spellman took office.[6] Voters tell pollsters they want competence and integrity; they say they're tired of all the shouting. But pizzazz still matters. Credibility, in the squirrely world of legislative politics, is a coefficient of moxie. The governor who loved to burst into song and play his Charlie Parker and Ella Fitzgerald albums as a guest deejay on NPR was curiously bad at schmoozing and arm-twisting. One critic christened him "Governor Dullman." George W. Scott, an historian who headed the Senate Ways and Means Committee during the most turbulent years of Spellman's term, calls him "The uncertain drummer."[7]

Spellman's muddled initial reaction to a ferry workers' strike undermined his credibility. When he balked at killing a Republican bill placing the ferry workers under Civil Service and went on to veto a raft of labor-backed legislation, he burned important bridges. Mixed messages obscured his achievements. "I don't think governors are supposed to make everybody happy," Spellman shrugged. "You don't get elected to get re-elected."[8]

Grimm was an up-and-coming legislator at the height of the 1981-83 budget battles. Negotiating with Spellman, he remembers, was "like a horse trader dealing with someone who doesn't know horses."[9] Sometimes the words Spellman plucked from his voluminous vocabulary seemed stilted. One drizzly winter's night when the revenue shortfall was a billion dollars, the leaders of all four legislative caucuses met with the governor. He sat there smoking his pipe, listening intently, nodding now and then, seeming to be more observer than participant. House Speaker Bill Polk, a conservative swashbuckler, grew disgusted and abruptly ended the meeting. As everyone was preparing to depart, Spellman said to everyone and no one in particular, "If I can be of any help as an interlocutor, please let me know." Polk stage-whispered, "What the (bleep) does that mean?"[10]

"They say I failed in dealing with the Legislature, but the truth is I got practically everything I wanted," Spellman retorts, conceding "it was a lot worse than I thought it would be."[11] (Gardner seconded the motion 90 days into his first term after he was dubbed "Prince Faintheart.")

Spellman opened the door to trade with China and boosted job creation statewide, especially in distressed counties. He created a Housing Finance Commission that allowed thousands to achieve the dream of home ownership. The Washington Environmental Council feted him as its Elected Official of the Year. The economy was recovering when Spellman stood for re-election in 1984, but he couldn't match Gardner's ebullience or bankroll, though the deepest wounds he suffered in that election were self-inflicted.

SPELLMAN ALWAYS SAID his management style relied "more on love than fear," yet he countenanced two campaigns that were landmarks in the use of attack advertising in Washington state politics.[12] The ads relied if not on fear, loathing. The first ones were decisive in electing him governor. His opponent was state Senator Jim McDermott, the doctor turned politician. Spellman's full-page ads in the Spokane papers asked, "Do you want a liberal Seattle psychiatrist running your state?" The same ad—minus one word: "Seattle"—ran in the Puget Sound papers. McDermott said it was appallingly divisive, "the politics of polarization," and a slam on a profession that has helped millions struggling with mental illness. Spellman says they were merely telling the truth: Jim McDermott is a liberal Seattle psychiatrist.

The second attack ad—actually an increasingly greasy series of three—sealed Spellman's defeat in 1984. Gardner had a huge lead after the primary. Spellman's strategists, desperate to close the gap, seized on an anything-you-want letter Gardner had written to union members. Spellman's ads depicted Gardner as the puppet of organized labor, with cigar-chomping "Big Labor Bosses" salivating over his letter. Spellman had misgivings about the ads but went along. It was the worst mistake of his political career, he says. "The ads were way over the top, and they negated everything I'd done over the previous 30 years as an ally of labor."

So, while politics never broke Spellman's heart, there were times when it bruised his conscience. He is an intensely spiritual man, a devout Irish Catholic, but also a fervent ecumenist who grieves over the ungodly things men do in God's name. As I pondered the portrait of Thomas More over the fireplace in the Spellmans' living room, I remarked mischievously that a new book reminds us that "The Man for all Seasons" coldly consigned at least six shrieking Lutherans to be burned at the stake. "Well," Spellman said with a wink of his own, "those were different times."

Some people who worked with Spellman for years keep telling me he's shy. One thing I know for certain is that he isn't. Granted, he's "not much of a hugger"—his words—but his reserve is the sense of modesty Jesuits inculcate at the seminary. Spellman loves his church and Lois Murphy, the strong-willed Democrat he married 59 years ago; he loves his six children and six grandchildren; his jazz record collection; well-bred dogs; steelhead streams on crisp mornings, and rainy days in front of the fireplace with a good book. He still goes to his law office several times a week and participates in several community betterment activities. Spellman offered ongoing support and advice to Governor Chris Gregoire on her staggering budget problems. She believes he is one of our most underappreciated governors.

From the 36th floor of a skyscraper overlooking Elliott Bay, Spellman can see the site of the plumbing company his stolid Irish grandfather established in the 1890s; the landmark Smith Tower where he practiced law as a young man; the county Courthouse, and the snazzy stadiums that succeeded his beloved utilitarian Kingdome.

"HOW ARE YOU DOING on the Spellman biography?" Peter Callaghan asked as I arrived for a panel on Washington State politics in the summer of 2012. Pete is a reporter and columnist for the *Tacoma News Tribune*. He has a knack for seeing things other reporters overlook and writing things others won't.

"Spellman did way more than we gave him credit for," I said. "All I really knew about his years as county executive was that he built the Kingdome. There's a compelling personality behind his mild-mannered exterior, but in 1984 when he was running for re-election and I was writing editorials, I never got much past his persona as a pipe-puffer."

"It's what we do," Callaghan said mordantly.

A headline in Brewster's *Seattle Weekly*, which offered the best coverage of the 1984 campaign, summed up what we were all saying: "How could such a decent and honorable man be such a disappointment as a governor?" [13]

John D. Spellman is a paradoxical politician. Yet the way we sized him up after his four fraught years as governor speaks volumes about journalism as the first rough draft of history. That's not so much a knock on journalism—first drafts are priceless—as it is evidence that history is not immutable.

Here's the sixth draft. Or maybe it's the seventh. I always lose count.

JOHN C. HUGHES
Olympia
January 2013

CHAPTER ONE

Matters of the Heart

When Irish eyes are smiling,
Sure, 'tis like the morn in spring.
In the lilt of Irish laughter
You can hear the angels sing.
When Irish hearts are happy,
All the world seems bright and gay.
And when Irish eyes are smiling,
Sure, they steal your heart away.

J ohn Dennis Spellman's honeymoon as Washington's 18th governor seemed to end about 30 seconds after he sang the last chorus of "When Irish Eyes are Smiling" at his inauguration in 1981. "Never run for public office," his father warned 30 years earlier. "Politics will break your heart." Spellman shared that story not long before his 86th birthday. "I never let politics break my heart," he said, leaning closer. "Politics is politics. Sometimes it's the best salesman who wins, but I have no regrets. I'm proud of what I did as governor. I did a lot before that too. Teddy Roosevelt talked about 'The man in the arena' trying to make a difference. I've never stopped trying to contribute." Then, as if to chide himself for not maintaining what the Jesuits call "the modesty of the eyes," he smiled semi-sheepishly. His hazel-green eyes are droopy-lidded but bright. His mind is still as agile as a cricket.

Spellman's ancestors include the Pilgrim deacon who chartered the *Mayflower.* But you must remember this: He's Irish-Catholic to the core. His Irish ambition propelled him into public service; his abiding faith sustained him through personal tragedy and political disappointments. Perseverance is in his gene pool. And he loves to sing. It's not just a parlor trick.

THE GOVERNOR'S great-grandfather, Bartholomew Spellman, almost 20, arrived in New York from County Roscommon in 1844 just before the potato blight decimated Ireland. Bridget Finney, the governor's great-grandmother, arrived soon thereafter. Back home, a million of their countrymen died of starvation. A million more fled in the squalor of steerage. Smug Anglicans clucked that Ireland was a nation of incorrigible slackers. "The Great Hunger," *an Gorta Mór*, surely must be "a righteous punishment from God on the Irish for their popery."[1] Even before the blight, poverty was endemic. Sixty percent of Ireland's 8.5 million souls lived in sod huts.

Around the same time as the Irish diaspora, the governor's Protestant ancestors, the Cushmans and Kirks, packed their wagons and set out along the Oregon Trail to the verdant Willamette Valley. The Spellmans were also on the move. His paternal grandfather, Dennis Bartholomew Spellman— "Denny" to practically everyone—arrived in Seattle from Minneapolis at the age of 26 in 1889, just before the fire that leveled much of the wood-frame frontier town. The youngest of seven children, Denny Spellman grew up on a farm in Wisconsin and apprenticed as a harness maker. By heading west, he hoped to become a plumber. He was also seeking a place with less prejudice. His parents had fled Boston for the same reason. "The American response to Irish Catholics was almost a mirror image of what had occurred in Britain. ... Both societies were based on a self-conscious Protestantism and on the aggressive anti-Catholicism that was central to it."[2] The West was the most ethnically and racially diverse region of the country. Though not as numerous as in other western cities, the Irish had a solid foothold in Seattle. They were among the first white settlers on Elliott Bay in 1851. It seemed like paradise. J.F. Costello, writing home to Ireland from the "far and distant shores of Paget [*sic*] Sound" in Washington Territory, declared that he was in "as good a country as there is in the world to day for a poor man. ...There are no Gentlemen here. If a farmer in Ireland made 3 or 4 thousand dollars in a Year you couldnt walk the road with them[.] You would have to go inside the fence or they would ride over you." On any given Sunday in his new home, Costello said, you could bring home a feast fit for a king. "Wild animals of all description abound here. And as for wild ducks they are as thick as the cows to home ...and nobody will ask where is your license. All you want is money enough to buy a gun."[3]

Denny Spellman took one look around and decided this was the place for him. He soon landed a job as a plumber's apprentice, equipping the new buildings sprouting up after the fire. By 1891 he had his own business. It grew as steadily as his waistline. A photo from the turn of the century shows him ensconced behind a giant rolltop desk, new oak-topped commodes arrayed behind him, in the offices of the D.B. Spellman Plumbing Company, 215 Columbia Street.

Denny Spellman, seated, in the offices of his plumbing company at 215 Columbia Street in Seattle around the turn of the century.

The Klondike gold rush of 1897 transformed Seattle into a city. Between 1890 and the turn of the century, its population nearly doubled to 81,000. By 1910 it was 237,000. Henry Broderick, a shrewd bon vivant who became one of Denny Spellman's best friends, made a fortune in real estate.

In 1892, Denny Spellman married Catherine McClory, another offspring of Irish immigrants. Their son, Sterling Bartholomew Spellman, Governor Spellman's father, was born in 1895. They called him "Bart." Grandpa Spellman by then was emerging as one of Seattle's most prosperous plumbers. He was also an artful dodger, somehow managing to be both an observant Roman Catholic and a member of the Masonic Lodge. Spellman supported the Republican Party but professed always to cast "an independent local ballot, voting for the candidate whom he considers best qualified for office." [4] In 1912, he backed Teddy Roosevelt, who bolted the GOP to run for president on the Progressive "Bull Moose" ticket.

The governor's father inherited his father's ambition, independent streak and powerful upper torso. Bart was a natural athlete, more interested in football than plumbing. In the years to come, the Oregon branch of the family would crow that the University of Washington passed up a chance to give a future star a scholarship. Football, to Bart Spellman, was not just a game.

ON NEW YEAR'S DAY 1917, Pasadena boasted a million roses and 27,000 football fans. The largest crowd ever assembled for a football game on the West Coast overflowed Tournament Park. The partisan crowd stood to roar, clanging cowbells when Oregon's 23-man squad took the field in lemon yellow jerseys. Denny Spellman was in the grandstands. His son, at 180 pounds and a tad under 6 feet, wasn't even big for a player in his day, but he was as strong as a bull and crafty. The senior right guard from Seattle was also fast. They called him "Speed Spellman."

Bart had spent two weeks in the hospital with appendicitis in the summer of '16. By fall, however, he was as tenacious as ever, opening gaping holes for Oregon's multi-talented quarterback, Charles "Shy" Huntington.[5] Coach Hugo Bezdek's undefeated Oregon team had outscored its regular-season opponents 230-16. Still, the University of Pennsylvania was the overwhelming favorite in Pasadena. The Ivy League champions had three All-Americans.[6]

The 1917 Rose Bowl was scoreless for nearly three quarters before Oregon began to outplay the Quakers at their own game—end runs and forward passes. Spellman played the entire game with a sore shoulder that turned out to be broken.[7] "A half-crazed mob" descended on the coaches and players when the game ended, 14-0.[8] Back in Eugene, where bulletins were announced by megaphone and each play replicated on a miniature gridiron in a downtown theater, cheering crowds swarmed the streets.[9] Oregon's victory elevated West Coast football to national prominence.

Forty years later, Bart Spellman's lawyer son John was at The Dalles, Oregon, representing the Steel Workers against Harvey Aluminum. "It was a big, notoriously anti-union company," John says. "They had a preliminary injunction against the workers for picketing their plant. I arrived at court not knowing a soul."

John introduced himself to the bailiff.

"Is your father Bart Spellman?"

"Yes."

"Did he play football with Shy Huntington?"

"Yes."

"Shy is from here."

They talked football.

It was a good day. The judge lifted the injunction.

WHEN THE U.S. entered World War I in the spring of 1917, Bart Spellman and several teammates left college to join the armed forces. Bart won his pilot's wings—Jimmy Doolittle was a flight school classmate—yet war's end found him still cooling his heels as an instructor in Texas. He consoled

SPELLMAN FAMILY ALBUM

Lela Cushman, the governor's mother, as a coed at the University of Oregon.

himself by exchanging letters with a pretty girl he'd met on campus. Lela Cushman, an education major from Brownsville, Oregon, had a delicate mouth, lovely complexion and dancer's body.[10]

Bart returned to Eugene in 1919. Shy Huntington was now head football coach. He named Bart as his principal assistant, charged with tutoring the linemen. Spellman proved to be an exceptional coach, but he had a temper. When he lost it, you wanted to steer clear. Shy's problem was a lead foot. When he appeared in Police Court to pay a $25 speeding ticket, with Bart in tow, Spellman proceeded to "roast and abuse" the cops and court recorder. Didn't they know Huntington was the hero of the 1917 Rose Bowl? Unimpressed, the judge slapped Spellman with a $10 fine for disorderly conduct. He was mortified when the story made the paper.[11]

Huntington and Spellman led their alma mater back to Pasadena in 1920, dropping a 7-6 heartbreaker to Harvard. Spellman was gaining a reputation as one of the best line coaches in America. In those days, however, being an assistant coach wasn't a full-time job. It was increasingly difficult for him to live part of the year in Eugene and part of the year in Seattle where he had embarked on a career in banking, real estate and insurance. Bart in the beginning worked with his friend Joe Gottstein, a go-getter who'd been a line coach at Brown University. Gottstein's father came to Seattle from Russia in 1879 and built the largest liquor distributorship in the Northwest. Every ounce his father's son, Joe was branching out even before the advent of Prohibition in Washington State in 1916. He steered

SPELLMAN FAMILY ALBUM

Bart Spellman as an aviation cadet during World War I.

a lot of his real estate clients to the D.B. Spellman Plumbing Company. Over the years, Gottstein "proved again and again his knack for correctly reading the Seattle marketplace."[12] He loved deal-making, college football and Thoroughbreds. Longacres near Renton, in its day one of the finest horse-racing tracks in America, was his baby. Bart Spellman was often in the owner's box.

Henry Broderick, the Irish version of Joe Gottstein, was another Spellman family friend. When Broderick arrived from Minneapolis in 1901, Bart's father was one of the first people he met. Besides their ethnicity and religion, they had Minnesota in common. They became good friends. Both enjoyed Gottstein's company and abhorred anti-Semitism. Broderick was impressed with Bart. He was a man of parts.

BESIDES BEING SMART, ambitious and well connected, Spellman was in love. On December 27, 1921, he married Lela, who was teaching school at Stevenson along the Columbia. The rites were conducted at St. Mary's Cathedral of the Immaculate Conception in Portland, the bride agreeing that their children would be raised in the church. It was a bittersweet occasion. Lela's father had died just two weeks before. The "mixed" marriage raised some eyebrows in the Cushmans' circle of friends. But Lela's mother—America Kirk Cushman, "Mec" to family and friends—was an intelligent, forceful woman who liked Bart. Her husband had too.[13]

Bart turned down several opportunities to become a head coach. Growing business responsibilities in Seattle and his father's death at the age of 61 prompted him to resign from the Oregon coaching staff in the winter of 1925. The backstory was revealed three weeks later: Spellman was coming to the University of Washington. Under a banner headline, George M. Varnell, the sports editor of *The Seattle Times*, reported that UW Coach Enoch Bagshaw had wooed and won Bart Spellman with a sweetheart contract that "would not necessitate his being away from Seattle except for short periods during the fall." Spellman's job was to study scouting reports and brief the "supervarsity" on plays sure to be sprung on Washington in big games.[14]

Dubbed the "Purple Tornado" by sports writers, UW teams made two trips to the Rose Bowl over the next five years.[15] Bart's boys included three notable future politicians whose careers would intersect with his son's. One was Charles O. "Chuck" Carroll, a multiple threat All-American in the late 1920s who went on to become Mr. Republican in King County. Four decades later he recruited John Spellman to run for county commissioner and would rue the day. He thought he was getting someone who would go along to get along. Knowing the father, he should have known

University of Washington Athletic Staff 1926.

The University of Washington athletic staff in 1926, the year John Spellman was born. Bart Spellman is third from left in the front row. Other legendary Huskies in the group are Enoch Bagshaw, head football coach, far left, front row; R.C. "Torchy" Torrance, assistant graduate manager, fourth from left, front row; D.V. "Tubby" Graves, head baseball coach, far left, back row, and C.S. "Hec" Edmundson, head basketball coach, fourth from left, back row.

better about the son.[16]

Starring in the backfield for the 1930 team was "Cowboy" Johnny Cherberg, another future member of the Husky Hall of Fame. Cherberg found his niche in politics after he was fired as head coach in the mid-1950s. He served as lieutenant governor for 32 years, a tenure that spanned five governors, including the line coach's kid.[17]

It was a walk-on who became Coach Spellman's most famous former pupil. Warren G. Magnuson was a lithe 5-9 scrapper, whip smart and movie-star handsome. During high school in Minnesota, he was a standout quarterback dubbed "Gritty Maggie" when he refused to come out of a game after injuring an ankle.[18] Bagshaw and Spellman doubted Magnuson was big enough to play major-college ball, but they liked his spunk. Bagshaw finagled a job for Magnuson delivering ice—a union job no less—to help him pay for school. The ice came in handy after practice. "I was on the scrub team and we used to go to the stadium every night and let the varsity and the stars run all over us in order that they might get in shape for the enemy," Magnuson recalled years later when he was one of the most powerful members of the U.S. Senate. "Jesus, they would slam us around! There was no grass, just dirt, and when the rain soaked the field long enough, when it dried it was like cement. I made the squad, though, and I got to play two minutes in the Rose Bowl."[19] Magnuson became an important mentor to Bart Spellman's two sons.[20]

MARY CATHERINE SPELLMAN, Bart and Lela's firstborn, arrived in 1924, David Bartholomew Spellman 15 months later. John Dennis Spellman was born on December 29, 1926, and made his first appearance in print a few days later. A box plopped in the middle of the sports section of *The Seattle Times* had this to say:

JOHN D. SPELLMAN
TO SHOW 'EM HOW

DID you ever hear of John Dennis Spellman?

No; and very few others in this world have, either.

But in September, 1947, the whole world will hear about him if his dad; one Bart Spellman, assistant coach of the University of Washington, is to be believed.

John Dennis; who arrived last Wednesday morning, weighed nine and one half pounds; a perfect foundation for a good fast running guard, his dad declares further.

"He'll show 'em a thing or two," is Father Spellman's further word.

It was a lot to live up to.

CHAPTER TWO

Growing Up

Lela Spellman was busy fixing lunch. She turned her back to the stove for a few seconds. Johnny toddled over and on tippy toes reached for the handle of the pan on the front burner. He let out a horrifying wail as the boiling water splashed over his head and shoulders. Don Palmer, the UW team doctor, hurried to the Spellman home and slathered the sobbing child's scalded skin with paraffin. The only scar that remained 84 years later was a small splotch on Spellman's right bicep. "I remember nothing, thank God, because it must have been intensely painful." Some memories from his early childhood are vivid. Knute Rockne, the legendary Notre Dame coach, died in a plane crash when Spellman was 4. "I can remember exactly where I was in the house when we heard the news." That's how important college football was in the Spellman home.

Seattle in the 1920s was a growing city of 365,000, basking in the boom before the gloom of the Depression. Major new buildings sprang up downtown where Bart was now the insurance manager for Henry Broderick Inc., one of the city's largest real estate and mortgage brokers. A community bond sale financed construction of the grand Olympic Hotel, christened in 1924 with a gala party that drew 2,000, including Bart and Lela Spellman. Future lieutenant governor Victor Aloysius Meyers' dance band could be heard six nights out of seven in a lower-rent rendezvous, the Rose Room of the Butler Hotel at 114 James Street. From the tony Rainier Club, where Broderick's friend Bill Boeing sipped his highballs, to blue-collar joints and living rooms humble and grand, Seattle snorted at Prohibition. Palms were greased from City Hall to the precinct house. Raids by federal agents "did little to slow the river of hooch gushing southward via land and sea."[1] A cop-turned-rumrunner became a legend in his own time.

Seattle underwent a temporary housecleaning by the first female mayor of a major American city, the redoubtable Bertha Knight Landes. October of 1929 put a damper on the backsliding as reverberations from the Stock

Market crash soon hit most of the Pacific Northwest. The Port of Seattle saw three-quarters of its cargo revenue evaporate; homebuilding dropped to zero; banks failed. A bedraggled village of tarpaper and scrap-lumber shanties sprang up south of Pioneer Square, about where the Seahawks and Mariners play today. Spellman and his sister Mary remember driving by "Hooverville" with their father. Bart wanted his children to see it. The message was clear: Dad still had a job. They should count their blessings, work hard in school and remember the Golden Rule.[2] The children were fascinated by their father's boss, for Henry Broderick was a remarkable character. In 1915, he sold a hotel to Mother Cabrini so she could start a hospital, accepting Rosary beads in lieu of a commission.[3]

BETWEEN UW faculty events and the socializing related to Bart's work downtown, plus her job as mother to three young kids, Lela Spellman grew frazzled. Her widowed mother-in-law, afflicted with arthritis, lived with the young family. Lela nearly had a nervous breakdown. She told Bart she'd had enough of the city. It was "the partying, the smoking, the drinking," John says. His father also came to view the social scene as a slippery slope. Bart was paranoid about the caliber of his children's friends, worrying that they might take up drinking or gambling.

In 1934, when John was 7½, the Spellmans moved from upscale Broadmoor to Hunts Point, a bucolic finger of land between Fairweather Bay and Cozy Cove on the east side of Lake Washington. Over the hill a few miles south, Bellevue was little more than a village surrounded by strawberry fields.

In the days before the first floating bridge transformed the East Side, a round trip ferry ticket to Seattle was 25 cents for foot passengers. Motorists could buy a five-trip commuter ticket for $1.25. A sign that said "When foggy please ring gong" was tacked to a

SPELLMAN FAMILY ALBUM

John, left, and David Spellman around 1931.

post at the Medina dock where the Spellman kids boarded the *Ariel*, a tired little boat that chugged from dock to dock.[4]

"My mother never had another sick day after we moved to Hunts Point," Spellman says. That's not quite so, according to his sister. Being two years older, and female, gave Mary a different perspective. Their parents were close, she says, but Lela's nerves were often frayed because the dynamics of the household were tricky. Bart maintained he was tough on the boys "for their own good" and had dark moods. Mother was "the nurturing, loving one in the family," fundamentally a down-to-earth farm girl. The children cherished their summertime visits to Grandma Cushman's place in Oregon. She was up by 5 to fix breakfast for the hired hands.

Though Lela Spellman never returned to the classroom, she was always a teacher. "She read to us at night—*every* night," John remembers, eyes brightening. There were family stories about their ancestors, including great-grandpa David Crockett Cushman and his wife Maggie. At 2, legend had it, Maggie was sucked out of her Kansas home by a tornado and plopped down unharmed two miles away. There were books about the Pilgrims, cowboys and Indians, and classics like Charles Dickens' *Nicholas Nickleby* and *David Copperfield*. "I was the youngest, so some of it went right over my head, but she believed in oral presentation and made the stories come alive."

Lela Spellman was more faithful about Mass than her cradle Catholic husband, taking pains to ensure her children were steeped in their faith. The nuns came over from Seattle every Sunday to teach the Baltimore Catechism. Lela was confirmed by the archbishop at the same time as John and set the standard for the piety that has been a large part of his life. Bart had a short fuse with officious priests. When one complained about the high cost of living and remarked that his shoes cost $125, Bart was scandalized. Lela had a falling out with the same priest over something to do with the Ladies' Altar Society and told him off in a letter. "Mother would have been a good women's libber," Mary Spellman says. "She really stood up for people's rights, which wasn't easy in those days."

Bart was a busy man, what with business, coaching and overseeing the judges for Golden Gloves boxing matches. He was also active in the Seattle Kennel Club. The Spellman kids met all the coaches and most of Seattle's bigwigs. They were nuts about sports, but Bart discouraged the boys—John in particular—from taking football too seriously. The fractures and sprains Bart had suffered took their toll as he grew older. He was 30 pounds heavier than in his playing days, though never fat. His business suits were impeccable. The real Bart Spellman was "a very bookish, private sort of man,"

SPELLMAN FAMILY ALBUM

John, David and Mary Spellman around 1940.

according to John. "When he went into something it was always all the way. He'd get interested in the Civil War and read three dozen books on the subject. He took up the subject of time, and the house was suddenly full of clocks. Then it was magic, and he acquired every book in the world on the subject. He had universal interests. For a shy man, he could charm any group." [5]

THE SPELLMAN KIDS were unmistakably Irish. Mary looked like a Bridget. John was the image of his father, except with a gentler smile. When he's feeling mischievous, it curls at the corners, leprechaun-like. David was strikingly handsome, with an elegant nose. He had a special relationship with Bart. Mary was a lovely girl, taking after her mother when it came to nurturing and objectivity. John understood instinctively that he was the number two son, but says he never felt ignored or jealous. Quite the contrary. He loved and admired his big brother, respected their father and adored his mother and sister. That David was better at sports made John more determined. When they moved to Hunts Point, he taught himself to swim, secretly slipping into the water near the pier to practice. He held his breath, kicked his feet and moved his arms around until he got the hang of it. He became a strong swimmer. "It was a great personal victory," he said with a satisfied smile 75 years after his accomplishment. The relationship between David and John Spellman, two bright Irish-Catholic boys with a successful, demanding father, was similar to that of Joseph P. Kennedy Jr. and his brother Jack.

"My brother was the natural athlete," John says. "I wasn't bad, but I wasn't good. I beat him at some things, though. He was a little bigger than I was but if I got really mad I could pin him. He was a very good student; better than I was. He was smarter, too." If so, John's intellect was more encyclopedic, their sister says. From an early age he amused his family and friends with his cartoons. "He loved to compile scrapbooks and did one on the top jockey at Longacres. John knew a lot about music. He closely followed politics. We went to hear Thomas Dewey, the young Republican who was running for president. John became very interested in things. David wasn't like that."

Hunts Point was a wonderful place to be a boy. The 13 members of Boy Scout Troop 430, including the Spellman brothers, could practice their crafts and pitch their tents in their own neighborhood. Adventures abounded. The hunt for a pesky beaver gnawing docks and trees was the talk of the lake. It was "as big as an Airedale" and had a pair of buck teeth like hedge shears, locals told a reporter *The Seattle Times* sent across the lake to investigate the hubbub. "Mrs. Von Norman couldn't figure out what was happening to her weeping willow trees," young John Spellman explained—his first recorded quote. "One day they'd be there. The next morning they'd be gone. When she found out about the beaver she sure was sore. Nobody ever gets close to him. He doesn't give a whoop about dogs—there are 87 of them on the point. ... When they swim after him, he dives." Spellman's pal, Ed Parker, 14, "gazed longingly at the stump of an alder and said: 'If I had teeth like that, I wouldn't be going to the dentist this afternoon.' " [6]

David and John attended the three-room Bay School through sixth grade. John had a knack for drawing and illustrating. He was a good talker, too, winning most arguments and arbitrating squabbles. Bart didn't want his children spoiled by mowing lawns or running errands for their prosperous neighbors. The boys picked berries and sorted flower bulbs for pennies when they weren't doing chores around the house and property. David "resented it terribly" when Bart had them doing hard work on weekends, according to his siblings.

Most of the painstakingly cultivated berry farms and greenhouses on the East Side were owned by Japanese. The Yabuki family greenhouses at Hunts Point were among the largest. When the Bay School principal made disparaging remarks about Asian students, the Spellman kids were shocked. "We weren't raised that way," Mary Spellman says. "John took everyone under his wing." They remember the day he arrived home from school with a Japanese friend in tow. Their mother was having a bridge party. Some of the ladies put down their tea cups and raised an eyebrow. Not Lela. When the Japanese were sent to internment camps the Spellmans were saddened.

One of John's classmates at the Bay School was Frank Messenger, who became a naval officer before a career as a telephone company engineer. "My family were the dirty Democrats in the neighborhood and his were the Republicans," Messenger said. He recalled lively political arguments with John as early as fifth grade. David was "the straight one." John was "a prankster, the loose one." When John was running for governor, *Time* magazine described him as "colorless." That didn't square with the boy Messenger knew. John was capable of withering put-downs when confronted by stupidity. During a recess baseball game one day, their teacher was pitching. "He was an exuberant jock and John was a little more frail than your ordinary kid." After lobbing three fastballs right down the middle, the teacher crowed, "Well, Spellman, sit down. You struck out again." John leaned on his bat for a moment before hitting a verbal home run: "Big deal; 39-year-old strong man strikes out 11-year-old boy." [7]

Like his father, John had a talent for working with animals. He helped train Bart's prize Chesapeake Bay and Labrador Retrievers. He watched over premature pups, rescued a cat from a pond of diesel oil and nursed other ailing critters. (When John was governor, a reporter looked on with awe as a whimpering dog stayed gentle in his hands as he removed a BB pellet from its nose.)

At Junior High at Kirkland, John was elected class president. He was also a self-described "goof-off" and gifted mimic. His parents—Bart in particular—felt he needed the discipline and academic rigor of a parochial school, so he commuted to St. Joseph's in Seattle for eighth grade before entering Seattle Prep. John decided his class needed its own newspaper, so he became editor, reporter and cartoonist for a sheet he dubbed *What One Sees,* assembling a small stable of contributors. They cranked it out weekly on a mimeograph machine. His publishing career was nipped in the bud by the principal after a teacher he parodied in a cartoon was indignant. "They were defamatory," Spellman admits with a sheepish grin.

The popular boy some called "Spelly" had a pleasing tenor, sang in the choir and dabbled at the accordion and piano. He loved the big bands and became a jazz aficionado. His record collection was carefully indexed. The radio was always on as he studied. He played freshman football, but was better at boxing. One bout left him with a permanent souvenir—a ski-jump nose. The girls thought he was good looking and a bit mysterious.

"If he really wanted to work, he could have been a

straight-A student," one of his teachers recalled. But he never settled for a "B" in debate. He was always well prepared and tenacious. "John had an ability to let you know when he was disgusted," a former opponent said. "He'd lace his rebuttals with sarcasm. And he had this look in his eye and a twist to his smile."[8] Philip S. Land, a Jesuit with a passion for social justice, helped him polish his style. He had John recite the Gettysburg Address. "I was impressed that Lincoln was able to say so much in so few words. Father Phil gave me lots of material on discrimination, and I wrote a speech about the evil of Jim Crow laws. It was not well received in tournaments in Seattle or at other schools but it helped shape my attitudes as a lawyer and my actions when I became an elected official."[*] John won the gold medal at one tournament with a speech defending George S. Patton after the flamboyant general slapped a GI being treated for battle fatigue. One of Spellman's most formidable Jesuit-school debate opponents was a lanky kid from Gonzaga Prep in Spokane. Tom Foley was destined to become Speaker of the U.S. House.

John's academic frustrations revolved around math. An emergency appendectomy, followed by complications, caused him to miss weeks of school, including introduction to algebra. He never caught up and invented his own system, "which is ultimately accurate but slow." His scores on scholastic aptitude tests were so high, however, that counselors and his father gave him a hard time for under-achieving and not following in his brother's footsteps.

John and his father had house-clearing arguments. Bart had a temper—"Oh Lord, horrible," Mary says—but he never laid a hand on John. "I think he was afraid he was going to hurt me," John says. "I shouldn't have irritated him the way I did. I think he was worried about me and trying to keep me in check. I was the one who got in trouble. Nothing like stealing or being dishonest, but after awhile I was running with a crowd that drank. That really worried him. At one point he was convinced I was going to end up an alcoholic." Mary recalls a similar incident. Home from college one summer, she returned from an evening on the town with friends to find a book on her bedspread. It was a cautionary tale about drinking. "It was just Daddy letting me know I had to be careful. He was a teetotaler toward the end of his life. He had oodles of liquor around the house (for guests), but he just wouldn't drink anymore."

Bart Spellman jumps out of scrapbooks and yellowed clippings as a case

---

[*] Land went on to become an influential voice for human rights, working in Rome and Washington, D.C. He and Spellman stayed in touch over the years.

study in early 20th Century manliness. The
son of a workaholic who shipped him off
to prep school in Portland, his pluck and
intelligence made him a football hero and
opened the door to success. He was ob-
sessed with inculcating self-discipline and
drive in his sons and protecting his wife
and daughter. "David really was just the
apple of his eye," Mary remembers. "David
was an exceptional person, but different
from John, who is so kind and so dear and
always has been. Yet Daddy was worried
about him drinking or gambling. John was
never really wild. He just wanted to have
fun and be his own person." Whenever
her brothers were at odds with their father
they would go down by the lake and toss a
football back and forth.

ON THE DAY AFTER Pearl Harbor, Bart
and the kids were headed for work and
school in the city. As they approached the
new Lake Washington floating bridge,
Bart abruptly took an exit. "We don't know
what's going to happen," he said solemnly.
There was widespread fear of a Japanese
invasion. Strategists believed the beaches
north and south of Grays Harbor on the

David, top, at West Point; John in
the Navy during World War II.

coast were ripe for amphibious landings. Boeing's Seattle factories were
soon swarming with workers and producing bombers around the clock.
The Bremerton naval shipyard sprouted barrage balloons to deter low-flying
enemy aircraft. Bart packed Mary off to college in Omaha and encouraged
David to work toward admission to the U.S. Military Academy. "You're probably going to be in this war before it's over," he told John, about to turn 15.

While Spellman conceded that Warren Magnuson was "pretty damn
liberal," they were great friends. Bart campaigned energetically for Maggie
in his 1936 bid for Congress, raising money, calling in favors. They celebrated all night at the Olympic after Magnuson won handily, buoyed by
another Roosevelt landslide. In 1943, after David Spellman graduated from
Seattle Prep with honors, he was off to West Point, appointed by Magnuson.

March, 2013

Thank you for your sponsorship of this wonderful biography of Governor John Spellman.

Your complimentary copy of the book is enclosed.

We are very grateful to the more than 85 friends of Governor Spellman who totally contributed $25,000 to fund the book and to help the Legacy Project.

At the book release event on February 22, attended by more than 130 people, Secretary of State Kim Wyman made these comments:

"John Spellman is a rarity in Washington politics - the first county commissioner and first county executive to be elected governor. This book captures not only John's rise through local politics to

The Legacy Project, a program of the Washington State Office of the Secretary of State, is proud to present this, our tenth printed book, as part of our series on Washingtonians who have made an important difference in our state. All our books are printed with contributed funds and not at public expense.

If you wish to purchase additional copies, contact our State Seal Store at www.sos.wa.gov/store or telephone 360-902-4151.

Thanks again for your generous support.

Sincerely,

Carleen

Carleen Jackson
Director of Development

Note: The fair market value of John Spellman Politics Never Broke His Heart is $35.

WASHINGTON STATE HERITAGE CENTER
LEGISLATIVE BUILDING, PO BOX 40222
OLYMPIA, WASHINGTON 98504-0222

TELEPHONE: 360-902-4126
FAX: 360-586-5629
WWW.HERITAGECENTER.WA.GOV

"I don't think he really wanted to go," Mary says. "Daddy stayed up 'til all hours coaching him for the exam."

WITH DAVID AT WEST POINT and Mary exiled to Omaha, John left Seattle Prep in January of 1944, midway through his senior year, to enroll in the Merchant Marine Cadet/Midshipman program at Coyote Point near San Mateo, California. He was 17. It was Bart's idea, and Magnuson doubtless helped. The Navy recruiter in Seattle told John he had posted the highest test scores they'd ever seen. "They misjudged me. They had me all wrong. I looked good on paper, but I was still just a kid. Steam and diesel and electrical engineering was stuff I could not do. I don't remember if they asked me to or if I just dropped out, but I was having a terrible time."

"When John left the Merchant Marine program *that was something!*" his sister recalls. "He really showed his independence. Daddy was on the phone trying to find out where he was."

He was in San Francisco. Going home was out of the question, so he signed on as a merchant seaman on a seagoing tug. His job was wiper— as low as it goes—cleaning the diesel engines with Carbon tetrachloride. "The fumes should have killed me," Spellman says. He soon made oiler, a rung up the ladder of seagoing flunkydom. When they delivered a dry dock to Kwajalein, a strategic atoll in the South Pacific, the Japanese Navy was greatly diminished but the tug was still a sitting duck. "We were going maybe four knots with this heavy load, and the wind often made us go backwards." That was more action, in any case, than David Spellman was seeing at West Point. He was envious of his kid brother's adventures.

When the *MV Matagorda* returned to port in June of 1945, the war in Europe was over. Japan was on borrowed time but digging in. John immediately joined the Navy and was disappointed to end up ironing shirts in the laundry at San Pedro, California. Finally, he was assigned to the *USS Cates*, a destroyer escort. By then, however, the shooting war was over for the *Cates*. As they traversed the Panama Canal, heading for decommissioning in Florida, the captain called Fireman 1st Class Spellman to the bridge. "I've seen your test scores. We really think you should be going to Annapolis." ("We" surely included Magnuson, who saw combat in the Pacific before FDR ordered him and his lanky pal, Texas Congressman Lyndon B. Johnson, back to the Capitol.) "I've been through all that before," Spellman said. "I wouldn't make it."

He was discharged early in 1946 and returned home with new self-confidence and a ticket to college, thanks to the GI Bill. He was eager to make his mark, perhaps as a professor or lawyer. He'd been giving some thought to the priesthood, too. One thing was certain: Bart's 1927 birth-announcement prediction that by the fall of '47 John Spellman would "show 'em a thing or two as a good fast running guard" for the Washington Huskies wasn't coming true. The Jesuits now did the coaching.

CHAPTER THREE

The Graduate
and the Novice

Seattle College bounced around in its first half-century, trying to find its footing. The enterprising Jesuit priests who kept it alive even operated a grade school that Bart Spellman attended in 1902. The mission was never in doubt. The Jesuits consider themselves the church's intellectual soul.

In 1931 the struggling school returned to its birthplace on First Hill, there to stay, with 46 students and a quartet of new professors soon nicknamed "The Four Horsemen of Loyola." One was the Rev. James McGoldrick, an irrepressible son of County Sligo, Ireland. He made waves all the way to Rome by instituting pseudo "night" classes that admitted female students. The ecclesiastical grumbling continued for years, but Seattle was now home to the first coeducational Jesuit College in the United States. In 1946, with Uncle Sam footing the bill for tuition for ex-servicemen ($180 per year), its enrollment more than doubled to nearly 2,500.[1]

Former Fireman 1st Class Spellman, a history-political science major, was a star on the debate team within three months of matriculation. Seattle College took 17 of the 20 rounds in the first Northwest intercollegiate tournament of 1946. It fought to a draw with the University of California in a 2½-hour debate over whether federal regulation of labor unions should be heightened. John began coaching forensics at Holy Names Academy, a prep school for girls, and became co-chairman of the annual debate tournament for Catholic high schools in the Northwest. His father, always impeccable, admonished him to pay more attention to his wardrobe. "You look like you're going to Longacres to play the ponies," Bart observed, one eye cocked over the morning paper.[2] Soon, John was classically collegiate in tweed jackets and dark slacks. He started smoking a pipe. He won the 1947 President's Cup as the school's outstanding senior-division debater and was elected president of the Gavel Club. Academically, he was on track to graduate in three years.

In Spanish class, he sat next to Lois Murphy, who was as attractive as she was brainy. Her raven-black hair complemented her Irish complexion. She was the school's only female labor-relations major. Her father, one of Patton's top officers during the war, was a railroad official. He had moved the family from Montana to Seattle a few years earlier so Lois and her two brothers—one became a renowned oncologist who received the Papal Medal for service to humanity—could receive a strong education. Lois remembers the first time she saw John Spellman. He was coming down a staircase. Their eyes met. Another co-ed saw the look on her face and declared, "That's the man you're going to marry." Lois laughed. "I felt, Well he's good looking. He certainly looks like he's in command of himself—very self-confident, good posture. When I transferred to Roosevelt High School from Havre High in Montana I had the same impression of [future governor] Dan Evans. There was a similarity there. You sensed their self awareness and confidence in themselves." [3]

For John, it was also like at first sight. Though she was a Democrat and a huge Harry Truman fan, he quickly concluded she was very smart—a good debater, too. They were both dating other people, so it took a while for their relationship to blossom. "We ended up having these long discussions about life and what was going on in the world," Lois recalls. "I'm a now person. I love reading newspapers." As a reporter for the college newspaper, the *Spectator*, she was assigned to interview Senator Magnuson, whom she knew to be a longtime Spellman family friend. As the interview was winding down, "I gave him my pitch: 'By the way, senator, I'm really looking for a job in labor relations to represent women.' And he looked at me intently and said, 'You sure have good looking legs.' Decades later, just before Maggie died, John and I were at a reception at the Washington Athletic Club. Maggie was in a wheelchair. He looks me up and says, 'You still have great legs.'" [4]

SPELLMAN FAMILY ALBUM

John as valedictorian at Seattle University 1949.

SEATTLE COLLEGE became a university in 1948 and acquired a dynamic new president, the Rev. A.A. "Arby" Lemieux. The ruggedly handsome 39-year-old Jesuit had been a dean at Gonzaga, his alma mater, and held a doctorate in philosophy. Unpretentious and approachable, his first stop most mornings was for coffee at the student union building.

Lemieux had his work cut out for him. "The school lacked firm connections to the Seattle business community and lacked an endowment to assure ongoing financial security. The physical plant was deteriorating," with prefab classrooms and housing all over campus and adjoining blocks. The faculty and staff were underpaid. Henry Broderick, one of the school's most loyal benefactors, took Lemieux under his wing. "He was like a father to me," the priest recalled.[5] Lemieux's circle of friends soon included Bart Spellman. He was also not the first Jesuit university president to understand that a great basketball team is a marvelous marketing tool.

Lemieux took an instant liking to Lois, inviting her to breakfast with Clare Boothe Luce, the famous former congresswoman. Afterward, Lois escorted her around campus before the school's golden jubilee fundraiser.[6]

That winter, the college president also took pleasure in calling her friend John at home one night to announce he had been selected valedictorian of the Class of 1949. At 280 graduates it was the largest in the school's history. The commencement speaker was a former managing editor of *The Daily Worker*. Louis F. Budenz had renounced communism, gone undercover for the FBI and become a born-again Catholic, landing a teaching job at Fordham University. The small man with a booming voice declared that communism was "the greatest slave system since the Roman Empire," dedicated to "the destruction of all who believe in God." He exhorted the graduates to rise and join the fight to "aid all mankind."[7]

Spellman, who was 22, confessed that he found the times "confusing." He spoke on the power of piety: "You have to somehow get your life focused—get in the right place, position yourself for success. And piety is a virtue that will help you get there."[8]

"I'm more proud of you than if you had been an All-American," Bart told his son. Father Lemieux and Bishop Thomas A. Connolly believed John would make a fine priest.

HE CAME TO THE SEMINARY with one suitcase, an open heart and a pocketful of change. It was a sparkling September day in the Willamette Valley about 50 miles southwest of Portland.

The Jesuits were on a post-war roll when John Spellman entered the Novitiate of St. Francis Xavier near the sleepy town of Sheridan in 1949. The order was flush with recruits, many of whom had found God in foxholes and B-17's. The synergy of war and peace summed up the first 400 years of the Society of Jesus. It was conceived in the 1500s by Ignatius Loyola, a swashbuckling Basque knight who embarked on a series of spiritual exercises while recuperating from a wound and was moved by the Holy

Spirit. From this conversion emerged a band of educated, adventuresome priests—many would become martyrs—who set out to spread the Gospel around the globe and promote intellectual enlightenment. "Loyola had joined to the mystique of the monk the parallel mystique of the Renaissance knight."[9] Jesuit notables include Robert Bellarmine, who defended Galileo against charges of heresy, and Francis Xavier, who established missions in East Asia and Japan. A host of Jesuits were among the "Black Robes" who arrived in the Northwest in the 1840s. Father Pierre-Jean De Smet, an intrepid Belgian immigrant, helped establish a landmark mission in Montana. De Smet paddled and proselytized his way down the Columbia and sang High Mass at the mission on the Cowlitz in 1842 before baptizing his way back East. His business development and marketing skills were put to good use propagating the faith.[10]

The Jesuits were remarkable shape-shifters, adapting to whatever environment and language they encountered, be it Mandarin or Chinook Jargon. So numerous and resourceful were they that Protestant clergy sounded the alarm. "The Jesuits, of all the men in our world, are the most to be dreaded," a prominent Presbyterian pastor warned a Massachusetts audience in 1847. These seductive papists were "establishing their institutions of learning all over the West."[11] (Today there are 28 Jesuit colleges and universities in the U.S., including Seattle University and Gonzaga. Georgetown is the oldest.)

While the Protestants feared lockstep Catholicism dictated by the high and mitred, the Jesuits had endured four decades of repression instituted in 1773 by a pope who bowed to pressure from European monarchs to rein them in. "They were now seen as a vast, intellectually arrogant, power-hungry and hugely ambitious organization, enmeshed in international intrigue and totally unscrupulous in their operations."[12] Over the centuries, in fact, the Vatican has frequently blanched at manifestations, both right and left, of their intellectual independence—from doctrinal chauvinism to "liberation theology." In the 21st Century, the order that has fostered so much knowledge and piety would pay dearly, literally and figuratively, for the sin of harboring pedophiles. But in 1949, when Spellman arrived as a prospective seminarian, a postulant, the novitiate at Sheridan was an oasis of spiritual tranquility. Wearing a cassock, a long Rosary drooping from the waist, he was soon steeped in Jesuit lore. Harold Small, Father Lemieux's predecessor at Seattle University, was now the Oregon Jesuit provincial. He knew Spellman was ambitious and offered counsel. St. Francis Xavier, Father Small noted, was also a very ambitious man—for God. Spellman had some nagging misgivings about the priesthood. He couldn't quite define

Jesuit seminarians at Mass at the Novitiate of St. Francis Xavier, Sheridan, Oregon, in 1949.

them; "they were just there." He trusted God would let him know if the collar fit. He devised a code to let his sister know how it was going.

SPELLMAN IMPRESSED everyone he encountered at the novitiate. "John was a model novice; very prayerful yet never stiff; always a joy to be with. He had a marvelous sense of humor and kindness," says the Rev. John Navone, a classmate who went on to spend years in Rome as a revered professor, theologian and writer. Another fellow novice, the Rev. Tom McCarthy, recalls Spellman as "just a really nice guy; obviously very bright, from a family that valued faith and education."

Their surroundings were perfectly pastoral. "It was a thousand acres of heavenly Oregon countryside overlooking the Yamhill Valley," Navone said wistfully, 62 years later. "The meat was wonderful—the bread wonderful, too. There were prune orchards, livestock and crops to tend. Our outdoor exercise was agricultural." Inside, the 85 novices lived in a big, long room. Their cells were fashioned from wooden partitions that stopped short of the ceiling. Each room had a drape for a door, a desk, a kneeler and a bed. "It was very austere, yet very cheerful," says Navone. They had a common washroom. From time to time there was a shortage of water, and when there was plenty it was often cold. Once to bed, no one spoke—the *magnum silentium*, the great silence—until after breakfast the next day. No newspapers, no radio. "When I was in the world" was the phrase they used for life outside.

The Spiritual Exercises of St. Ignatius of Loyola are a month-long pro-gram of meditations and prayers designed to help each Jesuit "follow Jesus and seek God's will in any circumstance, from the most mundane day of teaching, administrating or writing to a particularly trying experience of walking with people, experiencing grave suffering or social injustice."[13] The long retreat, punctuated by rounds of Our Fathers and Hail Marys, was "a profound experience," Spellman remembers. His biographer confessed to finding rote prayers boring. "Ah," said Spellman, leaning forward fatherly, "but it's nice to be able to fall back on something when you're not able to get your mind in focus; when you're distracted or when you're down. That's when rote prayer is really useful. It's what's going on in your mind when you're saying those rotes that can give you direction."

Sometimes, however, Jesuits just want to have fun. Spellman sup-plied it with a production that elderly priests recall with boyish mirth in their voices. He rewrote the entire libretto of Rodgers and Hammerstein's smash-hit musical, *Oklahoma!* In *Sheridan!*, where the beets "sure smell sweet when the breeze comes right behind the rain," the quiet monk who rambled around the grounds in an old pickup truck was saluted in Spell-man's take on "Surrey With the Fringe on Top":

> *Chicks and ducks and geese better scurry,*
> *Here comes Brother Bies in a hurry!*

Sheridan! featured an all-novice cast. Spellman was lyricist, casting manager, producer and director. The show was presented on the stage of the theater in the old novitiate. The audience numbered 200, including 15 priests, the novices and the third- and fourth-year students—and Brother Bies, of course. "John picked up on people's characteristics and wrote new lyrics, including them in the songs," Father McCarthy, a parish priest in Oregon, recalled in 2012. "It was very clever, very creative, and all in good fun. John is a big-hearted person who enjoys life and likes people." Father Navone agrees and then some: "John's show was a masterpiece—the cul-tural apex, the apogee, of my two years at the seminary. His putting on that musical was really him communicating himself, his sense of joy, to the whole Jesuit community. ...We all stood and sang the chorus, but instead of 'Oklahomaaaaa!' it was 'Sheridaaaaan!' "

THE SEMINARY was an intensely spiritual experience for Spellman. After nine months, however, he concluded the priesthood was not his calling.

In a letter to his sister, a newlywed whose spouse was in law school in Omaha, he wrote that "the weather was stormy." That meant he had decided to leave. He packed quietly and crept out while the others were at their kneelers or tucked in their spartan beds. When some coins spilled from his pocket onto the concrete floor, one of the novices heard the clatter. "He was trying to sneak away without making a stir, but the one who heard the coins drop told us he knew John must be leaving because we had no money," Father McCarthy recalls.

"It would be impossible to say anything unkind about John Spellman," says Father Navone. "He threw himself into it. We really knew he had tried to discern if this was his calling, so when he left you knew he had really given it everything and had concluded, 'This is not what the Lord is calling me to do.' "

John had resolved to become a lawyer and follow his interest in politics and public service. The church would always be his lodestar, he told himself, but he could serve it best as an energetic layman.

CHAPTER FOUR

Heartbreak

Spellman arrived in Washington, D.C., by train in the middle of the night with a footlocker and an old Royal typewriter. He caught a cab to a rooming house and enrolled the next morning in Law School at Georgetown University. Seven-thousand miles away, his brother David was landing in Korea with an M1 carbine and three days' assault rations. It was the fall of 1950. The Cold War had come to a boil.

When the North Koreans suddenly swept across the 38th parallel dividing the Korean peninsula into two nations, President Truman said the United Nations had no choice but to move decisively to contain the spread of communism. He ordered a "police action" to repel the invaders.[1] Others called it a "conflict." To soldiers, a war is a war. This one was a brutal slog, from the frozen Chosin Reservoir to the outskirts of Pusan on the Sea of Japan. The Spellmans said their prayers. David's wife, Bonnie, a charming Iowa girl, was living with his parents at Hunts Point during his deployment from Camp Campbell, Kentucky.

First Lieutenant Spellman, West Point Class of 1946, commanded a company of 200 paratroopers from the 187th Airborne Infantry Regimental Combat Team. "The Rakkasans" acquired their nickname during World War II from a fractured Japanese phrase for parachutists.[2] On October 20, 1950, the 187th descended nearly 3,000 strong just north of the North Korean capital of Pyongyang. They cleared the villages, seized the hills and set up roadblocks. Nighttime encounters in the wooded hills were fought with grenades and bayonets; sometimes hand to hand. Aided by British troops advancing from the south, the Americans secured the capital. Then 300,000 combat-hardened Chinese Communist soldiers joined the war.[3] As the new year dawned, the Communists recaptured Seoul. Spellman and the men of Bravo Company marched south, an icy wind howling out of Manchuria at their backs. They were soon in the thick of the Battle of Wonju, the "Gettysburg of Korea."[4] Back home, the Spellmans devoured the newspapers and listened intently to radio reports, wondering where David was.

On February 3, 1951, David Spellman and his men were near Chechon, an important rail terminal, when they were attacked by thousands of Chinese soldiers. The 1st Battalion held its ground throughout the night and next day, inflicting "appalling casualties on the enemy."[5] Company B lost 50 men, including three lieutenants. One was David Spellman, picked off by a sniper, according to the first official report. Accounts varied thereafter. Whether it was a sharpshooter's bullet or a random round marked "to whom it may concern" from a barrage of rifle fire is immaterial. David Bartholomew Spellman was dead at 25. Peace talks resumed about the time he was being laid to rest at Calvary Catholic Cemetery in Seattle.

MARY SPELLMAN TULLY, John's sister, had a bad dream. She and her husband, Gene, a fledgling lawyer, had just bought a house in Medina, not far from Hunts Point. They were expecting their second child. On Monday, February 19, Mary and her mother went shopping. "I had a dream the night before that David had been killed. It seemed so real. I didn't want to bring it up with her, of course, and add to her worry. That night the phone rang. I answered. It was my father. He asked to speak with my husband. I knew right away what it was." John got the news on the pay phone in the hall of his rooming house and escaped into the night. Figuring the closest church was closed, he wandered along the mall at the Capitol, praying and pondering. He paused at the foot of a statue of John Marshall, the longest serving chief justice of the United States, trying to collect his thoughts. It was so unfair, he told himself. David was a great guy. He had a great wife and was just getting started in life. Now he was gone. John didn't blame God. "I knew better than that." His head thrummed with confusion. His heart ached, literally, pulsing all the way to his throat. It took him 20 melancholy hours to get home. It was his first trip in an airplane.

"When I think back on it," his sister says, "it was Mother who stood up and took charge. She was great. She was the strong one when David died. Her daughter-in-law was now a young widow, so that added to the heartbreak. David's death had a profound impact on John, and Daddy took it hard. Even before David died, Daddy had come back to the church. He'd never left it, really, but he had become a very staunch Catholic. All the boys from West Point came out to Seattle. David's fellow officers from Camp Campbell were pallbearers. It was a houseful, and Mother just took over."

Bart Spellman was shattered, John remembers, in part because he had pushed David to go to West Point. He was nearing retirement as an insurance partner at Broderick Inc. and all the zest just went out of him. "In many ways, David's death broke him physically," John says. "His nerves went to hell. Mother convinced him they should go traveling." John's own grief was compounded by mixed emotions over his draft status. He had taken a pre-induction physical in Virginia because his hard-nosed draft board back home was making noises about calling him back into the Navy even though he was doing well in law school. Now, as the sole surviving son, he was exempt from further service. "I think my faith helped me a lot, including my time at Sheridan. In later years, I saw a letter I wrote to my parents at that time. It was terribly eloquent and filled with faith. I used big words that I don't use anymore. I had been prepared to deal with heartbreak—not intentionally—but by what I had done 'till then on a spiritual journey. It still wasn't easy."

Big brothers who die young often leave indelible heartache and asterisks about what might have been. A framed photo of David Spellman, bivouacked in Korea on a bleak day, occupies a place of honor in his brother's law office in a Seattle skyscraper.

IMMERSING HIMSELF in the study of law was great therapy. When he left the seminary, Spellman considered a career in the Foreign Service. "But few people get to the top in the diplomatic corps without a law degree, and if I was going to go to law school I wanted to go to one of the very best." It came down to Georgetown and Michigan. Georgetown is a Jesuit school, but where it was mattered more. "What else are you going to learn in Ann Arbor, Michigan? Washington had the Supreme Court, libraries, galleries and museums. It's just a great place to be a law student."

America's capital in the early 1950s was also the home front of the Cold War. With the loss of China, the eruption of war in Korea and the prosecution of Julius and Ethel Rosenberg, a frumpy couple from Manhattan, as Soviet spies, the Red Scare was at its apex. Joseph McCarthy and Richard M. Nixon, with matching five o'clock shadows, amped up the hunt for communists and fellow travelers. Nixon, shrewd and sober, was going places. McCarthy was an alcoholic bull in a china shop and headed for a fall, despite the counsel of Spellman's favorite professor, Edward Bennett Williams.

Spellman and Dewie Gaul, a future judge, lived in the same rooming house during their first year of law school. Gaul was a Democrat—still is—while Spellman was an enthusiastic Young Republican. Their political arguments lasted for hours, adjourning late at night only to be continued the next morning. One of the most heated concerned Douglas MacArthur, the U.N. commander in Korea. Truman sacked the imperious old five-star general after MacArthur groused publicly that his commander in chief was timid. Gaul backed Truman; Spellman MacArthur. Spellman had a personal stake in the outcome of the war. Gaul had his full sympathy on that score.

John and his roommate, Sam DeSimone, an Amherst grad, stretched an Eisenhower for President banner across E Street near their rooming house. From Sam's dad, a haberdasher, John received his first pair of grey flannel slacks. The package also contained a huge salami. "I think Sam told him

SPELLMAN FAMILY ALBUM

Spellman with Georgetown Law School classmates Dewie Gaul, center, and Robert J. Kresse. Gaul and Spellman lived in the rooming house in the background during their first year of law school and often argued politics way past bedtime.

I was poor and he felt sorry for me. The GI Bill paid for tuition and books, but they didn't give you much to live on. I spent a lot of time in cafeterias or eating beans out of a can."

During the summer of '52 John worked the graveyard shift in the metal-fabricating shop at the Boeing Company, which was developing a revolutionary swept-wing commercial jetliner that would become the 707. In his spare time he saw a lot of his Seattle U classmate, Lois Murphy, who was working at Peoples Bank in downtown Seattle. No one in Seattle, union or business, was willing to hire a woman for a job in labor relations. John and Lois talked politics a lot. She defended the Democrats. He liked Ike.

DWIGHT D. EISENHOWER was an athletic Kansas boy with an infectious grin and steely self-discipline. After he graduated from West Point, his career stagnated for decades as the Army shrank after World War I. February of 1940, found Eisenhower arriving at Fort Lewis, near Tacoma, finally a lieutenant colonel. Twenty-three months later he was a four-star general, propelled past men with far more seniority by his genius for strategy and diplomacy.

"Amid the finger-pointing mania of the early 1950s, Eisenhower emerged as a nearly ideal presidential candidate."[6] John Spellman was among thousands of young vets who rejected the isolationist conservative wing of the party personified by Robert Taft. During high school, Spellman had followed Thomas E. Dewey's rise from crime-fighting district attorney to New York governor and presidential candidate. Dewey's surprising loss to Truman in 1948 and stiff "man on a wedding cake" image obscured his progressive platform. Dewey opposed racial discrimination, defended Social Security and supported collective bargaining.[7] "His moderation and internationalism appealed to me," Spellman says, "and Ike embodied all that too." Dewey began recruiting Eisenhower as early as 1949 and played a key role in depriving Taft of the 1952 nomination. Adlai Stevenson, the Democrats' nominee, had no answer for Ike either. Ten days before the election, Eisenhower pledged, "I shall go to Korea."

Ike went. He extricated the U.S. from Korea. But the uneasy truce came too late for David Spellman and 34,999 other American soldiers. At Georgetown Law School, even as post-war prosperity bloomed, the students and their professors were intensely conscious of being caught up in the Cold War. The "Domino Theory" of Communism on the march was hotly debated.

EDWARD BENNETT WILLIAMS, poised to become one of the greatest lawyers of the 20th century, was a big man with intense hazel eyes and curly brown hair. Only 32 in 1952, Williams was teaching part-time at his alma mater and cultivating his law practice. Spellman vividly remembers Williams' hypotheticals, the grist of effective Supreme Court advocacy. For their final exam on Evidence one semester, his students mulled this:

> A, B, and C are indicted by a Federal Grand Jury for using the mails to defraud. The telephone wires of all of these men had been tapped by FBI agents and conversations which they had among themselves had been recorded. ... A and B immediately decided to plead guilty ... and agreed to testify for the government against C. At the trial, A and B are offered by the government as witnesses. Counsel for C objects to the admission of their testimony. Is there any way in which counsel for C can block this evidence?[8]

The way to an "A" was to have counsel for C point to the safeguards of the Fourth Amendment: "The right of the people to be secure in their persons, houses, papers, and effects, against unreasonable searches and seizures, shall not be violated ..." Williams became the Fourth Amendment's masterful champion, arguing four Supreme Court cases that hinged on its interpretation. He also testified before Congress, "sounding the alarm about the dangers of wiretapping and eavesdropping."[9] Several of his cases broke new ground or clarified important constitutional principles, Justice William Brennan noted. "It is not often that the same lawyer can be tough and quick and a tremendous adversary in the courtroom and also write law review articles and appellate briefs and make oral appellate arguments of excellent quality. Well, Ed Williams could do it all."[10] And without raising his voice or waving his arms.

"Williams had a commanding yet soft presence," Spellman says, relishing memories of his eventful second year of law school. He had Williams for Evidence and Criminal Law. "There was gentleness in his voice and demeanor. He conducted the class in the Socratic manner, but his lectures were the highlights. He would stand on the corner of the large platform, rarely using the lectern, and talk about legal principles, obligations and abuses. He was an idealist, always emphasizing the history of individual freedom and the Bill of Rights. Fairness. Due process. From Ed Williams I learned a great respect for our system of law and a passion for the rights of the accused: The presumption of innocence; the right to effective counsel; protection against forced self-incrimination; protection from illegal searches and seizures; freedom of speech. Platitudes? Perhaps, but without them we would be in deep trouble. I attended a trial where Williams defended a libel case and later adopted some of his tactics when I defended the rights of the United Steelworkers."

Some criticized Williams for representing the likes of Joe McCarthy, mob boss Frank Costello and Jimmy Hoffa. "A clergyman can give counsel to the worst sinner, but when a lawyer gives counsel to someone who has had the condemnation of society, people say it's shocking," Williams observed. A lawyer's duty, he said, "is not to admire his clients, but simply to defend them" within the limits of integrity and the facts.[11] Williams told his classes that when he was a student at Georgetown he often walked to the Supreme Court Building across from the Capitol. "I never failed to be thrilled when I looked up at the magnificent portico and saw the words chiseled into stone: Equal Justice Under Law."[12] Williams, and those words, made a lifelong impression on Spellman.

HE SPENT much of his spare time at the Supreme Court or in the galleries and hearing rooms of Congress. He studied the styles of the best debaters and soaked up the gravitas. Moot Court competition became his passion. Judged on the persuasiveness of their written briefs and skill in oral arguments, law school moot court teams argue both sides of their hypothetical cases before mock courts featuring seasoned judges and trial lawyers.

SPELLMAN FAMILY ALBUM

Georgetown's national champion moot court team in 1952: Seated next to Spellman is Richard Alan Gordon. Standing are A. Kenneth Pye, left, and Carl D. Hall Jr. Spellman and "Gordo," presented the team's arguments and became best friends for life.

Kenneth Pye and Carl D. Hall Jr., who excelled at research, anchored the briefs for the Georgetown team. All four members researched, polished and practiced. Spellman and Richard Alan Gordon presented the arguments. At the lectern, they represented a formidable one-two punch. John and "Gordo," a devotee of Gilbert & Sullivan theatricals, became best friends for life. Georgetown's brief in the 1952 competition focused on a law prohibiting aliens from owning land in California. Did it pass muster with the 14th Amendment, the United Nations Charter and its Universal Declaration of Human Rights? Gordon advanced the 14th Amendment.* Spellman cited the U.N. declaration. Some said it was an absurd argument. He holed up for days at the Library of Congress, studying old texts on human rights. He would assert that the Universal Declaration of Human Rights was a self-executing treaty. "John had a terribly difficult position to argue," Hall says, "but he was very imaginative and did a wonderful job. We all learned a lot from Ed Williams, who was spellbinding."

Georgetown won every round, defeating the University of Chicago to claim the national title at the finals in New York City. U.S. Supreme Court Justice Stanley Forman Reed, a swing-vote moderate who authored more than 300 opinions, was one of the judges.

Richard Gordon went on to become a revered professor and assistant dean of Georgetown Law School. Ken Pye became the dean at Duke Law School. Carl Hall had a distinguished career specializing in labor law and

---

* "All persons born or naturalized in the United States, and subject to the jurisdiction thereof, are citizens of the United States and of the State wherein they reside. No State shall make or enforce any law which shall abridge the privileges or immunities of citizens of the United States; nor shall any State deprive any person of life, liberty, or property, without due process of law; nor deny to any person within its jurisdiction the equal protection of the laws."

taught at the University of Tulsa and Oral Roberts. In a photo of the four-some, Spellman looks the very model of a serious young lawyer in rep tie and button-down collar. His flip side was the jazz aficionado who entertained friends by crooning popular tunes as they walked down the street.

Spellman graduated in the top 10 percent of the Class of 1953, and was admitted to the Washington State Bar on September 25. Over the years, he closely followed Williams' storied career. Their paths didn't cross again until the 1970s in the lobby of the Camelback Inn at Scottsdale. Williams was by then not only famous but rich. He owned the Washington Redskins and was in Arizona for a meeting of National Football League owners. "He was surrounded by press and admirers, but I reintroduced myself as one of his former students and told him I was now the King County executive, trying to get an NFL team for our domed stadium."

CHAPTER FIVE

Kane & Spellman

J udge Charles P. Moriarty, the newly-appointed U.S. Attorney in Seattle, had some advice for the polite young lawyer looking for a job:
"Don't be so modest."

Spellman had weighed an offer to clerk for a Supreme Court judge in
Oregon. It was tempting. "But if I go to Oregon," he said to himself, "I'll stay
there the rest of my life. I like Washington." So he went to see Moriarty, one
of his father's grade-school classmates and the ex-officio "family lawyer" for
Seattle University.[1] Moriarty's daughter Jean and Lois Murphy, now John's
steady girlfriend, were chums. The judge's son, Chuck Jr., was John's age
and friends with Frank and Joel Pritchard, Dan Evans and a whole crew of
bushy-tailed young Seattle Republicans. Chuck Jr. would soon land a job as
administrative assistant to Republican Congressman Tom Pelly.

John didn't mention to Judge Moriarty that he was Bart Spellman's
son—as if Moriarty didn't know. Connections were nothing to be ashamed
of, Moriarty counseled. "You shouldn't be reluctant to use your father's
name. He's well known. He's a good man, and that's a plus for you."

Moriarty was impressed by John's achievements at Georgetown. He
also seemed more mature than most 27-year-olds. "I don't have any open-
ings now," he said, "but I expect to have some in October. Stick around."
Lois mentioned that Joe Kane, one of their favorite professors at Seattle
U, was now practicing law. John paid him a visit on the 10th floor of the
landmark Smith Tower. "I'm up to my neck in cases!" Kane declared, evi-
denced by a desk awash in papers. "Why don't you help me until you get
the appointment?"

"Joseph Sylvester Kane was a very bright, principled guy—a civil
rights activist who had worked for the ACLU," Spellman says. "He was a
wonderful professor, but he hadn't practiced nuts-and-bolts law very much.
Pretty soon I was up to my neck in cases. When a job opened with the
U.S. Attorney's Office, I was already on track to becoming his law partner,

specializing in labor and maritime law. I never regretted my decision."

At lunchtime, Kane would be out schmoozing up business while Spellman ate an apple at his desk before heading to the Courthouse. Some saw them as unlikely partners. In practice, they were a good pair. Spellman reduced the chaos, if not the clutter, in the office, and his social conscience was as strong as Kane's. "It was a very idealistic practice," Spellman recalls. "We did considerable pro bono work for minorities and poor people." Two decades later when Spellman was running for governor, Kane observed that "John was not what you'd call a quick jumper. He was an academician; whatever he undertakes he'll have the facts. ... Politically I pegged him as an independent, quite pro-labor as we got into representing the ironworkers and the steelworkers."[2]

BART SPELLMAN had retired after 22 years with Henry Broderick Inc. Some say his departure was tainted by haggling over what was owed him. If so, Bart's long battle with depression, compounded by David's death, surely had a role in the dispute; he and Broderick had been friends for so many years. Lela suggested a change of scenery. They were packing for Europe as John and Lois were growing serious. Lela approved. Lois was a woman after her own heart—smart, industrious, thoughtful and pious. Lela gave her son a nudge: "Why don't you get married? You're going to be all by yourself for a year. Call up Lois!" John called up Lois. "We really should get married," he said. "My parents are going to Europe, and we could live in the house over at Hunts Point.' "

As proposals go, this is not the stuff of fairy tales, but she said yes. Their match is steeped in mutual admiration. "Lois was always one of the brightest students, all through school," John says. "In Havre, Montana, where she grew up, the priest even put her up on the altar to give a talk. That was against all the rules. She was a natural leader." Lois' eyes sparkle when she talks about her husband. From the Courthouse to the Governor's Mansion, John's friends, agency heads and staff came to regard her as an astute observer and tough cookie. "She is very good at reading people," says Steve Excell, a longtime Spellman friend and former chief of staff. "She could spot trouble. John was always inclined to give every dog a second chance to bite. It's the Jesuit in him. Lois was more wary. She has always been his biggest fan, sometimes protective but knowing deep down that that's not really realistic. They're both resilient people. He values her advice. It's a love story."

Lois Elizabeth Murphy and John Dennis Spellman were married on February 20, 1954, at Assumption Catholic Church in Seattle. The bride was

SPELLMAN FAMILY ALBUM

Lois Murphy on her wedding
day in 1954.

radiant in Chantilly Lace over taffeta, the groom
dark-haired, handsome and boutonnièred.

"Where you going on your honeymoon?"
Joe Kane had inquired the week before.

"I hadn't really planned one. I don't think
I can afford it."

"Well, why don't you go to San Francisco
and take a deposition for me?"

Red-faced, crusty Joe Kane had a romantic
Irish soul. It was a lovely wedding present.
The Spellmans' daughter Margo was born on
their first anniversary. Twelve days later their
joy was fractured by another tragedy.

JOHN WAS SUMMONED from a courtroom to
take an urgent call. It was Friday, March 4,
1955. His father was dead; his mother in critical condition with a brain injury and multiple
fractures in a hospital at Nogales, Mexico, 60
miles south of Tucson. When she was able to
talk, Lela Spellman could remember only a sweltering day; Bart changing
a tire on the small foreign car they had brought from Europe, and a group
of horsemen alongside the overturned car, which was subsequently looted.
Bart Spellman, 59, had died of a broken neck. Did he swerve to avoid a
collision? Was it a moment of deadly inattention on a primitive road? Me-
chanical failure?[3] Details were sketchy then and remain so.

"A brave and resourceful counsel general from the United States broke
all the rules and probably saved my mother's life," Spellman says. "When
he visited her in the hospital it was clear they had no idea how to treat
someone with such a catastrophic head injury. So he put her in a Piper Cub,
along with my father's body, and flew them out of Mexico. That was totally
against the law. He was our hero. She wouldn't have made it in Mexico.
They took her to a hospital near Dallas where there were great doctors.
Besides a fractured skull, she had a broken arm and a broken leg. When
she was better, she had plastic surgery. My sister spent months nursing her
back to health." Lela Spellman, the spunky daughter of Oregon pioneers,
lived another 30 years.

Bart was mourned on sports pages all over the Northwest and by a son
who named his first son Sterling Bartholomew Spellman. Henry Broderick,
who'd lost one of his best friends, took John to Seattle First National Bank

and arranged for him to receive a line of credit until Bart's estate and the medical bills were sorted out.

JOHN SUCCEEDED his father as president of the Seattle Kennel Club. He was elected president of the Seattle University Alumni Association and became one of the most influential members of Archbishop Connolly's kitchen cabinet. Thomas A. Connolly—"TAC" to friends—was a large, charismatic man. He had prowled the gritty docks of San Francisco as a young priest. Equally at home in a fashionable club or the banquet room at the Olympic Hotel, the archbishop was a hard man to refuse when he needed money to build a new school or church.

Spellman was increasingly in demand as a toastmaster and fundraiser. He headed the Archdiocesan Holy Names Society and, at Connolly's urging, traveled widely in the Northwest, giving speeches on "the Lay Apostolate," Catholic education and the dangers of pornography. In 1957, King County Prosecutor Charles O. Carroll—one of Bart Spellman's football stars at the UW—appointed Spellman to the King County Salacious Literature Committee. The "magazine probers" were spotlighted in *The Seattle Times*, where Carroll had friends in high places. Spellman and Deputy Prosecutor James A. Andersen, together with church ladies in hats and gloves, were shown gravely inspecting "girlie" and "exposé-type magazines" plucked from newsstands all over the county.[4] Spellman took some razzing and, for the first time, political heat. Liberals accused him of censorship. He was unapologetic, arguing that magazines depicting rape and murder, not just bare-breasted centerfolds, could be easily acquired by kids. By 1958, Spellman had three children of his own. Magazine distributors agreed to cooperate with the committee.

KANE & SPELLMAN developed a thriving practice. John's top clients were the unions. He represented the Steelworkers, Ironworkers and Communications Workers, as well as the Butchers & Meat Cutters, the Bakers, Transportation Workers and the National Maritime Union. The tiny law firm also handled the classic walk-ins—probates, bankruptcies, traffic cases and custody battles. In a case that reads like an episode of Maury Povich's tawdry TV show, Spellman did his best to win leniency for a 17-year-old who had fathered illegitimate children with two different girls, one 14, the other 15. As the mothers looked on from the front row in Superior Court, fidgety infants on their knees, Spellman argued for a deferred sentence on a morals charge so the defendant could finish 10th grade at Garfield High School. The judge was unmoved. Noting that the demonstrably promiscuous youth

had been expelled from several schools, he sent him to the state reforma-
tory for no less than 2½ years. Though the kid "appeared unconcerned,"
Spellman gave him a reassuring pat.[5]

Spellman absorbed few setbacks in personal injury cases, winning
settlements as high as $39,000—about $395,000 in today's dollars—for
seamen injured when a cylinder of chlorine gas burst in the hold of their
ship.[6] He fought hard for a railway worker who'd lost his left leg in a lift-
truck accident. The Great Northern claimed it was his own fault. Spellman
got his client a settlement from a federal court jury.[7]

If Spellman had gone to work for Carroll, as had so many of his peers,
he wouldn't have lasted long. The prosecutor expected all hands—from
deputy prosecutors to receptionists—to become lock-step members of a
political machine that controlled Republican politics in King County. Tub-
thumping was a condition of employment. "We didn't have a choice. It
was anathema to mention the word 'Democrat,'" says Charles Z. Smith,
who joined the Prosecutor's Office in 1956 as a young attorney and went
on to become a member of the state Supreme Court.[8] Robert Utter and
Carolyn Dimmick, two more Carroll recruits who became Supreme Court
justices, tell similar stories. All three escaped as quickly as practical. The
drill was too demeaning. Until Carroll's last hurrah in the late 1960s, one
of the chief deputies would go from desk to desk with a coffee can every
payday, collecting donations. The kitty had various names—the Christmas
Tree Fund, the Get Well Fund and the Flower Fund. What it was was the
Re-elect Chuck Fund. Not that Carroll was the lone practitioner. Most of
the other elected officials in the Courthouse had funds of their own. Carroll elevated it to an art form. He also had friends who bought ink by the
barrel. Ross Cunningham, the top political writer for *The Seattle Times*, was
his pal. The prosecutor's staff "timed big announcements for *The Times'*
afternoon press runs, and his secretaries waved *Times* reporters into Carroll's office without an appointment. *The Times*, in turn, produced a steady
stream of articles—Carroll's duck hunting ...tributes from admirers, and
his occasional interest in running for governor."[9] "Carroll had a big following," Spellman says. "Even people who had worked for him and seen all his
warts tended to forgive and forget and remain loyal over the years. Chuck
could fill a ballroom all by himself. He loved to have big Christmas parties
where some precocious 11-year-old would sing his favorite song, 'How Great
Thou Art.'"

Spellman had no regrets about joining Kane. In his first five years as
a lawyer he argued practically every kind of case, from police court to the
State Supreme Court; from Seattle to San Francisco. One made headlines
in 1955 and 1956.

EUGENE V. DENNETT, a small, balding man who favored dignified double-breasted suits, seemed older than 47. He looked more like the seventh-grade history teacher he used to be than what he was—a steelworker. His hobby was even more incongruous. He had taken up knitting. In his fingers, the needles moved with methodical precision as he produced a pair of socks during three days of headline-making hearings conducted in Seattle in 1955 by the House Un-American Activities Committee. For 16 years Dennett led a secret life as one of the most energetic communists in the Northwest. Now he was naming names—lots of names. Depending upon your persuasion, Dennett was a patriot, a shameless stool pigeon or a cunningly duplicitous communist operative. Spellman believed Dennett had never left the party and was busy boring from within at Bethlehem Steel's plant in West Seattle. "The Party distributed leaflets far and wide telling everyone that I was a renegade Trotskyite opportunist son of a bitch," Dennett wrote. "The union thought I was subversive, and the company hated my guts, and in the middle of all this, my wife leaves me too."[10]

Dennett led the rapt congressmen "through the mazes of subversion like a professor diagramming the parts of a sentence."[11] He also turned over a handbook—typed in red—for party operatives that included instructions on how to concoct invisible ink from onion juice. Party membership in the Northwest peaked at around 5,500 in 1939, Dennett testified, just before the comrades were confused and demoralized by the Nazi-Soviet Non-Aggression Pact and the Soviet invasion of Finland. The party's ranks were now "pretty well decimated" but America couldn't be complacent. "If you 'leave it to George,'" Dennett warned, "you'll wake up one day and find out that George has not done it the way you wanted it done." He was "warmly commended" by the committee for his patriotic cooperation.[12] Dennett, meantime, had filed libel suits against the United Steelworkers of America, seeking $160,000 in damages. The alleged defamation—the insinuation that he was still a communist—was contained in briefs and a petition recommending his expulsion from Local 1208. The local's Trial Board had concluded Dennett was "guilty of imposing his political views in the mind" of a fellow worker "and not working with the Local and International Union in harmony."[13]

Kane & Spellman took the Steelworkers' case, with Spellman as the lead attorney. Spellman and his co-counsel, Arthur Goldberg, the prominent labor lawyer who represented the national union in Washington, D.C., insisted on a jury trial. Proof positive that Dennett was "a very smart man," Spellman says, is that he was represented by Kenneth MacDonald, a fearless, principled liberal. When union officials declared that lawyers were to be excluded from one of the pre-trial meetings, "Kenny held onto his chair and they had to carry him out," Spellman recalls, laughing admiringly.

The steelworkers and their wives were frightened that they could lose their homes, Spellman says. Each household was served with a copy of the lawsuit. "The allegation against Dennett, which I believed was probably true, was that he had tried to indoctrinate a young, naïve steelworker by having him read a Marxist pamphlet by Lenin and then warned him about what they did to squealers. This young guy tried to commit suicide because he was so frightened."

Spellman rates the Dennett case as the most memorable of his career. The trial began in the fall of 1956 in King County Superior Court. Presiding was Judge William J. Wilkins, one of the jurists at the Nuremberg Nazi trials.[14]

During law school, Spellman attended a libel trial in which Edward Bennett Williams made skillful use of dramatic exhibits. Now, to buttress the Steelworkers' defense, Spellman displayed large blowups of the newspaper stories and photos headlining Dennett's appearances before the House Un-American Activities Committee. He asserted that union members had a "qualified privilege" to circulate petitions advocating Dennett's ouster. "I proved that Dennett had been a communist, which wasn't all that hard," and left it to the jury to weigh whether his expulsion from the party wasn't a cunning ploy to allow him to keep agitating under cover. MacDonald countered with witnesses who testified that Dennett's only crime was defying the company and its right-wing union patsies. The jury was pre-empted. Four days into the trial, Judge Wilkins granted Spellman's motion that the case be dismissed. The allegations that Dennett had engaged in subversive activity "were an internal affair of the union" and of common interest to the membership, Wilkins ruled, adding that Dennett "had not been maligned before a third party." [15]

SPELLMAN FAMILY ALBUM

Spellman as a young lawyer.

IN 1958, TO HELP a civil rights activist win a seat in the Legislature, Spellman took on another complicated, closely-watched case. It involved a fellow graduate of Seattle University.

Sam Smith, a 36-year-old Boeing Company manager, lived in Seattle's largely minority Central District. He had grown to manhood in segregated Louisiana, the son of a preacher and a teacher. Smith was smart and idealistic, an upstart Democrat at odds with some of the white party leaders in his legislative district. In 1954, when they blocked a black candidate from the ballot, Smith and other insurgents made good on a threat to help elect a white Republican. There were a lot of shades of gray as Smith made his way to the front of the bus. A black Republican, Charles M. Stokes, was one of the incumbent legislators in the 37th District. When Smith came to Seattle after World War II, he believed he too was a Republican. However, the King County branch of the Party of Lincoln, having elected Stokes in 1950, "didn't want any more blacks."[16] The Democrats accepted Sam warily. He had a whole headful of "radical" ideas about open housing and government intervention to force equal opportunity.[17] Barrel-chested and natty in a bow tie and pencil-thin mustache, Smith was frustrated and impatient. In 1956, he lost his first bid for the Legislature, convinced he'd been beaten by his own party. There was a conspiracy afoot in the 37th to keep uppity Negroes from being elected, Smith said. The primary-election ballot was stacked to split the vote. Losing stung, he acknowledged, "but I considered it was part of my purification."[18]

In 1958, Smith ran again. He talked two Democratic challengers into withdrawing; "the Lord took away" another with a heart attack.[19] One remained, and he was a carpetbagger, Smith's supporters charged. Kane & Spellman filed suit in Superior Court to clear away the last hurdle. The judge agreed with Spellman's assertion that Leonard J. Russell, a black real-estate agent, had been ineligible to file for state representative in the 37th District. Russell had recently moved from the 33rd to the 37th but did not register as a voter there until eight days after the filing period ended.[20] Russell immediately appealed the decision. Spellman made his first appearance before the Washington Supreme Court. His moot court experience served him well. His jitters evaporated the minute he took the lectern, looked up from his notes and uttered the time-honored words: "May it please the court." He enjoyed the give and take with the justices, and listened intently as they also grilled the attorneys for Russell and the county auditor. Justice Frank Weaver, a former law professor, wrote the affirming decision. He carefully parsed what the state Constitution did and didn't say, but Justice Robert C. Finley, a man of keen intellect, said it best:

> The meaning of the pertinent constitutional language is ambiguous. ... If there ever was a case which the court could easily decide one

way or the other, and a case which consequently poses a policy decision for the court, this is it. There has been much emphasis upon the importance and desirability of all citizens registering and voting in order to facilitate democratic management of the affairs of government by the electorate at all levels of government. The requirement of registration as a qualification for candidacy for the legislature imposes no serious burden upon any citizen who may aspire to such public office. For the reasons indicated, and with the forthright acknowledgement that the decision is a policy one, I agree with the majority opinion that the trial court should be affirmed.[21]

Sam Smith outpolled Charles Stokes by a thousand votes to win election to the Legislature. Six Republicans in all were ousted by King County Democrats that year. But the young progressive wing of the GOP had a breakthrough of its own to celebrate. In the 43rd District, their leader, 33-year-old Dan Evans, won re-election to the House, while Charles P. Moriarty Jr. and Joel Pritchard were victorious in the 36th. Their prize new recruit, Slade Gorton, was elected in the 46th. Jim Andersen—one of Spellman's fellow "magazine probers"—won in the 48th.

Smith went on to become Seattle's first black city councilman. He and Spellman were friends and frequent political allies for 40 years, notably on open housing and affirmative action, as well as legislation that paved the way for construction of the domed stadium that became the signature issue of Spellman's career as county executive.

Spellman also admired Stokes. In 1968, with Spellman's endorsement, he became Seattle's first African-American District Court judge.

CHAPTER SIX

The Swamp

What the 1956 Clinton-for-mayor campaign needed was an energetic Catholic. Joel and Frank Pritchard volunteered to enlist Spellman. He didn't need much persuading. Gordon S. Clinton, a former FBI agent, was an upstanding young family man. He promised to "put progress ahead of politics" and rekindle the reformer spirit personified by mayors Arthur B. Langlie and William F. Devin and the New Order of Cincinnatus—a cross between the Jaycees and the Salvation Army.[1] The Cinncinatans mobilized Seattle's young professionals during the Depression. They sang "Stout-Hearted Men" as they paraded in their white shirts and green hats, avatars of "absolute cleanliness and honesty."[2] When Langlie took office in 1938, Seattle cops were siphoning upwards of $160,000 a month from the swamp of vice. Draining it "took another 25 years."[3]

The Pritchards were the sparkplugs of progressive Republican politics in King County, raising money, recruiting doorbellers, drafting ads. "They were brilliant organizers," Spellman says, "and as witty as they were smart." Joel Pritchard, a future congressman, could have made a decent living as a stand-up comedian. His favorite parlor trick employed an imaginary telephone, à la Bob Newhart: "Hello, mother. Who's this? Joel. Joel *Pritchard*. Frank's brother. Yes, that nice Dan Evans is here." Joelisms are legendary, including "Some people are all propeller and no rudder" and "He who can be pressured will be pressured."[4]

"I fell in with the right people," Spellman says. "I was concerned about pollution, urban sprawl, vice and civil rights. I probably should have been a Democrat. I have a soft heart. I really do. But the Republicans I knew—the Pritchards, Dan Evans, Jim Ellis, Slade Gorton—were change agents. Like me, they were also embarrassed by some of the prevailing views in both parties on racial issues. The opposition to open housing was appalling."

GORDON CLINTON rose from an impoverished childhood with pluck and determination. He graduated from the University of Washington with honors and went on to Harvard Business School. After serving as a naval officer during World War II, he finished law school and became active in Scouting, the YMCA and the Municipal League. Clinton instigated Municipal League hearings on irregularities at City Hall and opposed the "tolerance policy" that ostensibly kept vice at tolerable levels and forestalled mob influence. Seattle cops had a standard joke: "If you cleaned this city up, we'd all have to go on welfare 'cause none of us could live on our salary."[5]

Spellman's name appeared in a political ad for the first time as one of "A Hundred Young Men for Clinton."[6] Clinton's election "was a passing of the baton from the sons of Cincinnatus" to the Evans Republicans. The "burgher-business civic matrix" was eroding.[7] To Spellman, "it was inspiring and exciting."

The Clinton administration, though honest and efficient, was also something less than dynamic, given its penchant for committees. Its achievements included the orderly planning for the landmark Century 21 World's Fair and its aftermath. A modern, livable city required more than a Space Needle and a couple of miles of monorail, Clinton said. He and Jim Ellis, a visionary civic activist, advocated lidding the freeway through downtown, a bold plan advanced by the noted architect Paul Thiry. The push for regional mass transit collided repeatedly with short-sightedness. "Metro," the Municipality of Metropolitan Seattle, denounced by some as a blend of Big Brother and Communism, was finally approved by the voters in the fall of 1958. It set out to clean up Lake Washington, which had absorbed the effluent of affluence. Fecal plumes, mixed with oil, antifreeze and insecticides, percolated unchecked for decades. Large stretches of the lake were unsafe for swimmers.

Clinton made good on his promise to investigate police corruption. The grafters lay low for a while. The best the mayor could do was put a dent in tolerance. It was systemic, with complicit "victims" and friends in high places. In 1961, City Council members pointed out, the revenue from licensing punchboards and pinball machines—"trade-stimulant" devices—was $225,000.[8] Unlicensed punchboards and pulltabs flourished in rural King County, together with sports betting, cardrooms and "bottle" clubs where patrons brought their own booze. The mayor said it was up to the county prosecutor to order a full-scale crackdown. Charles O. Carroll, Sheriff Tim McCullough and Police Chief Frank Ramon, professing deep concern, swapped news releases with the mayor. Deadlines were set. Not much changed, to the surprise of few.

Clinton appointed the city's first Human Rights Commission and pushed for open housing, only to see it rejected by the voters. Seattle was ballyhooing itself as a modern, cosmopolitan city, Sam Smith noted in a letter to the editor. But if it was truly progressive, Seattle and all of Washington State would declare "it to be public policy that a man's race, color or national origin should not be determining factors as to whether he should be able to purchase adequate housing." [9]

Provincialism still ran wide and deep even as Seattle's population topped 550,000 and King County's approached one million.

SPELLMAN WAS a deputy chairman of the Clinton campaign in 1960 as the mayor breezed to re-election. County Commissioner Scott Wallace, an upwardly mobile young Democrat, appointed him to the King County Library Board. The Spellmans' fourth child, Jeff, was born in 1961, a year in which John juggled a busy law practice and a growing list of extracurricular activities. He headed the Georgetown Alumni Fund Drive in King County, became chairman of the Library Board and was the Archdiocese of Seattle's leading layman.

In 1962, at the urging of Joe Kane, Mayor Clinton named Spellman to the Municipal Civil Service Commission. Spellman campaigned for progressive City Council candidates and helped elect his friend Johnny O'Brien county commissioner on the Republican ticket. O'Brien and his brother Eddie, the fast-breaking "gold dust twins," had elevated Seattle University to national prominence in basketball. They were both All-Americans in 1953. Seattle was a UW town, but Seattle U grads constituted a tight fraternity of their own.

On Friday, December 27, 1963, a few minutes before filing week ended, Spellman strolled into the city comptroller's office and declared his candidacy for mayor. "It was a spontaneous decision. Clinton had decided to not seek a third term, and I didn't see anyone worthy of filling his shoes. Lois was furious that I hadn't consulted her first. She would have said 'OK,' but she wanted to be asked. She had a right to be upset."

THERE WERE EIGHT candidates in all for mayor of Seattle in 1964, all white males; otherwise an assorted lot. The job paid $23,000-a-year. "Cowboy" John Cherberg, the genial lieutenant governor, wanted it. So did J.D. "Dorm" Braman, a city councilman who owned a lumber and hardware store. "The boys on the curb" saw it as "a Cowboy John/Braman the Brahmin one-two finish," Emmett Watson wrote in his popular *Post-Intelligencer* column. [10]

Braman was elected to the City Council in the 1950s and quickly became

SPELLMAN FAMILY ALBUM

The candidate.

chairman of the Finance Committee. He ably represented the city on the World's Fair Commission and played a key role in the redevelopment of the fairgrounds as a civic commons, the Seattle Center. Braman knew all the old-guard business and industrial leaders. He had friends in big labor. Chuck Carroll introduced him to the pinball people.

Mayor was a nonpartisan office but party regulars knew who their candidates were. Cherberg, 53, was a New Deal Democrat; Braman, 62, a lifelong Republican. Former sheriff Tim McCullough, viewed as the next most credible contender, thanks largely to name familiarly, was a Democrat. So was Irving Clark Jr., an attorney and property developer newly appointed to the State Highway Commission by Governor Rosellini. Spellman, identified with the Clinton-Pritchard bloc, was a distinct dark horse in his first political race. Billing himself as "A new face with a new pace," he doorbelled citywide and appeared before any group that would have him, from the PTA to Post Office retirees. A $15-a-plate dinner at the Edgewater Inn netted $600, peanuts compared to the frontrunners' war chests. Spellman learned early on that to get noticed he had to be more forceful, even interrupt. That was against his nature. Soon, however, newspaper accounts of candidate forums began to spotlight his views on government efficiency. The Seattle Center, post-fair, was now like "a beautiful new ship in the middle of a hurricane," Spellman said at one forum. "A half dozen different captains, each at a different wheel," were attempting to steer different courses while shouting different commands. What Seattle needed was one organization to oversee the center and promote tourism, including the annual Seafair celebration. "Overlapping executives and wasteful expenses" compromised efficiency. He saw similar problems "everywhere" in city and county government.[11] The mayor and council also had an obligation to plan for the future without forgetting the past, Spellman said. From his office in the Smith Tower, he had a bird's-eye view of a spectacular bay separated from its city by an ugly concrete-and-rebar motor vehicle viaduct. The Pike Place Market, which renowned artist Mark Tobey called "the soul of Seattle," had been branded blighted by developers. "It is far from that," Spellman said, quoting Emmett Watson, who wrote that "a flossy rehabilitation would be like placing a beanie on the bust of Teddy Roosevelt."[12]

None of the other candidates were as adamant as Spellman and Clark on the need to regulate high-rise buildings. Scenic views and waterfront locations "belong to all the people" and "should not be sacrificed," Spellman said.[13] He and Clark were poles apart, however, on the tolerance policy. "You can't eliminate gambling in a city the size of Seattle," Clark asserted. "The Wallingford Boys' Club shouldn't be barred from financing its activities through bingo games." Boys' Club bingo wasn't the problem, Spellman said, noting that no city in the United States outside of Nevada had issued more gambling licenses than Seattle.[14]

Spellman and Clark also emerged as the most outspoken advocates of the open housing ordinance on the March 10, 1964, municipal-election ballot. The measure made it there through the efforts of Councilmen Wing Luke, the first Asian-American elected to major public office in the Northwest, and Lud Kramer, another young progressive. Asians and Jews, as well as blacks, knew "the sting of bigotry" in a supposedly enlightened city, Spellman said. Braman opposed the open housing ordinance as an infringement on private property rights. The city should concentrate on finding more and better jobs for blacks. Until then, Braman said, "only a relatively few Negroes" could afford better housing outside the Central District.[15]

The *Seattle P-I* paused from its election coverage to profile Dixy Lee Ray, "the eminent zoologist" on leave from the University of Washington to direct the Pacific Science Center, the former U.S. Science Pavilion at the 1962 World's Fair. She was heading for the island of Mauritius in the Indian Ocean with eight grad students to study the impact of monsoons that blow one way for six months "then reverse course for the next half year." She said she found bacteria more interesting than politics.[16]

THE MUNICIPAL LEAGUE'S RATINGS, influential and controversial, ranked Braman alone as "outstanding." Spellman, Cherberg and Clark were judged "above-average." McCullough was outraged at being branded "below-average."[17] City-county finger-pointing over who should be enforcing gambling laws raged during his last term as sheriff.[18] The dailies and the *Argus*, Seattle's venerable weekly, endorsed Braman. Spellman earned a nod as a bright new face, handicapped by "no organized support except that provided by friends and admirers."[19]

The boys on the curb had underestimated Braman. With the top two advancing to the finals, he outpolled Cherberg by nearly 15,000 votes. Spellman won more respect than votes. He finished fifth, with 6,327 out of 137,000 cast. This was "somewhat short" of what he'd hoped for, he said, but he was "invigorated" by the experience.[20] Carroll and Ken Rogstad, the county Republican chairman, told him he had a real future in politics. Ed Devine, Braman's campaign manager, called to say he'd done very well. Spellman knew what was coming next: "Dorm would love to have your support for the finals." He got it. "Cherberg was a nice fellow and a gentlemanly presiding officer for the State Senate," Spellman says, "but he wouldn't have been the kind of mayor Seattle needed."

The King County commissioners, led by Scott Wallace, adopted an open housing ordinance the week before the general election. Although the law applied only to the county's unincorporated areas, it was one of the first in the nation. Gordon Clinton, frustrated by his council's reluctance to pass a similar measure, was on hand to applaud as the commissioners passed the ordinance.

BRAMAN WAS a tenacious campaigner. Emphasizing his own often-stated opposition to open housing, he styled Cherberg as indecisive. Braman won 53 percent of the vote. Open housing was defeated two-to-one. The World's Fair had been a Potemkin village, civil rights leaders said, warning that Seattle was in for "a hot summer." [21]

In office, Braman pleased high-rolling supporters of tolerance by maintaining that "vice was easier to police if it was licensed and regulated." [22] Reformers called it "Dormancy." But there were impressive progressive developments, too, thanks in no small part to Ed Devine's moxie as deputy mayor. Braman supported Ellis' Forward Thrust initiatives—light rail enthusiastically. He appointed Seattle's first black municipal court judge, Charles Z. Smith, a former top aide to Attorney General Robert F. Kennedy, and established a Special Citizens Committee to improve relations between the Police Department and the black community. Braman appointed himself to the group, together with Smith and Spellman. "Ed Devine was Dorm's secret weapon," Spellman says. "He was a Jersey City guy who ran Jack Kennedy's campaign in New York in 1960 and came out here to oversee development of the Pacific Science Center in the wake of the World's Fair. Dorm knew talent when he saw it." So did Spellman. The plump, rumpled Democrat "with large, worried eyes and an irrepressible ironic sense" would become one of Spellman's most trusted advisers.[23] Devine skillfully worked the corridors of power in Washington, D.C. Over the five years of the Braman administration, Seattle secured $100 million in federal Model Cities grants to fight poverty, improve housing, boost parks and recreation and improve mass-transit.

THAT NOVEMBER, the "new breed" Republicans achieved their fondest goal. Dan Evans defeated Al Rosellini to become at 39 the youngest governor in Washington State history and one of the few major-office Republican candidates to escape the Johnson landslide. Thousands of LBJ voters crossed over to Evans, while thousands of progressive Republicans, Spellman included, voted for Johnson. "There was no way I could vote for Goldwater."

Spellman, only 37, liked politics but figured the best he could hope for was a seat on the Superior Court bench. He was destined to find himself picking his way through the minefield of Courthouse politics during an era fraught with the challenges of change. Chuck Carroll had him pegged as someone who would go along to get along.

CHAPTER SEVEN

Fear and Loathing
at the Courthouse

Scott Wallace had a bull's-eye on his back and an $11-million albatross around his neck. It was the summer of 1965. As he geared up to campaign for a third term, the chairman of the board of King County commissioners was worried about the soaring cost of remodeling the Courthouse. Completed in 1916 and expanded in 1931, the 12-floor land-mark near Seattle's Pioneer Square featured wood-frame windows, antique mechanicals and dangerously overloaded electrical circuits. The jail on the top floors was overcrowded and equally outmoded.

When Phase I got under way there were unpleasant surprises. Ob-solescence and decay ran deeper than originally thought. Change orders pushed the work 10 percent higher to nearly $2 million. When bids were opened for Phase II on July 6, 1965, Wallace almost gulped. The lowest bid—$11.1 million—was more than twice as high as the architect's estimate. The escalating price of materials and expansive wish lists from the elected officials were key factors. They all wanted carpet, not vinyl tile, in a building that had 14 acres of floor space. The judges insisted, however, that it was the architect who suggested they should have fancy bleached paneling in their courtrooms and showers in their private bathrooms.

The growing impression that the commissioners were at best hapless and at worst engaged in kickback cronyism had its genesis in an off-the-cuff estimate three years earlier by then-Commissioner Howard Odell that remodeling would cost "about $3 million." That was just "a sidewalk archi-tect's guess," Wallace said repeatedly, "not the result of any detailed study."[1] Moreover, Odell was talking about *Phase One*, "but no one listened," Wal-lace said. "About $3 million" vs. the new reality of $13 million was invariably mentioned by the press and seized on by critics of Wallace and his fellow Democrat, Commissioner Ed Munro. Johnny O'Brien, the lone Republican on the three-member board, told reporters he was exasperated by the over-runs and dubious that the architect, Paul W. DeLaney & Associates, was up to the task. The cries of boondoggle began when Republicans, smelling blood, pointed out that Bernard J. Heavey Jr., the Democrats' recent county chairman, was an electrical engineer with DeLaney & Associates. The firm's fee was 11 percent of the total construction cost. In other words, the higher the better, critics said. DeLaney countered that Heavey was on unpaid leave during the time he headed the party and had no part in the Courthouse project. *The Seattle Times* asked the architect if politics played any role in his firm landing the job. "Personally, I don't think so," DeLaney said, making things worse in the next breath by telling the gospel truth about doing business in King County: "You get jobs from your friends. What one person might construe to be political influence, another does not."² Wallace explained that the commissioners tried to "pass around" work. DeLaney was a capable architect, experienced in big remodeling jobs. "That's the bottom line."³

Howie Odell's "about $3 million" guesstimate and DeLaney's "You get jobs from your friends" were the defining quotes of the growing controversy. In the shorthand of headline writing it quickly became a "scandal."

THE COMMISSIONERS rejected the bids and asked the Seattle Chapter of the American Institute of Architects to appoint a committee to review DeLaney's professional performance.⁴ Prosecutor Carroll was ginning up a grand jury.

C. Montgomery "Gummie" Johnson, the shrewd Republican state chairman, cut to the chase in an address to King County's 32nd District Republican Club. Right-wingers in the audience flailed him for joining Dan Evans in repudiating the John Birch Society. "Listen," Johnson said,

A flier from Wallace's campaign for re-election as King County commissioner in 1966.

wagging his cigar, "and I'll tell you some things we should all agree on." He proceeded to outline a five-point plan to elect more Republicans in 1966: Better organization; a lot more money; grass-roots foot soldiers; compelling issues and great candidates. The race for King County commissioner would be one of the most important in the state. "We must control the Court-house," Johnson declared. "There is more patronage available through the local government at the County Courthouse than even Governor Evans controls statewide. Remember the name Scott Wallace and go after him."⁵

Shelby Scates had pretty much seen it all as a wire service reporter, bouncing from Baton Rouge to Little Rock before landing at the *Post-Intelligencer*, Seattle's morning daily. He took stock of the atmosphere at the King County Courthouse: "As political offices go, it's about as glamorous as an end zone seat for the Idaho game in Husky Stadium. Or, in the words of John Spellman, 'What wife would want to say she raised her husband to be a county commissioner?' The pay isn't bad ($15,000) but the quarters in King County, not to mention a lot of the company you keep, are some-thing left over from the Last Hurrah. ... Trouble is just another word for the job. The tax assessor takes a dive and everybody gets a little dirty."⁶ Spellman lost his political virginity in the rough-and-tumble of the 1966 campaign for county commissioner. Remarkably, his friendship with Scott Wallace survived.

WALLACE was a third-generation dairyman in the Snoqualmie Valley. He married his childhood sweetheart when he returned from the war and received a degree in Sociology from the UW, where he was a light-heavy-weight boxing champ. Like Spellman, he had a slew of kids and seemed to be everywhere at once. He was elected to the school board and became a live wire in the Kiwanis Club, the Grange and Dairy Products Commission, promoting flood control and fighting pollution. When he filed for county commissioner, Marine Corps buddies, college classmates, fellow farmers and other neighbors covered a "Mile-a-night-for-Wallace," doorbelling 80,000 homes in the North District. "Wholesomeness shone from every bit of the old Wallace family farm home" on the morning after his victory in 1958.⁷ The commissioner-elect, a husky 32-year-old with an apple-cheeked smile, was wearing bib overalls and rubber boots when the press arrived. He had chores to do and cows to milk but he posed with his wife and kids, year-old Shelly in his arms, family pooch at his feet.

Wallace headed the "Dollars for Democrats" Kennedy campaign in King County in 1960, rubbing elbows with Rosellini, Magnuson and Jackson. He was a strong supporter of Jim Ellis's efforts to clean up Lake

Washington. After the State Supreme Court struck down a financing plan for the Evergreen Point floating bridge that Rosellini had championed for years, Wallace and his talented aide, Henry Seidel, saved the day. They came up with a loan proposal from Wallace's North District Road fund to guarantee the construction bonds. When the long-delayed second span across Lake Washington opened in the summer of 1963, *The Bellevue American* hailed the "Wallace Plan" as the key to the $27 million project. With heavy use, the span was quickly self-supporting. The East Side's already remarkable growth accelerated.[8] The Jaycees named Wallace one of the most outstanding young men in the state.

"John Spellman was a friend of mine," Wallace says. "We were the same age," two Catholics who grew up on the East Side and got interested in public service. "When I became county commissioner, John came in and said, 'I'd like to be on a committee or something.' I said, 'Take a look at them. Whatever you want you can have. I haven't appointed anybody yet.' He said, 'Well, I kind of like the Library Board.' And I said, 'Fine. I'll appoint you to the Library Board.' Pretty soon, John became the chairman of a board that oversaw a million-dollar budget and 39 branch libraries. He did a great job."[9]

Until the Courthouse scandal, Wallace seemed a shoo-in for a third term and likely destined for even bigger things. Chuck Carroll was intent on derailing a dangerous Democrat, while Governor Evans saw an opportunity to gain hegemony in King County through the Courthouse. There was another thing: When Wallace took office in 1959, Evans' 64-year-old father, Les, lost his job as county engineer. Wallace, Munro and Odell wanted a man of their "own choosing." What goes around comes around.[10]

DEMOCRATS HAD CONTROLLED the Courthouse since 1952. Jack England, a handsome lawyer, would have the support of both wings of the King County Republican Party if he took on Wallace. But England would have to surrender his seat in the State Senate, paving the way for the advancement of State Representative Wes Uhlman, an ambitious young Democrat. Don McKeta, a former star running back for the UW Huskies, was mentioned early on as another possible Wallace challenger.[11] Carroll and Rogstad quickly concluded, however, that Spellman was just the ticket. On this even Evans and Rogstad, sworn philosophical enemies, could agree. Spellman was clean-cut and hard-working, with a June Cleaver wife and five cute kids. Being the son of a Northwest football legend didn't hurt either. Carroll summoned Spellman to his office for a chat about "your future." Rogstad was there. So was seven-term Congressman Tom Pelly.

So was Bill Boeing Jr., a staunch conservative who headed the finance committee for the King County GOP.

"We think you should run for county commissioner," said Carroll.

"Why would I want to do that?" said Spellman. "I've never seen anybody go anywhere from being county commissioner."

"Yeah," Carroll said, "but what if somebody could? What if they could shake up the county government and turn it into a new and better government?"

"It was a good pitch," Spellman remembers. "They convinced me I could win—that I could reform county government and maybe go on to even bigger things. They assured me that raising money would be no problem. Crucially, I would be a coalition candidate, the focal point of cooperation by both extremes of the Republican Party in King County; the right and the left coming together."

Evans, the Pritchard brothers and Gummie Johnson were battling the Goldwaterites for control of the county GOP apparatus. They agreed to bury the hatchet with Rogstad for the duration of the campaign on the condition that Carroll would stay neutral in the intra-party fight. "Everything came together," Spellman says. "The Democrats had tried to draw the lines to keep me out, but my house remained inside the North District by about a block" after redistricting. Carroll and Rogstad assumed that Spellman, once elected, would be "a team player." He could smoke his pipe, wear his tweeds and have coffee with the archbishop, but not go overboard on the reform and modernize stuff. Above all, as Gummie Johnson had made clear, the prize was patronage—3,000 jobs. The Sheriff's Office was the only county agency under Civil Service, and even that wasn't much of a problem.

After his run for mayor in 1964, Spellman was focused on City Hall, not the Courthouse. When the remodeling controversy erupted, "I never thought for a moment that Scott had done anything dishonest. The 'scandal' was something Carroll obviously had engineered. It was a scandal of ineptness, and it wasn't entirely Scott's fault. But I wanted to be a county commissioner, and his seat was the one that was up for election. It wasn't personal."

A banner headline in the *Post-Intelligencer* in February of 1966—"GOP Finds Top Candidate for Commissioner"—announced that Spellman had been chosen. He claimed to be still mulling, but the story was unequivocal: "Republicans searching high and low for high-caliber candidates Wednesday came up with a top-notch opponent to go against North King County Commissioner Scott Wallace in the person of John D. Spellman, minor hero of the 1964 Seattle mayoralty race.... As a candidate, Spellman will have many things going for him. He is neither tabbed as a liberal nor conservative and could pull support from all segments of the party, an acknowledged requirement to unseat the entrenched Wallace.... Now only 39, Spellman is chairman of the Seattle Civil Service Commission which has jurisdiction over 8,000 employees." [12]

Scott Wallace would have many things going against him.

CHAPTER EIGHT

Psychological Warfare

Convened by Carroll on February 28, 1966, the King County Grand Jury began with a bang, bogged down in minutiae and finally fizzled to an anticlimactic close on May 3. It had been in session for 35 days, calling 84 witnesses. The first headlines heralded the sensational news that A.J. "Tony" Steen, 59, the county assessor, had resigned, together with his chief personal-property deputy. The Democrat admitted to accepting bribes from tax consultants to lower assessments. The Courthouse probe shared the front page with the escalating war in Vietnam, Boeing's plans to add 15,000 workers and the hotly debated proposal to install Namu, a kidnapped killer whale, in a pool at the Seattle Center.

Grand Jury witnesses were pressured to sign waivers of immunity from prosecution before entering the jury room. Bernie Heavey, who worked for the embattled architect, called it "psychological warfare."[1] Scott Wallace was pictured lugging box loads of subpoenaed income-tax returns and other personal records through a perp-walk gantlet of reporters and photographers. "I have nothing to hide," he said repeatedly. The board's mistake was in not hiring a nationally-known expert building consultant before embarking on the remodeling project, Wallace said. "That way the public would have known in advance how big a job this is." An urgent job, too. "Things were so bad that if this had been a private building, it would have been condemned. ... We knew we would be damned if we did and damned if we didn't."[2]

Wallace said he hoped the probe would lead to a sweeping reorganization of county government. With Boeing's expansion and the growing suburbs, King County was undergoing extraordinary change. Critical problems—mass transportation, air and water pollution, law and justice services, parks and recreation—couldn't be solved with a government that was an antiquated "carry-over of 100 years ago," he said. The workload was simply too much for three commissioners to handle. "It's amazing it works as well as it does." Wallace advocated a virtual county legislature of perhaps 18 to 24 representatives, with a mayor-like executive.[3]

LIKE THE VICHY police chief in *Casablanca* who professes to be shocked that gambling is going on under his nose, then deftly pockets his winnings, one of the Grand Jury's more entertaining pseudo-revelations was that practically every county office had a "flower fund," watered weekly by the troops. (A grand jury in 1937 had condemned the practice.) The fund in the Prosecutor's Office was voluntary, Carroll insisted. The men contributed $2 a month, the women $1 since they were paid less. The fund paid for get-well bouquets and funeral flowers, Christmas and retirement parties and tickets to the Policeman's Ball, church and charity dinners. "It is never abused" for partisan political purposes, Carroll said.[4] County Clerk Walter Renschler was more candid—and decisive. He fired the two employees who exposed to the Grand Jury the mandatory 2 percent-of-pay contribution system in his office, accusing both of disloyalty. "God, let's be practical!" Renschler told reporters. "This is a political patronage office and you have to have the loyalty of your staff."[5]

Bernie Heavey and Carroll swapped pleasantries outside the jury room. The electrical engineer called Carroll "a politically prejudiced nitwit" whose duplicity on gambling and other vice deserved a grand jury of its own. "This would appear to be another version of 'Smoke Gets in Your Eyes' by Bernard Heavey," Carroll suggested.[6] Three weeks later, Heavey's boss, architect Paul DeLaney, was indicted by the grand jury, arrested, booked and fingerprinted for a gross misdemeanor, "fraudulently presenting a claim to a public officer."[7]

The Grand Jury's final report chastised the commissioners for their method of selecting an architect and "failure to establish a centralized control for the project." It recommended firing DeLaney & Associates. However, after an exhaustive review of personal financial records it found no evidence that Wallace, Munro and O'Brien or their budget aides had violated any state laws. There was no "conspiracy." Presiding Judge William J. Wilkins immediately dismissed the indictment against DeLaney.[8] The jury also concluded that the flower funds violated no statutes and praised Carroll for the "personal guidance" he provided during its deliberations. He sent each juror a certificate of appreciation.[9]

Forty-five years after the ordeal, Wallace leaned over a plate of biscuits and gravy at his favorite diner and declared, "If they'd found five cents out of line they'd have stuck my ass in jail. Afterward, everybody kind of laughed about it, but the stress was terrible. They wanted to see all my farm stuff for seven years. All my campaign documents and income tax returns. I had to wheel all that into the Courthouse. That was the start of my arthritis. Inside the jury room, the line of questioning was 'When did you quit beating your wife?' You weren't allowed to be accompanied by legal counsel."[10]

What qualified as a bona fide revelation was the depth and breadth of cheating that had been going on for years on tax assessments. Hundreds of scofflaws, including major corporations, had evaded some $10 million in taxes since 1962 by filing fraudulent personal-property tax returns. Tony Steen, the assessor, was at worst a penny-ante player. Yet he went to jail, railroaded by Carroll, Wallace maintains. Many in both parties agreed. An editorial in the *Argus* concluded, "The poorly-paid public official is not as culpable as the affluent business man who took advantage of the opportunity offered, full knowing that he was breaking the law" by cheating on estimates of inventories, furniture and other taxable items.[11] In another broadside, the paper declared that the stubborn old was colliding with the irresistible new in King County: "The notion of King County's commissioners settling a multi-million dollar highway route in one breath, then weighing a decision to hire a carpenter with the next, may have been just the ticket for our Populist forefathers. But in 1966 it is absurd."[12]

SPELLMAN MADE his candidacy official on June 1st, calling for a merit system for county hiring, a full-time budget director and the "end of one-party rule." He accused Wallace and Munro of "gross political cynicism" for overriding the recommendations of the grand jury by retaining Delaney & Associates and pushing ahead with the project.[13] Carroll emerged from filing week home free, with no opponents. The prosecutor had "intimidated the hell" out of everyone, Wallace grouses.

For Spellman and Wallace, both unopposed, the Primary Election was a dry-run involving only North District voters. Spellman outpolled Wallace by 1,300 votes. Clearly wounded by the Courthouse remodeling controversy, Wallace probably could "count himself lucky to have virtually broken even with Spellman," *The Seattle Times* observed. But the whole county would vote on the race in the General Election. If recent trends held true, many more Democrats would be in the mix then. Wallace was an energetic campaigner. No one was counting him out.[14]

One casualty of the primary was a $38 million bond issue to finance a domed stadium. It had been heavily promoted by civic and political leaders and the media. But the issue was ill-timed, sharing the ballot with a Seattle school-bond issue and other bond-debt proposals. It needed a 60 percent supermajority and received only 51.5. Given that the Kingdome

Spellman addresses a campaign event.

would become one of the signature issues in Spellman's political career, it's ironic that in the 1966 campaign Wallace was one of the stadium's strongest supporters while Spellman was trumpeting Courthouse reform. Wallace wrote a well-crafted column—"This Time, Let's Come in Out of the Rain"—for KING Broadcasting's sophisticated new *Seattle* magazine. The stadium would cost the owner of a typical $20,000 home only about $6 the first year, decreasing thereafter, Wallace wrote. "King County is the largest metropolitan region in the U.S. without any major league team." With a domed stadium, it stood an excellent chance of landing the National

Football League's 16th franchise and probably a major league baseball team, too, Wallace added. Seattle also desperately needed an enclosed multipurpose facility to attract national conventions and trade shows and shed its small-town reputation "once and for all."[15]

GOVERNOR EVANS headlined a $50-plate Spellman fundraiser at the Olympic Hotel. It drew 400 Republican stalwarts, including Weyerhaeuser heir Norton Clapp, who made a handsome contribution. The Spellman campaign's steering committee acquired the assistance of Helen Rasmussen, a key player in Evans' 1964 upset of Rosellini. "The illusion was that harmony reigned among King County Republicans, and it played pretty well," Spellman says. Behind the scenes, however, trouble was already brewing. "The day after the primary, Carroll and Rogstad asked me to agree to get rid of certain people when I took office. I said, 'I can't do that.' Then they wrote me off." They were consoled by the notion he surely couldn't be worse than Wallace and might yet come around.

Given his record as a debate champ, old friends expected Spellman to mop the floor with Wallace. Spellman knew better. During one joint appearance, Spellman held aloft a Wallace campaign brochure that cited the Courthouse remodeling project as an example of leadership. "When you do business in this slipshod manner with political cronies, I'll bet this won't even wind up as a $13 million job," he said. "A new one," Wallace shot back, "would have cost in excess of $30 million." Branding hard-working county employees as "political hacks" was "totally undeserved and a cheap campaign trick," the Democrat said.[16]

Full-page Spellman ads in the dailies featured photos of allegedly slipshod work at the Courthouse. Governor Evans excoriated Wallace as part of "a continuing dynasty of incredible ineptness."[17] Wallace bristled, telling the governor to butt out and "tend to state business." He said the grand jury was "being used maliciously and untruthfully in an effort to paint me as some sort of crook."[18]

Spellman was growing queasy over the thrust of the campaign. And he was visibly upset when reporters told him the grand jury foreman, a fellow with the Dickensian name of John K. Wimpress, had been trotted out by Carroll to take umbrage at Wallace's criticisms of 16 "sincere and thoughtful citizens."[19] A few days before the election, fliers targeting Wallace as a crook popped up all over the county. "They were scandalous," Spellman says. "Horrible stuff!" says Wallace. Spellman disowned them and asked his friend Roman Miller, a legendary Seattle U athletic booster, to mobilize campaign workers to scoop them up. Spellman believes the handouts were the handiwork of Rogstad, who was locked in a no-holds-barred struggle with Evans for the 600 precinct-committee slots on the ballot. "I wanted to be county commissioner, but not that bad. I was convinced that the commissioners had botched the remodeling and that patronage had to end, whether it was the Democrats or Republicans dishing it out. But Scott Wallace was not a crook. Nor was Ed Munro."

Ed Donohoe, the hard-hitting columnist for the 51,000-circulation *Washington Teamster*, castigated Spellman, Evans and Carroll for under-handed tactics. Donohoe had long since christened Carroll "Faircatch" to lampoon his exploits as a football All-American and fearless champion of public morality. "With all the issues squarely facing the voters in this burgeoning county," Donohoe wrote, "we will wonder right down to the wire why Spellman and his backers continue to harp about a Grand Jury, conducted by C. Faircatch Carroll. ... The one indictment that was squeezed out after nine weeks of witch-hunting was quashed immediately for lack of evidence." Carroll was so crafty, Donohoe said, that he even made secret tape recordings of his "inquisitions" of Courthouse supervisors. The edito-rial was accompanied by a cartoon showing a puny Spellman in oversized

A cartoon in the *Washington Teamster* lampoons Evans and Spellman.

"Sorry, Johnny. This is about all you have to run with."

helmet being handed a football by Evans from the governor's "bag of tricks." The caption says: "Sorry, Johnny. This is about all you have to run with." [20]

SPELLMAN won his first election on November 8, 1966, outpolling Wallace by 31,000 votes. "I just feel like going out and shaking hands," he told reporters the next morning, posing with Lois, the kids and a Siamese cat named Cy. It was a *Father Knows Best* tableau. America was on the cusp of social cataclysm, but Lois was proud to be a stay-at-home mom, while John promised to be a fulltime commissioner committed to evolution, not revolution. "There won't be any mass firing," but "political hacks" on the payroll were in jeopardy. [21]

In Olympia, the governor was jubilant. Republicans had captured not only the King County Courthouse but control of the state House of Representatives for the first time in 14 years. Evans partisans had also won the lion's share of King County precinct committee spots. Rogstad maintained their schism had been "highly overrated" and said his last-minute get-out-the-vote drive was the key to Spellman's victory. Maybe so. Come December, in any case, Rogstad outfoxed Evans and was narrowly re-elected Central Committee chairman. [22] "Probably the most conspicuous absentee" from the tumultuous King County Republican Convention that drew nearly 1,500 delegates was Commissioner-elect Spellman, *The Seattle Times* reported. "The official explanation was that Spellman was tied up in a freeway traffic jam. But Spellman has made every effort to remain aloof from the intra-party struggle, figuring he will have to keep all fences mended during the coming four years." [23]

The inside story would have sold more papers.

"Two or three days after the election, Carroll got behind Ken Rogstad for county chairman, going back on his word that he would stay neutral in the intra-party fight," Joel Pritchard revealed when Carroll was under even heavier fire two years later. Spellman provided the rest of the story: "Carroll called a meeting and said we all had to help out Ken in his fight with the Evans forces to get re-elected county chairman. He asked me to sign a letter endorsing Rogstad's candidacy. I refused, saying that I had stated my neutrality in the fight during the campaign and I meant it. The prosecutor said something to the effect that I had to play ball with the guys who elected me. I refused. He went into a rage. Carroll then said, 'If that's the way you play it, you're through.' " [24]

Spellman also refused to give Carroll veto power over his selection of an administrative aide, choosing a young newsman named Gary Desharnais. The prosecutor prodded O'Brien to give his new colleague the silent treatment. "That ruptured all communications between Carroll, O'Brien and Spellman during the crucial month prior to the 1967 legislative session" when the commissioners could have been pressing their case for more taxing authority.[25] "The tension was such that I spent a lot of it wondering whether I should actually take office," Spellman says.

Wallace reserved his enmity for Carroll and Evans. "I'm convinced that John didn't have anything to do with the dirty, below-the-belt stuff. That was a faction within the party completely outside of him."[26]

On January 9, 1967, Spellman's first day at the Courthouse, Wallace dropped by as painters were erasing his name from the office door. "John, I'm going to warn you," he counseled. "Chuck Carroll is upstairs. You've got to be careful. If you go in his office, remember he's got a tape recorder under the desk. Don't say anything that could come back to haunt you. He'll get you if you do."[27] Richard D. Auerbach, a retired FBI agent who helped oversee finances for the Spellman campaign, offered a similar warning right after the election: "They will attempt to compromise you." Auerbach urged him to keep fastidious records on auto use, travel and gratuities. "I knew Auerbach and Wallace were not over-reacting," Spellman says. "Carroll and Rogstad weren't going to like my independence, so I was always super circumspect on all my activities. You never know for sure if there was an attempt—a trap—unless you fall into it, but there were a number of fishy things: A developer who had not contributed during my campaign but now sends a letter and a check; the offer of a free trip to Las Vegas. I had an Irish sixth sense that warned me when things didn't seem right. The threats against people I hired when I became commissioner certainly weren't subtle. I told Desharnais, 'I'll handle the politics here. You keep me out of jail by paying the strictest attention to details.'"[28]

Carroll and Wallace bumped into one another at a bipartisan fundraiser a couple of years after the election. "As we were coming out of the restaurant Chuck was getting his coat on and talking to somebody. He motioned toward me and I overheard him say, 'You know I worked like hell to get that Wallace out of there but I don't know if I did myself any good.' I guess I didn't do myself any good either when I gave John Spellman his start in politics," Wallace says with a *c'est la vie* laugh.[29]

CHAPTER NINE

Changing Times

The social seismometer was registering tremors along multiple fault lines across America when Spellman arrived at the King County Courthouse. Student activists opposed to the escalating war in Vietnam coalesced with civil rights advocates as the new left challenged the establishment. "I ain't got no quarrel with them Viet Cong," heavyweight champ Muhammad Ali said as he defied the draft. They'd never called him "nigger."[1] Still, 1967 was a garden party compared to 1968, the pivotal year in Spellman's political rise. "America shuddered. History cracked open and bats came flapping out," *Time* magazine wrote.[2]

In King County, urban planners, architects and exponents of the advancing environmental movement warned that a "Pugetopolis" was the shape of things to come unless someone put on the brakes. The Chamber of Commerce's drive to pave paradise and put up a parking lot accelerated with the completion of Interstate 5 between Tacoma and Everett. Business was booming. Farmland succumbed to factories, subdivisions and shopping malls. Boeing's best-selling 737 made its debut, with the jumbo-jet 747 close behind. A revolutionary supersonic transport, the SST, was on the drawing board. The federal Department of Labor was helping Seattle recruit more workers. Within four years, however, Boeing would come "within an eyelash of bankruptcy."[3]

Reformers were gaining a foothold at Seattle City Hall. New media voices emerged, from the underground *Helix* to *Seattle* magazine, KING Broadcasting's blend of new journalism, culture and cuisine. The Students for a Democratic Society and Seattle's intellectuals found additional common cause in their disdain for Charles O. Carroll. Spellman's sideburns crept an inch lower, but "violence, polarization and the erosion of civility," deeply troubled him.

"Where have you gone, Joe DiMaggio?" Simon and Garfunkel lamented as the nation writhed from assassinations and rioting. Incongruous as it may have seemed in the midst of a political-cultural revolution, Joltin' Joe had gone to Seattle to help Spellman campaign for a domed stadium.

SPELLMAN'S EARLIEST MEMORIES are of attending college football games with his father and listening to Seattle Rainiers baseball games on the radio whenever he couldn't make it to Sicks' Stadium, the Depression-era ballpark in the Rainier Valley. He even remembers its predecessor, Dugdale Park. Leo Lassen, a legendary broadcaster, offered play-by-play so vivid "you could almost smell the peanuts," Spellman says. "My enthusiasm for a domed stadium was also kindled by its multipurpose design. In addition to baseball and football, we could host everything from a national political convention to a rock concert."

What came to be called the Kingdome was an idea born in 1959. With work on the Century 21 World's Fair well under way, a $15 million stadium bond issue was placed on the ballot by the City Council in 1960. The booster spirit surrounding the fair was not infectious enough, however, to brush aside two key questions: If we build it, will a big-league sports franchise really come? And is $15 million really enough? Georg Meyers, sports editor of *The Seattle Times*, warned that if the bond issue failed "this neck of the wood can kiss good-bye all hopes of attracting major-league baseball or professional football here in this generation." But if it succeeded the odds were excellent that Seattle and King County would take their "rightful place among the nation's principal centers of sport." For the owner of a "typical" $10,000 home, "that ought to be worth the price of a package of gum once a week into eternity."[4] The ballot issue needed a 60 percent majority. Nearly 52 percent were opposed.

After the fair—a huge success that elevated Seattle's image internationally—two new stadium plans were floated, one literally. Seattle had floating bridges and houseboats. Why not build a truly unique floating stadium on Elliott Bay? A giant lily pad could rest on concrete pontoons, with variable ballast to ensure stability in the roughest weather. The proposed stadium featured a retractable roof and seating for up to 70,000. The city's Engineering Department squelched the idea as impractical. The other plan that died a-borning was a privately funded sports complex near Kent.

In 1966, the $38 million stadium bond issue championed by Commissioners Scott Wallace and Johnny O'Brien had strong support from civic leaders and the media. It was jinxed by sharing the ballot with several other tax proposals. Then, in late 1967 Major League Baseball awarded Seattle an expansion franchise. The Seattle Pilots would take the field in the spring of 1969 at rickety, undersized Sicks' Stadium. With a team on the way, it was hoped that voters would approve a big-league stadium. The likelihood of landing a professional football franchise was also in the air. The Legislature gave King County the authority to appropriate 2 percent of the state sales tax on hotel-motel stays within the county to retire bonds for a new stadium.

THE KINGDOME was one of the "Forward Thrust" bond propositions submitted to Seattle and King County voters in 1968. The driving force was Jim Ellis, a resilient visionary. During his 60 years as a citizen activist, Ellis has "left a bigger footprint on Seattle and King County than perhaps any other single individual."[5] At 91 in 2012, he was still closely following civic affairs and lamenting missed opportunities.

Ellis joined the Municipal League after graduating from law school at the University of Washington in 1948. He fell in with the post-war crowd of young progressives, notably the Pritchard brothers, Gordon Clinton and Dan Evans. In 1952, Ellis became the legal counsel for the citizen "free-holders" chosen to draft a new King County charter. He quickly ran afoul of Chuck Carroll, technically his boss. The prosecutor worked overtime to derail the freeholders' proposal for a nonpartisan county council that would appoint a county administrator. It was "a hostile environment" from day one, Ellis recalls.[6] Opposed by labor, courthouse managers and both political parties loathe to surrender patronage, the new charter was soundly defeated at the polls. "Losing can be a good teacher," Ellis says. "While licking our wounds, a few of us asked ourselves whether we had been on the right track. I asked myself whether improving the internal structure of county government would make much difference to the congested traffic, polluted water and sprawling developments that were spreading across the boundaries of cities and counties, beyond the control of either."[7] King County was one of the most segmented counties in America, with 31 municipalities and hundreds of special districts. The government of the City of Seattle was also "hopelessly out of date," one essayist concluded.[8] Ellis resolved to create "a new kind of government—a federation of municipalities—to improve water quality, garbage disposal, transportation, parks and land-use planning."[9]

Spellman witnessed Lake Washington's strangulation by civilization during his boyhood at Montlake and Hunts Point. The lake was awash in raw and partially-treated sewage. Places where Spellman swam as a boy were now off limits. The problem worsened exponentially as Seattle's suburbs grew by 110,000 in the 1950s. One of the iconic images in Seattle history shows a group of disappointed kids eyeing a "No Swimming" sign on a summer's day. They became the poster children in the 1958 campaign for "Metro," a new metropolitan sewerage municipality. Joel Pritchard's debate opponent in a televised forum "opened a jar of slimy green algae and proceeded to eat it" in an effort to prove that the gunk strangling the lake "was really good for us," Ellis recalls. Joel held his nose and rolled his eyes. "That was all it took to convince the audience that his opponent was out his mind." [10] Another member of the Municipal League's Metro debate team was Slade Gorton, a brainy transplant from the East Coast. It was the future U.S. senator's first civic foray in his adopted home state.

Defeated in its first try, Metro was shrewdly scaled back by Ellis to target pollution control and win over the smaller cities. Victory came in September of 1958.

SPELLMAN WAS AT the Olympic Hotel on November 3, 1965, for one of the landmark speeches in Seattle history. Ellis told the Downtown Rotary Club—350 movers and shakers—that if Seattle and King County united "in a total effort" they could usher in a "golden age" of livability within a decade. Rapid transit was a cornerstone of his vision. It would reduce air pollution, preserve the city's vital core and obviate the need for more intrusive, clogged freeways that would throttle growth. Ellis also called for a major-league sports stadium, new parks, swimming pools, open spaces, community centers, an aquarium, improved arterials, sewer bonds and low-income housing. It would take a bipartisan "Forward Thrust Committee" of 100 volunteers with "World's Fair zip" to cut through the politics of parochialism and sell the voters on an unprecedented package of bond issues, Ellis said. "Cooperation without rivalry will have to be unstintingly given by public officials." The next day, a columnist observed that "one who does not know Ellis might be tempted to ask what brand of hashish this 43-year-old attorney smokes." Anyone who did know Ellis understood, however, that this "bold new challenge to the metropolitan area he loves so well and serves so faithfully is not an idle pipe dream." [11]

The speech was front-page news and featured on TV and radio. Thousands of free copies were distributed. "That's all everyone talked about," Spellman remembers. Eddie Carlson, the hotel executive who had headed the World's Fair Commission, was on board with his usual ebullience. (His high school yearbook called him a "pint of dynamite.")[12] Mayor Braman, an exponent of rapid transit, was another Forward Thrust supporter.

Ellis worked 80-hour weeks for 18 months and inspired 40,000 man-hours of voluntary labor from the region's brightest people. "It was invigorating to be part of such an amazing brain trust," Spellman says. "With his track record, personality and speaking ability, only Jim Ellis could have galvanized support for a plan that ambitious. We'd known each other for years but became good friends after I was elected county commissioner and joined the Metro Council board." Ellis became "very fond of John as he became absorbed in Forward Thrust. The Kingdome was one of its landmark projects. John persevered to make it happen. With all the roadblocks the stadium encountered, a lot of people would have given up."[13]

When Forward Thrust was put to a vote on February 13, 1968, a typical home in Greater Seattle was worth $20,000. The total local cost for the entire package, $820 million, amounted to $49 a year for a home owner in Seattle, $36 for someone in the suburbs and $17.50 outside the Metro boundaries.[14] Factoring in state and federal matching funds, King County stood to achieve improvements worth nearly $2 billion. Opponents branded Forward Thrust the "greatest conceivable monument to socialism ever offered in our community" and "a death chant for democracy."[15]

The voters authorized $40 million for the multipurpose stadium, $118 million for parks and recreation, $81 million for arterials and $70 million for sewers. The casualty was rapid transit. With matching funds, the measure would have parlayed $385 million in local bonds into a total of $1.15 billion. It received barely a simple majority. Slade Gorton calls it "the stupidest 'no' vote the people of Seattle ever cast."[16] A second try also failed, Spellman recalls, shaking his head. "We left a lot of federal money on the table." Braman was glummer yet, predicting there would be "tragic results."[17]

As for the Kingdome, getting the money to build it was a snap compared to deciding where.

CHAPTER TEN

The Crisis
of the Old Order

Spellman and O'Brien flexed their majority early on by placing a freeholder election on the 1967 ballot and hiring a county administrator. John Porter, former executive director of the Puget Sound Governmental Conference, was a 41-year-old ex-Marine from Detroit with a master's degree in urban planning. The Republican commissioners also set out to hire a budget analyst and personnel director.

O'Brien, boyishly handsome and personable, nevertheless seemed less comfortable at the Courthouse than the ball park. The kid from New Jersey had spent six seasons in Major League baseball. Political hardball was another story. Carroll and Ken Rogstad were out to fracture his relationship with Spellman and undercut the freshman commissioner. "I knew Spellman was in for it," Scott Wallace says. "The fly in the ointment was always Chuck. Otherwise, O'Brien, Munro and I agreed on practically every important issue when we were commissioners together."[1]

Spellman grasped the full extent of Carroll's craftiness when he dropped by an official's office one morning. "I won't say who is was—that could be hurtful—but I'll tell you this: the man was lying on the couch in his office crying. He had gone to some party the night before and never got home until sunup. When he arrived at the office, Carroll called. 'I know where you were and I know what you were doing,' he said. He had him, in effect, in the palm of his hand. That was the way Carroll operated. Thank God he never had anything like that on me, but he certainly tried."

JOB ONE FOR THE Republican majority was the major piece of unfinished business from the 1966 campaign: remodeling the courthouse. Spellman endorsed a plan developed by Harmon, Pray & Detrich, an architectural firm picked by O'Brien. As the newly-elected chairman of the board it was O'Brien's call, Spellman says, "and the plan struck me as sound. Still does." Remodeling in phase one would focus on the floors housing the

courtrooms and jail and the offices of the clerk, coroner, sheriff and prosecutor. Simultaneously, work would begin across Fourth Avenue on an
annex to house the other administrative offices. The new plan, estimated at
$13.5 million, would give the county a largely refurbished Courthouse and
140,000 square feet of additional office space. All this for $37,000 less than
the old remodeling project alone would have cost, O'Brien and Spellman
said. The annex could be expanded by another 140,000 square feet in the
1980s, if growth predictions proved accurate, "to fill county office needs
into the 21st Century."[2] In Phase Two, O'Brien told reporters, remodeling
the remainder of the Courthouse and expanding the annex would bring
the final cost to $27.5 million, including the $3 million already spent by
Wallace and Munro. If the Democrats' approach were extrapolated to fill the
county's long-range needs the cost would have been more than $32 million,
the chairman said.

Ed Munro, now the lone Democrat, protested that $32 million was "a
figment of someone's imagination. ... I'm like the lonely end of Army (football team). I'm on the team but they won't let me in the huddle."[3] Spellman
scoffed, "We met with Mr. Munro this morning, as we do regularly when
he is in town."[4] The vote was 2-1 to proceed with the O'Brien-Spellman
plan. Behind the grandstanding, things were largely congenial. Spellman
and O'Brien liked Munro, an old pro who was fast on his feet. He'd served
in the Legislature, as Democratic county chairman and president of the
National Association of County Officials.

Poor soil conditions resulted in delays and $1.6 million in additional
expenses on the annex project. Stabilizing caissons had to be installed deep
into the hillside. The annex opened in the fall of 1970. Spellman and O'Brien
took more heat over the way it looks than what it cost. Critics denounced
its "unusually hideous" diamond-shaped exterior, with "stupid little port-
holes for windows."[5] Some liken it to a cheese grater. Ibsen Nelsen, the
award-winning architect who served on the Design Commission created by
Forward Thrust, pronounced it a disaster, declaring, "Seattle now has the
ugliest governmental center of any city in the country."[6] Munro crowed,
"We ought to name this abortion the Spellman-O'Brien Building!"[7] The
designers countered that the hexagonal panels created "a very exciting play
of lights and shadows ... like a well-cut jewel," but conceded the structure
was dumpy from certain angles. That would change in the years to come
with the addition of another six stories, they said.[8] With the construction
of a new jail and other accommodations, as well as seismic concerns, the
annex was never expanded. "It's ugly," Spellman concedes, joking that "it
was O'Brien's idea—he picked the architect!" The building should have

been twice as tall, he says. "That might have given some proportion. And it shouldn't have had that cement base. That was an accommodation to the city. It might not have been the prettiest design but it's an efficient building. Still is."

Scott Wallace muses that he was pilloried over a low bid of $11.1 million, "while what the Republicans built actually cost the $30 million that they claimed we wanted to spend. Yet no one called it a 'boondoggle.' "9

CARROLL WAS OUTFLANKED and the commissioners united on the need for a new county charter. With support from the League of Women Voters and other good-government groups, Spellman, O'Brien and Munro approved a primary to winnow the field of candidates for 15 freeholder positions, five in each commissioner district. There were 93 candidates on the primary ballot, which touched off an endorsement jamboree featuring the Municipal League, the Committee to Modernize County Government and the newspapers. KING Broadcasting joined the fray with ads promoting its own progressive slate.

The 1967 General Election produced an intriguing panel of freeholders—13 accomplished men and two talented women. (Only 10 women ran in an era when female candidates were still something of a novelty.) Their average age was 44. Seven were lawyers, mostly from the nation's top schools. Simon Wampold, a Democrat practicing law in Bellevue, had perhaps the perfect resume with which to address King County's complicated political calculus. He was a Harvard man who had spent five years as the "alter ego" to Teamsters boss Dave Beck, one of the most powerful and controversial characters in Seattle history.10 Though Republicans had a numerical edge among the freeholders, most were Evans progressives. From the outset, a majority of the freeholders favored keeping county elective offices partisan. They were split practically down the middle, though, on whether a county administrator/executive should be elected or appointed.

Richard R. Albrecht, a 35-year-old Republican lawyer who'd been active in the Municipal League, was chosen chairman. He handled the job with such aplomb that friends boosted him for county executive. Albrecht demurred, saying he was "just not the politician type," and went on to become general counsel at Boeing. Another influential freeholder was Lois North, 45, a past president of the Seattle League of Women Voters. She would serve in both houses of the Legislature and on the King County Council. James O'Connor, 31, was a Yale man. Virginia Gunby, 36, a charter member of the good government forces, had attended Reed College. Paul Friedlander, 55, a longtime friend of Magnuson and Jackson, was a public-spirited jeweler.

"In the beginning, there were roughly two slates," Albrecht says, "one supported by the Carrolls of the world, the other by the Muni League, which figured Carroll's slate would try to torpedo any change to the status quo. We achieved unanimity by finding one or two areas where you were better off leaving things well enough alone. Perhaps crucially, we decided that whatever's wrong with the elective process isn't necessarily due to the fact that someone belongs to a political party. We retained partisan elective offices and we ended up with a proposed new county charter that all 15 freeholders signed off on. No small achievement." [11]

The new charter was submitted to the voters in the fall of 1968. In it, Spellman saw his political future. And Charles O. Carroll saw trouble.

COUNTY GOVERNMENT in Washington State hadn't had a major overhaul in more than a hundred years, despite cries for reform. A constitutional amendment allowing counties to adopt "home rule" charters was approved by the voters in 1948. Yet when 1968 rolled around no charter change proposal had succeeded anywhere in the state.

The Municipal League, hoping to "lift King County out of the mire of the spoils system," backed a charter change that was thrashed at the polls in 1952. [12] The plan called for a seven-member board of nonpartisan commissioners who would select a county administrator. The only other elected officials would be the prosecutor, judges and county school superintendent. The charter's foes, including Chuck Carroll, Assessor Ralph S. Stacy, both major political parties and organized labor, warned of a dictatorial county administrator. "The elimination of partisan elections certainly will not put an end to politics in the Courthouse," they said. "It will, however, eliminate organized opposition to incumbents and insure the retention of the administrator and of county commissioners who do his will." [13] Stacy soapboxed countywide, warning that the commissioners would "balance their budgets by raising tax assessments." [14] The Muni League, led in 1952 by banker Ben R. Ehrlichman, dismissed the opposition as "gravy-train politicians ... who shudder at the new rules requiring that the coroner must be a doctor of medicine; that the county auditor must be a certified public accountant; that the sheriff must pass competitive examination..." [15]

Carroll, the sheriff and other standpatters were still shuddering 16 years later when home rule made it back to the ballot in King County. This time the freeholders had done their homework. Their plan featured a nine-member county council, an elected county executive with veto power and an elected assessor. All of the elected offices would be partisan, including the prosecutor. The executive would appoint a county administrative officer, as well as the heads of the executive departments, save for the assessor. All of his appointments would be subject to council confirmation. The charter even called for an Office of Citizen Complaints, an ombudsman. The freeholders noted that at 1.2 million, King County's population was greater than 16 states.* Dick Albrecht, the freeholders' chairman, said they hoped a new charter would help the citizens overcome their "blissful ignorance" of county government.[16]

Ironically, by raising the scent of scandal to oust Scott Wallace in 1966, Carroll had given momentum to the reformers and set the stage for his own downfall. In the long, hot summer of 1968, as charter change proponents geared up for the election, the *Seattle Post-Intelligencer* and *Seattle* magazine made Carroll the poster boy for King County's longstanding accommodation with vice. Don McGaffin, a KOMO-TV reporter who wore his trench coat with authenticity and had the instincts of an Irish street brawler, was assembling evidence.

EVEN BEFORE SEATTLE became the gateway to Alaska during the Klondike gold rush of 1897, vice was tolerated south of Yesler Way, the "Skid Road" of sawmill days. When the prospectors arrived, saloon-keepers, card sharks, itinerant hoochie-coochie dancers, hookers and madams hit their own paydirt. By the first world's fair in 1909, the Alaska-Yukon-Pacific Exposition, Seattle's industrial and cultural wonders were augmented by a host of licentious diversions. Beat cops collected the shakedown boodle like clockwork for their chiefs. At brothels, the going rate for protection was $10 per prostitute per month. Reform movements periodically rounded up the usual suspects. Invariably, though, it was back to business as usual when the stink blew over. Even the 1962 World's Fair, with its 21st Century theme, offered a taste of mid-20th Century bawdiness that many movers and shakers embraced with a leer: Gracie Hansen's "A Night in Paradise" burlesque show.

By "East Coast standards," defenders of tolerance asserted, Seattle vice added up to garden-variety corruption—semi-organized crime, so to speak, with the quasi-idealistic objective of keeping things local and within controllable limits. Ross Cunningham of *The Seattle Times*, Carroll's good friend, was a typical burgher in this regard, asserting that Chuck was their bulwark against The Mob.[17] With no mob, more people—respectable ones, too—certainly got a piece of the action. "Total profits of these various illegal businesses exceeded a hundred million dollars a year in Seattle, and this

---

*King County's population was 1.93 million in 2010, still greater than 14 states.

placed gambling, narcotics, fraud, usury and organized theft among the state's two or three largest industries," wrote William J. Chambliss, a young sociologist who went undercover during the early 1960s to explore vice in King County.[18] In a book entitled *On the Take*, he wrote:

> From 1956 to 1970 each of eleven bingo parlors grossed over $300,000 a year. The owner of one bingo parlor netted $240,000 a year after all expenses, including payoffs to police and politicians. ... From 1960 to 1970 there were over 3,500 pinball machines licensed in the state. These machines grossed over 7 million dollars a year. The investment necessary for purchasing and servicing the machines was minuscule. The taxes were nonexistent since all returns were in cash and could be hidden. There was one "master license" for the county. It gave one organization the right to place pinball machines in the amusement parlors, cabarets and restaurants. This small group of businessmen, closely tied to political and law-enforcement people, had a monopoly on one of the most profitable businesses in the state. ... A bagman collects an established payment from every enterprise engaged in illegal business. Cardroom operators were surprisingly consistent in their reports of how much they paid off. The large operators paid $350 a month to the police and $300 to "the syndicate." Smaller operators paid $250 a month. ...[19]
>
> It is not the goodness or badness of people that accounts for the emergence and persistence of crime networks. The people who run the network in Seattle are not amoral men and women. On the contrary, they are for the most part moral, committed, hard-working, God-fearing politicians and business people. ... "The Fourth of July oration is the front for graft," Lincoln Steffens wrote. It is often the sincere belief of the grafters that they are also performing a public service and living up to the principles of the Fourth of July oration.[20]

Robert F. Utter, a young King County Superior Court Judge dedicated to helping troubled youth, noted that streetwalkers were plying their trade within four blocks of the county juvenile court. Tolerance, he said, was a bigger danger than the vice itself because it systemically eroded society's self respect.[21]

"PINBALL KING IS TAILED TO HOME OF PROSECUTOR," the *P-I's* front page declared on August 21, 1968. Inside, four full pages, replete with grainy surveillance photos and diagrams, detailed the once-a-month visits to

Carroll's home by one Ben Cichy. He was an official with the "non-profit" coalition of local pinball operators that had held the master license for pinball operations in the county since 1942. They raked in an estimated $5 million annually. During a divorce trial in 1949, Cichy's income was revealed to be up to $60,000 a year.[22] "What could possibly be the nature of such liaison between men of such diverse callings, a prosecutor and a pillar of the pinball fellowship?" *P-I* reporter Orman Vertrees wondered. The *Post-Intelligencer* and *Seattle* magazine, which had joined forces for the investigation, hounded Carroll for an explanation. The prosecutor was far "too busy" to discuss the issue. Commissioner Spellman wasn't. He told reporters several stories that illustrated the consequences of crossing Chuck. Soon after taking office, Spellman said he had hoped to install an FBI man as the county's license director. Carroll prodded him and Johnny O'Brien to instead name a former Seattle Police vice squad sergeant. The license director's job "can get you in trouble the quickest," Spellman quoted the prosecutor as saying.[23]

A sidebar by Shelby Scates, one of the *P-I's* top reporters, probed the power and political longevity of an old-school politician who for 20 years had "played the angles like a guitar," his personality ranging "from charming to sulphurous; from persuasive to intimidating." In a blast at the *P-I's* afternoon rival, Scates detailed how Ross Cunningham of *The Times* had brow-beat the Municipal League into upgrading Carroll's rating from "above average" to "superior" in a recent election.[24] Moreover, the prosecutor and Ken Rogstad, the county Republican chairman, worked as a tag-team to place allies in key jobs:

> At Rogstad and Carroll's behest, O'Brien pushed Stan Gallup, a real estate man and stalwart in the King County GOP organization, for the airport manager's job. Spellman acceded ... in the interest of harmony. It was a less than happy choice. Gallup battled with clients, personnel and the Boeing Co., and finally got fired when—unbeknown to the commissioners—he filed as a GOP candidate for state Land Commissioner. While he was around, Gallup lunched frequently with Carroll, almost never with the commissioners who were, presumably, his bosses. ...
>
> Spellman's sharpest brush with Carroll came last year when he refused to buckle to the prosecutor's demand that Carroll be budgeted to hire an attorney to advise King County freeholders. ... Commissioner Ed Munro initially agreed with Spellman that the commissioners, not the prosecutor, should hire the freeholders' lawyer. But in the crunch,

he switched his position. Spellman held firm and Carroll didn't get the money. What followed was an investigation by Deputy Prosecutor Bill Kinzel and detective Ron Crider into a bill charged to the county by one of Spellman's road employees.... Spellman said, "We argued to a standoff. The upshot was that the equipment supervisor was fired, his boss wasn't. And I spent some months in late December with terrible apprehensions. I had the feeling that I and my staff was under investigation. I was worried about being framed." (Spellman said Carroll continued his attempts to divide and conquer by pressuring O'Brien.) "It had been agreed with O'Brien that he would be chairman (of the board) the first year, I would be chairman the second. Apparently Carroll will not tolerate it." [25]

The minute Spellman arrived back at the Courthouse from lunch with Scates, the phone rang. It was Carroll. He had spies everywhere.

ON THE MORNING the *Post-Intelligencer* sprang its scoop, Spellman studied the murky photos showing Cichy appearing to smile as he walked down the driveway to Carroll's house. He was trying to refresh his memory. "One day during my campaign for commissioner, Chuck came to the headquarters. He said he wanted me to meet somebody. He took me out on the street corner and introduced me to somebody whose name I recall as being Ben. I think it was Cichy. What Carroll was doing was showing he knew me; that he could get me to come outside and meet him. That's how he played that kind of politics—it was who you know."

If the *P-I's* exposé amounted to an uppercut, *Seattle* magazine landed a body blow a few weeks later. "REMOVE THE COUNTY PROSECUTOR" its September 1968 cover declared over a wanted-poster photo of Carroll. The once-handsome UW football hero now resembled a New Jersey mobster ambushed by paparazzi. The magazine indicted the prosecutor on four counts: consorting with "at least one well-known gambling kingpin"; failing to effectively enforce statutes against gambling and other vice; inflaming racial tensions by "overzealous prosecutions," and urging excessively high bail and severe sentences.[26] Three young black men had been sentenced to six months in jail over a sit-in at Franklin High School, just one of several incidents that elevated Carroll to "public enemy number one" in the black community.*[27] When Judge Utter, presiding over Juvenile Court,

---

*When an off-duty policeman shot and killed a black man in 1965, it was ruled "excusable" homicide. Four blacks, and one white officer, were charged with assault by Carroll. The Central District was outraged.[29]

refused to remand two of the sit-in defendants for trial as adults, Carroll was livid, dressing down the judge in a phone call. After another run-in, Utter received a call from Carroll's secretary. "I was told that that if Chuck ever saw me on the street, he would refuse to acknowledge me."[28]

"[N]o matter what the outcome of any official investigation ... Prosecutor Carroll should be removed from office forthwith," the editors of *Seattle* magazine concluded.[30]

Governor Evans and one of his leading Democratic opponents in his bid for a second term, Attorney General John J. O'Connell, engaged in what appeared to be bipartisan chop-

Charles O. Carroll on the cover of *Seattle* magazine in 1968.

licking at the prospect of gelding a mutual enemy. Carroll had better come up with some "substantial answers—fast" as to why he was rubbing elbows with the likes of Cichy, Evans told reporters, while O'Connell declared, "I am ready to act. You just can't leave that sort of thing alone."[31] O'Connell resolved to launch "a full-scale investigation into strong suggestions of organized vice in King County."[32] Martin J. Durkan, an influential state senator challenging O'Connell for the Democratic nomination for governor, convened a legislative committee to take testimony on vice. Evans quickly grasped that the headline-grabbing issue could complicate the race for governor. He pirouetted artfully, accusing O'Connell of being "presumptuous" and "jumping the gun." O'Connell needed his approval to conduct the investigation. "I proposed that any pertinent material in the hands of the *Post-Intelligencer*, the attorney general, and Senator Durkan be given to the senior judge of the King County Superior Court, who could determine if a grand jury should be called," Evans recalls.

Carroll invited the governor to his home—that Evans would go speaks volumes about Carroll's power—and urged him to review a trove of financial records. "Although he was extremely candid and displayed his extensive banking and investment reports ... I felt like a financial voyeur. ... I strongly suggested that he issue a public statement that in my view could have muted the controversy. He failed to do so," Evans told Spellman's biographer in 2012.[33]

After meeting with Carroll, the governor told reporters, "A man is innocent until someone proves otherwise. I was assured by the prosecutor he still maintains the office with the highest degree or integrity. I believe him. I have confidence in him."[34] Carroll, who had schemed to keep the governor from taking control of the King County GOP, and Evans, an agile pragmatist, were allies for the duration of the 1968 campaign.* As for his friendship with Cichy, Carroll kept stonewalling, even when KING-TV offered air time for a rebuttal. "You can just say I have no comment."[35]

DEMANDS TO CRACK DOWN on graft and corruption escalated. Raids on a Seattle gambling den produced fresh evidence of payoffs to people in high places, but Carroll wasn't up for election for two more years. He figured it would all blow over by then. His friends and admirers—numbering in the thousands—accused the media of gang-tackle sensationalism. They pointed to the prosecutor's long record of public service, which had produced an office wall crowded with plaques. B'nai B'rith, the Knights of Columbus and black ministers had honored Carroll for promoting brotherhood. The PTA and Boy Scouts hailed his campaign against salacious literature. Even Ed Donohoe, whose "Tilting the Windmill" column in the weekly *Washington Teamster* was the juiciest read in town, rose to defend "Faircatch." Donohoe also roasted the *P-I* and the "dainty darlings" of KING and *Seattle* magazine: "Perhaps someone would like to know what crime this fellow Ben W. Cichy committed by visiting Carroll's home on occasion rather than the office. Although the inference of skullduggery was there, I fail to see where Cichy or Carroll committed an unlawful act. For some reason the newspapers seem to write in all sorts of criminal activity where coin produced amusement games are concerned. Is Cichy a criminal? The story doesn't support such a thesis."[36] The Teamsters' influential house organ emphasized, however, that the expose did not amount to "trial by newspaper." Carroll was hardly "a helpless defendant." He had the demonstrably potent power of the prosecutor's office at his disposal yet "remained aloof" when given ample opportunity to respond to the charges against him.[37]

---

* O'Connell's campaign for governor was derailed down the stretch by the revelation that he liked to gamble for high stakes at Las Vegas casinos. Democrats cried foul, charging that the story was the handiwork of the Evans brain trust, including Gummie Johnson and Slade Gorton, who was elected attorney general in a photo-finish as part of the progressive Republicans' "Action Team." Evans easily won a second term.

As to what could possibly be the nature of a liaison between men of such diverse callings, associates explained that Carroll and Cichy "were friends from way back; they had grown up in Seattle at the same time."[38] Both were boating enthusiasts—*big* boats. Cichy, moreover, was engaged in a business that passed for legal under the tolerance policy, even though it was alleged that "he met regularly with and allegedly paid substantial sums of money to politicians ... and to members of the police department."[39] If guilty of nothing more than keeping suspicious company, the UW's "human battering ram" of 1928 now stood convicted in the court of public opinion of becoming a law, and a force, unto himself. His ego matched his ambition. "Carroll and a group of the boys were visiting with the governor" one day early in Evans' tenure," one of the exposés noted. "At one point Evans excused himself from the meeting, whereupon Chuck plopped himself down in Dan's chair under the state seal and looked just blissful."[40]

MRS. CICHY CALLED the Sheriff's Department when Ben didn't come home for dinner. It was May 30, 1969. He'd left the house around 1 to work on his 54-foot yacht. It was docked near their handsome home at Yarrow Point along Lake Washington. Divers recovered his body at 8:45 p.m. The 71-year-old was face down in about five feet of water not far from the boat. His glasses were unbroken, his watch still ticking. Reportedly a strong swimmer, Cichy had "conveniently drowned," Rick Anderson, a former longtime police beat reporter, observes in *Seattle Vice*. Many suggested that Cichy, like hapless Luca Brasi in *The Godfather*, had been sent to sleep with the fishes, yet reportedly there were no signs of foul play.[41] Christopher T. Bayley, who in 1969 was a 31-year-old deputy attorney general weighing a challenge to Carroll, talked with a young sheriff's deputy who was the first to respond to Mrs. Cichy's call. Bayley says he was told there were no law enforcement witnesses at the autopsy, a deviation from standard procedure in high-profile cases, "so that's what's very suspicious." However, the notion that the prosecutor had anything to do with Cichy's demise strikes him as illogical for multiple reasons. "Why would Carroll be trying to bump off Cichy? They were boyhood friends. ... There were no doubt payoffs going on from the tolerance policy, but Carroll did not get rich."[42] In *On the Take*, Chambliss writes, "On the day he died, Cichy had two appointments. The first was with two of the tolerance network's most trusted members, a former assistant prosecutor and an undersheriff in the county sheriff's office. The second appointment was with a special investigator whose evidence had been crucial in developing the case against the crime network. Cichy's death was seen by network members from top to bottom as a desperate move on the part of desperate men to keep the cracks in the wall from destroying the foundation. But it was too late. The foundation had already been moved." [43]

AGAINST THE BACKDROP of scandal, proponents of a new county charter said it would be the foundation for "a more just and orderly government."

Johnny O'Brien and Ed Munro, Spellman's fellow commissioners, were up for re-election on the same ballot as the charter change proposal, allegedly having made a deal that each would strive to keep their party from fielding a strong candidate against the other. The county's political bosses were pragmatically united on defeating the new charter. They figured O'Brien and Munro were the best bets to maintain the status quo. If the charter change passed and both were re-elected they would be grandfathered into the new government as county councilmen, together with Spellman.[44]

Munro joined Spellman in endorsing the charter. Both emphasized the need for a county executive. O'Brien had some reservations: Nine council members was excessive, he said, and too many officials would be appointed rather than elected.[45] The Conservative Club was categorically opposed to "more big government." Rogstad said he and other conservatives found the charter hard to swallow, especially because the sheriff, who "has stood throughout history as the pillar of the public community," no longer would be an independent elected official. "The people are afraid of creating bureaucrats instead of directly elected representatives of the people," the Republican chairman said.[46] Sheriff Jack Porter and the union representing his deputies shared that fear, also objecting to having the sheriff's civil service system absorbed into the new personnel system.[47]

The 75,000-member King County Labor Council also opposed the new charter. "The freeholders must have rocks in their heads if they think they are streamlining county government by replacing three commissioners with nine councilmen" at $18,000 per year each, plus $27,000 for a new county executive, *The Washington Teamster* said in a front-page editorial. "That means six more offices, six more staffs, and six more giant dips into the county till for expenses, not to mention such freeloading activities as the Stadium Commission, which traveled all over America at your expense just to see what other baseball parks look like." [48]

With support from the Municipal League, the League of Women Voters and City Council reformers, charter change proponents fielded an impressive bipartisan campaign committee. It included Norton Clapp, chairman of the Weyerhaeuser board; Dorothy Bullitt of KING Broadcasting; Mort Frayn, a popular former Republican legislator, and State Senator Wes

Uhlman, a young Democrat poised to run for mayor of Seattle. At Spellman's urging, the commissioners issued a joint statement disputing the notion that the new charter would increase the cost of government. It would save at least $500,000 a year, they said. "In fact, without instituting good management and budgeting practices now, the county may well be losing ground rather than gaining." [49]

In addition to the separation of administrative and legislative powers, the charter called for a career-service personnel system mandating hiring and promotion on merit. Conflicts of interest would be prohibited, "flower funds" banned. The anti-discrimination section was robust, stipulating that "the county shall not enter into any contract" with any organization or company that discriminated "on the basis of sex, race, color, national origin, religious affiliation or age... ."

But the proviso that gave the charter the best chance of passage granted job protection to all county employees on the payroll before June 1, 1968. The sheriff, auditor and coroner, heretofore elected, would be subject to appointment by the executive and confirmation by the county council. In any case, they would be guaranteed "equivalent" jobs until retirement age.

ON NOVEMBER 5, 1968, nearly 62 percent of the voters backed the new charter, topping the most optimistic predictions by 10 percent. O'Brien and Munro were handily re-elected. A primary election to select the finalists for county executive and six new County Council seats was set for February 11, 1969, with the general election a month later. The charter would take effect on May 1.

"If the charter had failed, I would not have run for county commissioner again," Spellman says. "County commissioner was a very frustrating job for someone who wanted to get a lot done. I was even developing stomach troubles. So there was no question in my mind about what I was going to do next: I was going to run for county executive."

CHAPTER ELEVEN

Making Al Old

Brock Adams, the man U.S. House Speaker Tom Foley remembered as "the young prince of politics," had a tough choice. With his boyish smile, Harvard degree and links to the Kennedys, Adams had just breezed to a third term in Congress. King County Democrats were urging him to run for county executive. Rosellini's hat was already in the ring. He appeared reinvigorated, and you could always call him Al. Still, the party's young liberals worried that the former two-term governor, pushing 60, would come off as old politics in a race with Spellman.

Adams announced his decision on December 6, 1968. Campaigning for county executive from 3,000 miles away would be too difficult, he said. With America blowing fuses right and left, he couldn't shirk his duty as a member of Congress. (His press conference was interrupted by young people making statements against the war in Vietnam and the college ROTC program.) In a backhanded compliment, Adams said Rosellini had been an excellent governor, but King County needed "new people" to modernize its government—people like Wes Uhlman and Renton Mayor Don Custer. The new job also would be a "good springboard for governor," Adams acknowledged. "It does not follow that I will not be a candidate for governor (in 1972), but the decision not to run for executive greatly reduces any chances I might have."[1] In fact, he was more interested in the possibility of inheriting Warren Magnuson's seat in the U.S. Senate, Maggie looking increasingly long in the tooth.

Spellman had just caught a break. Rosellini had too. A few days earlier, when a reporter asked Al about Adams, he quipped, "He's a fine congressman and I hope he stays there."[2] Rosellini declared that he alone had the "tremendous experience and background to meet the problems which will arise during the formative years of the new county government." Spellman's two years as a county commissioner hardly qualified him to take on "the second most important" political job in the state, Rosellini said.[3]

Spellman's rejoinder sounded the theme for his campaign: "We can no longer accept the 'old politics' which has produced patronage and paralysis in our county. We need public officials who are willing and capable of meeting the challenge of our times." [4] If there were any lingering doubts about his philosophical allegiances, Spellman sought to dispel them with a statement that county chairman Rogstad had to go: "We no longer can accept divisive disunity," especially at a time when the people of King County were embarking on an attempt to create a new government "untrammeled by political abuses." [5] The bitter factionalism in the King County Republican Party had contributed to Nixon losing the state to Humphrey by 27,500 votes.*

Rogstad, to the chagrin of the progressives, went on to narrowly defeat their candidate, James O'Connor, to win a third two-year term as county chairman. Despite the schism, Spellman was unquestionably the Republicans' leading contender for the plum new job. A nimble core group of supporters understood his strengths and weaknesses. Dick Schrock, a 25-year-old ad man with the Irv Stimson agency, was the wordsmith and press agent. "Patronage and paralysis" was his line. Joe McGavick, a former legislator, and Bob Bratton, a manager with IBM, were veterans of the Evans-Gorton campaigns. Harry Prior, a respected management consultant, headed the steering committee. Frank Pritchard, Joel's equally ebullient brother, was the chief strategist and sage—"our gray eminence," Schrock says.[6] Ritajean Butterworth, a seasoned campaign volunteer for mainstream Republicans, handled scheduling. The de facto campaign manager was her good friend, Helen Rasmussen, who oversaw Spellman's 1966 campaign for county commissioner. That Rasmussen had managed to keep the right-wingers and Evans forces on the same team most of the way was a remarkable achievement. "Helen was a great motivator," Spellman says. "She always reminded us to tell people what we were going to do, then do it and then tell people we did it. Her ability to recruit and organize volunteers was crucial. That was a time when volunteers were as important as money in political campaigns. That she was also a great cook was a bonus."

Lois Spellman was pregnant with Katherine, their sixth child, when Butterworth arrived at the house one afternoon to discuss scheduling just before the campaign got under way. "If she was going to let him become

---

* Spellman, like Dan Evans, was a Rockefeller supporter early on. At the 1968 GOP convention, Evans was on Nixon's short list of possible running mates, together with Oregon Senator Mark Hatfield. With an eye to the South's electoral votes, Maryland Governor Spiro Agnew, a blunt instrument, got the nod. Weighing the fall of first Agnew, then Nixon, and the probity of Evans and Hatfield produces a fascinating "what if?" asterisk.

involved in politics, which took him away a lot, she said she had to make some rules," Ritajean recalls. "And the most important thing to her was that John had to be home during at least part of the dinner hour to spend time with his children. I worked with a lot of candidates over the years and no other wife ever told me anything like that. So regardless of what events were on the schedule, my job was also to make sure that John spent part of the dinner hour with those kids every night. It could be soup; it could be salad; it could be dessert. But he was there. I really admired Lois for that. It says a lot about John, too. He's just built differently."[7]

THERE WERE A DOZEN CANDIDATES in all for King County executive in 1969. Rosellini's leading challenger for the Democratic nomination was former freeholder Robert Block, an energetic 46-year-old real-estate man. Spellman's main competition was Stephen J. Hall, 53, a conservative business consultant with a degree in economics from Yale. Hall was a forceful speaker. "If you're looking for a politician, I'm not your man," he said up front. "...What alternatives are there? There's Albert Rosellini with his cronyism, and John Spellman, who hasn't done one cotton-pickin' thing about what is wrong in county government. He's part and parcel of the mess we're in. ..."[8]

Spellman's ads, designed by Frank Pritchard and Don Kraft of Kraft, Smith & Lowe, were forceful, even by today's standards. "Only John Spellman has had day-to-day experience with the challenges of King County's government," one declared. "Other people talk about what should be done under the new Charter, but John Spellman has the know-how to make our new government really work. ...We know John Spellman. He can be trusted to keep cronyism out of King County's new government."[9] Arrayed below the text in the print version were the names of 300 of King County's most influential citizens, including Gordon Clinton, Dan and Nancy Evans, Jim and John Ellis, Slade Gorton, Mort Frayn, Charles P. Moriarty Sr. and Jr., Arthur Langlie, Dr. Richard Fuller and Keith Callow. Also featured were young activists like Chris Bayley, one of the founders of Choose an Effective City Council, CHECC.

The unions backed Rosellini, but not with as much vigor as might be expected. While the State Labor Council, led by the cagey Joe Davis, had enormous clout in King County, Spellman had longstanding ties to labor through his years with Kane & Spellman.

Rosellini and Spellman, as expected, advanced easily from the February 11 primary.

One of the also-rans for a seat on the new County Council was a 48-year-

Spellman and former governor Al Rosellini during a debate in the campaign for
county executive in 1969.

old commercial real estate developer, Frank Ruano. Remember that name.
Ostensibly a Democrat, he was invariably at odds with the party hierarchy
and a rebel at heart.

SPELLMAN AND ROSELLINI had exactly a month to make their cases. Rosellini, the immigrants' son, was warm and folksy off the cuff. In formal
settings, however, he was often inarticulate. Frank Pritchard was still antsy
about agreeing to debates. "Al had just slaughtered one of the young guys
running against him in a debate before the primary, so I wanted to be damn
sure it didn't happen to John. But one day after the primary John walked
into my office and told me he'd been thinking about it. He said, 'I just don't
feel good about not debating. If a guy can't debate he shouldn't even run.
I'll debate, and I'll beat him.' He'd been a champion debater in college, so I
guess I shouldn't have been worried." [10]

What worried Rosellini's brain trust was a nervous tic that popped up
when Al was under stress. He'd punctuate sentences with a sound that was
a cross between a slurp and a tooth-click. "It's not something you comment
on, but it was distractingly there whenever I got under his skin," Spellman
remembers, "and I think it hurt his image. The perception was that Al was
getting a little old, although we now know that he was going to live to be
101. I was 42. He was 59. I seemed young. He didn't. That was very much to

my advantage." Spellman's ads maintained the drumbeat: The choice was between "old politics" and "new direction."[11]

Payton Smith, Rosellini's biographer, says it was the perfect strategy: "[T]he circumstances that resulted in the passage of the new charter assured that Rosellini—who was almost totally identified with an older more partisan era—would be unsuccessful in his attempt to return to public office."[12] Smith had been co-chairman of the Committee to Modernize County Government. "In 1969, I didn't even support Al for county executive because that would have just been a return to the old days," Smith says, chuckling at the irony.[13]

"There was always a sense that Al was not quite clean," Joe McGavick says. "I don't think he was ever dirty, particularly. ... I don't think he ever got a fair shake in terms of his honesty, as good a man as he was as a governor. But at that time it was just easy to run against him."[14]

Rosellini tried to turn the tables by styling Spellman as part of the Carroll-Rogstad machine. "I think the people by voting for the charter and a new form of government indicated they want to get rid of the political-patronage spoils system my opponent has fostered and tolerated."[15] He was also out to settle a score for his vanquished friend, Scott Wallace—"one of the finest young men ever to serve this country." Rosellini reminded voters that Spellman had promised to rein in the cost of remodeling the Courthouse. Now, thanks to "the mess" created by Spellman and O'Brien, the cost had doubled during Spellman's two years in office. So much for "reform." The Spellman campaign counterattacked with a fundraising letter warning that "King County can't be turned over to Al and his friends."[16] On the surface, it seemed as if the only thing Spellman and Rosellini had in common was their Roman Catholic faith. Looking deeper, both were progressives; Seattle lawyers with strong ties to labor, family men and hard workers.

That the electorate was apathetic worked to Spellman's advantage. Dick Schrock recalls, "We carefully, deliberately avoided stirring up controversy within heavily Democratic voting areas in the city and throughout the county. We were happy to let Democrats sleep through the March special election, and most did."

While Rosellini's lingering problem was his image as a godfather, Spellman had a charisma deficit. Progressives like Ellis and Albrecht strongly endorsed his candidacy, but he was viewed by much of Seattle's intelligentsia as a bland pipe-puffer. "The most disturbing thing about these elections," an unnamed former freeholder told *Seattle* magazine, "is the lackluster quality of the leading candidates for county executive. I don't see how this could have happened." Also granted anonymity, "a local attorney" said of Spellman, "I like the man personally. He's honest as he can be, and I'm sure he wants to do the right thing. My only question is whether he is strong enough or politically savvy enough to do it."[17] Ed Donohoe dismissed Spellman as adept only at "asking folks to tithe for a new church." He exhorted labor to get out the vote. The Teamsters' Mencken said Spellman was "the best hindsighter the County Commission ever had ... kicking Sheriff Jack Porter when Fairview Fanny (*The Seattle Times*) was climbing Porter's back for the increase in county jail escapes. ... then rescinding the charges the next day. ..."[18]

THE SITE FOR THE $40 MILLION domed stadium approved by the voters was a major bone of contention in the Rosellini-Spellman debates. In the middle of the campaign, the State Stadium Commission—Spellman and O'Brien were members—unanimously endorsed a site near Seattle Center, the civic complex created in the aftermath of the World's Fair. Supporters of other sites were vociferous dissenters. South Park along the Duwamish River and the rail yard south of the historic King Street Station below Pioneer Square were far superior sites, they said. Frank Ruano early on advocated a privately funded stadium straddling the rail yard. Some said he hoped for a piece of the action. That was nonsense, he said. His projects were relatively modest—strip malls and condos. The issue was free enterprise, and somebody had to look out for the taxpayers.

Ruano was dismissed as a gadfly by Joe Gandy and other downtown businessmen. Gandy, who'd made his mark as the live-wire head of the world's fair board, was now chairman of the stadium site selection commission. The King Street site was not just summarily rejected, it was ranked dead last. "Ruano was petulant as hell" at being left off that committee, according to Bill Sears, who handled promotions and publicity for the Seattle Pilots before managing the Convention and Visitors Bureau.[19]

Whatever the true genesis of his pique, Ruano was "justifiably outraged by the unorthodox method of selecting the Center site," according to Hy Zimmerman, a sports columnist for *The Seattle Times*. South Park had ranked first, Seattle Center third. Ruano charged that a domed stadium would ruin the Center and carve up the city with yet another freeway. Worse, the voters had been "misled from the start" with a "phony" construction budget.[20]

Rosellini criticized the way Spellman and O'Brien handled the site selection process—"one of the greatest examples of political bungling I have seen in my career."[21] Which site did he favor? He refused to be pinned down. The whole process just needed immediate review. Spell-man said property condemnation proceedings at the South Park site would have delayed the project three to five years and caused construction costs to escalate way beyond the $40 million budget.

Spellman and Rosellini did agree on the need for rapid transit, more revenue-sharing by the state, less red tape and new measures to improve race relations and combat crime. Their last televised debate produced the most fireworks when Bryan Johnson, a cut-to-the-chase reporter for KOMO, observed that their goals would all require more money: "You both agree the county lacks money. Nothing in the Charter says the county has the power to levy taxes. If the question is resolved in favor of the county, would you favor that the county levy a head tax or sales tax?" [22] Rosellini pledged there'd be no new taxes on his watch. "We're being taxed to death right now under the present governor!" By cutting the waste and incompetence fostered by Spell-man, he would demonstrate how "a proven administrator" solves problems. [23]

For much of their debate a night earlier, Rosellini's attacks had Spell-man playing defense. Now Spellman looked right into the camera, shook his head and chopped the air with his right hand. "I'm amazed to hear that the former governor who doubled the state bonded indebtedness during his term of office and when unemployment was at an all-time high says he thinks there is plenty of money around to get the job done. If some-one can think of how we're going to hire an additional 300 policemen or sheriff's deputies in King County without some additional funds, well that person will be a genius. Now, I've suggested ways to do it by tightening the belt but we are not going to lick the problem without local government having the authority to provide local services and have the tax base to do it." [24] As for "the alleged Courthouse mess," Spellman said the voters surely would recall "the purchasing scandals" of the Rosellini administration. Rosellini flatly denied any such scandals. Spellman looked incredulous. "Your own purchasing director resigned after a long investigation." [25]

"[A]t stake is an immense new power base from which to shape the future of Washington politics," *The Seattle Times* said. [26] If so, an off-year election in the middle of March was not calculated to generate a strong turnout. Fractured though they were—with Carroll twisting arms for Rosellini in a marriage of convenience—Republicans got out the vote; the Democrats didn't.

On March 11, 1969, Spellman became the state's first elected county executive, outpolling Rosellini by 8,400 votes, 51.5 percent. The turnout was 12,000 lower than in the primary. Republicans won a 5-4 majority on the new County Council. [27]

Four-year-old Teresa holds a campaign sign as Spellman poses with his family outside their home on the morning after he was elected county executive in 1969. Margo, 14, is next to her mother. The boys are Jeff, 7, David, 10, and 12-year-old Bart. Lois is pregnant with their daughter Katherine.

Around midnight, Rosellini, trademark rosebud in his lapel, stood on the sidewalk outside his headquarters on Third Avenue, shaking hands and thanking campaign workers. He laid his defeat squarely on "apathy on the part of the people." Richard Larsen, the political writer for *The Times*, looked on:

> One young man grasped Rosellini's hand and said, "Well, at least you've had a wonderful political career."
>
> The tone of finality seemed to startle the ex-governor. But it stated a question in the minds of many: Had Rosellini reached the end of the political trail? ...
>
> After a pause, Rosellini told the young man: "Well, I've learned over the years you can't win 'em all." [28]

The next morning, Spellman posed with Lois and the kids on their front yard. Four-year-old Teresa hoisted a campaign sign. He was "very excited" over his new job and discounted the notion advanced by Adams that it would be a great stepping-stone to governor. "I have no aspirations to run for another political office. I've used up my family's political stamina." [29]

CHAPTER TWELVE

The Political Job

*"I don't look on this as a political job, but a governmental job.
The challenges are governmental, not political."* [1]
—Spellman at his first news conference as county executive-elect

Political realities, big and small, tactical and churlish, were the first
challenges. "The inability of King County to adequately finance
basic services and operations is approaching a crisis," the Municipal
League warned a month before the May 1, 1969, changeover to the new
government. A decade's worth of capital-improvement projects had saddled
the county with daunting debt-service obligations. It was like "a family so
overburdened with home-mortgage payments that it must live on a diet of
beans and ham hocks." [2] Unfunded state mandates and growing demands
for law enforcement and social-welfare programs made the pantry barer yet.
The citizenry was in a foul mood over property taxes. A revenue shortfall
of at least $5 million was projected for the 1970 county budget. Spellman
called for a "stop everything" attitude, including a hiring freeze, "until we
find out where we are and where we are going." [3]

Spellman went to Olympia, tin cup in hand, to testify before the Senate
subcommittee on Revenue and Taxation: "We're in dramatically bankrupt
shape, looking for emergency aid until we can get some type of tax reform.
We can no longer provide services as we have. The only alternatives are
to issue warrants or to lay off employees." Crime in unincorporated King
County was up 25 percent, Spellman said. The county needed at least 80
more sheriff's deputies. Commissioners from around the state joined him
in asking the Legislature for a direct appropriation or authority to boost the
tax on real-estate transactions. The crunch had roots dating to the Great
Depression. In 1935, an income tax having been held unconstitutional and
revenues down precipitously, state government siphoned off part of the
counties' taxing authority. [4] "I think the message is clear," Spellman said. "If
state government will not support local government in providing local-state

services, they are merely shortchanging the taxpayers of this state."[5] It took a year for help to arrive.

Chuck Carroll, meantime, was busy casting himself as the people's tribune, undermining Spellman at every opportunity. "I am always surprised when I read about county business in the newspaper," Spellman groused after the *The Times* headlined the prosecutor's opinion that lease rates at Boeing Field were still below fair market value. "I think Mr. Spellman should address himself more to correcting the problem at the airport rather than criticizing the line of communication," Carroll shot back, adding that if Spellman had been in his office on Saturday, "as a lot of us were," he would have received a copy of the opinion.[6]

Ed Heavey, one of the four Democrats on the new County Council—Bernie Heavey who'd been caught up in the Courthouse remodeling scandal was his brother—challenged Spellman to show spine and discount Governor Evans' criticism of Sheriff Jack Porter over the epidemic of escapes from the jail on the top floors of the Courthouse. Porter, a Democrat, was due to lose his badge in the changeover to the new government. He hoped Spellman would appoint him director of public safety.[7] Under the charter, Spellman was now "chief peace officer" for the county, a duty he took seriously. The jail remodeling project under way included electronic surveillance and more humane conditions. Younger prisoners were being subjected to sodomy, and cliques of hardened criminals were running a protection racket. Spellman was working with Senator Magnuson to secure federal funds for a new jail that would emphasize rehabilitation. He named Porter interim public safety director but immediately appointed a committee to recruit nationally-recognized candidates for the post. The panel included Gordon Clinton, a former FBI agent, and Will Bachofner, the longest-serving chief in the history of the State Patrol. In a small move that nevertheless signaled the end of an era, Spellman revoked 1,613 honorary deputy sheriff commissions. King County sheriffs—like sheriffs all over the state—for decades had bestowed the commissions on their favorite reporters, bartenders and morticians as a public-relations gimmick.

FOR DEPUTY COUNTY EXECUTIVE, Spellman chose a Democrat. John L. Chambers, 42, was executive secretary of the State Association of County Commissioners and a wiry, intense government expert. Joe McGavick became Spellman's administrative assistant. The hard-charging 34-year-old had served in the Legislature as the seatmate of Mary Ellen McCaffree, an architect of the redistricting plan that created crucial gains for Republicans. He also shared a desk on the House floor with Spellman's old friend, Sam

Smith. The idealistic Irish Catholic from Wallingford and the black Baptist from the Central District became friends and allies. Governor Evans had appointed McGavick chairman of the State Board Against Discrimination. His work ethic was legendary. The minute he returned from a meeting he'd start rearranging business cards in his Rolodex.

Many who found Spellman low-key to a fault would have been surprised to know how carefully he chose smart, strong-willed subordinates, tacitly promoting creative tension. "Integrity, competence and creativity were prerequisites, but not necessarily tact," says Steve Excell, who was an energetic Young Republican at the University of Washington when Spellman became county executive. Excell came to know all the players. "McGavick and Chambers were type triple-A guys who would pound on the table to order a sandwich. Bob Bratton, who succeeded Chambers, was a bit more laid back and less of a politician, but a tough guy too. He had worked at IBM and had a keen business mind. Today we talk about Lincoln and his celebrated 'team of rivals.' Spellman didn't want any yes-men, either. He gave people a lot of freedom. Sometimes he even gave the same assignment to two people to see who could come up with the best ideas."[8] Excell, who went on to become chief of staff in the Governor's Office, marveled at Spellman's equilibrium. When tempers and egos flared, he would calmly take depositions from the aggrieved and, ever the Jesuit, try to foster reconciliation. Cavendish smoke wafted from his professorial pipe as he reminded the combatants of their shared goals.[9]

"Chambers and I became kind of contentious over different things we wanted to get done," McGavick recalls. "He wanted total control. He wasn't into sharing. But he was really a great guy ... a very creative fellow. I was closer to Spellman than Chambers was, but Chambers was No. 2. Spellman was just a terribly decent, honest man—a very caring guy, though not a very politically efficient guy. He just did what he thought he should do. He pushed you to be honest, to make sure you were getting stuff right. We were looking for performance, not perfection. We wanted to make sure it was a goal-oriented, merit-based kind of government. My objective was to get the job done. That's what politics is about. Sometimes I was probably a pain in the ass."[10] Ed Heavey agrees, conceding in the next breath that it takes one to know one. "I was pretty much of a hard nose myself. ... John didn't really work closely with the County Council. McGavick was the one who pushed the (executive's) policies—McGavick and later on Chuck Collins, another Spellman assistant. Joe and I were in the Legislature at the same time. He and I differed on some policy issues, but he was someone you could trust. As a matter of fact, I gave him more credit for putting together the county

Spellman with
his top aides at
the King County
Courthouse
in 1970:
John Chambers,
left, and
Joe McGavick.

government than I did John. I thought Joe was really the brains of the outfit, in there doing the grunt work" early on.[11] "That means I was a good manager," Spellman says with a smile. "Half the challenge is picking the right people to get things done and then giving them the leeway to do the job." He had freewheeling weekly brown-bag luncheon meetings with his department heads and key staff, as well as suburban mayors and city councilmen, but rarely attended County Council meetings. On Fridays, however, until the state Open Public Meetings Act took effect in 1971, he would meet privately with the council as a committee of the whole to discuss upcoming issues. "What had been productive problem-solving closed meetings between the council and executive became open meetings attended by the media and filled with play-acting and grandstanding," Spellman says. "It's the flip side of openness."

"In one of these sessions, John was making a proposal," Heavey recalls. "I forget the specifics, but I was opposed to it and I was going after him. Finally he got *really mad* at me. And he says, 'What are you doing for the county?' And I said, 'Well, I'm not working seven days a week, if that helps!' After we came out of the meeting McGavick said to me, 'You know that's the first time I've seen John Spellman get really mad at somebody.' " [12]

Practically everyone liked Barbara Schmidt, Spellman's loyal and resourceful secretary, who remained with him throughout his political career. Her mother had been the secretary at Kane & Spellman. When the job became her own, the transition was seamless. She knew what Spellman shouldn't eat, what kind of pipe tobacco he smoked, when it was time for his tea and, especially, Lois' rule about him being home for dinner. Schmidt and the office receptionist, Mary Tedesco, an Italian Earth Mother from Central Casting, had things well under control.

SPELLMAN, CHAMBERS and McGavick rolled out a host of executive house-keeping orders and initiatives, including travel restrictions and creation of a motor pool. All county vehicles, save for a few needed for undercover police work, henceforth would be plainly marked. Budget data was to be computerized. The new personnel director would review all policies, oversee a salary study and draft rules to promote diversity. Contacts for public works were to be submitted to the Department of Planning for review on whether the work was congruent with a comprehensive plan. Drawing the line between the executive and legislative branches of the new government, Spellman emphasized that all requests to department heads, as well as the prosecutor, should go through him. His office also drafted a strong conflict-of-interest ordinance. County employees were prohibited from drinking alcohol during working hours. No more bottle in the bottom drawer; no more "flower funds." Citizen requests for information were to be answered within seven days.

"Early one morning after I first took office, I'd been out late the night before and was feeling mean," Spellman recalls—mean equating to mildly cranky, but he was not a morning person. He called the county treasurer. "How much money do we make on our bank accounts?" The treasurer seemed startled. "Why, the banks are very good to us. They give us all this service and we don't have to pay anything for it." Flabbergasted, Spellman said, "Well, as of tomorrow, we're going to get interest on everything we've got in the bank." He had kicked over another rock and could only wonder how many more there were. "Talk about police scandals—this was a big-time financial scandal. We not only handled our own money and the tax money that comes in, we handled it for many of the cities. *No interest!* You can't tell me there wasn't something going on there. Presumably it had been going on for years, so I'm not saying it was the treasurer. He seemed like a good ol' guy, but that in itself was a big part of the problem."

As Spellman and his team settled in and started making changes, a steady stream of aggrieved lifers flowed into the Prosecutor's Office to vent. From day one, "Chuck Carroll was constantly looking for something to embarrass John," McGavick says.[13]

ABOLISHING "TOLERANCE" was an important plank in Spellman's platform. Slade Gorton shared Spellman's antipathy for gambling, although he strategically soft-pedaled the issue during his 1968 campaign for attorney general, which he won in a photo-finish. Gorton gave Spellman a big hand the day before he was sworn in as county executive. In a decision that reverberated from the legendary Poodle Dog café at Fife to the Knights of Columbus hall in Spokane, Gorton ruled that multi-coin, multi-odds pinball machines, "even without proof of payoffs," were illegal gambling devices. Cardrooms also violated the law, while Bingo, when played for money or merchandise by persons who have paid "a valuable consideration to play," constituted a lottery in violation of the State Constitution. Punchboards and pulltabs, likewise, were illegal gambling devices. Any way you cut it, Gorton said, tolerance was "very debilitating." However, he agreed with Spellman that "a law that bans a Little League raffle to purchase uniforms or bingo games in a church is a bad law." The shades of gray were the purview of the Legislature and courts, Gorton said. He could only recommend clarifying legislation. Enforcement was the same story. "I don't have criminal jurisdiction. A prosecutor can obey or refuse to obey."[14] Carroll responded with duplicitous I-told-you-so's, asserting that his own legal opinions as far back as 1961 had pinpointed what constituted legal and illegal activities.

Spellman urged the County Council to commence revoking licenses for pinball machines and cardrooms. The loss of revenue was pegged at about $24,000—peanuts compared to the $160,000 the City of Seattle was reaping from its licenses. Even that was peanuts compared to the under-the-table take. Seattle Mayor Floyd Miller, Dorm Braman's successor, ordered a ban on gambling. He was already probing police corruption.

Spellman used his veto for the first time to quash a revised pinball licensing ordinance drafted by Heavey. He said it lacked teeth. He wasn't happy with the second version either since it still lacked a penalty clause. Spellman enlisted Gorton to testify before the council on its shortcomings. The attorney general warned that the ordinance would encourage the invention of new gambling devices under the guise of "amusement" machines. While Republicans held a one-vote majority, the divide usually boiled down to urban vs. suburban interests. In this case, the council made a declaration of independence and unanimously approved the ordinance. The license-issuing authority, however, rested with the executive.

Spellman served notice on every municipality in the county that tolerance was over. The police chief in Tukwila was unimpressed, and reporters noted that county workers were avidly engaged in at least four office pools on the World Series.[15]

CHAPTER THIRTEEN

Breaking Barriers

RACIAL RELATIONS in King County were brittle as Spellman prepared to deliver his first major speech as county executive, "Breaking the color barrier." Four months earlier, on January 26, 1969, Edwin T. Pratt, the 38-year-old leader of the Seattle Urban League, was shotgunned to death in the doorway of his home. Pratt was a widely respected moderate who lobbied tirelessly for better housing and job opportunities for blacks and other minorities, shrugging off death threats as part of the price of progress. Seattle had not one African-American firefighter and only a handful of black police officers. Area labor unions were overwhelmingly white. A commission on the Causes and Prevention of Civil Disorder had recently concluded that "the failure to provide bias-free services in the ghetto"— outright racism, over-reaction to unrest, and police brutality—fomented hatred with an unlimited shelf life.[1]

Spellman and McGavick closely followed the work of the commission. It was headed by their friend, Secretary of State Lud Kramer, a former Seattle councilman. Its executive director was Bruce K. Chapman, one of the idealistic young Ivy Leaguers who migrated to Seattle in the 1960s. Soon after the report was released, Chapman wrote that business and labor leaders, police chiefs, politicians, preachers and teachers, would do well to read and heed the recommendations of the commission's report, *Race and Violence in Washington State*:

> It argues that terrorism and civil disorders are quite possible in our state if underlying social problems go unattended, and even says that the perpetuation of those problems is a greater danger to community well-being than is more sensational, overt violence. The report also argues that ghettos, not to mention hardened hearts, lead to misspent lives, depriving society of untold individual contributions, communal trust and, if you care to look at it that way, economic power.[2]

Spellman looked at it precisely that way.

There was anxiety in the air as a crowd assembled at Mount Zion Baptist Church to hear the new county executive address the 23rd annual dinner of the Central Seattle Community Council. Leaders of the Black Student Union at Seattle Community College were a few blocks away, planning their next move. Walt Crowley, a Seattle historian who came of age as a student activist and underground journalist during the turbulent era, was there with his notepad—a skinny John Lennon look-alike in wire-frame glasses, boots and jean jacket. The militants had discovered "plans to shift most of the college's academic programs to the North Campus, leaving only vocational programs for the mostly nonwhite students attending the Central Branch on Broadway."[3] The Black Student Union, with support from the Students for a Democratic Society, vanguard of the new left, staged a noisy demonstration on the day of the Community Council banquet. A few hundred protesters stormed Edison Technical School and refused to leave. It took the police Tactical Squad to finally clear them out.

"The problems of the Central Area are not its own problems, or the problems of the city," Spellman told the tense room. "They are all of our problems. Unless we work together to solve them we will all fail." Looking on from the front row, his friend Sam Smith nodded. Spellman said it wasn't enough for the county to promote equal opportunity in its own hiring. "We must do better than that." He had issued a directive that all those with whom the county did business—from office supplies to major construction projects—would be required to promote diversity. He was asking the County Council to allocate seats on the Harborview Medical Center Board of Trustees to Central Area residents. "If the government is weak, it is because many of us are weak—weak in our determination to make government work. ... If it is corrupt, it is because our own standards are too low as individuals and we not only tolerate a little graft but expect it in our elected officials. ... I see the Central Area as a microcosm of King County, of its problems and of its opportunity. It presents an opportunity to prove that the democratic system works; that all people can be represented effectively in government and that inequality of opportunity cannot be tolerated. If we cannot in this country, with our vast resources, high ideals and abundance of men of good will, give all men an opportunity to live with human dignity, within just laws and with peace, how can we hope to achieve it in the world?"[4] They applauded warmly, hoping it was more than rhetoric. "We saw it as a real opportunity for us to speak out," McGavick recalls. "John spoke from the heart. We were all worried about the atmosphere after Ed Pratt's murder."[5]

"I always felt John was on target in civil rights—human rights, as we say today," says Charles Z. Smith, the first ethnic minority on the King County Superior Court bench. "With John, integrity was part of the package." [6]

AFTER A SERIES of settling-in skirmishes, the new County Council, with its tenuous Republican majority, proved more collegial than many had expected. Bob Dunn, an affable Evans man who owned an auto dealership, bonded with petite Bernice Stern, a vivacious Democrat. The offspring of German Jewish immigrants, Stern was the only woman on the council. In the 1950s, she battled red-baiters and book-banners. She was a tireless advocate of women's rights. "The Bernice and Bob Show" became the foundation of a progressive coalition that helped Spellman derail patronage, modernize the criminal justice system and build a domed stadium. Dunn was "as close to a nonpartisan in actions and in conduct of his office as anyone I had ever known," one colleague recalled. "What he brought to the council was civility and an ability to deal and work with everyone," said another. Dunn organized a prayer group that Spellman often attended, together with judges and other county officials. "Bob might not always go along with everybody, but he was never offensive about it," Spellman says. "He was an important player, especially in tandem with Bernice, who was such a vibrant person." [7]

Ed Munro was another straight shooter. Although he'd been duty-bound politically to denounce O'Brien and Spellman's Courthouse remodeling project and was part of Rosellini's inner circle, Munro genuinely admired Spellman, and vice versa. While Ed Heavey self-admittedly was the most ambitious and political of the council members, he was a strong ally on social-justice issues. Heavey called Spellman's job-training programs for minorities "one small step on a long and tortuous road" toward equal opportunity. "For the first time a local government official has moved without hesitation into a dangerous situation." [8] The council unanimously approved the program, although Councilman Dave Mooney, a former Kent mayor, worried that the county was becoming embroiled in a dispute between contractors and blacks. So be it, said Spellman, Heavey and Stern.

Heavey, who'd spent part of his boyhood in an orphanage, was a pugnacious self-made man. During the first year of the new government, the Republicans on the council blanched at his caustic tongue as chairman of the Operations and Judiciary Committee. He declared that Dunn and the Republican "reformers" were giving only lip-service to conflict-of-interest rules. They bounced him at the first opportunity. "Mostly, however, we all got along pretty well" after a while, Heavey says. "I cooperated with Bob

Dunn on a couple of efforts and Bernice Stern and I agreed on a lot of issues. She was very strong on civil rights and accountability of public officials." Spellman was a model of civility, Heavey says, but no pushover. "John was one of these people who wanted to accomplish things and make compromises. He wasn't hide-bound by some ideological issue that he just had to defend till his death, like politics today. ... Unfortunately, I tended to be one of those (partisans) and John tended to be someone who tried to work out the things to solve the problem. Even though I was more than willing to compromise I never gave people the credit they deserved" back then.[9]

Tracy Owen, another of the Republicans, was a friendly Savings & Loan president and former Realtor who emerged as a proponent of land-use planning. Bill Reams, a 36-year-old Republican from Redmond, played an important role early on as chairman of the council's Environmental Planning Committee. In 1970, he succeeded O'Brien as council chairman. O'Brien's appetite for elective politics was waning. He wanted to manage the domed stadium.

THE COUNCIL BACKED Spellman's call for fiscal austerity until all programs could be analyzed. On a 5-4 vote that crossed party lines, it authorized a telephone tax and a surtax on the state business-and-occupation tax to help balance the $89.3 million 1970 budget. Thanks to Forward Thrust, the Parks Department would open six new swimming pools in 1970. However, it needed at least 60 more workers. Nixon's proposed revenue-sharing plan offered a ray of hope, especially for the county's hard-pressed Public Safety division.

As Apollo 11 was preparing to lift off for the moon, Evans, Spellman and McGavick attended a White House conference on a down-to-earth issue: local government deficits. The old federal grants-in-aid system—600 programs in all—was a model of expensive inefficiency. The turgid reports it produced were gathering dust on courthouse shelves all over America. "We have studies until we are blue in the face. Those dollars are not providing services," Spellman told the president's aides, chief among them former Seattleite John Ehrlichman.[10] Another important stop for the delegation was Senator Magnuson's office. Maggie confided that he was impressed with Nixon's "New Federalism" domestic agenda. Spellman was too. Revenue-sharing finally won congressional approval in 1972, funneling $4 billion annually to states, counties and cities.

Spellman was an admirer of Peter Drucker's "management by objectives" and IBM's innovation in workplace computer systems. His team set out to overhaul the county's budgeting and personnel departments. A private company was hired to help the county assessor with reassessments. Del Ruble, a retired executive with Pacific Northwest Bell, oversaw the personnel department. A nationwide search brought 36-year-old George D. Church from Solano County, California, to King County in the summer of 1969. With a master's degree from USC and wide-ranging experience in county government, his job was to establish the "career service" personnel system mandated by the charter, one that blended the best of Civil Service and merit while prohibiting patronage, nepotism and conflicts of interest. Told he couldn't run for the Kent City Council and keep his job with the county medical examiner's office, one employee said, "They're trying to make county employees into second-class citizens."[11]

Minorities in King County felt like third-class citizens.

ON AUGUST 29, 1969, at 11:06 a.m., as Katherine "Kat" Spellman was busy being born, Seattle's black contractors and construction workers were on the march. They shut down work on the new County Administration Building and a research facility at Harborview Medical Center. Their leader was a sturdy electrician by the name of Tyree Scott. Given the tension in the air, many were surprised to find an ex-Marine so self-effacing. Scott was "more interested in results than rhetoric," observing that "people like labels—they're easier to deal with—but labels don't mean a thing. I talk to church people and they call me radical. The Panthers call me an Uncle Tom. Union people call me a communist and a guy at the University called me a fascist. It must mean I am doing something right."[12]

The newly organized Central Contractors Association demanded more work, especially opportunities for minorities to climb the ladder to skilled jobs. Their attorney was Lembhard "Lem" Howell, a flamboyant, shrewd Jamaica-born civil rights activist with a degree in history and a disarming smile. Howell reveres Gandhi but loves nothing so much as a good fight.

Buttressed by wives and children and a group of white clergymen, the workers marched from one site to the other, asking contractors to halt work until they were in compliance with the Equal Employment Opportunity provision of the 1964 Civil Rights Act.

Spellman kissed his wife, admired his new daughter and collected McGavick. After they met with Scott's group, he said he would ask the County Council to pass an ordinance requiring minority hiring on all county projects. Bolstering apprenticeship programs for minorities was a key part of the equation, Spellman said. The 15 building trades unions in the state had only seven non-white apprentices among their 29,000 members. Governor

Evans pronounced it appalling. He warned that discrimination would not be tolerated by any company, union or contractor doing business with the state.[13] Spellman and Evans had an influential ally. Art Fletcher, the black Republican from Pasco who in 1968 had lost a close race for lieutenant governor, was now assistant secretary of labor and the point man for the Nixon Administration's push for affirmative action.

Revenue to forestall major cutbacks and jump-start new initiatives like the apprenticeship program was Spellman's top priority. Evans had called a special session of the Legislature for January of 1970. Spellman and Chambers jawboned King County legislators to redouble their efforts to help the counties out of their revenue crisis. The effort paid major dividends. The Legislature at long last gave local governments the power to impose a half-cent sales tax, which generated about $5 million annually for King County. Commissioners from around the state became Spellman fans. Gorton's push for legislation targeting tolerance was one of the session's casualties. Those who favored liberalization of gambling gained an upper hand.

Boeing layoffs were the chill that chastened Olympia and shivered King County that winter. When Thornton A. "T" Wilson became president of the Boeing Company in 1968 and CEO a year later he set out "to create a leaner, meaner Boeing. ... "[14] Demand for the 747 jumbo jet, which had added 50,000 workers to the payroll, "fell way short of expectations" as the air travel boom that began in the mid-'50s tapered off.[15] The SST, a revolutionary supersonic airliner, was encountering multiple problems— engineering, environmental, economic and political. The first round of layoffs, 12,000 workers, proved to be the tip of the iceberg.

Nixon famously chronicled the "Six Crises" of his checkered career. Spellman would persevere through at least five of his own in one tumultuous year—1970: The Boeing Bust, the battle over the domed stadium, the loss of the Seattle Pilots, the fight for affirmative action and an attempt to have him recalled.

CHAPTER FOURTEEN

Way Out Front

As they paraded toward the King County Courthouse, 3,000 strong, on October 8, 1969, some of the construction workers chanted "Impeach Spellman!" Others demanded "Equal Rights for Whites!"[1] Tim Burgess was impressed by the size of the crowd, which grew with each passing block, but not surprised it had come to this. The tension had been building for months. Only 20 years old, Burgess earned his spurs that summer as a reporter covering the civil rights movement for KJR, Seattle's No. 1 radio station.

By September, Tyree Scott's Central Contractors Association had shut down practically every publicly-funded construction project in the county, including the Medgar Evers Memorial Swimming Pool near Garfield High School in the Central Area. Unemployed blacks had looked on with escalating chagrin as white workers built a landmark to a murdered brother in their front yard. Scott's followers were outraged by assaults on their members and the intransigence of the lily-white building-trades unions. The blacks and their allies clashed with police while picketing a project at the University of Washington. Two trucks and a bulldozer ended up in a pit excavated for a new parking garage. In all, some 700 white workers were idled by the disputes, including $47 million worth of improvements to Seattle-Tacoma International Airport.

The National Labor Relations Board arrived in Seattle to investigate unfair-labor-practice charges against the iron workers, bricklayers, electrical workers, operating engineers, plumbers and pipefitters. White unionists seethed over the threat to their apprenticeship programs, bastions of who-you-knew nepotism that doubly discriminated against minorities.[2] Black workers deserved a chance to prove themselves through programs that led to skilled jobs, "not just pushing dirt," Scott said.[3] "Either black men work or nobody works," Herbert Hill, national labor director of the NAACP, declared.[4] Some 3,000 blacks had applied unsuccessfully for construction jobs. To Spellman, it was a "fundamental human rights issue." Some of the contractors, meantime, realized he would soon have a carrot far bigger than his present stick: Multi-million-dollar contracts for the domed stadium. The rank and file had yet to see the light. Unions boycotted most of the peace talks called by the county executive.

The "Seattle Plan" embraced by Spellman and Ed Devine, Mayor Miller's savvy deputy, called for a change in the ratio of skilled to unskilled workers. After 30 hours of talks over three days in Spellman's office, five members of the Associated General Contractors agreed to hire one black trainee for every four journeymen on a project. Each craft union would have a ratio of its own. Spellman, with the council's support, pledged to underwrite the job-training program with an initial investment of $15,000. Under a new anti-discrimination ordinance, every county administrator was directed to prepare a plan to address the "gross imbalance" in county employment. Contractors bidding on county projects henceforth would be required to submit a certificate of compliance, pledging to uphold affirmative action guidelines.[5]

The unions remained defiant, insisting the job-training agreement amounted to a breach of "bona fide, federally recognized" apprenticeship programs and collective-bargaining contracts.[6] A group of irate ironworker wives clutching unpaid bills, kids in tow, met with Spellman for 40 minutes. Departing unmollified, they told reporters he just passed the buck to the contractors. "We're here to find out who is going to pay our husbands' wages," one angry housewife declared, voice quavering with indignation. "Our taxes are supporting the projects that are shut down."[7]

"Bright and early on the Monday after the five white contractors endorsed the agreement, we sent a black trainee to a construction site, and the unions immediately walked off the job!" said Lem Howell, anger and astonishment undiminished by the passage of 43 years. He filed suit in federal court, asserting it was now a full-fledged civil rights case. Spellman and Evans were steadfast in solidarity. The governor told the unions he was confident the Legislature would enact an open door to apprenticeship rolls if they failed to get with the program. Spellman said the county wasn't bluffing. "By their own reports prepared for the federal government," he said the unions admitted their minority representation amounted to less than six-tenths of one percent while the county's minority population topped 10 percent.[8] The International Brotherhood of Electrical Workers in Washington State had about 20 nonwhite members and zero minority apprentices among its 7,000 members.[9]

"Spellman could have taken a hard line and said, 'Hell no—nobody will

violate the law!' No demonstrations!" Howell says. "In fact, he told me that
Charles O. Carroll threatened to throw him in jail! ... Spellman issued the
change-order that said the county would be responsible for any additional
expense for the hiring of the black trainees. ... He was the first public official to agree to a plan like that. I was not familiar with all his leanings as a
progressive in race relations. I just knew that I thought it took a whole lot of
gumption to have issued that change-order and to get us to where we were
and into court. ... It would have never happened but for Spellman." [10]

Seattle was just one battleground. Across America, the construction-
worker wing of the civil rights movement grew more militant by the hour,
even as the AFL-CIO dug in. At a federal hearing in Chicago on September
25, a thousand angry hard hats blocked the entrances to the U.S. Customs
House. Art Fletcher was hustled into the building through a basement door
as reinforcements wielding batons arrived and shots rang out.

TIM BURGESS and a gaggle of other reporters accompanied the shouting,
sign-waving throng of angry white construction workers who set out for the
Courthouse and City Hall at 9 a.m. on Wednesday, October 8, 1969. Led
by a worker carrying the Stars and Stripes, they paraded 20 blocks down
Second Avenue, cheered on by sidewalk crowds and office workers leaning from windows. At one corner, the marchers spotted workmen atop a
building under construction. "Get off the job!" they yelled. "Come join us!
They'll have your job next!" A half-dozen men climbed down the scaffold-
ing and accepted signs. One said, "No Work, No Taxes." Another, "For Every
Building-Trades Trainee, One Lawyer Trainee, One Judge Trainee, One
Governor Trainee, One County Excutive [sic] Trainee." [11]

At Second and Yesler, they turned toward the Courthouse and massed in
front of the Fourth Avenue entrance, chanting, "We want Spellman! Whites
have rights, too!" Four of their leaders were ushered into Spellman's office.
"We're a profession just like doctors and lawyers," said Leroy Mozingo,
an electrician. "We don't want our standards lowered." Spellman said he
had represented unions for years as a lawyer and understood their pride
in professionalism. "No one is talking about putting unskilled trainees in
skilled jobs. This amounts to a drop in the bucket in what has to be done
to alleviate poverty and racial discrimination." He urged the union men to
embrace programs that would give well-qualified minority workers a chance
to become skilled workers. "We're talking about basic justice—fairness, not
favoritism." [12]

"Spellman is a pretty smooth character," said a 41-year-old electrician
named Jim Koehler, one of the protest leaders. "He starts out by agreeing

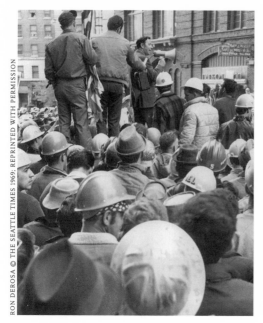

Spellman addresses a construction worker protest march outside the Courthouse.

with everything you say. Then he starts talking, and by the time he's through, he's disagreeing with everything you've said."[13]

Around 10:30, Spellman resolved to address the crowd. Aides were nervous because security was thin. Spellman climbed onto a truck and was handed a bullhorn. He was booed and taunted. Reporters leaned forward from all sides, tape recorders and microphones outstretched. To most of the onlookers he was a speck in a sea of hard hats and bobbing signs.

"The deal is, we don't mind the blacks coming in the union," one worker shouted, "but we want them to serve the same amount of apprenticeship we served. I served five years of apprenticeship. *They serve five years of apprenticeship!* Not six months and get the same pay I'm gettin'!"[14]

"Lots of people have received bad information on this subject," Spellman began, only to be drowned out by jeers and groaning. A union leader standing next to him gestured for silence.

"I've been up there meeting with your committee," Spellman said.

Demands hailed down before he could start his next sentence.

"If you want to hear the answer to the question, *somebody's going to have to listen,*" Spellman said, voice betraying annoyance at the incivility. "What we talked about was a way to give more people an opportunity to work in this area."

A clump of glowering workers demanded to know whether he had agreed to the job-training program. "Yes or no? *Yes or no?!*"

It was yes. "But it is a temporary solution to prevent work from being halted. At no time have we suggested that a single member of any labor union in this city or this county would find his job in jeopardy because of this program."

The crowd turned surlier yet when Spellman denied the county had refused to maintain law and order on construction sites. "King County is prepared to protect all citizens from threats of violence," he said.[15]

He spoke for about five minutes, deciding to return to his office when it was obvious he wouldn't, and couldn't, be heard. As Spellman climbed back down into the crowd, reporters clustered around. They were all cheek by jowl with the protesters, barely able to inch forward, let alone conduct an interview. "I'm going to go back inside," Spellman told Tim Burgess.

"We all turned as a tight little group and started moving toward the Third Avenue entrance to the Courthouse," Burgess remembers. "I was right next to John or one person removed from him. Suddenly this fist comes from my right on a direct line for the right side of Spellman's face. I just put my hand up—I think it was more of a reflex instinct—and I blocked the fist. John was kind of startled and we all started walking much faster. When we were inside the Courthouse he turned to me and said 'Thank you.' I wouldn't say he was shaken, but he still looked kind of startled." [16]

Spellman isn't certain the fist was malevolent. Maybe it was someone trying to help clear the way or just reaching out to him. *The Seattle Times* reported there was "a brief pushing match between some workers and plain-clothes detectives clearing the way for Spellman." Burgess, who went on to become a police detective and, in 2007, a Seattle City Council member, is

BARRY SWEET PHOTO

Tim Burgess, a reporter for KJR radio, clears the way for Spellman as the county executive tries to move through a crush of angry construction workers outside the King County Courthouse on October 8, 1969.

certain it was a fist. Shooting from above, Barry Sweet, an award-winning photographer for the Associated Press, captured Burgess's outstretched protective arm. *The Times* captioned it "Spellman Faces Hard-Hat Man."[17] Burgess remembers being impressed that Spellman had waded into a huge, hostile crowd, appealed for civility and stood his ground. He sees the scene in even sharper focus now. "For the times, he was way out front."[18]

Eight days later, white construction workers marshaled 4,000 for a march on Olympia. They demanded that Evans be impeached too. The governor faced them down from the steps of the Capitol building, standing firm for affirmative action on his 44th birthday while being interrupted by booing and jeers more than a dozen times.[19]

LEM HOWELL'S FIRST federal case remains the most far-reaching of a long, colorful career. U.S. District Court Judge William J. Lindberg ordered the construction unions back to work, ruling that his court had jurisdiction because racial discrimination complaints transcend collective-bargaining agreements. Then, after conducting wide-ranging hearings on hiring practices, Lindberg ordered four Seattle-area construction unions to cease discrimination against any person "because of his race or color." Howell had hedged his bets by filing a complaint with the National Labor Relations Board. The Department of Justice also brought action against the unions under the Civil Rights Act of 1964.[20]

"Let me tell you about this prince!" Howell declares. "William Lindberg is the only federal judge I know who was not affected by Federalitis—the notion that one is God's gift to mankind. He was such a humble man. He had hearings going into the night. He understood the issue at hand and ended up mandating hiring and apprenticeship classes and other programs to boost minorities' chances for skilled jobs."[21] Spellman agrees: "I had tried maritime and union cases before Judge Lindberg as a young lawyer. He was an even-tempered man, ready to change his views if the facts or law required it. I testified in the apprenticeship case. He was fair and intelligent. What more can one ask of a judge?"

Tyree Scott, who died in 2003, went on to many more victories for human rights. He used to say that the black Central Contractors Association set out to "take a fort with a popgun." It won the war with persistence and the support of some righteous white friends in high places, Howell says. The minority-hiring protests that began in Seattle "precipitated the first federal imposition of affirmative action upon local governments and industries."[22]

THE HARD HAT MARCH, one of the most significant civil-rights showdowns in King County history, was bumped to the bottom of the *Post-Intelligencer's* front page by a double-deck, banner headline:

Mayor Says Policeman Offered
Assistant Chief $40,000 Bribe

A trio of assistant chiefs—dubbed the "Young Turks" by the media—had staged a coup over corruption in the Seattle Police Department. While the chief was vacationing out of town, they ordered a raid on one of the city's leading bingo parlors. The proprietor, one Charlie Berger, and some 80 regulars at the Lifeline Club off seedy old First Avenue were stunned when 34 cops barged in and scooped up evidence of illegal gambling, payoffs to politicians and revenues that ran as high as $2 million per year. Berger, 72, a convicted felon, sat forlornly at his desk as they carted out files by the box-load. He thought he had greased all the right palms. Effrontery became gall when Berger was cuffed and hauled off to jail.[23] Former sheriff Jack Porter, heretofore hoping Spellman would name him public safety director under the new government, provided an embarrassing Exhibit A for the vice probers. Reproduced on the *P-I's* front page was a $1,000 check from Berger's club for 20 tickets to a 1966 Porter re-election campaign fundraiser. Not that he was the lone beneficiary. State legislators Gordon Walgren, John Bagnariol, Leonard Sawyer and John Rosellini had also received campaign donations from Berger's clubs, as had Congressman Brock Adams. It was Assistant Chief Tony Gustin, head of the vice squad, who'd been offered $40,000 by one of his officers "to look the other way on gambling," the mayor said. Gustin clarified that it was not so much a bribe as a warning that the gambling lords were willing to pay that much for his complicity. Gustin, Eugene Corr and George Fuller, his fellow whistle-blowers, denounced tolerance as a pox on the community and a slap in the face to the honest cops who made up 90 percent of the department.

Chief Frank Ramon, who had hurried home to spring Berger from jail, was forced into retirement by Mayor Miller, who ordered "a complete halt to all gambling activity in the city." Spellman instructed sheriff's deputies to redouble their enforcement efforts county wide. He asked the mayors of the smaller cities to follow suit and launched an investigation into Porter's conduct.[24]

At the Prosecutor's Office, it was business as usual. Don McGaffin, the crusading TV reporter whose year of legwork played a pivotal role in the revelations, told viewers that the cops who conducted the raid left

Carroll's office "in a state of shock" after their evidence against Berger was discounted. "They felt they had acquired more than enough" evidence to sustain a felony gambling conviction. "To their astonishment," the Prosecutor's Office charged Berger with possession of gambling paraphernalia, a misdemeanor. Carroll said he hadn't "personally" handled the case. His understanding was that as his deputies were reviewing the evidence, Chief Ramon called and asked that the cases be returned to the Police Department because the suspects had been held for 18 hours and he wanted to get charges filed immediately in Municipal Court.[25]

Spellman was neither shocked nor astonished.

CHAPTER FIFTEEN

Mudville

n a Milwaukee tavern, a factory worker hoisted a beer, waved it toward a waitress named LaVerne and offered a toast: "Baseball is back! This is the greatest thing since Polish sausage."[1] It was April Fools' Day 1970. Seattle was a joyless Mudville. Boeing had jettisoned 16,000 workers since the first of the year. Now it was handing out 3,600 more pink slips as the Seattle Pilots—balls and all—were headed to Wisconsin to become the Brewers and go down in history as the only team in Major League Baseball history to move after one season and the first to declare bankruptcy.

Spellman, Governor Evans, Attorney General Gorton and Wes Uhlman, Seattle's new mayor, had flown to Oakland on January 27 to urge the American League owners to accept a local ownership plan to keep the Pilots in Seattle. Hotelier Eddie Carlson, Teamsters official Arnie Weinmeister, the Nordstroms and other leading Seattleites had raised nearly $2.5 million in pledges for a line of credit to cover the team's interim operating costs at rickety Sicks' Stadium. They were optimistic the new domed stadium would be ready for the club's home opener in the spring of 1973. Practically the only Seattleite who hadn't been tapped for a contribution was J.P. Patches, the popular clown on after-school TV. Jim Ellis marveled that more money was "collected in 10 days to save the Pilots than was collected in six months for the World's Fair."[2] The franchise would be operated as a "public trust," a nonprofit corporation overseen by a blue-ribbon board. Joe Cronin, the league president, told them there was no rule barring such a plan. He offered the league's "whole-hearted cooperation to Seattle."[3]

"They assured us the Pilots were going to stay in Seattle," Gorton recalls with a sardonic smile. "It was 'We'll find a way to do it. We don't want to move them. Thank you, gentlemen, for all your hard work on behalf of baseball!'" After the delegation departed, the owner of the Washington Senators reportedly chortled, "Well, I hope we gave those guys enough rope to hang themselves."[4] Gorton concluded "that if an American League owner moved into your neighborhood, he would lower property values."[5] He filed suit in federal court. It would take six years to bring baseball to trial.

Spellman had been county executive for 11 eventful months when the Pilots made their galling exit—a preview of coming attractions. The loss was a double disappointment, throwing into doubt the domed stadium project. But there's no crying in baseball; it's only a game, although Jim Bouton, the legendary former Pilots pitcher, observed that "They call baseball a game because it's too screwed up to be a business."[6]

BUSINESS DEFINITELY was screwed up. King County's jobless rate was climbing one percent a month. Miner Baker, the highly regarded economist for Seattle-First National Bank, warned on New Year's Day 1970 that Puget Sound's "Soaring '60s" were over. "Reality would prove far more dire than Baker's forecast."[7] Over the next two years the Boeing Bust rippled exponentially though the region, leaving heartache in its wake.

Spellman called Magnuson, Jackson and other members of the congressional delegation, including Tom Foley, the up-and-coming Democrat from Spokane. On January 17 Spellman caught a red-eye for the other Washington, the first of many such trips in the months to come. At the White House, John Ehrlichman promised he would do everything he could to expedite assistance. Spellman urged taxpayers to write letters in support of Nixon's Revenue Sharing plan, which was bottled up in the House Ways and Means Committee. He called it "the most important bill regarding local government" in half a century.[8]

King County unemployment hit 8.3 percent in March, more than double the national average. Puget Sound qualified as a "redevelopment area."[9] The Legislature's approval of a half-cent local-option sales tax for counties and cities was a welcome development after Spellman's yeoman lobbying, though now little more than a tourniquet, given the magnitude of the job losses.

Seattle's winter of discontent was punctuated by a federal grand jury probe of police corruption, protest marches, explosions and the stench of tear gas. Thousands took to the streets, "occupied" freeways and disrupted university classes, demanding an end to the war, the draft, ROTC, racism, sexism and corporate capitalism. And no more freeways either! Riot police repelled some 200 demonstrators who rushed the Federal Courthouse and kicked in two glass doors in protest of the contempt-of-court sentences handed down against the radical anti-war Chicago Seven. Demonstrators—2,000 in all—retaliated with rocks and bottles.[10] Uhlman told a U.S. Senate fact-finding committee that his city had the "dubious distinction" of being No. 1 in the nation for bombings and arson fires per capita, trailing only New York and Chicago.[11]

WORKING WITH Evans and Uhlman, Spellman appointed a 32-member Economic Development Planning Committee to make the county's case for low-interest industrial loans and public-works grants. The group was headed by Seattle attorney Jerry Grinstein, Magnuson's trusted former chief of staff. Grinstein had recruited many of the senator's bright young "Bumblebees," including Norm Dicks, Stan Barer, Harley Dirks and Ed Sheets. Grinstein was the son of Magnuson's physician. Dr. Alex Grinstein was a good friend of Joe Gottstein, the lord of Longacres. Politics came as naturally to young Jerry "as his analytical brilliance and humor."[12]

Spellman hired Ed Devine, the former deputy mayor with whom he and McGavick had worked so effectively, to be the county's liaison on Capitol Hill. Devine was a master of "the art of the possible."[13] Like "an old Irish song-and-dance man," he could charm everyone from campus radicals to senators' wives, Spellman says.

"In those days, earmarks were not the dirty word they are today," Grinstein says. "That downturn at Boeing was so damn dramatic that we were looking for any source of funds that would provide employment, whether it was for transit or waste disposal. My work was largely with Maggie and Scoop, and they in turn worked on the administration."[14] The president, his brain trust and Republican businessmen with deep pockets thought highly of the hawkish Jackson—so highly in fact that GOP strategist Gummie Johnson groused that it was practically impossible to raise money for a credible challenger to Scoop, placing the two-party system in the state "in serious jeopardy."[15]

Devine's role as the county's inside operator was enhanced by his relationship with former mayor Dorm Braman, who in 1969 joined the Nixon Administration as an assistant secretary of transportation with a special portfolio for "Urban Systems and the Environment." A new package of Forward Thrust issues set for the May 19, 1970, ballot in King County included a $1.3-billion regional mass-transit plan for which Magnuson and Braman had secured 75 percent federal funding, outflanking the highway lobby and Nixon's initial opposition to such projects.[16] Spellman said the project would create at least 2,000 construction jobs, spin off thousands more and relieve traffic congestion. Unaddressed, the problem would only get worse, he warned, stifling recovery and "compromising our area's quality of life" for decades to come.[17] The other Forward Thrust issues included storm-water control, a regional correctional facility to replace the aging county jail, community centers, public health clinics and improvements at Seattle Center.

Spellman, McGavick, Devine and Grinstein concentrated on job-creation projects that would utilize the county's large pool of skilled labor. Spellman, characteristically, saw the glass as half full. "Painful as this is," he said, "we can come out of this stronger if we set aside partisan politics, work together and look out for our neighbors. A lot of people need help."[18] Spellman championed the jobs program that in 1973 won passage as the Comprehensive Employment and Training Act—CETA. It focused on the long-term unemployed and youth. King County put it to good use.

While pushing projects that would create more jobs at military bases, Jackson also conducted an important series of hearings on the unemployed and under-employed. "Scoop got that right, which a lot of people still don't get right," Grinstein says. "Under-employment was a serious problem then—and still is today (2012)."[19]

Magnuson secured millions for cancer research as he redoubled his efforts to promote Seattle as a cutting-edge center of health care in the West, a hallmark of his years in Congress. Maggie had a soft spot for Spellman, and not just because John's father had been his coach at the UW, according to Grinstein. "John is just a disarming man. He was never the kind of guy where you couldn't get between him and a TV camera. He didn't toot his own horn. He just wanted to get things done in the right way. Maggie liked that."[20]

Grinstein felt the same way about Pete Rozelle. The commissioner of the National Football League was "a dead-straight guy" who, even as the Pilots were leaving for Wisconsin, made one thing perfectly clear to the media: "I always have thought highly of Seattle and still do ... as an excellent city for a franchise."[21] Grinstein became the Rozelle-Spellman go-between in the years to come. But no stadium, no team—football or baseball.

ON THE DAY BEFORE the Pilots were sold to Milwaukee auto dealer Bud Selig, the Washington State Supreme Court issued a provisional decision that set the stage for Frank Ruano's biggest victory. His initiative campaign to keep the domed stadium from being built at the Seattle Center had won a place on the ballot.

Fizzing with indignation, Ruano took his case to court after Spellman ignored his demands to halt spending on the project, pending the outcome of the challenge. Spellman instead signed a $780,000 contract for the second phase of design work. Charles G. Prahl, a former state highways director, sided with Ruano, charging that even with federal funding "it would be a miracle" if the proposed Bay Freeway to expedite stadium traffic to and from Seattle Center would be ready by 1973. In one breath, Ruano beseeched the County Council to overrule Spellman; in the next he charged it had "robbed and cheated" the taxpayers.[22] "My wife tells me I shoot from the hip, anger too quickly and am not overly diplomatic," Ruano once conceded with a sheepish smile. "People who know me only from

An artist's rendering of a domed stadium at Seattle Center.

my newspaper write-ups may be surprised to learn that I am basically a very sensitive person and not the ornery S.O.B. they have heard about." [23]

"I understand that Frank is a fine husband and father," Spellman said, unable, however, to swallow "very sensitive person."

At the time, and for three decades to come as he challenged public financing of sports stadiums, bond issues, mini-prisons and assorted other causes, critics called Ruano a goofball and "misdirected egomaniac." [24] That someone who seemed so squirrely was also a sophisticated political operative caught many by surprise. When Ruano died in 2005, Seattle historian Walt Crowley concluded that the commercial real estate developer was "probably our first suburban rebel." [25]

A CASE CAN BE MADE that Harley Hoppe was actually the first. Bursting onto the political scene at 27 in 1957, the car-wash entrepreneur founded a group called Overtaxed, Inc. By 1969, it claimed 130,000 members around the state. In this, Hoppe was the godfather to Tim Eyman's latter-day tax protest movement. Hoppe, however, got himself elected to public office—county assessor, no less. Then, while "scrupulously doing the opposite of nearly all the things he pledged to do," he aimed much higher.[26] But all that was still more than two years away.

In 1970, in the middle of the debate over the fate of the Pilots and the site for the domed stadium, Hoppe announced a petition drive to repeal the county charter and return to a three-member board of commissioners. Spellman and other "so-called progressives" had bamboozled the voters into believing the new charter would save money and decrease bureaucracy, Hoppe declared. "In fact, it has been extremely costly" and not "the panacea of all our problems that it was to have been. ... Our county executive has been more concerned with baseball and football teams than with the plight of the taxpayers." [27]

Spellman, who found Hoppe's populist bravado disgusting, dismissed the assertions as "complete nonsense." Under the old system, "debt was hidden by borrowing from other county funds," he said.[28] The new government, though only a year old, had eliminated waste, improved services and promoted transparency. It was also promoting countywide consolidation of police and fire protection and recruiting "some of the top people in the country" to modernize county government, Spellman said.

Harley Hoppe in the early 1970s

One of those was Norward J. Brooks, a 35-year-old computer expert and minority-jobs activist. A Democrat, Brooks had worked with McGavick at the Boeing Company. McGavick was impressed with his can-do personality and ability to harness new data-processing machines. Spellman named Brooks director of the Department of Elections and Records, winning confirmation after wrangling with the County Council over a salary of $18,000. There was also considerable sentiment at the Courthouse for Ed Logan, the acting director and longtime elections superintendent. Logan stayed on in that role under Brooks, the county's first black department head, who immediately began computerizing the real-property and corporations records that had been laboriously entered by hand. And on his watch, the Elections Department was a pacesetter.[29]

WHEN THE NEW government had its first birthday on May 1, 1970, Richard Larsen, the astute political reporter for *The Seattle Times*, took stock of the county executive's achievements. Though wracked by challenges, Spellman seemed remarkably calm. He was genial John, smoking his pipe, twisting arms in his own low-key way; overseeing the reform of personnel policies, shunning the role of patronage broker and insisting on top-flight appointments, regardless of political persuasion, even if that took longer than expected. Everyone was wondering, for instance, about ex-sheriff Jack Porter. He never had a prayer of becoming Spellman's public safety director, even before the bingo club scandal. Yet Porter was still acting chief. Some 300 department employees and two of the county's biggest unions were pushing for his appointment, while reformers wanted him fired. Spellman said the only pressure that moved him was the "appalling" unemployment rate, now rising toward 11 percent.

When he was running against Rosellini, many said the prize was the second most powerful political job in the state. "I always said it wouldn't be," Spellman told Larsen with a puff and a shrug. Spellman had become an important political figure, Larsen concluded. "But buried in the flow of details spawned by a new form of government," he was far less visible than the transparently ambitious Uhlman. Around 7 a.m. most days, the prematurely gray 34-year-old mayor could be spotted hopping out of a Chrysler Imperial limo to jog around Green Lake in his bright white sneakers. Then he'd change out his sweats and roll up his Brooks Brothers sleeves at City Hall, with a news conference to follow.[30] Spellman was annoyed by the perceived vigor gap. Despite his demurring, he had ambitions of his own. He cared that his accomplishments seemed less sexy than Uhlman's. McGavick, Spellman's alter ego and tail twister, was there to say "sic 'em, chief!" Neither of them trusted the mayor. McGavick correctly suspected Uhlman was wooing John Chambers, the deputy executive, to jump ship. "Wes was a very bright young guy. We were capable of working together but it was not a good relationship," Spellman says. "I would come up with a great proposal and Wes would have a news conference on it before we were ready to announce it. I felt he was devious in terms of joint relations and joint programs—always looking out for Wes first. My staff was furious, and I didn't feel very good about it either."

When Chambers, sure enough, left in the summer of 1971 to become Uhlman's top deputy it was seen at first as a political coup for the mayor and an embarrassing moment for Spellman. Sooner or later, Uhlman and Spellman seemed destined to be running against one another for governor or U.S. senator. On the other hand, the Uhlman administration almost from the get-go "had earned a reputation as an often-frustrating, perilous place for bright people with ideas and a desire for action," Larsen observed. "Hopes rose anew when the mayor lured Chambers away from the county executive's office. Perhaps, some thought, he might cause a rebirth of executive excellence in the mayor's office. But the able Chambers, still deputy mayor," was soon "shifted into partial isolation at the Smith Tower—away from the hour-to-hour executive action of City Hall."[31]

Though he lacked the mayor's panache, Spellman knew talent and didn't squander it. Chambers' successor, 40-year-old Bob Bratton, proved to be a decisive administrator. He also took pains to never be seen as upstaging Spellman, which sometimes seemed the case with his predecessor. To no

one's surprise, Bratton and McGavick, now the director of budgets and program planning, periodically clashed. Their problem, however, had nothing
to do with petulance and everything to do with self-confidence. "They were
two very bright guys," says Spellman, who harnessed the creative tension.

Chambers was back at the Courthouse within two years. The County
Council, envious of Spellman's power and itching to be more assertive,
hired him as its first chief administrator to oversee the 54 employees in
the legislative branch. Chambers was soon authorized to hire three planners as part of a new policy-development unit. One was Ken Eikenberry, an
attorney representing the 36th District in the House as a Republican. His
seatmate, Democrat Helen Sommers, was a legislative aide to the council.
It wanted all its bases covered.*

WHILE UHLMAN ASPIRED to be the Democrats' rising star, Evans and
Gorton were grooming Chris Bayley, one of Gorton's brightest deputies,
to challenge a wounded bull elephant. When Charles O. Carroll first
took office, Bayley was 10 years old. Now, at 32, he looked and sounded
a lot like Dick Cavett, the urbane talk show host. Bayley was the son of
a respected Seattle businessman. He'd met Evans and Gorton as a Young
Republican leader during college and joined the progressive Ripon Society
during law school in Boston. Returning home, Bayley became a charter
member of Choose an Effective City Council and Action for Washington,
which promoted public service and "mainstream" politics as an antidote
to extremism. During the summer of '70 Gorton shrewdly had Bayley, his
consumer-protection deputy, all over the radio dial, warning the citizenry
about con artists.

Mort Frayn, a Republican sage, convinced Bayley he should pay a courtesy call on Carroll to inform him of his candidacy. "OK," Bayley said, "if
you'll go with me." They were ushered into the prosecutor's imposing office. Carroll, glowering imperiously, was seated at a huge conference table,
Bill Boeing Jr. at his side. "Carroll was like Charles de Gaulle. He didn't
think anyone else could do his job," Bayley says. Oozing contempt, Carroll suggested that Bayley was little more than a puffed-up pipsqueak hot
out of Harvard. "I have deputies who've tried 10 murder cases and they're
not qualified to run against me!" As Carroll continued, practically wagging
his finger as he told of 2 a.m. phone calls and weighty decisions, Bayley's

---

* In 1976, Eikenberry gave up his safe seat to run against Sommers, saying, "She embodies the
epitome of the philosophy that I am opposed to."[32] Incensed, Sommers vowed to win. And she
did—decisively. Both had long and eventful political careers.

initial jitters turned to indignation, then confidence. "It was perfect timing and great luck because he was a perfect target. He thought he could bull his way through—that the Cichy scandal didn't matter. ... If you were a black kid from Franklin High school he'd throw the book at you, but he wouldn't do anything about other crimes. I refused to be intimidated." [33]

Making an increasingly wider political splash was Dixy Lee Ray, newly appointed by Nixon to a special task force on oceanography. She was much in demand as a guest speaker and TV show panelist. When she became chairman of the federal Atomic Energy Commission, Johnny Carson invited her to "explain" nuclear power on *The Tonight Show*. She radiated quirky charm and was able to demystify science without seeming to talk down. It was Mr. Wizard recast as your maiden Aunt Madge, Wellesley '44, in a Pendleton skirt and knee socks with a poodle named Jacques in tow.[34] Ray was the author of a treatise on *Marine Boring and Fouling Organisms*. In the years to come she would be accused of fouling. No one ever said she was boring.

CHAPTER SIXTEEN

Thrust Backward

I f timing is everything, Spellman, Jim Ellis and Eddie Carlson had a well justified sense of foreboding that Forward Thrust's second chance was about to lurch into reverse. Events beyond their control—20,000 layoffs at Boeing since January and the loss of the Pilots—spelled big trouble for the domed stadium and mass transit in the countywide May 19, 1970, special election. They urged voters to consider both the immediate and long-term benefits: sorely needed jobs; nearly $900 million in federal funding to relieve gridlock; revenue from major conventions and the likelihood that the city would acquire a new major-league baseball team as well as a pro-football franchise. "The truth is that we will either build the stadium at the Center site in the next three years or we will not have a stadium … during the next 25 years. It is that simple," said Carlson, leader of the businessmen's group that backed the Seattle Center site.[1]

It wasn't that simple. And Spellman, truth be told, had nagging doubts about the Seattle Center site, even if the Bay Freeway linking the neighborhood to Interstate 5 was built. Traffic to the Center, especially along Mercer Street, was already "a bloody mess," dissenters on the City Council said.[2] Imagine 60,000 more people heading to a stadium. In 1968, when the State Stadium Commission visited other venues, Spellman was hobbled by a painful knee injury from a fall on a slippery ramp in a downtown parking garage. "The commission members who had seen the other new stadiums around the country said Seattle Center was by far the best site for ours. I didn't know any better, so I went along. But in hindsight my early reservations snapped into focus."

At the time, however, Spellman had no choice but to frame the choice like this: "Are we voting against the Seattle Center site because we are angry and discouraged with the economic climate or the loss of the baseball team? If so, is it wise to abandon the project, thereby worsening the economic climate and doing away with all future hope of obtaining major-league baseball and football teams?"[3] The 1968 bond-issue proposition mandated that the stadium be built at a site "to be selected by the State Stadium Commission." If the voters rejected the Seattle Center site, how and by whom would another site be chosen? Given the rate of inflation, the time it would take to choose and acquire another site likely would push the cost past the already tight $40 million budget "and make it questionable whether the stadium could be built at all," Spellman warned.[4]

Spellman was under some pressure to skew the referendum by placing the previously considered stadium sites on the ballot together with Seattle Center. That way, the Center likely would have emerged with the most votes and been saved. "I could have, but that would have been a terrible mistake. It would not have been an appropriate use of my office."

The three other Forward Thrust issues on the ballot were also vital to resuscitating the economy, Spellman said. Eighty-million dollars was earmarked for storm water control; $55 million for community centers and libraries; $40 million for public-safety projects and public-health centers. Though improvements had been made to the County Jail, Spellman said it was still a "crime hatchery."[5] The chief justice of the U.S. Supreme Court, Warren Burger, cited the jail for a glaring lack of rehabilitation programs.

The Boeing Company endorsed the Forward Thrust package, saying the improvements, especially the transportation proposal, would be a boon to both business and quality of life.

ALL FOUR Forward Thrust proposals took a thrashing from the antsy electorate. Only 46 percent supported the mass-transit proposal. Nearly 61 percent rejected the Seattle Center stadium site. Ellis was crestfallen, although he assured Spellman and several hundred other stalwarts gathered at the Washington Athletic Club that "no campaign could have done better. ... We have rowed against a tide that simply was impossible."[6] Looking back, Ellis says, "People were just scared. Fifty-thousand people had left Seattle. It was just night and day between 1968 and 1970." Gallingly, the mass-transit money Magnuson had earmarked for King County was snapped up by Atlanta, "and they built a beautiful light rail system!" Ellis says, all but slapping himself on the forehead.[7]

Ruano and Hoppe said it was distrust of the downtown business establishment, not fear, that motivated the voters. "I don't mean to gloat, but we worked hard and long without a dime," Hoppe said on the morning after.[8] "Now that the voters have spoken," Ruano said he was thinking about launching a recall movement against Spellman.

Spellman urged Uhlman and other local-government leaders to join him in developing a less expensive regional mass-transit plan based on the bus component of the defeated Forward Thrust proposal. "This region still needs rapid transit, and eventually it must come," he said. "But we cannot let our disappointment turn into pessimism ... and stand by as even greater numbers of people are forced into cars, clogging our arterials and choking our air." [9]

Regrouping paid some dividends. With Spellman, Uhlman and Ellis pushing hard, an all-bus Metro Transit system won approval at the polls in the fall of 1972. Not until 1996, however, would Puget Sound voters finally fund light rail—the $3.9 billion Sound Transit system. [10]

AFTER MEETING WITH SPELLMAN, Governor Evans on June 18, 1970, authorized a new six-member State Stadium Commission. He named James L. Wilson, a Seattle physician active in civic affairs and renowned for civility, as its chairman. The governor's second appointment was Spellman's friend Arnie Weinmeister, a twofer. Weinmeister was an important Teamsters leader who knew stadiums from the ground up, having starred at defensive tackle for the New York Giants in the 1950s. [11] Spellman's appointees were County Councilmen Ed Munro and Bill Reams. Uhlman named City Councilmen Wayne Larkin and Ted Best. None of the appointees had served on the commission that picked Seattle Center as the stadium site. Dr. Wilson promised the commission would meet "with regularity and dispatch." [12] He was as good as his word.

Spellman kept his eye on the ball. Critics to the contrary—and he won over many during the next five years—he could be decisive and dogged. Never more so than in rescuing the domed stadium time and time again, but also in pursuing federal aid to ease the pain of the Boeing layoffs. David Brewster, a talented young writer for the Seattle *Argus*, observed Spellman's "fastidious scorn for demagoguery," his high-mindedness and command of facts; his penchant for sharing political credit and "unshakeable reserve." Unfortunately, absent an angry throng of hard hats, Spellman's self-effacing competence gave off "a pervasive sense of dullness." [13]

" 'Dull' definitely didn't apply to my second year as county executive," Spellman says with a rueful laugh. "In fact, if there was a dull year out of all 11 I must have blotted it out. People used to ask me how I stayed so calm when so much was happening, seemingly all at once. I found out that I was very good at switching topics, almost in mid-sentence. It was my ambition to know more about the county than anybody. I set out to acquire enough knowledge on any topic so that I could discuss it intelligently and not get blindsided. In the beginning, Lois had apprehensions about me becoming an executive—and rightly, because I didn't have experience. But I had the temperament. Maybe I would have been a more successful politician if I had been more showy. That just wasn't me—not that I was going to let anyone push me around."

In events that presaged one of his most determined stands as governor a dozen years later, Spellman collided in the summer of 1970 with Bert Cole, the state's imperious commissioner of public lands, over leases for oil drilling in Puget Sound. Spellman had asked Cole to delay action until the county had a chance to review the proposals. Cole accused him of "emotionalism." Spellman bristled: "Far from responding emotionally concerning this issue, we are responding from a perspective of factual information about the damage potential to beaches, property and fish life in Puget Sound." While he was anxious to promote new jobs, Spellman said the potential for economic and recreational damage from an oil spill "approaches a scale which is incalculable. ... My advice is that you forget oil drilling in Puget Sound until such time as spills become absolutely avoidable."[14] Cole backed off. In 1971, an oil spill from an Atlantic Richfield tanker plying the waters off Whatcom County, where a refinery was under construction at Cherry Point, prompted Senator Magnuson to call for stringent new tanker regulations and a vessel traffic control system starting at the Strait of Juan de Fuca, the gateway to the Sound. For Magnuson and Spellman, Puget Sound—already sloshing with civilization's runoff—simply couldn't absorb more "progress."

AS THE FALLOUT from the Boeing Bust drifted across Puget Sound, Jerry Grinstein's Economic Development Steering Committee rolled out a new package of applications for $360 million in emergency federal funds to develop industrial parks, mitigate environmental problems, upgrade utilities and help existing companies expand. Fifty-thousand King County residents were jobless and 100,000 were receiving public assistance. The Fourth of July, 1970, found 68,648 receiving food stamps vs. 20,497 a year earlier. Spellman had jawboned the Nixon Administration into broadening eligibility for the federal program. He was also accelerating county public-works programs. The county's new $6.5 million Administration Building, with its controversial cheese grater façade, was nearing completion. Spellman and McGavick went east for the third time in three months to meet with Ehrlichman, Magnuson and Jackson. The Department of Labor soon provided relocation money for skilled workers who could find work elsewhere, and the administration accelerated funding for several job-creation projects. Crucially, unemployment benefits were extended.

Spellman at this juncture acquired a new aide who proved to be a star, 28-year-old Charles T. Collins. After a tour of duty in Vietnam as a decorated Army officer, Collins enrolled in the master's of public administration program at the University of Washington and came to the Courthouse as an intern. Spellman was immediately impressed: "His combat experience gave him wisdom beyond his age. He was serious-minded but good to be around and immediately became a trusted player at a time when we needed someone with his intelligence and instincts." Bratton and McGavick found Collins to be, as McGavick put it, "a phenomenal guy." [15]

There was also a new sheriff in town. After nearly 16 months of searching, Spellman finally found someone with the experience and integrity to transform the Department of Public Safety. Lawrence G. Waldt, the police chief in Hayward, California, was a lanky, 50-year-old bachelor who reminded Spellman of a sheriff from Central Casting. Waldt earlier had spent 22 years with the Alameda County Sheriff's Department, the last five as a division chief. Before that, he oversaw the county's maximum-security jail. From a field of 90 applicants, Waldt won the unanimous endorsement of Spellman's selection committee. The clincher was an impressive, highly public audition. While a finalist, Waldt was in town to head the investigation into payoffs and perjury in the Seattle Police Department. He comported himself with a professionalism that drew admiring reviews and was also a candidate for police chief. Spellman snapped him up. "One of the best decisions we ever made," McGavick says. [16]

FILING WEEK for the fall elections, to Spellman's delight, found Carroll facing multiple challengers—Chris Bayley for the Republicans and Ed Heavey and Lem Howell for the Democrats. Spellman was for Bayley but believed any of the three would be "a long overdue breath of fresh air." In the wake of the perjury conviction of M.E. "Buzz" Cook, a former assistant police chief, and the ongoing federal grand-jury probe of organized crime, reformers on the City Council were pushing a wholesale review of what tolerance had spawned. The council's president, Charles M. Carroll—no relation to the prosecutor—made a clean breast of it in an entertaining interview with reporters. Known as "Streetcar Charlie" because he once worked for the city transit company, he readily admitted receiving contributions from jukebox and pinball interests over the years. "Sure it influences my vote, but I don't sell my soul to them," said the former longtime chairman of the council's License Committee. Councilman Carroll said his goal was to prevent big-time mobsters from gaining a foothold in Seattle. Perhaps emboldened by having a priest among his sons, Charlie uttered what many considered the

quote of the year: "May God strike me dead if I know of racketeering in the industry!"[17]

Political combat was breaking out on multiple fronts. After expelling the 173-member King County delegation over its opposition to Governor Evans' tax-reform plan, the State Republican Convention adopted a platform embracing the ballot issue. Ken Rogstad led his unrepentant conservatives out of the hall and onto the lawn where they caucused noisily to draft their own platform and assail Evans and Gummie Johnson as the leaders of a pack of liberals who were Republicans in name only.[18]

Hoppe, a Republican candidate for the state Senate, was disappointed in mid-campaign when a Superior Court judge restrained county officials from placing on the November ballot Overtaxed, Inc.'s nebulous initiative to repeal the county charter. Spellman had already named a 13-member committee to review the charter, in keeping with the charter itself, which mandated a review every 10 years. In a deft move to disarm Hoppe, he named him to the group, together with Richard Albrecht, Virginia Gunby and Paul Friedlander, three of the original freeholders, plus Payton Smith, the Democrat who had been co-chairman of the 1967 Committee to Modernize County Government. Hoppe now said he preferred a five-member County Council and appointed executive rather than a return to the old-style three-member commission.*

AROUND 10 P.M. on September 15, 1970, an excited crowd of volunteers and well-wishers—mostly young, stylishly dressed and coiffed—learned that Chris Bayley was on his way to campaign headquarters. Beneath a bucket of melting ice a pool of water was spreading. "Shouldn't we mop that up before he gets here?" someone said. "Never mind," a campaign aide quipped. "Bayley could walk on water tonight."[19] Charles O. Carroll had lost the Republican nomination for King County prosecutor by more than 40,000 votes. Bayley was not

Norm Maleng and Chris Bayley in the 1970s.

---

* The cloud hanging over the charter finally cleared in the spring of 1971 when the State Supreme Court, in a 5-3 decision, ruled that the entire charter could not be repealed by initiative.

as ebullient as many expected, acknowledging that his victory was inflated by Democratic crossovers eager to knock out Carroll one way or the other. Heavey had blitzed Howell for the Democratic nomination. Bayley knew he was in for a tough fight.

Heavey styled himself as the people's candidate facing a slick Ivy Leaguer backed by the entrenched downtown business community. He was going into battle with "just Ed Heavey and his helpers, and I'm $6,000 in debt." [20] Evidence that Bayley had arrived came when Ed Donohoe took note of his dreamy eyes and christened him "Bambi" in *The Washington Teamster.*

One of the most memorable election battles in King County history was finally decided five weeks after Election Day, when a recount declared Bayley the winner by 1,453 votes out of 337,000 cast. Spellman, who ordered the absentee ballots placed under armed guard, joked that he'd been waiting anxiously for a puff of white smoke from the balcony.

Among Bayley's campaign volunteers was Norman Maleng, an exceptional young lawyer—yet another former Magnuson "Bumblebee." Maleng's boyish smile, impeccable manners and work ethic sprang from growing up on a dairy farm at Acme, pop. 300. For Spellman, the best thing Christopher T. Bayley did as county prosecutor was hire Maleng and name him liaison to the county executive.

IN A MOVE that shocked many, Spellman organized a retirement party for Chuck Carroll in the ballroom of the Olympic Hotel. Lou Guzzo, executive editor of the *Post-Intelligencer,* surveyed the room, spotted Spellman and strolled over with an air of incredulity. "What in the world are you doing? This guy doesn't deserve to be honored." Spellman felt like saying, "So why are you here?" Instead, he just smiled and said, "Lou, even the mafia sends flowers."

Soon thereafter, Bayley asked the county's judges to convene a grand jury. It indicted Carroll, ex-sheriff Jack Porter, former police chief Frank Ramon and 16 others for conspiracy in connection with vice and kickbacks dating to the 1950s. Porter was accused of accepting $2,000 from Ben Cichy to grease the skids for tolerance countywide, with the prosecutor as the alleged go-between. When the key witness admitted to perjuring himself before the grand jury, Porter and Carroll were acquitted. By the time the trial sputtered to a close, only two of the original defendants—Buzz Cook and an ex-captain—stood convicted. Carroll crowed that Bayley's best efforts had produced "a big fat zero." The sole purpose of the grand jury "was to get Charles O. Carroll." [21] Bayley denied any vendetta. He said he knew going in that it was a crap shoot, so tangled was the web of police payoffs and back-scratching. Spotlighting the institutionalized corruption was an important learning experience that "effectively dismantled the system," he said.[22]

Politicians keep score at the ballot box. When Bayley stood for re-election in 1974—a rematch with Heavey—he won by a landslide. Carroll collected more awards and for years was feted annually on his birthday. Spellman was invited and attended several of the get-togethers. So did Maleng, who in due course became Bayley's successor, serving for 28 years. When Carroll died in 2003 at the age of 96, Maleng waxed nostalgic: "He was really a giant of his era .... He was a grand old man, and I miss him. I really do."[23]

"That comment was vintage Maleng, whom I really do miss," Spellman says, reflecting on his friend's death of a heart attack at the age of 68 in 2007. "In his later years, Chuck was an old, sick man, so it was time to bury the hatchet. That's why I organized the retirement party and in the years to come periodically showed up with everyone else to sing 'Happy Birthday.' It's the only way to live life. There's no denying that Chuck personified old Seattle."

SPELLMAN WOULDN'T face re-election until 1973. Ruano wanted him out within the next six months. Shortly after the 1970 primary, Ruano stepped to the microphone in the County Council chambers and with his usual staccato delivery put the council on notice that if it couldn't rein in the executive, he would. A committee was being formed to gather the 50,560 signatures it would take to force a recall election over Spellman's conduct, mainly "misuse of county funds" on the stadium project.[24] The recall petition charged that Spellman: "Conspired with others to suppress and withhold relevant information from the voters" concerning the cost of building a multipurpose stadium at the Seattle Center; contracted with the stadium design team for the second phase at a cost of $780,000 when the site was being challenged at the ballot box; unlawfully exceeded his authority by boosting Norward Brooks' salary after he was confirmed as director of the Department of Elections and Records, and violated the "employment rights" of construction workers by ordering a work stoppage during the minority-rights protests. The final charge—that Spellman had refused to enforce county gambling laws—was so vague that even Carroll, a lame duck, blew it off until Ruano filed an amended version. Carroll duly certified that four charges, though not proven, were legally sufficient to prompt a recall election if the required number of valid signatures could be obtained.[25]

Spellman was infuriated by Ruano's accusations, especially the transparently cockamamie charge that he didn't clamp down on gambling after Slade Gorton issued his decision that tolerance was at odds with the state Constitution. "That was the one that hurt the most," Spellman says. He issued a statement blistering the recall petition as "a form of base harassment that strikes at the very heart of orderly government. ...Mr. Ruano has used a legal mechanism in an irresponsible fashion, and for this reason deserves the same opprobrium and scorn that we as the public hold for those who promote anarchy to benefit their special interests." [26] Ruano said Spellman should resign.

Tellingly, even the King County Democratic Central Committee refused to support the recall initiative, and the Labor Council's early enthusiasm quickly petered out. Ruano groused that the unions had promised to drum up 25,000 signatures but managed only a thousand. By May of 1971 fewer than 10,000 had been gathered. Ruano glumly conceded defeat. "I have had my chance and the recall hasn't materialized. I don't believe I should misuse the law." To his consternation, the County Council that week approved King Street as the new site for the domed stadium. Recall cloud lifted, Spellman set out to make the stadium a reality.[27] "It means jobs," he said, "and we can also demonstrate that King County has a bright future."

First, however, it grew darker.

EVEN SCOOP AND MAGGIE, arguably the most formidable tag-team in Senate history, couldn't get Boeing's supersonic airliner off the ground. A Citizens League Against the Sonic Boom warned that the SST could create a fish-killing sonic wasteland as it soared over the Atlantic at 1,750 mph. Other critics said vapors from the plane's exhaust might alter the Earth's climate and weaken the ozone layer, leading to an epidemic of skin cancer. A Sierra Club leader charged that a fleet of SSTs could deplete America's petroleum reserves in the space of 20 years. Magnuson rushed through a bill banning supersonic speeds during domestic flights. And Jackson said nothing less than U.S. superiority in aviation was at stake. The specter of Americans circling the globe in Russian-built supersonic planes failed to chasten Senator Charles Percy. The $290 million loan to cover Boeing's prototype development costs was a lousy investment, the Illinois Republican said. "There isn't a bank in the world today that would accept a loan on this basis." Maybe so, Maggie said, "but there wouldn't have been a banker in the world that would have accepted a loan for Grand Coulee Dam, either. ... I've got about 100,000 people walking the streets in my home town. I don't know a better way to put them to work. It's better than raking leaves." [28]

On December 3, 1970, despite desperate horse-trading by Jackson and Magnuson, the U.S. Senate effectively killed the SST. Another 7,500 Boeing workers soon hit the bricks. An ironic backstory emerged. The dispiriting 52-41 vote, one of the few battles Maggie ever lost on the Senate floor, "may have saved the Boeing Company from financial disaster," according to Shelby Scates, Magnuson's biographer. He wrote:

> Engineers had wind tunnel difficulties with the SST airframe, never really solving the question of where to locate the craft's engines given its "swing-wing" design. Economists were seriously in doubt about how soon the plane could make a profit, given the high cost of jet fuel and low interest of airline passengers. By putting the SST aside, Boeing forged ahead with the slower but enormously profitable 747, 737, 757, and 767 aircraft, and thus, prospered.[29]

At the time, though, no silver lining could be seen beneath the ozone. Two real-estate salesmen paid for the billboard that famously declared, "Will the last person leaving SEATTLE—Turn out the lights." What they were trying to say, they insisted, was that the rumors of Seattle's death were greatly exaggerated: "The ridiculous idea that there ever would be a last man leaving town and turning out the lights seemed to us a spoof on all the doom-and-gloom talk."[30] It was more than talk. "Month after month, an avalanche of homes, cabins, powerboats and cars—at fire-sale prices" filled the classified columns of the two dailies. Laid-off machinists applied for food stamps, the jobless rate hit 14 percent and "an anti-suicide net was deployed on the Space Needle...."[31]

CHAPTER SEVENTEEN

The Kingdome

I t was two weeks before Christmas 1970, and Frank Ruano was a con-
flicted Scrooge. When the new commission chose the area below King
Street Station as the site for a domed stadium, Ruano practically said
"Bah, humbug!" Then, in the next breath, "It was my idea first!"

It took the panel appointed by Evans, Spellman and Uhlman less than
six months to settle on a new site after Ruano's initiative led to the rejection
of Seattle Center. Consultants concluded that the rail yard abutting Pioneer
Square and the International District had a clear edge over the other finalists. King Street was best in three crucial categories: accessibility, environmental impact and cost—$48.6 million, including parking. A stadium on
a site near Longacres race track in suburban Renton was estimated at $50.7
million. Building at Riverton, just north of Sea-Tac International Airport,
would cost $50.5 million, while utilizing the Sicks' Stadium property in the
Rainier Valley was pegged at $64.4 million, even though the city owned the
land. Parking was the problem there. King Street was close to downtown,
Interstate 5, I-90 and the Alaskan Way Viaduct. The parking facilities would
cost $9 million, but a City Council bond issue could cover that. Downtown
needed more parking in any case.

A stadium at King Street would "spiff up a seedy section of the city,"
usher in professional football, the return of major-league baseball and
attract conventions, Hy Zimmerman wrote in his *Seattle Times* sports-page
column. It would also create new jobs, "so highly imperative at this time."
King County contractors said 3,000 family-wage jobs would be opening up
that very month if the stadium hadn't been delayed. Burlington Northern
was amenable to a speedy deal for the 36 acres—at a reasonable price, too,
rail traffic having declined. Bob Dunn, the chairman of the County Council,
said morale was an important intangible. The stadium would "be good for
the community's spirit."[1]

Frank Ruano questioned the honesty of the report and demanded a detailed cost analysis. "There is already a petition set up to fight this thing," he told the Stadium Commission."[2] He couldn't resist reminding everyone, however, that it was he who first suggested the rail yard as the optimum site, "only to be shot down" by the business clique intent on building at the Seattle Center. Seemingly mellowing for a moment, Ruano added, "I think people want a stadium. I am for a stadium."[3] Ruano suggested putting King Street and a suburban site on the ballot in March. Two allies, Tony Ferrucci and Dick Young, were still trying to make a case for a site at South Park along the Duwamish. It had ranked first in the 1968 survey but was brushed aside by the original commission. Ruano went away muttering something about "no stadium at all."[4]

Zimmerman had had enough. In a Christmas column that Spellman clipped and saved, he wrote the equivalent of an open letter to Ruano. It could have been headlined, "Yes, Frank, there is a Grinch."

> Are we to have government by petition? The situation is much like the one in which the little kid, unhappy with the way the game is going, takes his ball and goes home. But Frank, this is not your ball. Once, Joe Gandy, when he headed the site-seekers, was reminded and cautioned that the stadium was that of the people, not his; Mr. Ruano needs the same reminder, the same cautioning. We deplore Mr. Ruano's tangent flight, for we have found him a warm human being with a steel-trap mind, a citizen of merit. But always, there is the human equation. And some there are, Frank, who get blinded by camera flashes. And some there are, Frank, who grow giddy from a mere sip of power. ... Frank, 62 percent of us voted for a stadium. ... We suppose that you presently represent a handful more than just yourself. But you do NOT represent 62 percent of us. So who are you to decide for us?[5]

Even Ross Cunningham, Chuck Carroll's old pal on *The Times'* editorial page, cut to the chase: "Looking strictly at the county's legal position, the sole mandate from the voters is to build a stadium. None of the by-play during the past 30 months has altered that mandate in any way. While County Executive John Spellman has been taking some criticism for his persistence in pursuing the project, he has been acting under the only stadium mandate he has from the voters in refusing to abandon the project."[6]

With inflation and interest rates on the rise, Spellman was worried. The original timetable called for completion in the spring of 1973. Now Ed Heavey was urging separate facilities for football, baseball and conventions. Mayor Uhlman wanted to study whether council-issued bonds would be appropriate. Private investors insisted they could put together a deal for a stadium near Kent. "I wondered if we would ever get going," Spellman says. "It was one delay after another. The costs were rising, and I knew Ruano would have a field day with that."

After more wrangling over yet another feasibility study, the County Council endorsed the King Street site, optioned the property and deputized Johnny O'Brien to help Spellman and Norm Maleng expedite construction of a 65,000-seat domed stadium. In December of 1971 Spellman signed a $1.8 million contract with Naramore, Skilling & Prager of Seattle to design the stadium.

Ruano wouldn't go away. He organized a drive dubbed CASH—Citizens Against Stadium Hoax—and submitted petitions calling for a referendum on whether the voters still wanted to spend $40 million on a stadium. He sought a preliminary injunction against any further expenditures. And if Spellman challenged another referendum on the stadium, Ruano threatened to petition for a new freeholder election to terminate the home-rule charter. "Every time someone gets 20,000 signatures on a petition, you can't stop government," Spellman said, jaw set, Maleng at his side.[7] Heavey was also out of patience. "I think we should have that election as soon as possible. ... As a matter of fact, I'm calling Mr. Ruano's bluff."[8]

Heavey, whose County Council seat wasn't jeopardized by his run for prosecutor, boycotted the swearing-in ceremony for the re-elected council members and the new county assessor, the inimitable Harley Hoppe. Heavey groused that the 5-4 Republican majority was hiring "political hacks" as aides and depriving the Democrats of any meaningful role. There was unanimity, however, on the stadium. Tracy Owen, the new chairman, said the council was determined to "follow the mandate of the people and build our covered multipurpose stadium with the foundation laid from the bricks that have been thrown at us."[9]

DENIED A HEARING in King County Superior Court, Ruano took his case for an injunction to Kitsap County in the winter of 1972. Maleng led the county's legal team, emphasizing that bonds totaling $10 million had been issued and $7.5 million spent on design. The call for bids was being advertised even as they spoke. The voters may have changed their minds about the site, Maleng told the court, but the commitment to public financing of a multipurpose stadium still stood, four long years after the election. A handful of embittered opponents were still "mucking around with the system." Enough was enough.[10]

Judge Oluf Johnsen, a stolid Scandinavian, dismissed Ruano's lawsuit and declared the initiative invalid. He said King County was "completely and irretrievably and irrevocably committed to the King Street site," and Spellman was following a clear directive of the voters to proceed with the project. Undaunted, Ruano teamed up with Central Area and International District activists worried about the stadium's impact on their neighborhoods. "Frank was sort of a loose cannon, but we found common cause," says Lem Howell, who headed the Central Seattle Community Council Federation. "Spellman and I were on opposite sides on this one." [11]

When he met with the federation, Ruano quipped, "I've been on this stadium kick so long that I now look like a stadium!" [12] A new "Citizens Coalition on the Domed Stadium," with Ruano and Howell as co-chairmen, petitioned the City Council to deny a building permit pending a referendum. The city held that insufficient signatures had been submitted and issued the permit. A Superior Court commissioner rejected the coalition's request for an injunction.

Ruano's court of last resort was the State Supreme Court, which on January 18, 1973, unanimously upheld the lower court ruling. It agreed with Maleng's contention that "without a point of finality—a line of demarcation," the whole process of municipal finance could be destroyed. The county's only remaining decisions concerning the stadium were administrative, the justices said, and not subject to an initiative under the home-rule charter. [13]

By then, work on the stadium was well under way. It also had a name. "The Kingdome" was first suggested by Rod Belcher, a popular former sportscaster, *Times* columnist Don Duncan wrote in 1972. Belcher, at 91 in 2012, demurred. "I was just one of many who submitted that it would be a good name" since the county and the railroad station were both named King and a group called the Seattle Kings was pursuing a pro-football franchise.*[14]

SPELLMAN HAD so many irons in the fire—including countywide Medic 1 and 911 systems and a regional airport authority—that he was giving little thought to a re-election campaign in 1973. The biggest guessing game was whether Governor Evans would run again in 1972 in defiance of the third-term jinx. Slade Gorton, Secretary of State Lud Kramer, Spellman and Evans' trusted aide, Jim Dolliver, were considered the Republicans' leading possible successors.

---

*The name became "official" on June 27, 1975, as the dome was taking shape. Ted Bowsfield, the stadium manager, told reporters, "As far as I am concerned it's the official name." He proceeded to order "Kingdome" letterhead. [15]

Another opportunity arose. Congressman Tom Pelly, who had survived a spirited challenge from Joel Pritchard in the 1970 Republican primary, was urging Spellman to seek his 1st District seat in 1972. "Pelly was 69 years old and in his tenth term in Congress," Spellman remembers. "The challenge from Joel, who was nearly 25 years younger and absolutely at the top of his game, took a lot out of him." The Pritchard brothers had deployed 700 volunteers to doorbell practically every house in the district.

Pelly perceived that Spellman was more conservative than Pritchard, which was slightly true. He offered Spellman his endorsement, together with organizational and financial help from Rogstad and Bill Boeing Jr. Though philosophically aligned with the Evans wing, Spellman did his best to get along with both factions of the party. He had enormous respect for the Pritchards and not much use for Rogstad. There was another thing: Pelly was now an important go-between to the administration as Spellman pursued federal aid. Pelly and Nixon had been young congressmen together.

"Soon after he lost, Joel said he wasn't going to run again. He changed his mind in due course but I didn't think I was stepping on Joel's toes to meet with Pelly, who had me back to D.C. and introduced me to all the congressional leaders. I'd been there several times in the previous months, meeting with Scoop, Maggie, Ehrlichman and Nixon, so I wasn't awed. But I'd watched what happened to people with trans-continental marriages. I really couldn't do that to Lois and our six young kids. Lois didn't think I should do it either." Pritchard and Spellman had what Joel called a "face-off" until he learned the facts. Pritchard chalked it up to "Rogstad and his crew," always looking for angles.[16]

Pelly retired from Congress in 1972. Pritchard kept the seat in Republican hands. Evans won a third term by defeating Al Rosellini, who nearly made a stunning comeback from his loss to Spellman. Rosellini had a double-digit lead down the stretch. Then, during a debate with Evans, he condescendingly dismissed his successor as "Danny Boy" and the tide turned overnight.

SPELLMAN WAS GRATEFUL for the administration's support of beleaguered local governments. He agreed to be Nixon's 1972 state chairman. Nixon's people wanted someone who could bridge the factions. Gummie Johnson's divide-and-conquer strategy wouldn't do. Given McGovern's haplessness and the tenor of the times, winning the state for the president turned out to be a cakewalk, with Gwen Anderson and Helen Rasmussen, two organizational whizzes, overseeing the troops. As Washington went, so too every other state in the nation except Massachusetts. Every pollster and pundit accurately predicted the landslide. Nixon's paranoia still knew no bounds. His cloak-and-dagger Committee to Re-Elect the President—aptly abbreviated as "CREEP"—led to the Watergate burglary, a cancer metastasizing on the presidency. "The tragedy of that character flaw and the divide over the war in Vietnam obscure Nixon's achievements," Spellman says. "He had a remarkable domestic agenda." Spellman points to the creation of the Environmental Protection Agency, headed by the estimable William Ruckelshaus; Revenue Sharing that brought $10 million to King County; Affirmative Action; the food stamp program; advances in civil rights and opening the door to Red China. "I never felt apologetic about being Nixon's state chairman." That spring, however, as American B-52's pounded Hanoi and Haiphong, a bomb fractured the foundation of the ROTC building and shattered a hundred windows at Seattle University, Spellman's alma mater. He wondered if Nixon and Kissinger could actually produce "peace with honor" in Vietnam.

CHAPTER EIGHTEEN

Groundbreaking

Someone forgot to bring a flag for the groundbreaking, so they pledged allegiance to the bulldozers chugging in the background. The project had been buffeted by controversy since its inception so it seemed perversely fitting that the first pitch thrown at the site of the Kingdome was a mud ball on a gray day.

It was November 2, 1972. When Spellman was introduced, an angry cluster of college students, most of them Asian, began to chant "Stop the stadium!" The International District, Seattle's Chinatown, abutted the stadium site. Community activists, including Sabino Cabildo, Bob Santos, Al Sugiyama, Michael Woo, Frank Irigon and Pete Bacho, a UW Law School student, had inspired the troops to disrupt the establishment's photo-op. Some merchants in the "I.D." were eager for new customers. Many residents worried, however, that commercialization would displace elderly apartment dwellers, clog the streets and shutter family-owned cafes and shops. A McDonald's, replete with gaudy golden arches, in place of the venerable Tai Tung was unthinkable. "Hum bows, not hot dogs!"—a reference to steamed Chinese pork buns—became a rallying cry for the protesters.[1]

Spellman shouted into the microphone to be heard above the ruckus, promising that mitigation projects and the new land-use rules he and Mayor Uhlman supported would protect the area "better than it ever has been protected." "Bullshit!" someone shouted. An angry young Filipino responded with the middle-finger salute when a sheriff's deputy tried to restrain him. A pushing match erupted as he was handcuffed. Spellman looked dyspeptic. "For every small group who have opposed the stadium, there are hundreds of thousands who will attend when it is completed," he declared. The chanting grew louder. "Stop the stadium!" "Down with the Dome!" [2]

"Construction has begun," Spellman continued. "The stadium will be built. It will be a major asset to all the people in this community. Let's get on with the building!" Hugh McElhenny, a former UW Husky and NFL star, presented Spellman with a helmet featuring the logo of the Seattle Kings, the football franchise McElhenny was promoting. Protesters jostled with security as Spellman gamely left the dignitaries' stand to place a gold-painted home plate in the newly smoothed sod. He was supposed to throw out a ceremonial first pitch and kick a football through makeshift goal posts. A dozen protesters formed a tight circle to block his path. Some lobbed clods of mud, splattering Spellman and Johnny O'Brien. McElhenny's scowl made it clear he'd love to stiff-arm the first protester who got in his way. "I'd never make it as a politician," the Hall of Famer said. "As a football player, when things get tough you just go get them." [3]

Wayne Field, a self-made millionaire from Minneapolis, watched the commotion from the scrum below the speakers' platform together with Herman Sarkowsky, his Seattle rival for an NFL franchise. Standing alone, the ubiquitous Frank Ruano told reporters, "I am not responsible for this demonstration and I don't approve of it. I put my faith in the courts, not in elected officials who lie to the people, as John Spellman did in court and is doing here now." [4]

When the program dissolved in disarray, several young Asians confronted City Council President Liem Tuai as he stepped from the platform,

A demonstration against the Kingdome in 1972 featured college students, most of them Asian, and other residents of the International District.

accusing him "of being everything from a traitor to a pawn of the establishment." Tuai stood his ground. "I believe in the stadium. I think it has to be
built. I think the people of Seattle want it to be built and I represent all the
people of Seattle."[5]

THE YOUNG ACTIVISTS represented a potent faction in the conflicted Asian
community. Santos, a charismatic Filipino-American, found common cause
with black, Latino and American Indian leaders during the civil rights era,
notably Tyree Scott, Larry Gossett, Roberto Maestas and Bernie Whitebear.
As they grew simultaneously more sophisticated and stubborn—picketing
job sites, seizing Seattle's decommissioned Fort Lawton for a tribal center
and demanding neighborhood input on Urban Renewal and Model Cities
programs—their power grew. Santos was the director of the International
District Improvement Association, Inter*Im for short, which tapped federal
funds for a variety of projects. They kept the heat on Spellman and Uhlman
to make good on promises concerning the Kingdome.

"The opposition to the Kingdom coalesced into the Committee for Corrective Action in the International District, which presented Spellman with
six demands: a percentage of stadium profits for neighborhood social and
health services; a voice in hiring a stadium manager; an Asian American on
the stadium administrative staff; neighborhood preference in stadium hiring; a percentage of stadium jobs for Asian-Americans, and free admission
to all stadium events for elderly International District residents."[6]

"Spellman gave us a verbal commitment that all six demands would
be met," Santos wrote in his autobiography. "We should have known
better. Always get commitments in writing, especially from politicians."[7]
The coalition flooded the media with press releases. Several times it sent
upwards of 50 sign-waving "concerned citizens" to the county executive's
office. The county did provide money to jump-start a health center for the
International District but the "major grants came from the state and federal
governments," Santos wrote.[8]

Spellman says that's not the whole story. "My administration played a
key role in securing those grants. We kept our promises, including stadium
jobs for Asians and other minorities. However, there was no way I was going to give them a percentage of stadium profits. I didn't have the authority
to do that, and wouldn't have done it if I'd had the authority. If we did it
for them we'd have to do it for everyone else. I like Bob. He was a very resourceful activist with some worthwhile goals. We came to a meeting of the
minds—although there were tense moments. Barbara Schmidt, my secretary, was outraged by the poor manners of some of the people who barged

into my office." A golden spike presented to the county executive in 1971 when the tracks were removed from the Kingdome site turned up missing after one visit. Spellman was not amused, and Santos was chagrinned. The troops otherwise had been on good behavior that day.

Spellman appointed Santos to join him on a committee to pick the stadium manager. The job went to Ted Bowsfield, a former major-league pitcher who by all accounts, including Santos', proved a good choice.*

A mellower Santos—"Uncle Bob" to most in the International District— says he came to respect Spellman. "Don't forget, Spellman in the beginning was the enemy. Then through the years as the Kingdome was being built, one of his aides was a guy named Jerry Laigo, who I grew up with. I'd go by Jerry's office whenever I was in the Courthouse and say, 'Hey, Jerry, we're here again!' and he'd go, 'Oh, shit! Not again!' and run around and tell the boss, 'Hide, John. They're here again!' But John was very professional with us. He never promised anything he couldn't deliver. That's what I liked about John. I found out that he was a collector of jazz. That impressed me because that means he's down-home somewhere, some way. In his being, he's with it. It was refreshing to talk to him about something other than politics and the Kingdome. Our committee realized the stadium was going to be built and used it for leverage. We marched on HUD. We marched on the mayor's office. The City Council came up with 17 resolutions that included support for housing for low-income seniors. Between Spellman, Uhlman and their councils we were able to implement almost all of those one way or another."[10]

"A legal clinic and community culture center were opened, as was a food bank, nutrition programs, and a food buying club," Frank Chesley wrote in a HistoryLink.org essay on Santos. "Neighborhood produce gardens would later be carved out of blackberry-infested vacant lots with help from volunteers. ... After 1973, when HUD released funds for low-income elderly housing, Inter*Im worked with several property owners to rehabilitate or build housing projects in the neighborhood. ... In 1978, HUD designated the International District as a Neighborhood Strategy Area and provided assistance for private investment in elderly low-income housing programs. Tapping into that program, the Chinatown-International District PDA was able convert the New Central Hotel and Jackson Apartments into 45 low-income apartments for the elderly."[11]

---

* O'Brien had dearly wanted the job. He left the County Council in 1973 and became No. 2 to Bowsfield. That the two former sports stars formed a solid management team is another point on which Spellman and Santos agree.[9]

"We got a lot out of our activism," Santos says, "even though there were sacrifices—the traffic; fans taking up parking spaces on Seahawks game days, which prohibited families coming down for dim sum Sunday. And very few of the stadium-goers would stay in the I.D. for dinner. But we have to give John credit for working with us. Because of the lessons we learned we were better able to deal with the issues after the other two stadiums were built." [12]

THE HOT RUMOR around the Courthouse was that Spellman was in line for a Nixon appointment to the federal bench. The call never came, nor was it expected. If it had, he says he wouldn't have accepted. Close friends knew he hoped to end his career on the bench, but he was telling the truth when he downplayed the story, telling reporters "not at this point in my life. I'm too interested in what I'm doing now." [13] At 46, he felt increasingly confident of his abilities as an administrator despite the crisis du jour at the Kingdome construction site. And there were robins on the lawn.

All seven speakers at the Seattle-King County Economic Development Council's New Year's luncheon agreed that the economy was on the rebound. No one had turned out the lights. "Last year at this time things were still bad, but they were no longer getting worse," said Seafirst's Miner Baker, no Pollyanna. "This year the improvement has been dramatic!" [14] Boeing's sales in 1972 were a billion dollars higher than expected. Work on the Trans-Alaska Pipeline would soon begin, spurred by the oil crisis. Housing starts were also promising, according to Norton Clapp, chairman of the Weyerhaeuser Company. He was seated next to his stepson, Booth Gardner, newly installed president of the Laird Norton Company. Despite a lackluster term in the State Senate, Gardner harbored an ambition to become governor.

"FOUR YEARS AGO," Spellman said as he launched his campaign for re-election, "the people of King County said they wanted a solvent government. Since that time we have not only lived within our revenues each year, but eliminated the $6.8 million inherited county debt. ... By adopting a county charter, they also said they wanted a progressive government and better law enforcement." The Public Safety division now had nearly twice as many deputies, Spellman said. The crime rate was down by more than 5 percent, and the corrections department was no longer "just a warehouse." The county had reformed its personnel practices, instituted comprehensive land-use planning and improved mental health and drug-abuse prevention, while reducing the number of departments from 13 to five. Emergency employment and food-bank programs had helped the county weather the Boeing Bust.[15] In 1973, for the first time in county history, King County did not levy the full tax millage allowed by law. "No new taxes and living within the budget are pledges of John Spellman's administration," the campaign's full-page ads declared.[16]

"How about that half-cent sales tax increase you campaigned for?" said his opponent, 34-year-old Mike Lowry, aiming high in his first bid for elective office. Lowry was a protégé of State Senator Martin J. Durkan, a savvy, old-school Irish politician who would have been equally at home in Boston. Lowry proved to be a quick learner when he became a fiscal

Mike Lowry as a candidate for county executive.

analyst for Durkan's Ways and Means Committee. He was that rare combination of policy wonk and stump speaker. Spellman never for a moment took him lightly.

Lowry aggressively challenged Spellman's boast that he had lowered property taxes. For whom? An elderly person with a home valued at $13,000 stood to save $4.38, Lowry said, while Pacific Northwest Bell got a $102,000 break. As for the Kingdome, he questioned the site and doubted the stadium would produce a profit—at least for the taxpayers. Why should they get stuck with the bill? "I want to develop a revenue program so that those extra costs of the stadium will be picked up by the downtown business establishment who wanted it down there."[17] Lowry noted that Spellman himself had warned the council that 1974 would be a bumpy year. Federal funding to ease unemployment—$8 million—would expire, while a new state property-tax law would slash revenues by $3.7 million. Fallout from the OPEC oil embargo doubtless would have a major impact on operational expenses. As for "streamlining" county government, Lowry said Democrats on the council had instigated steps Spellman was taking credit for.

Spellman immediately warmed to the challenge, charging that Lowry's solution to the county's funding problems was an unconstitutional corporate income tax. "If the county has the authority to levy a corporate income tax, it has the authority to levy a personal income tax or any other type of tax," Spellman said during one of their debates. "Believe me, if the county has that kind of power, you should be afraid as citizens."[18] Lowry said the proposed 1 percent tax on corporate net profits in excess of $10,000 was not only constitutional but realistic.[19] He acknowledged that Spellman possessed solid executive skills, quipping, "If I win, I'd like to make him stadium manager."[20] Spellman laughed as hard as anyone in the audience. Party politics aside, they had formed a mutual admiration society. Amid the escalating global oil crisis, Watergate and a bruising Uhlman-Tuai mayoral contest, "It has been one of those welcome rarities in politics," the *Post-Intelligencer* said, "a race run on the issues alone without the faintest trace of smear or mud."[21] Both dailies endorsed Spellman.

Also trailing badly in the fundraising race, Lowry lost by 50,000 votes. What he won was credibility. So too Spellman. His impressive victory affirmed he would be a strong contender for governor in 1976.

Nineteen-seventy-three was not the typical off-year yawner. The voters crushed a graduated net income tax for the second time in three years even though the measure would have limited special levies for schools. Harley Hoppe, with gubernatorial ambitions of his own, was one of the measure's most animated opponents. Uhlman narrowly survived the challenge from Tuai and would face a recall threat of his own in next 18 months. Ruby Chow, a vivacious restaurateur, became the first minority on the County Council. She captured the fifth-district seat O'Brien was vacating, narrowly defeating Spellman's friend Walt Hubbard in an all-Democrat contest. Hubbard was the contract compliance supervisor for the State Human Rights Commission and one of the leading Black Catholics in the nation. Many Democrats questioned Chow's true colors. She considered running as a Republican and purchased two $50 tickets to an "appreciation dinner" for Spellman. Politics in King County was a smorgasbord.

Tracy Owen won re-election to the County Council, handily outpolling Frank Ruano, who promptly returned to his role as the Kingdome's naysayer-in-chief. He would have plenty to keep him busy over the next three years.

CHAPTER NINETEEN

Sand Jacks and Smoke Screens

t was bigger, taller and more commodious than the Roman Colosseum, and there were days when Spellman felt like the first Christian fed to the lions at the season opener.

The Kingdome boasted the largest self-supporting thin-shell concrete dome in the world. It contained 52,800 cubic yards of concrete and nearly a million pounds of structural steel. Getting it built generated 16 tons of trouble. Like the relative who came for a week and stayed a year, Frank Ruano was looking over Spellman's shoulder every inch of the way.

Bids on the innovative roof were sought first. Peter Kiewit Sons' Company, a respected Omaha firm with a Seattle branch, submitted the lowest, $5.8 million, in the spring of 1972. But that was for a dome of its own design. It would cost $6.6 million, Kiewit said, to construct the dome designed by the county's team of architects and engineers. Resembling a circus big top on steroids, the double curvature hyperbolic paraboloid would be 660 feet in diameter.

The Donald M. Drake Company of Portland won the contract to build the dome the county preferred. Its bid of $5.9 million squared with the designers' estimate. The dome—only five inches thick—was to be poured in place between concrete-beam ribs 250 feet above the floor of the stadium. The design was computer tested. It offered the promise of lower long-term maintenance and insurance costs, Spellman said.

Three months later, Drake underbid Kiewit by $1.6 million to win a $29.6 million contract for the stadium's superstructure, which one wag described as a layered hamburger supporting a concrete bun. The cost of the Kingdome, including artificial turf, a sound system and 65,000 seats, was estimated to be $42 million upon completion. The due date was December 16, 1974. With $2 million from interest on the sale of the $40 million bond issue authorized by the voters, "We're right in the ball park," Spellman said. "It is going to be an austere project," Jerry Schlatter, the county's project manager, promised.¹ The smaller capacity Houston Astrodome, which opened in 1965, cost $35 million. The Superdome under construction in New Orleans was at $130 million and climbing.

Kiewit's people were privately skeptical Drake could turn a profit on its bids, but Drake boasted a half century of wide-ranging experience. It posted a performance bond for the full amount of the contract, $31.6 million after mutually agreed upon changes. In the months to come, Drake would argue that things came to grief for a whole series of events beyond its control. Schlatter, a detail man, saw the contractor falling behind early on. He repeatedly documented his concerns. Crucially, Drake failed to grasp the ramifications of not promptly placing orders for important construction forms, Schlatter says. "That issue then drove all the suppliers and subs" (subcontractors).² The cost of building materials was escalating, interest rates rising. Drake faced a $1,500-a-day penalty if it missed its completion date. The contractor was not only burning daylight, as old straw bosses used to say, the meter was running.

WHEN SIX STEEL TOWERS toppled like dominoes on January 10, 1973, it was an omen that building the Kingdome wouldn't be a walk in the park. Bill Fenimore, a 26-year-old ironworker, was about 25 feet up the first one when an eyebolt holding a guy wire snapped. The 20-ton towers destined to be the Kingdome's support columns were cages filled with rebar. They fell in what seemed like slow motion. Fenimore went along for the ride most of the way. When he finally decided to jump, the guy wire snagged him. Steel rods slammed into one of his legs. He was lucky to be alive. It was remarkable that no one else was hurt. About 50 workers pouring concrete footings for additional 40-foot towers scurried for safety when the first one fell. The mass of twisted steel now encircling them resembled an Erector Set squashed by Godzilla.³

In the months to come it was one thing after another. Someone wondered if they were building on an Indian burial ground, which was unlikely. When the white man arrived on the shores of Elliott Bay, the stadium site was tide flats and salmonberry marshes. As Seattle boomed, the land was filled with sluiced-down dirt from the regrades that leveled many of its hills. The Kingdome rested on nearly 2,000 pilings.

To control costs, Spellman and Schlatter came up with a private-financing plan for the stadium's power plant and trolled for grants. When the County Council endorsed an application for a $765,000 federal grant to install removable artificial turf, Ed Heavey was mad as hell. The taxpayers had been "lied to and misled" about the true costs of the stadium, the councilman said. Eighty million was more like it. Maybe Ruano was right all along. "Is this the first of a long series of jokes on the people?" he barked at Schlatter. "I wouldn't want to classify it that way," Schlatter said, ignoring the bait. "Anything we can do to embellish the stadium should be done." [4] Schlatter was an architect as well as a builder, "our eyes and ears on the job—tough and knowledgeable," says Spellman. "We were lucky to have him, especially when things got really contentious."

The county won the grant for the turf, together with several more. The concession-stand contracts, a lucrative enterprise for both concessionaire and county, generated more debate. Was 85 cents too pricey for a Domeburger? Eighty cents for 18 ounces of "mountain fresh" Rainier beer? On a 5-4 vote, the County Council finally approved Spellman's recommendation that the concessionaire finance its own facilities. It was another way to control rising costs. The county's share of the concession revenue was estimated at upwards of $7 million over the first 10 years.

Herman Sarkowsky, the astute part-owner of the NBA's Portland Trailblazers, was leading a consortium of Seattle business executives crunching the numbers on a National Football League expansion franchise. Wayne Field's showy efforts to land the franchise offended Sarkowsky's financial teammates. All but two were University of Washington alums active in every facet of civic life. It was "a distasteful thought" to them that someone from Minnesota could own Seattle's pro football franchise.[5] These were serious guys, Spellman told NFL Commissioner Pete Rozelle, all remarkably successful in retail, real estate, banking or heavy construction. "We'll have a stadium. Give us a team." Rozelle liked Seattle. He liked Spellman, too, according to Jerry Grinstein, but underestimated the county executive's gumption, connections and knowledge of sports.

IN THE SUMMER OF 1973, 4,000 ironworkers in Washington and Oregon struck over pension plans and travel pay. That fall, work on the stadium was threatened by the oil crisis. Drake and a hive of subcontractors had 17 diesel-powered cranes at the job site. The Seattle Chapter of Associated General Contractors scrambled to secure adequate allotments of fuel. Construction workers, some 250 in all, demanded gas to get to work.

By January of 1974, however, the stadium's superstructure was nearly complete. NFL owners were poised to announce their agreement on expanding the league by two franchises. Spellman, Bob Bratton and Norm Maleng were summoned to Manhattan in March to meet once again with Rozelle's brain trust. It was hard bargaining. The NFL owners planted stories about King County's "excessive lease demands, then left Spellman to twist slowly

Spellman and Gerald Schlatter, left, the county's Kingdome project manager, give Baseball Commissioner Bowie Kuhn a tour of the construction site in the summer of 1974.

under the pressure," David Brewster wrote in the *Argus*. "Our local papers readily obliged, the *P-I* in particular urging a quick desertion to the fledgling World Football League, lest we be left with a $40 million stadium and no big-league teams to play in it. For its part, *The Times* circulated self-serving stories from other NFL owners, all trying to get Spellman to cave in." [6]

Spellman didn't cave. The *Argus* headlined its story "John Spellman: Single Safety Against the NFL... Have Stadium, Won't Grovel." The county's proposal was right down the middle of current leases for other stadia. "We wanted 10 percent of the team's ticket receipts, plus day-of-game expenses—cleanup, ushers, security," Bratton says. It was "a far cry from the 22 percent scare figure that some NFL owners were bandying around. ..." [7]

Senator Magnuson was not amused by the league's roadblocks. For games sold out 72 hours in advance, his Commerce Committee had imposed a three-year ban on TV blackouts. The league dearly wanted it lifted. Maggie dearly wanted pro football for his city. "This is a game the NFL will lose," Brewster predicted. For Spellman, though, it was "a terribly dangerous

game of poker ... with his gubernatorial chances riding on the outcome." [8]
The election was 30 months away, yet Spellman was already viewed as a
leading contender for the Republicans, especially if Evans retired.

Major League Baseball, meanwhile, was playing a dangerous game of
poker with Slade Gorton, a baseball fan since boyhood in Chicago. The attorney general was unwilling to await baseball's beneficence: Seattle wanted
a new team and it was tired of waiting. Gorton was suing the American
League in state court, asking $32 million in damages over the loss of the
Pilots. Spellman and Gorton attended several Major League winter meetings. It was the same condescending routine every time. They were forced
to cool their heels for a couple of days before being granted a 15-minute
audience. The owners would stand, shoot their cuffs, shake hands and pre-
tend to listen. After one meeting, Baseball Commissioner Bowie Kuhn told
Seattle reporters he saw no expansion "in the immediate future," although
his director of public relations acknowledged, "When you have a dome, you
have an advantage." New Orleans had one. It wanted a team too, as did
Washington, D.C., Toronto, Honolulu, Orlando and New Jersey.[9] "Bowie
Kuhn and I actually got along famously," Spellman says. "It was the owners
and their lawyers who wanted to fight." He prided himself on his skills as a
negotiator, and for a while played good cop to Gorton's bad cop. Finally, he
was as fed up as Gorton. "They underestimated Slade," Spellman says.

THE STADIUM was about 60 percent complete, the first roof sections in
place, when a messy strike-lockout in the summer of 1974 halted work
once again. Hundreds of projects and 45,000 workers were impacted
around the state.

Profit margin evaporating by the hour, Drake's anxiety accelerated. The
completion date had already slipped to July 1975. Drake found itself in a
trifecta of trouble. It was at odds with the county, the unions and the Associated General Contractors. AGC secured restraining orders to keep Drake
from negotiating separately. The association and other employer groups
then sued Drake for $2 million for undermining their bargaining rights.
Drake halted work in exchange for a promise the suit would be dropped.
It asserted that it had entered into interim agreements with the unions at
the behest of King County and complained that the county had refused
reimbursement. "We said no," Spellman acknowledged. "It would not be
a proper expenditure of county funds. There was also a mutual agreement
to proceed without a promise of indemnification. ... The contractor has an
obligation to finish." [10]

After weeks of tedious talks between the unions and contractors, work at last resumed. Cement Masons and Ironworkers—their skills vital to the project—had won substantial wage increases. Spellman said the county would consider "reasonable" compensation for Drake's losses. Completion had slipped another five months to "late in 1975." A messy divorce was brewing.

IN OCTOBER OF 1974, Drake filed a $10.5 million claim against King County. Design changes instigated or approved by the county—allegedly 512 in all—plus the strikes and lockouts, had been ruinous to its bottom line, Drake said. Key subcontractors were threatening to walk unless they received $3.6 million in extra compensation. Drake also wanted its deadline extended 411 working days to February 1, 1976. "Unacceptable," said Spellman. Schlatter had assured him the design changes were minor, amounting to only about $500,000. The county was willing to negotiate over issues genuinely beyond Drake's control, but the contractor had only itself to blame for the lion's share of overruns, Spellman said. Drake had been paid $21 million to date. Now it wanted to renegotiate on a cost-plus basis, with no maximum limit and a minimum of $8 million more, according to Spellman. The county's best offer was an additional $1.5 million to cover contingencies.

A month of fruitless talks ended when Drake closed up shop at high noon on November 22, 1974. Two-thirds complete, the Kingdome stood silent. Franklin G. Drake, the company president, arrived at SeaTac Airport for a one-on-one with Spellman. "[B]oth men knew the colossal game of chicken they had played for two months was drawing to an end."[11] Spellman was resolute, once again risking all his political capital. For Drake, the stakes were millions in potential damages. He took his case to the County Council, hoping it would second-guess Spellman. In a long letter, Drake denied demanding $8 million more. Spellman had agreed to negotiate a cost-plus contract and asked for a "ball-park" estimate of what it might cost to finish the job, Drake said.[12]

The real issue behind the work stoppage, Drake wrote, was that the prescribed method for freeing the completed concrete roof segments from the temporary supports—the "falsework"—didn't work. "We have not refused to proceed with the project. Rather we have simply demanded that the county assume its clear contractual obligation to provide explicit design instructions regarding the work."[13]

IT WAS "darned lonely at the top" of the dome, *Times* reporter Polly Lane discovered after ascending a maze of ramps and narrow portable stairways. "There, against the spectacular background of the city, stood the dome rib that has refused to part from its form and the falsework supports below." Lane explained:

> The falsework beams rest on railroad tracks so they can be revolved into 40 positions for pouring of the ribs that will form the dome. The falsework rests on sand jacks—devices which hold two inches of sand between plates. When the contractor was ready to remove the forms from the first roof segment, the crews blew out the sand. This slowly lowered the falsework, which in turn was supposed to loosen the bracing for the forms so it could be removed. But the two inches allowed by the sand wasn't enough to free the concrete from the forms.[14]

"We aren't designers, just darned good builders," Drake said. "But we are unwilling to assume responsibility for the safety and integrity of a complex and potentially hazardous procedure. Only the county's design team has the knowledge to coordinate the critical factors involved in this project."[15]

Schlatter was disgusted. He told Spellman the falsework was a smokescreen. John Christiansen, the dome's proud designer, was also indignant. John Skilling, one of the structural engineers, said the primary responsibility for designing the falsework rested with Drake.

"Johnny O'Brien and I decided to check out the sand jacks," Spellman remembers. "We went down to the Kingdome with some apprehension because Drake was saying the falsework or the dome segment itself might fall. The architects and engineers assured us there was no danger. Johnny and I gave the sand a poke with hooks like the tapers you use to light a fireplace." As the sand flowed out, the falsework slowly, surely, came loose from the concave concrete panel it supported. "The clearance was a couple of inches." Drake still refused to modify the falsework without the county's "unequivocal assumption of responsibility. ..."[16]

"They got way behind schedule and wanted us to pay," Schlatter says. "The rest of that stuff about the sand jacks was all nonsense. It was their own incompetence. ... Everyone was saying the Kingdome wouldn't get finished for several years, but Spellman was calm and resolute."[17] He fired Drake and issued a new call for bids. Drake would not be allowed to submit a new offer. To do so would amount to a "total abdication" of the county's legal position. It was the lawyer in Spellman as much as the executive. A contract was a contract. King County filed a breach-of-contract suit against Drake, seeking damages for the delays and compensation for expenses beyond the original contract price. Also on the hook was Travelers Insurance

Company, which held one of the performance bonds. It was siding with Drake.

THE CONTRACT to complete the stadium went to Peter Kiewit Sons', which offered to do the job for $500,000, plus actual costs, including 4.5 percent of any change orders. Its performance in the months to come made Spellman and Schlatter wish they had chosen Kiewit in the first place. Kiewit modified the sand jacks and came up with its own method of repositioning the falsework to pour the remaining 36 sections of the dome. However, completing the stadium would cost another $28.8 million—some $13.6 million more than budgeted. The good news was that investing the money from selling the stadium bonds had generated an additional $6 million.

Ruano was at the print shop, ordering a batch of petitions to prevent the county from using property-tax money to help complete the stadium.

Spellman and Bratton met with Seattle's leading bankers. They agreed to loan the county $13.6 million at 5.7 percent, 65 percent of the prime rate. "I knew many of them from Forward Thrust and other civic projects over the years, but Bratton had a lot to do with pitching our plan. What it came down to was that they had faith in the project and what it would do for Seattle. We told them we were confident of winning our lawsuit against Drake. Best of all, we now had a football team."

On December 5, 1974, the day after Drake and Spellman drew their lines in the sand, the NFL awarded a franchise to Seattle Professional Football. The Seattle consortium had raised the requisite $16 million. Rozelle's "51 percent rule" required someone to be first among equals. The Nordstrom family consented to become the majority partner. Sarkowsky, however, was "the glue that held things together" as managing partner.[18] "Before they acquired a single player, named a coach, signed a lease on the stadium or attended a single league meeting together, they had sold 59,000 season tickets," Emmett Watson recalled.[19]

"Lloyd Nordstrom, sadly, never lived to see the Seattle Seahawks take the field," Spellman says. "Those men—the Nordstroms, Sarkowsky, Ned Skinner, Howard Wright, Monte Bean and Lynn Himmelman—personified the 'Seattle Spirit.' They certainly weren't in it for the money." Wright, third-generation president of the construction company that built the Space Needle and many other major buildings, agreed. Two years earlier, they figured it would cost $24,000 to field each player. Now it was up to $43,000 and rising. "It's not a good investment," Wright said, "but we all have the good fortune to live here, and it was time we stepped up and pledged a responsibility to the community."[20]

WORK ON THE KINGDOME resumed in March of 1975. A second shift was added to make up for lost time. By June, the roof was three months ahead of schedule. Opening day was only seven months away. Billy Graham was booked for a week-long Crusade for Christ. Spellman's motto amounted to "In God we trust, but a great lawyer is the best insurance." He and Bayley hired William L. Dwyer, master litigator and renaissance man, to assist Norm Maleng on the case against Drake. Dwyer and Jerry McNaul, his tenacious associate, were already advancing Slade Gorton's lawsuit against Major League Baseball over the loss of the Pilots.

Dwyer ended up hitting grand-slams in back-to-back trips to the plate.

CHAPTER TWENTY

Off and Running

With the Kingdome back on track, Spellman made up his mind to run for governor in 1976, even if Dan Evans decided to seek an unprecedented fourth term. Those who already knew there was an ambitious politician behind Spellman's nonconfrontational image were still impressed. He wanted it.

Spellman was not a member of Evans' inner circle. He was, however, a longtime admirer. They were both devoted family men; progressives, especially on social-justice issues and—increasingly for Spellman—the environment. A number of influential businessmen, wary of Evans' chances or otherwise convinced he shouldn't run—12 years being enough, many felt—were now in the Spellman camp. Evans was conflicted. He loved being governor, but maybe it was time for something new. Maybe outside politics altogether, although Evans found it tantalizing to be on Gerald Ford's short list of possible running mates, never mind that Nelson Rockefeller, one of Evans' role models, had found being vice president boring after less than a year. "I never wanted to be vice president of anything," Rockefeller conceded.

In the summer of '75, Spellman paid a courtesy call at the Governor's Mansion. He informed Evans he was running regardless. Evans understood, but urged him to run for lieutenant governor. Spellman found that unpalatable for several reasons. For starters, he wanted to be governor. And why would he relinquish a plum job as executive of the state's largest county and take a dramatic pay cut to preside over the State Senate and pose with pages and Campfire Girls? Also, while Lieutenant Governor Cherberg was now thought by some to be vulnerable, he was undefeated at the ballot box since 1956. "Cowboy Johnny" was way better at politics than coaching football. They shook hands. No hard feelings. Do what you gotta do.

On October 14, 1975, when Spellman announced his candidacy, Evans was on a Pacific Rim trade mission. Adele Ferguson, the *Bremerton Sun's* feisty Capitol correspondent, cut to the chase when he returned to Olympia:

"Governor, will the fact that many of the Republican leaders and most of the established party machinery have been committed now to John Spellman for the governor's race next year, is that going to influence you in thinking about whether or not to run for a fourth term or would you risk a bloody family battle?"

"Well, first ... you have to wait until filing time to make sure there is a battle. Secondly, I don't believe it would necessarily be a bloody family battle. Healthy competition is, I think, probably a pretty good thing. And as far as the commitment of all the party machinery and the party fundraisers, I think that's a long way from being true...."

"Do you think John Spellman would be a good candidate for governor?" said Gordon Schultz, the bureau chief for United Press International.

"Sure."

"Would you like to see him be the next governor?"

"At what time?" Evans said, nimble as ever.

He reminded them that for several months he'd been saying the odds were against another run, but not because he was losing interest in the job. "It would be purely and simply a family decision ... to step aside from public life entirely." And if he had made up his mind—he honestly hadn't—why would he tip his hand and become a lame duck with 14 months left in his term and a special session looming?[1]

Evans was a far more instinctive campaigner than Spellman. He also correctly surmised that Spellman's organization wasn't what it was cracked up to be. Pathetic was closer to the truth. The campaign manager was Doug Jewett, a bright young Yale Law School graduate on leave from the County Prosecutor's Office. Jewett was politically ambitious and, by several accounts, in over his head. By the time Spellman grasped that this was no time for beginners, valuable months had passed, although Evans' indecision was what hurt the most.

ONE YEAR from Election Day, County Assessor Harley Hoppe was also weighing his maybes. He told reporters he might run for governor or Congress in 1976 or county executive in 1977. He still had $25,000 in his war chest, and there was more where that came from. Hoppe had well-heeled fans. He was fresh from a resounding re-election victory and a trip to Longacres, one of his haunts, in a red Cadillac. At 6-3, 280 pounds, Hoppe cut a memorable figure in his checked sport coats, flashy ties and blue suede shoes. He was Colonel Tom Parker, Howard Jarvis and Archie Bunker rolled into one; in other words, a character but no clown. As the reigning short-order cook in his own kitchen, his specialty was "The Hoppe Sandwich"—peanut butter, jelly, bologna, a slice of onion and a pickle. Perhaps the perfect metaphor for his personality.[2] The prevailing caricature of the assessor as a bumptious flake ignored his competent performance of late and the appeal of his mavericky, anti-tax persona. After a bumpy start at the Courthouse, Hoppe hired as his top aide Vito Chiechi, Boeing's politically ambidextrous former lobbyist. It was Chiechi who computerized the Assessor's Office and helped Hoppe crunch the political numbers.

Always good for a quote, Hoppe was even more expansive than usual as he talked with reporters about his chances as a candidate for governor. "I want to make sure we're going to win. I don't want to go in just for the exercise, just to soften John up for the Democrats."[3] Then again, he might join them. He'd done so well in blue-collar Renton that he was toying with running as a Democrat. Another option was running as an independent because there was such "strong statewide support" for a third-party movement.[4] With Hoppe you just never knew. He filed as a Republican.

Spellman was confident he could beat Hoppe and convinced that Evans wouldn't run. In the General Election, he expected to face Wes Uhlman and win. He was psyched. Uhlman annoyed him almost as much as Hoppe, which was saying a lot. The mayor had crushed a recall attempt by firefighters and City Light workers angered by budget cuts and the firing of the fire chief. Uhlman believed he had dispelled his old image as a slick liberal. The "kid from the U," elected to the Legislature at 23 in 1958, was now running as "a hard-nosed, commanding executive who made unpopular choices and took on powerful interest groups for the good of the city he loved."[5] Most of that was even true. Uhlman had grown into the job. Now he wanted to be governor. He expected to face Spellman and win.

A funny thing happened to both frontrunners on the way to Olympia. Dixy Lee Ray, like Jimmy Carter, picked the perfect year to aim high. The quirky 61-year-old scientist and the Baptist peanut farmer were political outsiders in a year when the electorate awoke from the long national nightmare of Watergate with a dry-mouth hangover.

When Dr. Ray resigned in a huff from the State Department after being snubbed by Henry Kissinger, she summoned her aide, confidant and future biographer, Lou Guzzo:

"What would you say if I told you I am thinking seriously of returning to Washington to run for governor?"

"Mind if I sit down?" Guzzo says he said, mouth half open.

Friends back home were encouraging her to run, she said, and it sounded like fun.

The former newspaper man volunteered to canvass his own sources for a reality check. Heading for the door, he says he realized an important question was unanswered: "What kind of political animal are you—Republican, Democrat, Independent, or Tory?"

"Hell, I don't know. You tell me. What am I?"[6]

Guzzo walked her though her options. While she'd worked for Nixon and Ford, and most of her influential friends back home were Republicans, the party in Washington State was perennially split between progressives and conservatives. Evans was unlikely to run, Guzzo said, and Spellman was out front regardless. If she ran as an independent she would be hammered left and right—by Democrats united behind Uhlman and Republicans solid for Spellman.

Finally, Guzzo said, "Do you know what you are?"

"No, what?"

"You are a conservative Democrat."

Her eyes took on the "foxy twinkle" he had come to admire.[7]

Former colleagues concluded that Lou hadn't just crossed to the Dark Side, he was on a sugar high from Dixy's Kool-Aid. Shelby Scates, one of Guzzo's most enterprising reporters when he ran the newsroom at the *Seattle P-I*, would characterize Guzzo as "the Henry Higgins to this unfortunate Eliza Doolittle." In the beginning, however, their collaboration was blessed with more than a little bit of luck.

The dark horse Democrat in the race was Marvin Durning. The former Rhodes Scholar and Yale economics professor had never held public office, but he was one of the nation's leading environmentalists. The 46-year-old lawyer had been running for governor since 1974, asserting that the political process in Washington State was being poisoned by special-interest campaign money, "slick advertising images and few facts."[8] Other Democrats considering the race were State Representative John Bagnariol of Renton; former state senator Martin Durkan, who had run twice before; King County Labor Council leader James K. Bender and Pierce County Commissioner Clay Huntington. Al Rosellini was the wild card, watching and waiting.

At a turn-the-tables roast for Ed Donohoe, the union-paper editor famous for his acidic pen, it was also open-season on Spellman and Uhlman. Spellman's travails with the Kingdome inspired a musical number based on "Ya Got Trouble!" from *The Music Man*: "Trouble! Oh, we got trouble! Right here in Rainy City. With a capital 'T' and that rhymes with 'D' and that stands for 'Dome'!"

When it was Donohoe's turn, he squinted through the stage lights toward a who's-who crowd of 900 in the ballroom of the Olympic Hotel.

Spellman sells Frank Ruano, his dogged adversary, two tickets to the Kingdome's grand opening celebration in 1976. Ruano pronounced the stadium an "unbelievable … feat of engineering," but still said it should not have been publicly financed.

"Is Wes Uhlman out there?" The mayor's hand shot up and he scooted back his chair, preparing to stand for a round of applause. "Too bad!" Donohoe said.[9]

FROM HIS OFFICE at the Courthouse, Spellman used binoculars to keep tabs on the Kingdome, rapidly nearing completion. The Capitol was 50 miles farther south, as the crow flies. "But for Spellman," a reporter wrote, "both are in the same picture." Would the stadium be an albatross or landmark achievement? At 48, Spellman was "at the crossroads of his political career. If he isn't elected governor, he says he would not be a candidate for re-election as county executive in 1977 and probably would return to private law practice. 'The stadium is the most visible thing we have done, but it's not the most important. It's symbolic,' he says in his quiet manner through a wreath of pipe smoke."[10] Consulted for counterpoint, Ruano offered quite possibly the most rancorous words every uttered in public about John D. Spellman: "He misrepresents and he steals from the public. He has created an empire for his own selfish ends."[11] Perhaps thinking better of it, Ruano agreed to don a hardhat and pose with Spellman inside the Dome for a bury-the-hatchet photo. Unsmiling, Ruano pretended to buy two tickets for the grand opening. After a tour, he conceded it was an "unbelievable" feat of engineering.[12]

Two days before the festivities, the state's top political guessing game ended. Eyes misty, wife Nancy and three young sons at his side, Evans announced he would not seek re-election. After 20 years in public office, it came down to family. "They've contributed enough. I will end this term because I love my family so much."[13] The First Lady seemed relieved. Watching her reaction, Lois Spellman had a sense of foreboding about life in a fishbowl. Polls showed the decision boosted Evans' popularity. Many believed it also increased his stock in the competition to be Ford's runningmate.*

It would be the first wide open governor's race in 20 years.

MARCH 27, 1976, is one of the red letter days in Spellman's life. Not only was he the Republican frontrunner for governor, the stadium some had called "Spellman's Folly" was now a reality, with two big-league sports franchises as coming attractions. Bill Dwyer's indictment of baseball's double-dealing was so withering that the American League owners had thrown in the towel a few weeks earlier, 20 days into the trial over damages for the loss of the Pilots. They agreed to award Seattle a new franchise, the Mariners.

The 54,759 spectators who attended the Kingdome's grand opening cheered as Spellman presented a giant-size key to a group of grade-school kids "representing the future of our state." Uhlman's reception, predictably, was less robust, but the standing ovation accorded Evans eclipsed anyone's. "Be careful or I may change my mind," the governor said with a grin when the cheering stopped.[14]

The 3½-hour Bicentennial "Spirit of America" pageant featured a cast of thousands. There were covered wagons, square dancers, banjo bands, gospel singers, drill teams, gymnasts, log rollers, massed choirs, more than 76 trombones and Rufus, "the Frisbee-chasing" sheep dog.[15] The crowd came to ogle the humongous roof, sail paper airplanes from the upper levels, belt out "The Battle Hymn of the Republic" and eat expensive hot dogs, "not because they were hungry, but because at a buck and a half a throw they were setting dietary precedent," John Hinterberger wrote in *The Times*. "Gabe Castillo, 16, came to dance, to leap over the Astroturf and to discover that, for a barefoot Filipino dancer, it tickled. ... But the spectacle wasn't really the 7,000 performers on the floor. It was the dome itself. The consensus

---

* Diehard conservatives denied Evans a spot as a delegate to the GOP National Convention. He went anyway and was disappointed when Ford picked Robert Dole.

was that, as spectacle goes, the dome was pretty spectacular."[16] Old sports writers inspected the 175-seat press box, took note of the profusion of electrical outlets, "for all the new devilish methods" of transmitting their prose, and concluded that the "ink-stained wretches" never had it so good.[17] In a burst of old-time Hearstian hoopla, the *Post-Intelligencer* declared 1976 the "Year of the Dome," adding a stadium icon to its front-page nameplate.

Activists from the International District, young and old, stood outside the stadium, offering mimeographed leaflets decrying the plight of low-income residents forced out of their homes. New parking restrictions were being imposed, including meters that operated 12 hours a day. Chinatown would never be the same, they said. Frank Ruano was there too, reminding passersby and TV crews that the concrete "boondoggle" had cost $67 million. When the cameras swiveled to Spellman, he emphasized that nearly $10 million of that was privately financed. Construction costs had soared 59 percent during the four years it took to construct the stadium, Spellman went on, and Mr. Ruano's delaying tactics and Donald M. Drake's dissembling had cost the taxpayers millions. He predicted the county would win its lawsuit. Ruano scoffed. Asked why he'd left the dedication early, he said, "All that self-eulogizing got to be too much for me."[18]

Spellman and Uhlman handshaked their way through the crowds. Dixy was elsewhere, raising prodigious amounts of money. Her opponents had another challenge: How do you run against a force of nature who also happens to be a woman?

CHAPTER TWENTY-ONE

Primary Colors

Steve Excell was a sizable young man with a boyish face and frisky mind. He'd been a political junkie since high school. After law school at Georgetown he went to work for Congressman Joel Pritchard. Now, in the summer of 1976, he was holed up in a windowless room at Spellman's campaign headquarters with a high-mileage IBM Selectric typewriter and a trove of clippings about Harley Hoppe, Wes Uhlman and Dixy Lee Ray. Hoppe was, well, *Hoppe*—his own worst enemy. They had ample ammunition against Uhlman too. But Dixy was even more of a moveable feast than Excell had realized, not that they expected her to beat Uhlman. Other campaign workers could hear him cackling as he worked, collecting all the juicy things she'd said over the past 10 years. His favorite was right out of *Dr. Strangelove*: "The first atomic warhead I ever saw was like a piece of beautiful sculpture, a work of the highest level of technological skill. It's the point of a spear." The Darwinian Dixy was captured in a 1969 interview about the folly of America "rushing in to save starving populations" around the world. "I don't see this obsession with the lowest strata of humanity against all biological experience." As for the armchair environmentalists who thought electricity "came from a plug in the wall," Dixy said nuclear power plants were "infinitely safer than eating because 300 people choke to death on food every year." [1]

Excell also understood instinctively that "Dixy Lee Ray's whole persona—her dogs, her Jaguar sports car, her knee socks and her iconoclastic one-liners—made her a fascinating character in a year when being a tell-it-like-it-is 'non-politician' translated into political capital. 'Little lady takes on big boys' was a compelling theme." [2]

The 1976 gubernatorial primary was a landmark event in Washington politics. A woman—albeit not a very feminine one—was making a credible bid for governor for the first time. Though Dixy was famous for blunt talk, her opponents, with the exception of Marvin Durning, were apprehensive about giving as good as they got, lest they seem unchivalrous. Durning, who was tall and intense, found it appalling that a marine biologist seemed so cavalier about the environment. The media vacillated on what to call her: Dr. Ray, Miss Ray or just plain Ray? Most newspapers were still resisting "Ms." Dixy professed to being confused by feminism. She didn't mind being called Dixy, the name she invented for herself in childhood. She'd been christened Marguerite and hated it. It never fit. Too prim for a tomboy who at 12 became one of the youngest girls to climb Mount Rainier.

In March, two weeks before Evans bowed out, Dixy dove in. She was way behind in the fundraising race and didn't have much of an organization. However, she was well ahead of everyone but Evans in terms of fan base, according to a surprising new statewide poll. Evans was favored by 25.9 percent, Dixy by 15.5. Spellman was a disappointing third at 7.1; Rosellini next at 5.9, while 5.3 percent wanted Hoppe. Martin Durkan was favored by 3.1 percent, Uhlman only 2.9. Durning barely generated a blip. The biggest bloc was the undecideds, 31.6 percent.[3]

DIXY'S CAMPAIGN LANGUISHED though June, with her widowed sister, Marion Reid, doing double duty as treasurer and scheduler. "Chaos was the order of the day" at her King County headquarters, which had three staffers and two telephones.[4] A physician who found Dixy intriguing but uninformed on health-care issues suggested she meet Blair Butterworth, one of his classmates. Butterworth was a tall, self-assured young man with a mop of curly hair and rakish aviator glasses. After volunteering with Ed Muskie's 1972 presidential campaign he arrived in Seattle to head a health-policy grant program at the University of Washington. He had worked closely with House Speaker Leonard Sawyer and August Mardesich, the Senate majority leader, on health-care issues in what amounted to a crash course in Washington State politics.

Dixy invited Butterworth to lunch. Afterward, they repaired to her trailer. "We had this roaring argument about social service issues, welfare and health care in particular. She was very smart but thought she knew everything. There we were, drinking Scotch, surrounded by her dogs, with Marion wanting us all to get in the hot tub. Out of the alcohol-laced steam, I volunteered to write some position papers. She was outrageously interesting, and it was obvious that she needed help."[5]

Dixy was making enemies in the press by bristling at questions she deemed ignorant or impudent. Outside Seattle this would prove to be good strategy, à la Spiro Agnew. But Uhlman and Spellman were both gaining. The mayor had moved up to a solid third. His war chest was three times Dixy's.

WASHINGTON STATE ARCHIVES

Dixy Lee Ray with her beloved poodle, Jacques.

Spellman's campaign had benefited mightily from reinforcements. Joe McGavick was on board. Frank Pritchard was now chairman of the steering committee. Brian Ducey, Spellman's friend since their days at Seattle U, was once again the treasurer. Republican campaign stalwarts Helen Rasmussen and Ritajean Butterworth—no relation to Blair—were overseeing volunteers and scheduling. Pat Dunn, Chris Bayley's smart, charming cousin, was the campaign's field director. Dunn had worked for John V. Lindsay, New York's progressive mayor, after law school at Hofstra and for the first Democrat to be elected governor of Vermont. Mary Ellen McCaffree, the state director of revenue, gave the campaign access to the latest estimates on real revenue growth over the next biennium as it drafted its fiscal platform. The campaign's major catch was a masterful Seattle ad man, Dick Schrock. When Schrock joined the campaign as its communications strategist in late July, one poll showed Hoppe still too close for comfort. The Kingdome was a big plus for Spellman, respondents said. Name familiarity, however, was a major problem outside King County, especially in Eastern Washington.

At Dixy's headquarters, Blair Butterworth and campaign manager David Sternoff were on a collision course. On August 20, at a team meeting Sternoff had called to defend his strategy, Dixy unceremoniously fired him. Butterworth was now in charge, the candidate said. He was the go-getter they needed.[6] Lou Guzzo says he warned her that Butterworth's "Ivy League cuteness" and association with "wheeler-dealers" like Sawyer and Mardesich—both recently forced from leadership—"spelled instant poison with the news media and much of the public."[7] Evidence of this is scarce. What's undeniable is that between Guzzo and his new rival for Dixy's ear there was no love lost. "While Butterworth was flaunting his past and his friends, I was reassuring the news media and anyone else who would listen that Dixy was no captive of the Sawyer crowd," Guzzo wrote in his 1980 biography of Ray. "Had I walked out of the campaign when Butterworth brought in his crew, there might have been a swing of more than 7,000 votes in King County, where I was identified as a crusader against corruption."[8] Butterworth stifles a yawn: "I never bothered to read that book."[9] Schrock and Excell maintain that Butterworth saved the day for Dixy. "Blair is one of the smartest guys I ever met in politics," says Schrock.[10]

Butterworth, crucially, brought on board Orin Smith, a 34-year-old Harvard MBA with Touche Ross & Co., a consulting firm, to assist Dixy's sister with campaign finances. As the campaign progressed, Smith's role grew steadily. His wife, Janet, was already the campaign's communications director.

SPELLMAN FORESAW a general election showdown with Uhlman. It had been "a long time coming—kind of like *High Noon*," he said that July as his campaign gained steam. In theoretical head-to-head matchups with Uhlman and Ray, Spellman's polling gave him a four-point lead over the mayor. Against Dixy it was a statistical dead heat. Still, they figured Dixy would be easier to beat. Polls indicated two-thirds of Uhlman's supporters would opt for Spellman in the General Election.[11] Another statistic was less encouraging: Female voters and independents strongly favored Dixy.

Hoppe, meantime, groused that Spellman was refusing to debate. He was merely Evans' puppet—"Daniel J. Spellman." Hoppe had raised a heap of money from loyal benefactors but he was spending it amateurishly. For a conservative, his flashy image was "at odds with the required style of stiff Christian solemnity."[12] A B'nai B'rith-sponsored forum at Temple De Hirsch Sinai was also the wrong place to take a poke at Spellman for accepting a campaign contribution from Herman Sarkowsky, a leader in the Jewish community.

Spellman, an ardent fisherman, won endorsements from anglers after he called for exempting steelhead, designated as a game fish since the 1920s, from the landmark 1974 Boldt Decision on Indian treaty fishing rights. The Teamsters stuck with Spellman, but Dixy picked up a key endorsement from the Seattle Building & Construction Trades Council. Austin St. Laurent, the council's executive secretary, was a force behind the anti-Spellman hardhat march on the Courthouse in 1969 over minority hiring. They were also peeved with Uhlman, who opposed raising Ross Dam and delayed the new West Seattle Bridge.

The King County Democrats and the 35,000-member Washington Education Association snubbed Uhlman to back Durning, who dismissed Dixy as a "right-wing Republican" masquerading as a Democrat and Uhlman as a slick fence-sitter. Durning wore his brainy liberalism as a badge of honor. He supported a corporate profits tax and an income tax. It was time to be honest with the voters, he said. "We will have to raise taxes."[13] Uhlman favored "some form of an income tax," but said tax reform and spending reform had to go hand in hand. He touted his experience as a legislator.[14] Dixy waffled on an income tax for the time being. She was certain, however, that "anything business can do the state can do worse."[15] For Spellman, an income tax was off the table until "strict budgetary accountability" revealed the truth about how much money was being spent on "nonpriority" programs.[16] They all agreed that funding education should be the state's top priority, although Dixy maintained that special levies "provided a certain degree of local control."[17] All three frontrunners opposed the "Nuclear Safeguards" initiative on the general election ballot—Dixy adamantly—because it was more of a ban on nuclear power than a moratorium. Dixy alone was unconcerned, sanguine in fact, about oil tanker traffic on Puget Sound, accusing her opponents of being worry-warts.

Bob Gogerty, Uhlman's energetic campaign manager, was pursuing a 39-county strategy. His polls had Dixy slightly ahead but Wes gaining by the day. The undecideds still topped 40 percent. By Election Day, Uhlman had spent $316,000, largely on media buys, compared to only $96,000 by the Ray campaign. "Even counting in-kind contributions, we never hit $100,000," says Butterworth. "I think we lied to get it close."[18] Spellman outspent Hoppe $316,000 to $290,000. His polling accurately indicated Hoppe was floundering, though they weren't taking any chances.

Spellman with Seattle Mayor Wes Uhlman at a news conference.

Spellman's down-the-stretch TV ad, designed by the Kraft-Smith agency with fine-tuning by Schrock, was the best 30-second spot of the primary, David Brewster wrote in his sophisticated new paper, *the Weekly*. The fast-paced commercial featured Spellman at the Kingdome, cheering for star quarterback Jim Zorn and the Seahawks, "thus identifying himself with the fans, not with the fat-cat contractors" who had tried to screw the county. It was fun to watch, Brewster wrote, and the message was clear: If he could build that cavernous domed stadium, persevering at every turn, he could be a good governor. The commercial was "right over the plate."[19]

ON SEPTEMBER 21, 1976, Dixy's day began at sunup on her 63-acre Fox Island farm. After taking her dogs for their morning walk she made huckleberry hotcakes for herself and her sisters. They voted, then picked green beans before heading out to visit campaign volunteers. "Thanks to you," Dixy told them, "we're going to win," but it might be a long night.[20]

The returns see-sawed for six hours. Finally, at 2:12 a.m. on the 22nd, her lead was several thousand votes. "How does it feel, Dixy?" someone said. "How SWEEEET it is!" she exclaimed as one of her sisters rubbed her feet. "I'd love to see Charles Royer with crow feathers hanging out of his mouth."[21] The liberal commentator for KING-TV was prominent on her list of media enemies.

Dixy Lee Ray, in her first try for public office at the age of 62, won the Democratic nomination for governor by 6,896 votes out of 852,000 cast. Spellman was third, some 20,000 votes behind Ray, but genuinely pleased.* He had shellacked Hoppe, winning the Republican nomination by 73,000 votes.[22] Uhlman, deeply disappointed, could point to Marvin Durning, with 136,000 votes, as the spoiler. While Durning co-opted the left, Dixy won the right. Overexposed and cross-ways with labor, Uhlman ended up with a shrunken center. The mayor's fourth-place showing in his own back yard was decisive. In King County, Uhlman lost the enviro bloc to Durning and the Scoop Jackson wing to Dixy. Still, his statewide strategy nearly succeeded. Uhlman carried 22 counties to Dixy's seven, including most of Eastern Washington. Dixy's victory was stitched together from her strong showing in King, plus an 11,000-vote margin in Pierce, her home county, and solid support from Snohomish and Benton, home to the Hanford nuclear reservation.

In an open primary where voters can cast ballots for whomever they choose, regardless of party, divining the impact of crossover voting is one for the Ouija boards. Spellman, in fact, did much better than he had hoped or expected, yet one statistic was sobering: The combined Democratic vote

---

* If the state's "Top Two" primary, instituted by initiative in 2004 and upheld by the U.S. Supreme Court in 2008, had been in effect in 1976 two Democrats, Ray and Uhlman, would have advanced to the general election. It's arguable, however, that fewer Republicans would have crossed over, improving Spellman's chances of making the general election. At this writing (2012) Republican Arthur B. Langlie, elected in 1940, is the only Seattle mayor to become governor.

was 239,000 higher than the Republican vote. Evans, however, had faced a similar-size deficit in 1972 and gone on to win handily.

There was a potential wild card that worried the Spellman camp for a few days. The thought of Dixy as the Democratic standard bearer was so unpalatable to a large bloc of party regulars and liberals that even as the nomination was slipping away from Uhlman they were assembling at the Renton Musicians Hall for an ad hoc third-party convention. There, 125 registered voters, self-described "real" Democrats led by County Councilman Mike Lowry, nominated Martin J. Durkan as the Washington State Independent Party candidate for governor. Durkan, a strong contender for the Democratic nomination in 1968 and 1972, was flattered but antsy. He had serious reservations about Dixy, but "I don't want to be a spoiler. I have a week to make up my mind." [23] He needed only five days. Durkan demurred.

It took Uhlman nearly a month before he could put his shoulder to the wheel for Dixy. Even then, he came more to damn Evans and Spellman than praise her. The Spellman brain trust—and Blair Butterworth as well—believe that if Uhlman had defeated Dixy, Spellman would have become Washington's 17th governor.

CHAPTER TWENTY-TWO

Dixyland

Dixy Lee Ray had been "far more worried" about Spellman than Wes Uhlman, especially when it came to debates, according to Lou Guzzo, her aide-de-camp turned biographer. The mayor was demonstrably unpopular in King County, Guzzo wrote, while "the untouchable Spellman was a darling in the press" and with the establishment. "It was considered sacrilege to criticize John Spellman over the Kingdome—until Dixy came along. ... Spellman didn't like the heat; he rattled when criticized. ... That's how the 'Dixy Zingers' were born—tactical poison arrows I believe put her in office and kept him out."[1]

Whether the arrows made Spellman quiver is debatable. He shot some of his own. If Guzzo had written that the political calculus of 1976 was all about change and the zingers helped italicize it, that would have been a bull's-eye. Four years earlier, Nixon was re-elected in a landslide. Then, as Watergate began to simmer, his vice president, so fond of alliterative tirades, was revealed as a throwback to the Harding Administration. Nixon, if not a crook in the conventional sense, emerged as a paranoid hypocrite who suborned burglaries and perjury—a laundry list of high crimes and misdemeanors.

Toss in the fallout from Vietnam and it's easy to take America's pulse in the Bicentennial year. The voters were disillusioned and cynical about conventional politicians. The lack of faith in government that was spawned in the '70s persists to this day. *Time* magazine acknowledged another powerful crosswind. Instead of a "Man of the Year," it put a dozen notable women on its cover in December 1975.

Though he found them great sport, Blair Butterworth, Dixy's campaign manager, isn't certain the zingers were decisive. "And I don't think the strategy came out of the Kingdome; I think the Kingdome came out of the strategy."[2] Unquestionably, their plan was to catch Spellman off guard—make him nervous about what she might lob at him next time. Guzzo and Janet Smith worked the press into zinger anticipation during the last month of the campaign.

THREE-HUNDRED SPECTATORS, evenly divided between the candidates' supporters, filed into Spokane's Civic Theater at noon on October 8, 1976, for the first of four debates to be televised statewide. The topic was "The Economy and Environment." For 54 minutes, it was a feeling-out affair, though battle lines were drawn more clearly on supertankers, a volatile issue for the west side of the state. Two weeks before, in a surprise blow to Spellman and other protectors of Puget Sound, a three-judge panel of the U.S. District Court overturned the state law banning supertankers larger than 125,000 deadweight tons from the inner Sound. The court also tossed out the requirement that smaller tankers en route to refineries at Anacortes, Cherry Point and Ferndale have multiple tug escorts.

Dixy had maintained the supertanker issue was moot because of the state law. It was mostly "an emotional thing" for an uninformed public, she said, because tankers had been delivering oil to refineries for years with no major mishaps. In any case, "those refinery areas are, technically speaking, not in Puget Sound." That artifice enraged environmentalists and Senator Magnuson, a staunch supporter of the law. As a favor to Scoop, Maggie had signed on as honorary chairman of Dixy's campaign.[3]

Spellman adamantly opposed supertankers in the Sound, saying its narrow passages presented "substantial risk" of catastrophic accidents. "I am convinced we don't have to settle for something that is spoiling our physical environment."[4] He was wary but reserving judgment on Northern Tier Pipeline Company's proposal to build a supertanker hub at Port Angeles along the Strait of Juan de Fuca and pipe oil to Midwestern refineries. Dixy couldn't understand "all this fear" of modern technology. "We must have some kind of equal balance between development and environmentalism. In making energy, there are bound to be some things detrimental to the environment." She proposed "economic impact statements" to balance environmental impact statements.[5]

On other issues, it wasn't much of a debate. Dixy believed an income tax had to be considered as part of any tax-reform package. Spellman had twice backed Governor Evans' tax-reform proposals, only to see them soundly defeated. Introducing an income tax all over again would bog down the executive and legislative branches, Spellman said. What was needed was a sea change in government efficiency. "No new taxes are necessary." Both said funding for public schools, the state's constitutional "paramount duty," was a top priority. They reiterated their opposition to the initiative restricting nuclear power plants. Both supported capital punishment. Neither Spellman, a devout Catholic, nor Ray, raised in a Southern Baptist household, would interfere with a woman's right to an abortion under state law. As political theater, it was ho-hum until Dixy's three-minute closing statement. She said Spellman had been talking a lot about good management, certainly an important issue. And it was true that he had balanced King County's budget and wiped out a large deficit. "But I think it's fair to point out that that was done not by revenues generated in the county but from a combination of things," including federal revenue-sharing funds and the local-option sales tax. These were "windfall funds that will not happen again." As for the Kingdome, the issue "of whether there has been good fiscal management is still open. For example, there's a $13.5 million payment going to come due next March and there's no way for the county to pay it without an increase in the property tax." [6]

Spellman shrugged it off. Literally. He had the last word but stuck to the theme of economic and environmental issues: "The crucial issue is the quality of life in the State of Washington as it affects our people, as it affects the opportunities for people." In King County, "we have solved problems, paid debts," persevered.[7]

When reporters swarmed him afterward, Spellman realized he'd made a mistake. While Butterworth, Guzzo and Smith were high-fiving Dixy, he groused that she had read the charge from prepared notes, a violation of the ground rules. "I was certainly tempted to reply, but explaining something like that would have taken up my final three minutes and it (the issue) wasn't a proper part of a summary statement." Besides, the Kingdome "had nothing to do with the debate." It was "an obvious attempt to distract me ... a red herring. I'm surprised a 'non-politician' would act so political. Even the typed-out statement that Dr. Ray read shows an embarrassing lack of understanding about fiscal matters." The $13.5 million loan from the banks "was the best decision possible" for taxpayers, and he was holding the contractor's bonding company liable for the sum.[8] As for windfalls, King County, like every other county in the state, had received revenue-sharing funds. But that was six years ago, he said. While many other counties were now in financial trouble, his county was debt free and had imposed no major tax increases.

Dick Larsen, one of the media panelists, observed that Spellman's procedural personality had cost him points. "Dr. Ray, supposedly a political amateur, flicked the only stinging punch or their first bout."[9] Spellman called a press conference to emphasize there would be no new taxes to repay the $13.5 million loan. Reporters asked if he "smarted" from Ray's jab.

"I never smart when people make misstatements," he said, smarting.[10]

Jackson and Magnuson joined Dixy for a campaign commercial shoot at the Lake Union offices of the National Oceanic & Atmospheric Administration. Scoop smiled as she sparred with reporters over her managerial skills. Maggie looked as if he'd rather be having a root canal.

THE SECOND DEBATE, sponsored by the Seattle Municipal League, was televised live starting at 10 p.m. because the Yankees and Kansas City Royals were playing for the American League championship in prime time. Don Hannula, the wry Finn who covered the debate for *The Seattle Times*, stepped up to the bat: "Dixy Lee Ray threw a ninth-inning fastball at John Spellman and he unloaded on it." [11] In her closing statement, she questioned once again how Spellman was going to repay the Kingdome loan without shaking down the taxpayers. She had a suggestion: The leases at the county airport. In 1967 Boeing was paying only about $131,000 for a lease that should have cost at least $700,000, Dixy charged. Smaller companies had had their lease rates doubled, tripled even quadrupled since 1967, she said. Spellman, cheeks flushed, was ready. "Dr. Ray's closing statements are always interesting. They bring out this brand-new topic." But first, the Kingdome: "There are people like Dr. Ray who said it never could be built, who said the roof would fall in, who said there never would be tenants, who said there never would be parking." [12] Dixy was shaking her head and

The candidates eye one another warily during a debate.

muttering that she hadn't said those things. Then he had a zinger of his own: "I suspect that if the contractor walked out, Dr. Ray would say, 'We can't do it ... Maybe the Seahawks can play in the Pacific Science Center!'"[13] The audience erupted in laughter. Dixy had to grin, too.

As for the airport, Spellman said Boeing had a long-term lease but there was an arbitration clause. The issue was on appeal in the courts, with the county pursuing a settlement. "I'm always amazed when I hear people from the federal government in Washington, D.C., tell people how we must be more efficient in budgeting and spending at the local level." A project in Tennessee estimated at $700 million ended up costing $1.95 billion when Ray headed the Atomic Energy Commission, Spellman charged. "And the federal government bureaucrats tell us about efficiency in local government. We've operated within our budget without new taxes for six years and we've provided the services needed—not just bombs and things..."[14]

"John got a little fire in his belly," a spectator told Larsen, who observed that Spellman looked every inch a governor but usually seemed so calm you'd think he was running for state museum curator.[15] Polls found that everyday people found Dixy refreshing. They liked her self-deprecating humor. "Nature did not make me willowy," she quipped when someone said her wardrobe seemed to consist of plaid skirts and knee socks. Her aphorisms were catchy, reassuring: "We live in a society where half the people think science can do anything it wants to, and the other half is afraid that it will." Her stand on oil tankers won her the endorsement of the Puget Sound Maritime Trades Council.

A SPATE OF INSULT SWAPPING worked to Dixy's advantage. Evans said she demonstrated "abysmal ignorance" of state finances.[16] "The oil companies will dance in the streets" if she's elected, he warned.[17] Dixy retorted that she was "running against at least two opponents—the incumbent governor and his hand-picked successor ... his little shadow candidate."[18] Slade Gorton reprimanded her for saying that if elected governor she would not appeal the decision overthrowing the supertanker law. "It is the duty of the governor to enforce a state law banning supertankers whether or not he or she likes it," the attorney general said. In any case, as governor she would not have the authority to refuse to appeal the decision. "Decisions on legal matters are made by the attorney general. I have made the determination that the case will be appealed and I will go forward."[19]

For Spellman, and Evans, it was Catch 22: While taking pains to emphasize he was his own man, Spellman needed the Evans vote. For his part, Evans was appalled by Dixy, yet whenever he ripped into her the

implication was that Spellman didn't represent change. "We kept pushing 'Little Lady takes on the big boys,'" Butterworth remembers. "A lot of
people said the political establishment and media seemed to be ganging
up on her." [20] When Spellman called a press conference to outline his 1977
county budget proposal, reporters instead zeroed in on his new gloves-off
vigor as a debater. Had he been apprehensive about attacking a female opponent? Yes. While he was a supporter of women's rights and the father of
three daughters, he had "a psychological" aversion to lashing into her the
way he would a male opponent. He feared he would be accused of sexual
discrimination. "Isn't that reverse discrimination?" a female reporter asked.
Tricky stuff, said Spellman. "How do you deal with a female opponent in
this modern era of absolute rights for all (when) chivalry should be swept
aside? ... It is a new experience for most candidates." He was still inclined
to "give additional deference" to a female opponent, "and I don't apologize
for that." *[21] Meeting with a group of female leaders, Dixy admitted that at
62 she had only recently become "keenly aware" of women's issues. "I want
to learn more about the variety of problems women face." [22]

Spellman courted crossovers and independents. He won the endorsement of a coalition of conservationists and sportsmen, including Jim Whit-
taker, the famed mountain climber and Kennedy family friend.

POLLS RELEASED just before the final debate, in Richland on October 26,
found the candidates virtually tied, with about 24 percent still undecided.
Spellman was determined that the last zingers would be his. The format
suited him fine: Classic Lincoln-Douglas–head-to-head, no moderator.

Spellman said there were curious disconnects between what Dixy advocated and what she actually did. She maintained that special levies were
part of the answer to school-funding problems, yet she hadn't bothered to
vote on any of the school issues on the ballot in her Pierce County district in
recent years. He was also appalled by her attitude toward the less fortunate.
"If we treat people like experiments in a biology lab," Spellman said, we
lose touch with our souls. "I think a society is known not by its efficiency
alone, or by its science alone, but by its humanity. As the next governor, I
won't give up on a single human being." [23] Dixy was furious. She said it was

---

* How not to deal with a female opponent was demonstrated definitively by Congressman Rod
Chandler, R-Wash., in 1992, the Year of the Woman. Tall and handsome, Chandler was rated the
favorite for a seat in the Senate against Patty Murray, a tiny, self-styled "mom in tennis shoes." Then
he ended one of their debates with a chauvinistic rendition of the refrain from a popular Roger
Miller ditty: *"Dang me, dang me/They oughta take a rope and hang me/High from the highest tree/Wom-
an would you weep for me!"* With 54 percent of the vote, Murray moved from the suburban school
board to the U.S. Senate in the space of four years.

the same let-the-children-in-Biafra-starve big lie Durning hatched before the primary to portray her as "some kind of scientific monster," and the liberal media played right along. "The United States cannot feed the world for free. But I do care about people. To take quotations out of context and try to make it sound as if I have no compassion and no care for those who are unfortunate is not only untrue, it is a rather despicable tactic." [24]

On the stump, when hecklers asked about the starving children, she'd say, "Come on up if you want to feel my horns." [25] *Time, Newsweek* and *People* found her fascinating, especially compared to the "colorless" Spellman. [26] That line especially annoyed Lois Spellman. John took it in stride. "I'm not a celebrity. Never have been one and don't expect to be one." [27]

The writer who painted the most revealing portrait of John Dennis Spellman was David Brewster. His new paper, *the Weekly*, was a blend of the best of the late *Seattle* magazine, the *Argus* in its progressive heyday and *The Village Voice*. Besides being at the top of his game with a paper all his own, Brewster had observed Spellman's quiet, steady rise over the past decade. "The man behind the mask" was *the Weekly's* cover story as Election Day approached:

> [T]he more I look at Spellman, the more I see a much more interesting figure trying to break free. This personality, in turn, has a lot in common with an emerging style in American politics. It is a style with roots in Eugene McCarthy's deflationary rhetoric about imperial government, Jimmy Carter's straightforward Christian striving, Jerry Brown's hard-headedness, and the collapse of big-spending liberalism.
>
> What binds these styles together is a certain detachment from government. This Spellman certainly has. The other day, as he finished an excellent speech before the Seattle Rotary Club, outlining in remarkable detail his agenda for the coming four years, he remarked to a reporter that Dixy Lee Ray, who had failed to come to what was supposed to have been a debate, would have done well here. "I remember I once introduced her to this club and said she had won the hearts of everyone in this room." It was not the typical remark of a candidate in a close race. On his way out, even more remarkably, I witnessed the spectacle of Spellman being introduced for the first time to his pollster, who was conferring with Spellman's strategists. The notion of a candidate with only four weeks to go in a tough race meeting his pollster for the first time and then only to shake hands is, well, shocking. It was an indicator of Spellman's distance from campaigning and, incidentally, statistics, (which he finds to be dehumanizing). ...

What all this suggests is an unshakeable reserve in John Spellman, which, while it is certainly not a disdain of politics, is an unusual desire to keep psychic space from it, to preserve a personality, a private life, a steadier grasp of what's important. ... When he earned a day off from the campaign grind this week, he announced he would spend it as he most wanted to: reading and listening to music at home in his study and with his large family...

If you try to fathom what makes John Spellman tick, then you find mask after mask. First there is the public one of pipe-smoking delibera- tion, a judicial mask of a man who hears people out and later reveals his own analysis. Then there is the family man, the North End square, the careful organizer of his leisure time (championship dogs to be walked, steelheading to be done, reading at home almost every night, a few nights playing bridge with members of a small circle of friends). And then one begins to get beyond the masks to the Irish dreams—of being a Renaissance man like his father, of civic justice and Catholic idealism, of connoisseurship of culture and the finer things of life. ...

He is uncommonly good in crises, whether pulling the dome out of the fire one more time or deciding that black laborers had justice on their side and standing fast for minority jobs in the construction unions. He can be very decisive as when he faced down Bert Cole's plans to prospect for oil in the Sound. He's a fine negotiator, never getting mad (unless his integrity is attacked) and more interested in results than scoring points. ... He does not play political games with his employees, from whom he draws a high standard of work. ... There is his refusal to falsify his ungregarious personality out on the hustings. ... There is his inability to suffer a dirty joke in his presence. And there is his Jesuit's understanding of how people fail, and his concern in get- ting them another position before easing them out. ...

Whether this standoffish and cautious personality can attract and hold a good staff, fight the daily political wars in Olympia or stir the electorate to renewed confidence is difficult to say, although I would bet he can. It is, after all, a peculiar and ironic time, when such negative vir- tues have a lot of positive appeal. Hence it is that John Spellman, while seeming most welded to the status quo and a conventional business outlook, is probably the most disruptive candidate of them all because of his philosophical detachment from politics as usual. The least eccentric candidate, one whose only peculiar trait seems a fondness for pipes and fine wine, has a richer inner life and a fuller vision than all the others.[28]

In *the Weekly's* endorsements a week later, Brewster wrote a remarkably prescient paragraph: "Dr. Ray seems ever more ominous, not so much for her views as for the relentless way she holds them. A palace guard is already closing around her, shielding her from significant access, preparing enemies lists. She is not the kind of leader who draws strength from people; she is a person who imposes her views—mostly dated ones, at that—hard upon the benighted populace, however charming the smile as she does so. Badly out of touch and incapable by temperament of getting into synch with this evolving state, she would be a bitter and embattled leader." [29]

Butterworth and Orin Smith told themselves "she was going to be either the best or the worst governor the state had ever had." [30] Given her velocity, there was no looking back. They sealed the deal with a pitch-perfect ad: "Do you want the same old pipe dreams or a breath of fresh air?" Spellman's signature briar pipe was tucked into the copy. Below was an engaging photo of Dixy, who promised "new ideas and common sense ... creating a climate leading to more jobs rather than more taxes." [31]

One week before Election Day, John D. Ehrlichman, the former Seattle lawyer who had risen to No. 2 in the Nixon White House, entered a federal work farm to begin serving a 2½-to-8-year term as a Watergate conspirator.

ON NOVEMBER 2, 1976, Jimmy Carter lost Washington State and the entire West but won the presidency. It was close practically everywhere. Some maintain the decisive moment was Ford's self-inflicted debate zinger—"There is no Soviet domination of Eastern Europe." Others point to his pardon of Nixon.

The local change agent

The Ray campaign targeted Spellman's trademark pipe.

WASHINGTON STATE ARCHIVES

won in a breeze. Dixy defeated Spellman by nearly 135,000 votes, 53 percent. She carried 26 of the state's 39 counties, including King and even reliably Republican Lewis.* Butterworth believes he knows why: "On the road with her for all those hours, often just the two of us in a car, I learned that she had a serious boyfriend who was killed in World War II. It was a devastating blow. Her planned life imploded. She felt she had to make a decision between a career and a 'normal' married life. There were huge numbers of women her age who understood that. They fantasized about what if they had gotten a master's or a Ph.D. or otherwise had a career outside the home. Everyone paid attention to her colorfulness. But nobody really paid much attention to the symbol she was. Undecideds traditionally have been overwhelmingly female. I think that that's what happened. At the end the women broke for Dixy." [32] Jackson's support also helped burnish her Democratic bona-fides. Eighty-seven years after statehood, Washington had elected its first female governor.

In Tacoma, the governor-elect "locked arms with a banjo player, clutched a Scotch and soda and led almost 1,000 followers in a serpentine dance" to the beat of "When the Saints Go Marchin' In." [33] She paused long enough to gloat that 16 papers had endorsed Spellman. "Our success tonight is the failure of the newspapers to elect the people they wanted to elect. ... Do you think I'm going to forget that right away?" [34]

Butterworth had promised to stop smoking if she won. "I was wandering around, glass of wine or beer in hand, cigarette in mouth, everyone congratulating me, when all of a sudden at the stroke of midnight this pudgy hand reaches up and grabs the cigarette from between my lips, throws it down on the gray cement floor, stomps it out and says 'A deal is a deal!' " [35]

In Seattle, a four-man band played on, but the first two rounds of disappointing returns sucked the energy out the Georgian Room at the Olympic Hotel. The Spellmans appeared at 11:15 to cheers and tears. John thanked them for "keeping the faith." Disappointment etched on his face, he nevertheless conceded graciously.[36]

"What went wrong?" a reporter called out. "I'll let the experts decide that. If I knew what went wrong, it wouldn't have happened." He said he wouldn't seek a third term as county executive in 1977. Watching him hug

---

* The Owl Party provided some levity in 1976. It was founded by Spellman's friend Red Kelly, a former Big Band bassist who owned a Tumwater jazz club. Their motto was "We don't give a hoot"; slogan: "Unemployment isn't working." The Owls fielded an entire slate in 1976, including "Fast" Lucie Griswold for secretary of state. Kelly received 12,400 votes for governor at no harm to Spellman, as it turned out. Unamused, the Legislature tightened the law on minor-party candidates the next year.

campaign volunteers on his way to the door, Lois said, "I think our family won tonight." [37] At 49, Spellman figured his political career was over. His campaign manager, figuring his own was just beginning, appropriated the mailing lists. The souvenir they sent to the faithful was a thermometer engraved with "Thanks for your superb help in the 1976 campaign for governor" and a facsimile of Spellman's signature. Some wag dubbed it "the rectal thermometer." Pointing to a T-bar at its tip, Spellman deadpans, "Inserting it there would have hurt."

Pretty good zinger.

CHAPTER TWENTY-THREE

Second Thoughts
and Third Terms

Spellman's Election Night announcement that he would not seek a third term as county executive in 1977 surprised and disappointed his staff and department heads. "Never say never" was a cardinal rule of politics.

"As my schedule returned to normal, I realized how much I liked being county executive. Pat Dunn and some other bright new young people came to the Courthouse after the campaign. Mike Lowry had won election to the council in 1975. His activism was infectious. My batteries were being recharged."

Lowry, 12 years Spellman's junior, was championing farmland preservation, land-use planning and merging Metro with county government. "Those issues increasingly resonated with me," Spellman says. "Mike's ambition rankled some people, and some of his ideas seemed radical, but he has a good heart and a first-class mind. It's hard not to like Mike. We worked well together. But I still believed third terms were rarely successful. So I challenged my team to come up with what we could achieve with four more years."

Political alliances at the Courthouse were more fluid than usual as 1977 dawned, given the expectation that Spellman was a lame duck. Tracy Owen, the affable banker who had been a Republican county councilman since the charter government's inception, announced his candidacy for county executive. Harley Hoppe was being coy, which fooled no one. He could run for executive without risking his job as assessor since he wasn't up for re-election that fall. Lowry said it was likely he too would run. Aubrey Davis, a former Mercer Island mayor, was for the time being the Democrats' leading contender. The distinguished-looking 59-year-old had played a key role in the growth of Group Health, the landmark consumer cooperative. Davis' track record as a public transportation advocate was equally impressive. Thanks to him, Mercer Island had refused to be assaulted by a 16-lane, four-story freeway. Davis was now chairman of the Metro Transit Committee. He had silver hair, a Phi Beta Kappa key and a serious name-familiarity deficit.

When it came time to elect a new council chairman, Lowry campaigned as the change agent. Though most County Council members admired Spellman, they were envious of his media exposure and the impression that the executive branch outshined the council. With the votes of two Republicans, Owen and Paul Barden, Lowry elbowed aside fellow Democrat Bernice Stern, whose turn it was. Stern was mad as hell. Lowry felt bad about that but said some things were too important to wait.[1] Spellman was on good terms with both Stern and Lowry before, during and after.

When R.R. "Bob" Greive, the former Senate majority leader, joined the County Council in 1976 he was both bemused and impressed by Spellman's lack of guile. Fellow Catholics, they had worked together on Forward Thrust issues a decade earlier. Greive assured Spellman that the council's machinations amounted to a cakewalk compared to the Legislature, and if anyone knew wheeling and dealing it was the bow-tied West Seattle Democrat.

"AFTER A LOT of agonizing and self-searching," Spellman announced his candidacy for re-election on February 23, 1977. "I thoroughly intended not to run again," he told a press conference. "I was sincere about it. Very frankly, I've changed my mind." A department heads' retreat convinced him "we have a chance to achieve some things that are essential" to a more livable county, including preservation of open spaces, a new jail, improved social services and a merger of Metro with county government. "I think I'm more in touch with people in the county than I was eight years ago."[2] He was becoming noticeably grayer but seemed younger than 50. The "new" Spellman had shed some pounds and was cutting back on the Grecian Formula. There was another thing: Becoming governor was still in his system, and Dixy was busy burning bridges. No amount of cranial fracking by her advisers or legislative leaders could extract a pint of political subtlety from the governor's combative brain. Blair Butterworth extricated himself early on.

Spellman was appalled when Dixy cut the proposed social-services budget by $5.1 million. About $1.7 million of that had been earmarked for King County's community mental-health centers, already "strained to the breaking point," Spellman warned. He supported deinstitutionalizing mentally ill people who were no danger to themselves or others, but without adequate funding at the community level "there's no place for them to go." Mental-health professionals told him 12,500 seriously disturbed people in King County were already receiving no treatment. Many were homeless, often jailed. "That is a terrible waste of their lives, and an unnecessary misuse of already over-taxed police and jail resources," Spellman said.[3] He was staking a fresh claim on the Evans coalition of progressive Republicans, independents and environmentalists.

With Spellman in, Owen immediately opted out of the race for executive. Lowry thought it over for six weeks. He said Spellman was honest, hard-working and sincere about reining in sprawl. Barring some dramatic change in the situation, he had too much on his plate as council chairman to get involved in a campaign. He was excited about the opportunities at hand and moving to a more strategic Courthouse command post to better oversee council staff. "Where is he going to put the throne?" Stern snorted.[4]

How about Hoppe? On June 20, the assessor sent Spellman a letter assuring him he wouldn't be a candidate. "It is my humble opinion that you have done an outstanding job as county executive and are most worthy of being re-elected."[5] A month later, Hoppe was basking not-so-humbly in the success of a signature-gathering blitz to put a gas-tax rollback on the November ballot. He also pointed to an auditor's report critical of the county's handling of Forward Thrust road funds. A movement was building for him to run, Hoppe said, "and I've tried to put it down. ... I honestly do not see myself becoming a candidate."[6]

On July 29, 10 minutes before filing closed, Hoppe dispatched Jennifer Dunn, his administrative assistant for media relations, to file his name as an independent candidate for county executive "to give the people an alternative." What changed? "I guess what pushed me over the edge are hints of serious wrongdoings" in the Spellman administration.[7] The assessor had also "quaffed a heady Hoppe opinion poll with a double-ego chaser," Dick Larsen observed in his column.[8] There were suspicions that Dixy and her "inner circle" had encouraged him to run, hoping to derail Spellman as a challenger in 1980.[9] Earlier, the governor and Karen Marchioro, the King County Democratic chairwoman, had urged Jim McDermott to enter the race for county executive. The senator begged off, saying he was exhausted, physically and financially, from the last legislative session.[10]

Hoppe days were here again. "He's like one of those guys you see at the circus moving a pea around under some shells," Spellman said in one of the best quips of his career.[11] Davis, who launched his campaign believing he was running for an open seat, was more troubled than Spellman by this development. If Hoppe polled at least 20 percent of the primary vote, a distinct possibility given his diehard following, he'd be on the November ballot as a potential spoiler.

The first credible poll gave Spellman, with the advantage of incumbency, a sizable lead in a three-way race. Davis flogged his opponents as "two tired Republicans" tapping the taxpayers' money for "self-serving, pandering" campaign mailers.[12]

THE CONTROVERSY over the road funds dogged Spellman during the campaign. County Auditor Lloyd Hara discovered that $8.5 million in the Forward Thrust account had been tapped improperly by the Public Works Department in the early 1970s. The money went to build or improve roads not included in the omnibus 1968 bond issue. In all, 34 Forward Thrust road projects had been scratched for a variety of reasons and 31 others sub-stituted in their place. By the early 1970s when the projects were under way, "the world had changed," Spellman said. New arterial standards had been set by the state. Increasingly tighter environmental regulations came into play, together with new priorities in transportation planning. "All combined to render some of the Forward Thrust concepts obsolete." For instance, resurfacing of the Old Brick Road near Redmond was set aside when it was placed on the register of historic places.[13] The County Council had approved the changes recommended by Jean DeSpain, the public-works director, with Spellman's blessings. They had done a limbo under the letter of the law. "Frankly," Spellman said, "we goofed."[14] Lowry said the council "equally" shared the blame. It boiled down to "a technical question," he said. "There is not a dime we cannot account for."[15]

Kent and Renton also admitted to overreaching on Forward Thrust road funds, while Seattle was looking to cover its tail with a public vote on its desire to "reprogram" park funds authorized by the bond issue. The whole Forward Thrust program had become "slightly aromatic," David Brewster wrote.[16] Norm Maleng, the chief civil deputy in the Prosecutor's Office, said the question likely would be moot if the county agreed to complete $6 mil-lion in Forward Thrust projects. The auditor offered two choices: Pay back the money illegally appropriated for unauthorized roads—$9.5 million, interest included—or "pay whatever it takes to finish building the roads voters thought they would get."[17] The second option was duly exercised by ordinance. All of the projects were scheduled for construction regardless and ample funds would be available from county road revenues over the next five years, said Donald Horey, the county road engineer. "We didn't have to add them (to our budget). They just fell in there. Maybe it was just plain luck."[18] Or maybe it was a plain old Republican cover-up, Davis sug-gested. He called for an independent outside investigation, asserting that Chris Bayley, co-sponsor of Spellman's most recent campaign fundraiser, had a clear conflict of interest. Bayley said there was nothing more to in-vestigate. The auditor's report documented illegal transfers. The executive and County Council admitted to the oversights and took corrective action. No evidence of criminality could be found. Case closed. "What no one gets to the heart of," Davis observed, "is how the director of public works got the authority to initiate new projects and approve spending Forward Thrust funds for them."[19] That was an easy one, Spellman says, though he didn't admit it at the time. "Of all the departments, the one that was the most autonomous was the road department because it had separate funding. County engineers traditionally ran the small counties and certainly also had a great influence within the big counties." DeSpain, rightly or wrongly, was now on a shorter leash.

AUBREY DAVIS ARGUABLY is the brightest opponent Spellman ever faced. In terms of retail political skills, however, he was a campaign manager's nightmare—and Spellman, by comparison, Tip O'Neill. Davis one night passed up a chance to press the flesh at the Ballard Elks Club to attend a meeting of the Puget Sound Council of Governments. "We threw up our hands," remembers Don Munro, a longtime friend. "It was an epiphany. Aubrey was completely detached from running for office."[20]

Increasingly frustrated, Davis hit Spellman even harder than Hoppe but with infinitely more finesse. It was the difference between a blunderbuss and a rapier. Hoppe railed against "the financial skullduggery of the last eight years" and Kingdome leases "that are a license to steal." Davis carefully parsed the budget and scoffed at Spellman's boast that the loan to finish the Kingdome had been paid back and the stadium was now producing a profit. Current-expense budget funds were being used for Kingdome operations, Davis said. "So it's a little like giving the kids a dollar to start a lemonade stand and they come back and say, 'Here's 45 cents. We made money.'"[21]

"I feel a little like the guy hit by a shotgun blast while he's climbing over a fence," Spellman said. "I don't know which pellet to dig out first. But I'm not ashamed of King County and you shouldn't be either."[22]

When the county wooed the Seattle SuperSonics from the city-owned Coliseum to the Kingdome, Frank Ruano became a Davis man. Together they observed that the NBA franchise essentially was getting free rent for the first seven years of its lease, while the city stood to lose perhaps $500,000 a year, to the detriment of Seattle Center programs. Spellman countered that landing the Sonics was part of a long-term investment in creating one of the premier sports venues in America—"the only major stadium in the United States housing (professional) baseball, football, soccer and basketball." In the space of five days, Spellman had conspicuously

joined 42,000 fans at a Seattle Sounders soccer match, 62,000 rooting for
the Seahawks and 55,000 for the Mariners. Adding a basketball configura-
tion, theater-style, to accommodate 28,000 spectators would also help the
Kingdome attract a college basketball national championship tournament,
Spellman said.[23] Ruano announced a referendum-signature drive to block
the Sonics lease agreement. It died aborning. The Seahawks won two in
the Dome before Election Day. The roar of the Kingdome crowds was the
beginning of the team's legendary "12th man."

"MY NAME IS Aubrey Davis and I'm *not* running for governor," Davis declared during a Seattle Rotary Club debate. Everyone laughed, including
Spellman. But the Rotarians rolled their eyes when Hoppe called Spellman
"the king." And when Spellman said he was proud of the Kingdome "and
you should be too," the applause rocked the room.[24] At every appearance,
Spellman emphasized his enthusiastic support for the farmland preservation program. Tom Ryan, the longtime county planner, was now
overseeing a new Office of Agriculture. It recommended that the county
buy the rights to 24,000 acres of farmland. Hoppe called it "socialistic
... the most foolish idea anyone ever thought of."[25] Davis favored a pilot
program before asking voters to back a multi-million-dollar bond issue.[26]
Liberals questioned the sincerity of Spellman's new incarnation as a
land-use activist, while a Bellevue land developer at a candidates' forum

Spellman, Aubrey Davis and Harley Hoppe during a debate at Ballard's First Lutheran
Church during the 1977 race for county executive.

called him a sell-out. They went nose to nose. "I'm not anti-development," Spellman said. "I'm for orderly growth." A hundred-thousand acres of farm land in King County had been lost to subdivisions and malls since the 1950s, he said. There were 1,400 farms vs. 6,500 three decades earlier.[27]

Spellman won bipartisan praise when he intervened on behalf of special-education children caught up in a federal-state funding snafu. Members of his staff counseled that education was not a statutory responsibility of county government. And some disability advocates, even the irrepressible Katy Dolan of Troubleshooters, warned that emergency aid would let the bureaucrats off the hook. But Spellman was unshakable. He told the County Council It would be the moral equivalent of ignoring flood or earthquake victims if they failed to help 1,500 handicapped kids. The council approved an emergency allocation of $376,000 to keep the programs afloat. It was a "very sensitive and marvelous thing," said the chairman of the County Developmental Disabilites Board.[28]

IN THE WANING DAYS, it was a tossup as to who was more frustrated—Hoppe or Davis. With three candidates on the podium, "It's not a dialog. And there's no such thing as a trialog," Davis said. Increasingly, he sensed that Hoppe was taking more votes from him than Spellman. Hoppe knew it too and was consoling himself by stumping for his gas-tax rollback. He suspected he'd been a pawn in the Democrats' game. Looking back at the encouragement he'd received from Dixy's operatives, "I think there was a lot of intrigue," Hoppe told Dick Larsen. "There was a lot of conjecture (at the time) that if I got into the race that I'd give it to Aubrey Davis." Or maybe they were worried the gas-tax initiative would pass and wanted him preoccupied, Hoppe mused.*[29] It wouldn't be the last time Dixy Lee Ray, the "nonpolitician," demonstrated an appetite for covert activities, though she flatly denied any involvement in back-channel activity.[30]

In *the Weekly*, Brewster bemoaned the dailies' lack of coverage of the race for county executive, "a far more important" job than mayor. Spellman was a Johnny-come-lately to the crucial issues of "coordinating public services and mitigating economic and racial segregation," he wrote, thinking better of the positive portrait he had painted a year earlier when Spellman was running for governor—although Spellman's opponent then was Dixy Lee Ray. "Everything argues that Aubrey Davis ought to replace

---

*Asked in 2012 if he still felt he'd been used by the Democrats, Hoppe said he couldn't recall telling Larsen "there was a lot of intrigue." However, he considered Larsen "one of the best—a tremendous" journalist.The 82-year-old's recall of other events from the 1970s was impressive. And he emphasized that he ran for county executive in 1977 "because I still wanted to be governor."[33]

John Spellman," Brewster wrote, "yet everything conspires to prevent Davis from mounting the serious campaign he should have."[31] Davis made a last-minute appeal to Hoppe's supporters. If you vote for Harley, he warned, you "may accidentally re-elect John Spellman."[32]

On November 8, 1977, Spellman easily won a third term, outpolling Davis 160,000 to 113,000. Hoppe, with 68,000 votes, had faded to a distant third. His gas-tax rollback failed by 884 votes out of nearly a million cast. If Dixy had a plan, part of it backfired. Hoppe's candidacy clearly helped Spellman. The governor also noted with disappointment that Charles Royer, the TV newsman she loathed, had defeated Paul Schell to become the next mayor of Seattle.

Spellman had hoped for an outright majority, but said he was satisfied with 47 percent. "The next four years are going to be exciting," he said, nuzzling Lois, who looked radiant and relieved. "There are going to be some changes in county government. Nobody should be surprised to see us taking the lead, especially in the area of open spaces and the preservation of our agricultural lands. ... We're not going to let King County become a Los Angeles-type slurb."[34]

Would he run for governor again? That was too far down the road to contemplate. Never was no longer in his vocabulary. Dixy, meantime, had made a game-changing blunder: She underestimated Warren G. Magnuson.

THE GOVERNOR WAS FED UP with "pinheaded environmental overkill" so she set out to circumvent the coastal zone management plan adopted during the Evans administration. She vetoed a bill that would have banned a supertanker hub at Cherry Point just north of Bellingham. From there, oil from Alaska's booming North Slope would be piped to the Midwest. Magnuson believed that could spell catastrophe for Puget Sound. What happened next was "the political equivalent of the *Exxon Valdez* crashing into a reef ...," wrote Shelby Scates, the senator's biographer.[35]

Maggie, his resourceful aides and a bipartisan coalition of Washington State congressmen quietly greased the skids for a rider on a routine bill reauthorizing Magnuson's Marine Mammal Protection Act. On October 4, 1977, Magnuson offered a "little amendment" prohibiting supertanker traffic east of Port Angeles. Twenty-four hours later, the amended bill was headed for President Carter's desk. Livid, Dixy accused Magnuson of "being a dictator."[36] He had a name for her too: "Madame Zonga" because she reminded him of the tattooed lady on bawdy First Avenue when he was a young prosecutor.[37]

"Crossing swords with Maggie was a fatal political error," Spellman says, compounded by her decision to portray the 72-year-old senator as moribund, literally and politically. Spellman had to agree with the governor on one point, though. While Cherry Point was off the table, Northern Tier, a consortium that included Getty Oil, U.S. Steel and Burlington Northern, was still proposing an oil port at Port Angeles. Getting the oil from there to Midwestern refineries would be another story. "The environmental impact of 450 miles of pipeline across this state ... has not begun to be laid before the public," Dixy said.[38]

CHAPTER TWENTY-FOUR

Fully Justified

There was an important piece of unfinished business. The trial over the dueling Kingdome lawsuits had been set to begin just before the 1977 Primary Election. Stuart Oles, the attorney for the Donald M. Drake Company, won a delay, arguing that Spellman's bid for re-election might taint the proceedings. U.S. District Court Judge Morell E. "Mo" Sharp may have taken silent umbrage, since he would be hearing the case without a jury. Sharp rescheduled opening arguments for November 28.

Oles and Bill Dwyer, the county's lead attorney, sparred for 72 days over the next six months. It was a high-stakes match, especially for Spellman. Hoppe predicted the county would lose and end up in a financial pickle.

Oles was a tall man with a booming voice. Cocksure was the adjective that popped into Spellman's mind as the trial got under way. "Oles was a tough-minded conservative and a talented lawyer. I knew him well. We were confident, however, that he had overplayed his hand by convincing Drake and its insurance companies he would win. Dwyer, by comparison, seemed brilliantly well-prepared, calm and likable." The handsome outdoorsman was an author, art collector and actor, fond of quoting Shakespeare. If all the world's a stage, a trial with national implications is a lawyer's Broadway. Dwyer's famous 1964 libel-case victory for John Goldmark, the former state legislator smeared as a communist, was followed by his perfect game against the American League, a decision that brought the Mariners to Seattle. "I took a lot of flak over our legal fees, but hiring Dwyer was money well spent," Spellman says.* Norm Maleng, who played an important role in developing the county's case, also had a lot riding on the outcome. He hoped to succeed Chris Bayley as prosecutor.

---

*Dwyer's fee was $60 per hour, 20 percent less than his firm usually charged for his services. In all, the county's legal and consultant expenses amounted to $1.4 million before it was over, some $400,000 of that to Dwyer's firm.[1]

KING COUNTY sought damages totaling about $13 million for Drake's alleged breach of contract in walking off the job that gray November day three years earlier. The Portland firm counterclaimed for approximately $12 million, charging that the county compounded the soaring cost of materials and labor with hundreds of design changes.

"Almost from the first day," Dwyer told the court, "it became apparent that Drake would not, or could not, do things on time. Work started off on a poorly organized basis and stayed poorly organized." Some of the subcontractors performed badly, but that was Drake's problem, not the county's. The county and the stadium design team "went out of their way to try to help." By then, however, Drake had self-induced cash-flow problems. The contractor made things worse by replacing its project superintendent with a man who had never before overseen a major project. Then, as a way out, Dwyer said, Drake attempted to coerce King County into a cost-plus contract by threatening to halt work. At high noon, Spellman had called their bluff.[2]

Bob Sowder, a member of the stadium design team, used a 2½-foot model of the Kingdome to show the judge the technical aspects of its design, including the dome segments Drake said wouldn't safely separate from their supports, the famous falsework raised or lowered by sand jacks. Over Oles' strenuous objections, a consultant hired by the county to analyze the project was allowed to testify that the plans issued to Drake and other bidders in 1972 were sufficient for accurate cost estimates. If it had had its act together, Drake should have been able to turn a profit, the consultant said. He admitted, however, that he was no expert on construction project scheduling. Such "hearsay" from a man who'd been paid more than $300,000 by the county was hardly credible, Oles told the judge.[3] He called to the stand Drake's former project engineer, who told of exasperating delays in the arrival of materials as a result of design changes.[4]

In January, at Judge Sharp's urging, Spellman and Franklin Drake, president of the company, met for the first time in three years to explore an out-of-court settlement. "He was a pleasant man. I liked him, but he was backed into a corner," Spellman says, "and we were confident."

When the trial resumed, Dwyer called Henry Dean, an attorney for the design team. With the project falling farther behind schedule, Dean said the contractor asked for a letter in the fall of 1974 outlining how to handle its problems with the roof. But the instructions were already "crystal clear." And the wording they wanted would have resulted in the county accepting responsibility. A reasonable claim for more money might be entertained, the designers told Drake. A request for $10.5 million was "preposterous."[5]

Franklin Drake was incensed by the county's refusal to make a deal, according to John Skilling, senior partner in the structural-engineering firm for the Kingdome. After a tense meeting with Spellman, Skilling and others, Drake threatened to have Oles call a press conference and embarrass the county. He warned that Oles was a "political-action expert," Skilling testified.[6]

Spellman took the witness stand on February 23, 1978. He acknowledged that the county's $30 million budget for the Kingdome was "on the razor's edge." He conceded, too, that there'd been "tremendous inflation" in the construction industry between 1968 when the voters approved the Forward Thrust project and 1973 when work got under way in earnest. He "assumed" that Drake, an experienced contractor, knew what it was doing when it submitted the winning bid of $29.6 million. Spellman denied that eleventh-hour talks with Franklin Drake in 1974 had produced a tentative agreement. What Drake wanted would have amounted to "a total capitulation on the county's part"—an admission that the county and its design team were responsible for the roof problem. "I didn't even come close to such an agreement."[7]

With that, King County rested its case.

Oles relished his turn "to present the facts." He said there'd been a lot of talk about breach of contract by Drake, when in truth it was the county that did the breaching. The county made more than a thousand design changes, driving up construction costs by several million dollars, yet it paid "not a nickel" in compensation. The towering falsework for the dome was "grossly incapable of performing the function for which it was designed." So ham-handed was the design team that it "even overlooked" the city's building codes. As for the assertion that Drake "demanded" a new contract from the county, it was Spellman who "agreed unequivocably" to a plan that would cover Drake's actual construction costs, then reneged. Jerry Schlatter, the county's project manager, had deliberately delayed granting Drake deadline extensions and extra payments, all part of the county's strategy. They were "holding a hammer" over Drake's head, Oles asserted.[8]

Franklin Drake testified that Spellman assured him the county would cover the company's actual construction costs and a reasonable profit, based on an audit of the company's books. Two days later, Spellman offered only $1.5 million to finish the project. "This was a 180-degree turnaround. ... I was flabbergasted by the turn of events."[9]

Spellman sat silently, but couldn't believe his ears.

June finally brought final arguments. Dwyer said Drake blew it, then "decided to go for broke" with a "campaign of threats, walk-offs and shut-downs." Oles cited "gross and grievous errors" in the roof design—problems the county attempted to cover up. "The contractor never lost the capacity to finish this project. The county did. ... Now the financial life of my client is at stake."[10]

ON JULY 7, 1978, it was the Fourth of July all over again for King County. In a strong, clear voice, Judge Sharp read his decision to a crowded courtroom. It was notable for its lack of flatulent legalese. Sharp minced few words. Spellman's decision to fire the contractor and seek new bids was "fully justified." The county executive had "no reasonable alternative." Drake's abandonment of the project at a crucial stage with winter at hand was "deliberate, intentional and inexcusable." [11] Although the county and its design team were responsible for some of the roof problems, "It is further my opinion that the so-called falsework decentering problem was not the real issue between the parties." It never presented "an unusual or unreasonable

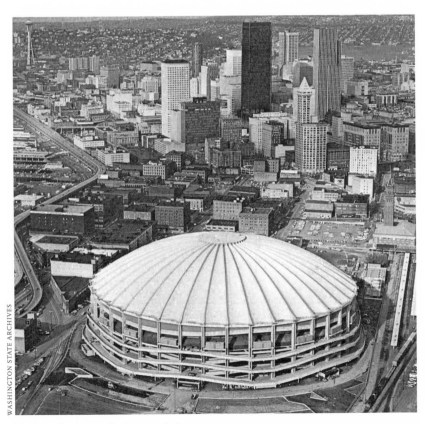

The Kingdome just after its completion.

safety or engineering problem" and "provided no justification whatsoever for abandoning the job." Drake had seized on the issue "as a lever to obtain county acquiescence with its cost-plus demands. ...The real issue all along was money. ...Suffice it to say, in my opinion, in the middle of the summer of 1974, Drake became aware that it faced a huge financial loss if it completed the job under its contract." It proceeded to wage "a deliberate public campaign to upset the lump-sum" deal it had agreed to. "County officials, mindful of the fact that they were in a position of public trust, fiduciaries of the people's bond issue, did everything they reasonably could to keep Drake on the job and satisfy its demands." [12]

The insurance company defendants that bonded the contractor were in "no sounder position than Drake," having fully supported the contractor's position despite being given "ample and timely notice and opportunity to take over the job." Their claim that they had been awaiting further notification as the walkout loomed "borders on the ridiculous," the judge said. "No, they made their decision. They must live with it." [13] Sharp ordered the defendants to pay King County $12.2 million in damages, including interest dating to 1974.

Spellman pronounced it "a complete and satisfying victory for the people of King County." He packed his pipe with a fresh fill and smiled broadly as reporters gathered round. The award was slightly less than the county had sought but "more than enough" to offset the loan, already re-paid, that he secured to complete the stadium.[14] The decision had national ramifications, Spellman said, because it affirmed the validity of competitive bidding and the right of governments to stand by fixed-fee contracts. The judge was saying, "You don't have to automatically cave in to the demands of contractors for more money." [15] In New Orleans, he noted, the Superdome had been a veritable cost-plus Mardi Gras for contractors.

DIXY'S APPROVAL RATINGS were tanking. Independent polls said Spellman would win a rematch. The cloud over his head was gone. Was he ready to announce his candidacy for governor in 1980? He tap-danced. "I have just been elected to a third term as county executive. I am not running for anything else." A few seconds later, he added a qualifier: Another office was "always" worth considering.[16] Spellman was more candid with Lyle Burt, who covered the Capitol for *The Seattle Times*: "I would still like to be governor. I haven't ruled it out. ... I just don't want to have people judge my programs on the basis of whether they are good for my political future. ... My wife is certainly not anxious for me to take on a new campaign. But there are people interested in my running. I talk to them." [17]

As Spellman was being hailed for "hanging tough," Franklin Drake issued a terse statement: "We strongly believe the court erred. We will appeal and are confident that we will ultimately prevail." [18]

Ultimately, the Travelers Insurance Company cut its losses. In the summer of 1980, without consulting Oles, it settled out of court for $12.8 million, a half-million dollars more than Judge Sharp had awarded, due to accrued interest. "Had I been asked," Oles fumed, "I would have recommended most vigorously against such a settlement. ... We had every confidence that on appeal" the judgment would have been reversed. A spokesman for Travelers had a narrower definition of "we": "His client isn't going to be settling this claim—we are." [19]

CHAPTER TWENTY-FIVE

You Win Some,
You Lose Some

Spellman's final three years as county executive sped by in a blur. While he kept one eye on Olympia, his partner in the push for land-use reforms and merging Metro with county government departed for the other Washington.

"If I lose will you give me a job?" County Councilman Mike Lowry said, less than half-jokingly. "Of course," Spellman said, meaning it. Lowry didn't lose. After 22 eventful months at the Courthouse, he defeated Jack Cunningham, a movement conservative, in a bare-knuckle 1978 campaign for the 7th District seat in Congress. Cunningham's election had been an aberration in a heavily Democratic district. Lowry was in Congress to stay for the next 10 years. "Early on I was a mentor to Mike. Then he became something of mentor to me. I was sorry to see him go," Spellman says, "but the goals remained the same."

The greening of John Spellman continued apace.

The same election elevated Norm Maleng, Spellman's counsel and friend, to county prosecutor. In Bob Bratton as deputy executive Spellman had a decisive, loyal, detail man. A trio of versatile young aides, Pat Dunn, Pete Shepherd and Shani Taha, a Smith College graduate who had worked for Henry Kissinger (she was brainy, beautiful and black), were Spellman's eyes and ears on a panoply of issues: recycling, herbicide spraying, farm-lands preservation, drug-treatment programs, a new jail, Enhanced 911 and federal assistance for low-income housing.

After months of delicate negotiations with the county's Superior Court judges, Spellman won County Council approval for a new Department of Youth Services. Juvenile detention and probation, overseen by the formidable, chain-smoking Edna Goodrich, were now in the executive branch. Goodrich, the first female superintendent of a Washington state prison, shared Spellman's passion for rehabilitation programs.

The Affirmative Action office was in the same fourth-floor suite as

Spellman and his staff. That too sent a message. The new Office of Agriculture, headed by Tom Ryan, was in charge of the farmlands preservation pilot program. There were now eight agricultural district advisory committees. Jack Lynch oversaw Planning and Community Development. Karen Rahm, the 33-year-old director of Seattle's Office of Economic Development, was recruited to manage the planning division. Jim Guenther, a Clark County administrator with a "sensitivity to the challenges of urban growth," replaced Jean DeSpain, the Public Works director who'd been on the hot seat over the Forward Thrust road funds.[1]

Sometimes there was no substitute for experience. Mary Ellen McCaffree was named director of the Department of Budget and Program Development. The veteran former legislator had overseen the State Department of Revenue during the last three years of the Evans administration. McCaffree and John Rose, the multi-talented budget manager, had their work cut out. Federal revenue-sharing funds were declining, inflation and interest rates escalating. The exodus from Seattle to the suburbs continued. Boeing, biopharmaceutical firms and fledgling computer software developers drew talented engineers and scientists from around the world. "In three short years, the average price of a single-family home outside the city more than doubled to $72,200 in 1980." Despite a slowdown in home building, subdivisions were still consuming dairy farms, horse pastures and woodlots.[2]

The growth-management strategy Spellman and Lowry developed focused on preserving productive farmlands. Regional planners had warned since early in the decade that the land base needed to sustain a viable agricultural economy was being eroded by panzer divisions of bulldozers.[3] Spellman and Lynch were roundly denounced when the county denied permits for a 120-acre shopping center between Bellevue and Redmond.

A consultant told the County Council that Spellman's first-steps plan to preserve 17,000 to 23,000 acres had the added advantage of boosting gross farm income by as much as $6 million annually. The biggest gains would be in the dairy industry, which accounted for 90 percent of all farmland in King County. If farmers were insulated from development pressures, the plan could lead to 5,000 more acres being used for milk production and considerable savings for consumers.[4]

The County Council adopted an 18-month moratorium on development of agricultural land. The Office of Agriculture and the Agricultural District Advisory Commission mobilized to develop a bond issue to purchase development rights. It went on the ballot in the fall of 1978.

Scott Wallace, the personable dairyman Spellman defeated to win election as a county commissioner 12 years earlier, enthusiastically joined Jim Ellis on the Save Our Local Farmlands Committee. With the indefatigable Ellis as chairman, they raised $50,000 for a campaign that featured hundreds of volunteers. Pat Dunn, Spellman's liaison to the campaign, donned a carrot costume for one rally and, together with an ear of corn, handed out decals that declared "Give peas a chance!" Wallace's standing as a longtime farm-group leader added important credibility to the effort. He and Spellman teamed up for several events, while Mayor Royer and Spellman made a joint appeal for the $35 million proposal. It was vociferously opposed by developers and Realtors despite repeated assurances that the program would be voluntary.[5] "If this bond issue passes, it will represent one more element in the ever-increasing encroachment of government into our private lives," one critic warned.[6]

Out of nearly 300,000 cast, the proposal fell 678 votes short of the required 60 percent supermajority. A revised $50 million plan that made its voluntary nature even more explicit was supported by 77 percent of the voters in the 1979 primary. This time it ran afoul of a turnout validation clause. Spellman, Ellis and Wallace urged the council to place the proposal on the November ballot. "The support for this is greater than any issue I've ever been involved in," even Metro and Forward Thrust, Ellis said.[7] "L.A. is suffering the worst smog in that area's history, and the reason is wall-to-wall asphalt. ...Do we want that here?"[8]

The third try, boosted by even more doorbelling and leafleting vegetables, produced a resounding victory. "It is a significant national landmark," Spellman said, hailing "an army of amazing volunteers." For the first time in American history voters had approved taxing themselves to preserve agricultural land and open spaces.[9]* "People tend to take it in stride when government does something," Ellis said, "but when voters take it on themselves to do a job, that gets attention. This vote may be the first step in a national revolution in the way people view our ever-diminishing agricultural resources."[10]

KING COUNTY VOTERS in that election also strongly supported expanding the county version of Seattle's nationally famous Medic 1 program. What they weren't buying was the consolidation of Metro and King County government. On this one, Spellman found himself in league with Labor

---

* There was yet another hitch: Prevailing interest rates on bonds were far higher than the 8 percent ceiling stipulated by county statute. When the County Council upped the limit, opponents blocked the move with a successful lawsuit. The council issued bonds in 1982 to begin protecting farmlands from development.[12]

Council leader Jim Bender and County Democratic chairwoman Karen Marchioro and at odds with Ellis.

When Lowry and Spellman set out to win merger-enabling legislation from the Legislature, Ellis called it "a transparent power play."[11] He recruited a host of allies, including the Seattle City Council, suburban mayors and the Municipal League. A truce ensued. Spellman agreed with Ellis that the issue ought to be decided by the voters. Lowry went along, grudgingly. He feared the merger could be "killed forever" by a referendum.[13] The County Council was also divided on the proposed merger. Councilman Bill Reams said Metro seemed chastened by the debate. "I've seen some changes. However, if this goes to the voters and gets massacred, then the (Metro) staff might feel it has a mandate to return to operating somewhat autonomously. That would be bad."[14]

Governor Ray thought long and hard before signing the bill. There was "a little question about people's political ambitions and interests," she admitted, loathe to do anything that might help Spellman.[15] The dogfight was on. City councilmen who served on the 37-member Metro Council complained "this was no merger ... but rather the county's bold-faced attempt to take over Metro's $158 million budget, 2,400 employees and critical transit and sewer functions."[16]

Bender chalked it up to "pure jealously" at City Hall and "the ego trips of a group of suburban mayors." Not that he was making a wholesale endorsement of Spellman and the County Council. "They may be lightweights, but at least the voters can recall them," the labor leader said.[17]

John Miller, president of the Seattle City Council, and County Councilman Paul Barden, a leading proponent of the merger, went nose to nose at one meeting. Miller said his council and its constituents had no confidence that county government would "look after the interest of Seattle citizens." "Why don't you level with us?" Barden retorted. "You are opposed to the concept of one man, one vote in the representation on the Metro Council, and that's because you have disproportionate control and don't want to lose it."[18]

Spellman said Metro unquestionably was a landmark in county history. "Having grown up on the shores of Lake Washington," he said he knew first-hand that Metro had "saved a jewel." But managing rapid growth required less bureaucracy and more efficiency, as opposed to "two separate, large, entrenched area-wide governmental units competing and duplicating." Further, Spellman said, the composition of the Metro Council short-sheeted rural taxpayers. "Institutional pride" shouldn't stand in the way of achieving area-wide solutions.[19]

Ellis and Spellman remained good friends, agreeing to disagree on this one. Ellis was confident that voter skepticism and the shining image of the utility he had worked so hard to establish two decades earlier would derail a merger. The proposal was crushed, three-to-one.*

KING COUNTY'S HOPES of landing $35 million in state funds for badly needed jail improvements ran afoul of the governor, who said a full-scale study by the Office of Financial Management was a prerequisite. "I think Spellman jumped to a conclusion," she said at her weekly press conference. "Just because the state is underwriting the bill does not mean that it is open season to public funds for just anything that any group wants." [20] In answer to a reporter's question on another topic making headlines, the governor said she wasn't worried about escalating cost overruns at the nuclear power plants under construction at Satsop just west of Elma in Grays Harbor County. They weren't out of line "compared with today's prices." Washington Public Power Supply System managers had things well under control, she said. [21]

If the Spellmans—Lois was John's most trusted political adviser—had any lingering doubts about a second bid for governor, Dixy Lee Ray was doing her best to dispel them. John was confident he could beat her and eager for the challenge. Fundraising accelerated in the spring of 1979. County commissioners from around the state, Democrat and Republican, were among those encouraging him to run again. No county commissioner had ever been elected governor. Spellman had moved through the chairs to become first vice president of the National Association of Counties. After losing the governor's race, his involvement with NACo was the tonic he needed, friends recall. Pat Dunn in tow, Spellman went from delegation to delegation at the group's 1977 national convention in Detroit, campaigning for fourth vice president. He won the endorsement of the California and New York delegations, largely composed of Democrats or Rockefeller Republicans. Farm belt states like Iowa gave him their votes, too. He lost narrowly to a conservative from Texas. The next year he was elected without opposition by delegates who wore buttons that said "John Spellman: Leadership for the 80's." The leftover pins would come in handy.

---

* Bill Dwyer, who altered Washington state history as a judge as well as a trial attorney, was newly appointed to the Federal District Court bench in 1990 when Metro arrived on his docket. The linchpin was a U.S. Supreme Court case decided on the principle of "one man, one vote." Dwyer overruled Metro's resistance to a merger, declaring that just because "the buses run on time cannot justify a dilution of any citizen's right to vote." A merger was approved by the voters in 1992. [22]

ALTHOUGH STATE REVENUES remained strong well into 1979, inflation was rampant. State spending increased substantially, siphoning away reserves. Governor Ray's relationship with the Legislature, tenuous from the beginning, had grown more toxic by the month. She regarded John Bagnariol, the Democratic co-speaker of the House, and Gordon Walgren, the Senate majority leader, as hacks and potential rivals. She played a fence-sitting game over full funding for basic education. She was intransigent over energy issues and indifferent to overcrowded jails and prisons. A contentious 2½-month special session heightened the tension. Spring saw President Carter curtail oil imports from Iran in the wake of the Ayatollah Khomeini's rise to theocratic power. Frustrated motorists were soon queued up at service stations.

Against this backdrop of anxiety and infighting, "Governor Ray threatened legal action against House Republicans for failing to enact a budget pursuant to statutory requirements. This did absolutely nothing to help in solving the budget issue. Finally on June 1, 1979, Duane Berentson, the Republican co-speaker, provided the 50th vote to pass a budget ..."[23] The Legislature broke camp with a sense of bipartisan certainty that the governor was on borrowed time.

On September 28, banners for the "John Spellman Committee" went up in an office building in the heart of Seattle's University District.

CHAPTER TWENTY-SIX

A Real Governor

Spellman was practically bouncing on his toes before the press conference began. Dick Schrock, Steve Excell and Jim Waldo, the dexterous young Evans Republican the campaign had recruited, were impressed.

"This state has not had a governor in the real sense of the word for the past three years," he began. "There has been an arrogance, an insensitivity, an attitude that technology knows best, that defies belief. ... This governor has given us a parade of agency directors and staff members that reminds me of a cross between *The Gong Show* and *Saturday Night Live*. I think I've been silent long enough. I gave her a fair chance to show what she could do." [1]

It was November 17, 1979. Spellman seemed to be channeling the boxer of his youth. And this time he was determined not to leave the ring with a broken nose. He was trimmer and "far feistier" than he'd been in his bout with Dixy Lee Ray three years earlier, one reporter told her notepad. [2] Slamming a palm with a fist, Spellman said the state needed a multi-faceted energy policy that respected the environment. Instead "we've got the country's most vocal press agent for the nuclear-contracting industry occupying our state's highest elective office, actively and repeatedly trying to persuade us, against considerable evidence to the contrary, that the only answer lies in a big nuke farm." Geothermal, solar, wind and tidal energy sources merited study, he said. Conservation too. "A real governor would be seeking ways to manage what energy we have, to distribute it wisely and efficiently and to plan for future growth." The state's prisons, meantime, were "another Attica, just waiting for a trigger," Spellman warned. To ease overcrowding, he said he was working with Senator Magnuson on the possibility of leasing the McNeil Island penitentiary from the federal government, yet the Ray appointee at the Department of Social and Health Services had told him to butt out. Real governors were not "petulant and stubborn." [3]

On her watch, Spellman went on, partisan bickering was undermining the state's higher education system, once "the envy of the nation." Frustrated legislators from her own party, notably Jim McDermott, had taken the lead in defining basic education and boosting funding for the public schools. Unfortunately, given the absence of leadership from the governor, they'd said, 'Well, let us take all of this money we've accumulated with inflation and deal with one problem—schools—and let us forget about all the rest of the problems.'" The bow wave from excessive spending was on the horizon, Spellman warned. He called her administration "a rudderless ship of governmental chaos," a "breeding ground for waste, for inefficiency. And it is the citizens, the taxpayers, who pay and who will be paying the price for this chaos for years to come.... She is a total failure as a governor."[4]

As fighting words go, it was the best speech of Spellman's career. He had been rehearsing it for weeks. The campaign's catchphrase—Schrock's handiwork—would be "A Real Governor."

"We got a 'New Spellman' headline above the fold in the Sunday edition of *The Seattle Times*," Schrock remembers, still savoring the moment. "That alone was huge positive exposure coming out of the box, literally and figuratively. Our first mission was accomplished. Spellman had taken a major step to leave the 1976 loss behind him."[5]

Governor Ray was "astonished that anyone would be so foolish as to declare his candidacy this early." Asked for her reaction to Spellman's assertion that the state hadn't had a real governor for three years, she smiled thinly. "I'll give him my phone number and a map to Olympia."[6]

Secretary of State Bruce Chapman and Duane Berentson, co-speaker of the House, were also poised to enter the race for the Republican nomination. For the Democrats, McDermott, Co-Speaker John Bagnariol from

Three GOP candidates for governor in 1980: Duane Berentson, left, and Bruce Chapman, center, listen to Spellman criticize Dixy Lee Ray.

Renton and Booth Gardner, a wealthy Tacoma businessman, were all "sufficiently discouraged with the governor to toy with the idea of challenging her."[7] The growing number of Democrats disillusioned with Dixy worried, however, that even two challengers would allow her to survive the primary.

To shore up her re-election campaign, the governor recruited former Republican strategist C. Montgomery Johnson. Blair Butterworth, who had played a key role in her 1976 victory, was now working for McDermott. The 42-year-old state senator from Seattle's liberal 43rd District was a child psychiatrist by training, a politician by calling.

Bagnariol, a jowly, rumpled 47-year-old insurance broker, was a centrist Democrat who understood the dance of legislation. When it took two to tango, given the unprecedented 49-49 tie in the House, "Baggie" and Berentson emerged as remarkably collegial partners. Party politics aside, they were old pros who genuinely liked one another and shared a distaste for the governor's sour-bellied amateurism.

Gardner, who had served an undistinguished, abbreviated term in the State Senate in the early 1970s, was the dark horse. At 42, he was an enigmatic figure—brilliant, charming and ambitious, yet insecure and conflicted by his inherited wealth. In the 1960s he self-identified as an Evans Republican.

Berentson's biggest problem was name familiarity. The veteran legislator from Skagit County was, at 50, a conservative family man with a gentlemanly style and engaging Scandinavian smile. He prided himself on being a team player. As a jump-shooting guard, he was a star for Anacortes High School in the 1940s and a solid collegiate player on a Pacific Lutheran team Marv Harshman coached to national prominence. Berentson had been a biology teacher and inspirational basketball coach at tiny Burlington-Edison High School before becoming an investment broker.

Chapman, the last player of substance, was only 38, but he'd been immersed in politics since his college days at Harvard. Before Evans appointed him secretary of state in 1975, he'd been a progressive sparkplug on the Seattle City Council, helping lead efforts to save Pioneer Square and the Pike Place Market from Urban Renewal run amok. While Chapman struck many as too intellectual to succeed on the baby-kissing circuit, he was no slouch at zingers, quipping that "the harmless-looking Winnebago Governor Ray drove into Olympia three years ago was actually a Trojan horse. She promised change, change, change and what we got was drift, drift, drift."[8]

MARKED BY GEOLOGICAL and political eruptions of the first magnitude, the next 12 months were among the most eventful in state history. The "misery index"—inflation plus unemployment—that served as a barometer of Jimmy Carter's chances for re-election against Ronald Reagan was also documenting the precipitous decline of Washington State's revenues. Whoever became governor, it was soon clear, would be facing an enormous budget deficit.

On April 2, 1980, as Bagnariol and his friend Gordon Walgren, the gregarious Senate majority leader, were poised to announce their candidacies for governor and attorney general, they were charged with conspiring to legalize gambling in return for a piece of the profits. The intermediaries they'd been meeting with, together with a lobbyist, were undercover FBI agents posing as gambling promoters from California. In one fell swoop, two of Dixy Lee Ray's antagonists, one a potential direct rival, were out of commission, and the State Patrol had been in on the operation. Sid Snyder, the widely respected secretary of the State Senate, smelled a rat. So did Adele Ferguson, the veteran *Bremerton Sun* political columnist. Ray Moore, a plain-talking old senator from Seattle who had radar for what he called "low cunning," also saw Dixy's "pawprints" all over "Gamscam." [9]

Angling for Walgren's support with full knowledge that the sting was under way, the governor had disingenuously offered him Magnuson's seat if the senator should expire or resign due to poor health. And Walgren wasn't the only one. Gummie Johnson acted as her emissary to his college chum, former congressman Brock Adams, who had bailed out of Carter's cabinet. Adams, unlike Walgren, tacitly accepted the unseemly quid pro quo, and "to the utter dismay of his liberal backers," became the nominal chairman of Dixy's re-election campaign. [10] The governor was either too naïve or too headstrong to care whether all this got back to Maggie, as it surely would. Johnson and Adams, without question, should have known better. ("Forget *Saturday Night Live* and *The Gong Show*," Spellman quipped. "I'd like to amend that to a cross between *Let's Make a Deal* and *Truth or Consequences*.") [11] When the scheming filtered back to Magnuson, he said little to his aides. Silently seething, he was also facing the toughest challenge of his long career in the person of Attorney General Slade Gorton. But, dammit, he wasn't dead yet.

Mother Nature provided the next explosion. At 8:32 a.m. on May 18, 1980, Mount St. Helens in southwest Washington erupted with a blast 500 times more powerful than the atomic bomb that leveled Hiroshima. "A cloud of superheated volcanic ash and acidic incandescent gases traveling at nearly 400 miles per hour sped along the ground," killing 57 people, countless creatures and all manner of vegetation. Millions of trees lay strewn like Tinker Toys in the peak's valleys and foothills. [12] The blast clogged lakes, riv-

ers and bays and wiped out highways and bridges. When Carter and Magnuson arrived a few days later to survey the disaster, TV cameras caught the
75-year-old senator stumbling on the stairs as he descended from Air Force
One. Maggie had a diabetic sore foot that wouldn't heal.[13] At the volcano
relief staging area in Cowlitz County, Magnuson exchanged chilly greetings
with the governor. When Carter asked what the government could do to
help, Dixy spelled it out: "M-O-N-E-Y." He turned to Maggie, who just nodded. The old lion secured nearly a billion dollars in emergency relief. Spellman contrasted Magnuson's effectiveness with the state's "weak, politically
oriented" Emergency Services Office under Governor Ray.[14]

WARREN G. MAGNUSON'S first and last palpable hurrahs came 44 years
apart in Grays Harbor County, home to the Siamese-twin timber towns of
Aberdeen and Hoquiam—as reliably Democratic as anyplace in America
since the coming of the New Deal.

In the spring of 1936, "pandemonium prevailed" at the State Democratic Convention in Aberdeen as delegates from the leftist Washington Com-
monwealth Federation clashed with centrist New Dealers over an initiative
that was unvarnished socialism.[15] Magnuson, King County's swashbuckling
young prosecutor, broke two gavels and lost his voice after a 16-hour stretch
at the podium, repeatedly yelling "Sit down and shut up!" When he was
named permanent convention chairman at 3 a.m. he relinquished the gavel
to Lieutenant Governor Vic Meyers and went looking for cough drops or a
stiffer elixir, according to contemporary newspaper accounts.[16] In truth, he
was holed up in a hotel room, brokering a rhetorical comprise that patched
up the party.*

On June 14, 1980, sign-waving McDermott delegates had a huge majority as 1,400 Democrats packed the new Hoquiam High School Gymnasium
for their state convention. The governor and Scoop Jackson were side by
side on the platform, together with Mrs. Magnuson and Lieutenant Governor Cherberg, as Magnuson addressed the rapt crowd.

> He told a new generation of Democrats about the fisticuffs and
> fire hoses that marked the knock-down, drag-out 1936 party conven-
> tion in Aberdeen. It was vintage Maggie and everyone was pleased,
> including Governor Ray. Her smile began to wilt and delegates began
> to squirm when Maggie paused, smiled and started, "This state is

---

*That fall, Magnuson, only 31, was elected to Congress. The initiative calling for socialized medicine
and state-owned factories, farms and banks was defeated three to one.

not going to be a dumping ground for nuclear waste and there are not going to be any supertankers on Puget Sound. Little monkeys in trees have thrown coconuts at me from time to time. I've even been called a dictator!" A wild cheer interrupted. Ray's face went red. She turned to talk to Scoop Jackson, himself looking uncomfortable.[17]

"Now, one more thing," Magnuson said. "While I've been back in Washington working on problems of the state and nation, I hear that some have been bartering my job. Well, I want to tell the governor and any future governor there ain't gonna be no vacancy in the U.S. Senate!"[18] A joyous, full-throated, fighting roar reverberated to the rafters as delegates sprang out of their seats, bobbing their Magnuson and McDermott signs in a swirling sea of blue balloons and confetti. Scoop was hoisting Maggie's arm. The old prize fighter was the winner by TKO on all cards and still champion, for a while at least. "I don't have to put up with this!" the governor hissed as she fled the platform and escaped through a side door, reporters and photographers in pursuit. "I'm late for an appointment." She hopped into a state car that sped away.[19]

Next up was a jubilant McDermott, who declared, "I am a Democrat of conviction, not convenience," proud to share a platform with "giants" like Magnuson and Jackson. "Maggie has been a senator we've always been proud of, and we should begin the new decade with a governor we can be proud of *again* ... not Gummie Johnson's current client!"[20]

McDermott left Hoquiam on a roll, with the de facto endorsement of his party. The "M&M ticket" was born.

"Hoquiam was some show, but we still thought Dixy had enough of a

Scoop declares Maggie still champion as Governor Ray glowers in the background before bolting the Hoquiam High School Gymnasium.

base to survive the primary," Steve Excell remembers. "Spellman and Berentson were just licking their chops to take her on in the general because she was so controversial. She was our Jesse Ventura before anyone had ever heard of Jesse Ventura, and her own worst enemy. In the final analysis, everyone was running against Dixy." [21] Schrock says, "It was a very tough three-way primary, but Dixy was still *the* issue." [22]

Schrock and John Brown, the brilliant Seattle ad man who sold a lot of shoes for Nike and acres of clams for Ivar Haglund, collaborated on Spellman's first round of TV spots. In one, the camera pans an array of actual front-page headlines, including "Ray angrily stalks out of Democratic Convention." The noise in the background is the rata-tat-tat of a wire service teletype. Voice over: "You've seen the headlines. You're read the embarrassing stories. And deep down you know we've got problems in Olympia. Well, now's your chance to change all that. This time let's elect a real governor for a change—*John Spellman*." A week later, a model of the state Capitol literally blew its dome. Flames and lava burped out and the same Walter-Winchellesque announcer recited a litany of bad news: "February 1980: Governor Ray tells an elected official one of his voters can go to hell! April 1980: Governor Ray admits she offered to trade a legislator a high political office for favors. May 1980: Governor Ray's budget office admits our state may face up to a billion-dollar deficit. We've had a lot of eruptions in Olympia in the past four years but no real governor. Elect John Spellman and we'll have a governor who will work with people instead of against them." [23]

"They were amazing commercials, especially for an era before computer-generated graphics came into their own," Excell says. "We were killing her. The way things turned out, we would have done better to keep her on life support." [24]

ADELE FERGUSON, who wrote in 1976 that Spellman had all the appeal of "a mashed potato sandwich," covered a Republican spring smorgasbord and was impressed to discover he had become a reasonable facsimile of *pomme frites*: "Not only did he let his hair go natural ... but he dropped some poundage and quit wearing his father's old suits. Somewhere along the line he got rid of the pipe, thank the Lord, and fired up his speaking style. There was a marked contrast between him and the other two Republicans. Chapman was reserved and scholarly.... Berentson has always suffered from a tendency to hesitate at making definitive statements. If the crowd had voted that night, I think Spellman would have won hands down." [25]

Chapman's candidacy never caught fire, especially in the fundraising race. In terms of GOP factional passions, he was straddling the conservative and moderate wings, while the media styled him as an Evans liberal. Berentson had all the right stuff. Positioning himself as "the real conservative in the field," he received a rousing reception at the state convention, campaigned his heart out down the stretch and nearly dashed Spellman's hopes of ever becoming governor.[26]

Berentson's consultant was the nationally known GOP strategist Paul Newman, who was also the image engineer for Slade Gorton's flawless campaign to elect "Washington's next great senator." The strategy now was to contrast Spellman's zero legislative experience with Berentson's 18 years. They said he knew little of the workaday world beyond King County. While Berentson had all but closed his investment office to run for governor, "John Spellman has been running for five years at King County taxpayers' expense. I think if he was in earnest and was confident he could win ... he ought to resign his present office and campaign full time," Berentson said. Spellman said he was spending "a reasonable amount of time" in the office and staying in close touch with his staff and department heads. "I'm literally on call 24 hours a day, every day."[27] On the hustings, the biggest philosophical difference between the two was that Spellman was more leery of the hazards and expense of nuclear power. Everyone *was* running against Dixy. Gummie Johnson called it an "un-election." He said he'd never seen anything like it.[28] Butterworth, who helped her defeat the "big boys" four years earlier, was now one of them. "McDermott," a barrage of ads declared, "is the primary choice." Every poll confirmed his steady rise. The consensus was that it was now too close to call. Butterworth predicted victory "by 18,000 votes!"[29]

On September 16, 1980, McDermott outpolled a sitting governor by 87,000 votes to seize the Democratic nomination. The Republican crossover vote to ensure Dixy's defeat nearly sank Spellman right then and there. He bested Berentson by only 7,702 votes out of nearly a million cast, or about one vote per precinct. Chapman was a distant fifth overall.* Berentson carried nine counties outright, including much of Eastern Washington, and finished ahead of Spellman in 12 others. Spellman's 27,500-vote margin

---

* In all, 71 percent of those who voted for McDermott did so because they wanted to be rid of Governor Ray, according to a poll for *The Seattle Times*; 58 percent cited dumping Dixy as their *only* reason for voting for him. The undecideds, together with the crossovers, broke McDermott's way heavily down the stretch. Thirty-five percent of those who had named Chapman as their favorite candidate in an earlier poll jumped ship to McDermott. Spellman lost 33 percent of his base. Those who preferred Berentson were the most loyal. Only 21 percent deserted the Skagit County conservative, hoping to ensure they wouldn't have Dixy to kick around anymore. In 1980, as in 1976, if a "Top Two" primary had been in place, the finalists for governor would have been two Democrats—McDermott and Ray.[30]

in King County saved the day. Absent Chapman, "I think we'd have probably won it," Berentson said years later. "Gamscam" likely hurt him as well,
he said, since he and Bagnariol were co-speakers and Dixy's spokespeople
"implied several times ... that we were all a batch of thieves...."[31]

Berentson swallowed his disappointment, conceded gracefully and
endorsed Spellman. Chapman quickly came aboard, too. But the Spellman
campaign, fractured by anxiety and second-guessing, was scrambling to
regroup. "The morning after the primary, I told Lois I wasn't sure we had
won anything other than seven additional weeks of hard work," Spellman
remembers. "The first head-to-head poll had McDermott with a 26-point
lead." It felt like déjà vu all over again. In 1976 Spellman was primed to
run against Uhlman, only to end up getting dumped by Dixy, "the consummate non-politician in the Year of the Non-Politician."[32] Now there'd be no
rematch. McDermott was the new giant killer. "And we probably helped
nominate him," Waldo said.[33] "It was a surprise," Excell agreed, "... and we
agonized."[34] "Suddenly, four years of anti-Dixy research, four years of Dixy
zingers, all the ads, and the accumulated animus were wiped out."[35]

"I didn't think McDermott had a chance in hell of beating Dixy," said
Ron Dotzauer, the Democratic nominee for secretary of state. "But I'm sure
glad he did. Frankly, it would have been tough to run with Dixy at the head
of the ticket." McDermott had given every Democrat on the ballot a booster
shot, the quotable young Clark County auditor said, adding that Spellman's
problem was figuring out how to "turn that momentum around" in the
space of less than two months.[36]

CHAPTER TWENTY-SEVEN

McDermott
is the Question

Dick Schrock, Spellman's longtime campaign strategist, media adviser and friend, was the first casualty of the fallout from the near-debacle in the primary. His intensity grated on many campaign staffers. Steve Excell, Schrock's protégé, tried to smooth things over, saying everyone just needed more sleep. When several aides put their "him-or-us" grievances in writing, Spellman "regretfully concluded it would be best for Dick to leave the team." Lois Spellman was also a Schrock fan, which made the parting more painful. The news that he had stepped down over differences he called "irreconcilable" broke right after the primary, confirming rumors that the Spellman campaign was in disarray.[1] Blair Butterworth, who admired Schrock, surely figured Spellman's loss was his candidate's gain. McDermott was riding high, campaigning with Magnuson and President Carter.* Democrats up and down the ballot were now reaching for McDermott's coattails.

"Our job is to unsurge the surge," Spellman said.[2] "We were at a crossroads," Excell remembers. "We needed outside advice and a quick transfusion of money to buy it." Howard S. Wright, the construction company owner, and Hunter Simpson, president of Physio-Control, a medical electronics firm, were among the major donors who funded a $25,000 poll on how the candidates were perceived. "We called them 'The Magnificent Seven,' and we might have been dead in the water without them," Excell says, "because the survey told us everything we needed to know."[4]

Asked, "Have you ever heard of John Spellman?" 98 percent said yes. Ditto for McDermott. Next came an open-ended question: "What can you tell me about John Spellman?" Smokes a pipe. Built the Kingdome. King

---

* As it became increasingly clear that identifying with Carter could cost McDermott votes, the campaign downplayed the "M&M's and Peanuts" slogan that popped up after the primary. One McDermott staffer would refer to the embattled president as "the tar baby in this race."[3]

County executive. Moderate Republican. Family Man. Silver hair. They knew a lot about John Spellman. However, the only thing they knew about Jim McDermott was this: "He beat Dixy." What pollsters call the "push" questions—If you knew this or that what would you think?—produced real grist for the campaign. "What's your general impression of psychiatrists—very positive, somewhat positive, somewhat negative or very negative?" It was "very negative," says Excell. "Their general impression of candidates from Seattle was also negative. So if you put it together—'Would you be more likely or less likely to vote for Jim McDermott if you knew he was a Seattle liberal?'—Down he goes! 'Would you be more likely or less likely to vote for Jim McDermott if you knew he was a psychiatrist?' Down he goes!"[5]

Excell, the Pritchard brothers and Jim Waldo, the campaign's chairman, met with Spellman's inventive ad man, John Brown, to review the survey data. Joel Pritchard, whose nice guy image belied his instinct for the jugular, nailed it: "Well, just put it all together. All you need to do is tell everyone in the state that he's a liberal Seattle psychiatrist. You'll win." [6]

The shoe fit, and they were going to make him wear it. In politics and image, McDermott was Kennedyesque (think Ted), a tall, handsome Irishman, with a winning smile and thick, wavy hair that spilled over his forehead. Smart, stubborn, proud to be a liberal, McDermott would have been equally at home in Massachusetts. Seattle liberals loved him. Eastern Washington was another story. In Colfax and Ritzville, even Spokane, men in particular believed there was something effete about seeing a

A flier from the 1980 Spellman campaign

psychiatrist—the couch and all that. Lunch-bucket communities around the state had the same prejudice, the survey found. Moreover, they saw Seattleites as uppity. Nor were they impressed by McDermott's radio ads featuring actor Robert Redford, an environmental activist.

When Spellman's strategists reassembled in Brown's office a few days later, Brown had a mock-up of the first ad facing backward on the rail of a whiteboard. Then, *voilà*, he flipped it around. "McDermott is the question," it said. "Spellman is the answer."

"Conventional wisdom is that you never mention your opponent's name," Brown says, "but when you're 26 points behind with seven weeks to go you can throw conventional wisdom out the door. It turned out to be a pivotal moment in that campaign. But 'McDermott is the question' was just the tag line. The bigger question was crucial: 'Do you want a liberal psychiatrist running your state?' "[7]

"It was like, 'OK, the discussion is over. That's it,' " Excell remembers. "Brown was so confident it was a winner that he already had mockups of a whole array of material with that theme—newspaper ads, posters, brochures, bus cards. The whole ad campaign was basically striking that difference on what kind of guy you wanted as your governor."[8]

McDERMOTT WAS CONFIDENT of his lead and his skills as a debater. He was invariably well prepared, forceful and fast on his feet. He agreed to three debates. As the frontrunner, he should have known better. Spellman was determined not to repeat the mistakes he'd made four years earlier when Dixy ambushed him with her zingers. He reprised the painstaking preparation of his days as a moot court champion at Georgetown and holed up for days with a stack of opposition-research binders. Excell and two other researchers, Dennis Michaels and Pam Calvert, had written the book on McDermott's every public utterance since 1970 when he was first elected to the Legislature. The team took turns tossing him the fastballs, curves· and sinkers he could expect from McDermott: Why had he supported Evans' income-tax proposals—*twice*? Why was the King County budget up 151 percent on his watch? What would he do about the relentlessly escalating cost of the WPPSS nuclear-power plants? Spellman was ready. No more Mr. Nice Guy, either.

Eastern Washington was crucial. Pat Dunn got that assignment. He moved to Spokane for the duration, with a room in the then-decrepit Davenport Hotel as his ex-officio campaign headquarters. Gurus like the Pritchards and seasoned young pros like Excell, Waldo and Dunn anchored a campaign that otherwise was "an ideological mixed bag," according to former *Post-Intelligencer* reporter Frank Chesley, who signed on as a press aide. There were "some mercenaries, some zealots, young and old, little old ladies, tireless young go-fers, bright ambitious acolytes in their first campaign, a couple of certifiable crazies. And at the center of the anthill was the candidate." In 16 years of campaigning, Spellman had long since lost his political virginity, fighting with crafty characters like Chuck Carroll. But he had never worked this hard—or hit so hard. He wanted to be governor. "Not only was his every day stuffed full, from pre-dawn darkness to late-night collapse, but the pressure was constant to shoehorn in one more fundraiser, one more meeting, one more plant gate, one more interview." 9

Spellman and McDermott addressed the annual meeting of the Spokane Area Chamber of Commerce a week before their first debate. McDermott arrived late, due to airplane problems, which was just as well. He missed most of a "Private Sector" pep assembly, complete with balloons, straw hats, hot dogs and a brass band. Spellman strode to the platform to the strains of "The Battle Hymn of the Republic" and, channeling Ronald Reagan, declared that the business of government is to "preserve and enhance the economic well-being of business. ... And we don't need all those government regulations!" He and McDermott were "diametrically opposed on many key issues," Spellman said, especially taxing and spending. He then uttered a no-new-taxes pledge that would haunt him for the next five years. The qualifier was largely forgotten. While he never said, "Read my lips," neither did he italicize "as a last resort," a variation of what he said on this day to hedge his bets: "... I can tell you the Republican Party and this Republican candidate favor a program of getting by on a balanced budget without using new taxes or income taxes as the first recourse in the solution of our problems." As phrases go, "the first recourse" is a clunker that probably went right over the heads of the 400 business people who interrupted his speech with applause nine times and gave him a standing ovation at the end.10 Nevertheless, he would rue the day.

Spellman departed when McDermott arrived. Told what his opponent had said, McDermott was forceful: "I would not ... try to fool you or the voters of Washington that our state's economic position is so rosy that I could make some blanket promise that if our deficit remains as it is now projected we could escape a possible short-term tax increase. Someone always has to pay the bill, and you have to be honest about that when you run, or nobody will follow your lead when you're governor." The crowd "clapped politely for 17 seconds ... and the band played 'Happy Days Are Here Again.'" 11

THE FIRST DEBATE, before a crowd of 700 at Gonzaga University and a

P-I cartoonist David Horsey's take on the debate.

statewide TV audience, was a free-for-all. The crowd, largely students, was more sympathetic to McDermott but Spellman was on message with a finger-wagging vigor that surprised many and jolted McDermott. "You are a liberal, big-spending Seattle psychiatrist versus a moderate, experienced administrator," Spellman declared. "I'm a sleeves rolled up, very hard-working leader. ... And he has no real experience as a manager." McDermott observed that the King County budget was six times higher than when Spellman first took office, "and he's saying that I'm a big spender." [12]

A day later, Excell exulted over their latest tracking poll. They had peeled eight points off McDermott's lead in the space of a week. Slade Gorton, jogging daily to underscore his vigor, was gaining on Magnuson. Reagan was thought to be in a dead heat with the hapless Carter, burdened with a bleak economy and the ongoing, ignominious U.S. hostage crisis in Iran. Washington Democrats winced when a federal "Gamscam" jury convicted John Bagnariol, Gordon Walgren and lobbyist Patrick Gallagher of racketeering to expand gambling. John Rosellini, Al's son, was an embattled candidate for attorney general, dogged by allegations he improperly borrowed from estate funds entrusted to him. Former speaker William "Big Daddy" Day of Spokane, a legendary Democratic deal-maker, had been busted for soliciting prostitution.

On October 12, readers of the Seattle dailies encountered a large Spellman-for-governor ad that boldly asked, "Do you want a liberal psychiatrist running your state?" The next day, it ran in the Spokane papers with one additional word: "Do you want a liberal *Seattle* psychiatrist running your

Do you want a liberal Seattle psychiatrist running your state?

We have nothing against psychiatrists or Jim McDermott.
He means well. But good intentions aren't enough.
We can't afford someone with little or no experience as our Governor.
McDermott is a part-time legislator with a reputation for doing almost nothing in Olympia except voting for nearly every spending proposal that came along.
He has one of the worst attendance records in Olympia.
But somehow he's managed to arrange for personal contracts with state agencies that will pay him $83,000 for his services as a psychiatrist.
McDermott is a big question mark.
But we *know* John Spellman can do the job. He's been the leader of the second largest political constituency in our state for 12 years.
Since he took office as King County Executive, the County has come from a deficit of $4,000,000 to a surplus of $15,000,000.
He's built roads. Helped create new jobs. Attracted new industry. Promoted new housing. Protected open lands. Added 150 new police officers. Guarded social and health services. And helped create a transportation system second to none.
All *without* adding new taxes over the last decade.
We *know* John Spellman can do the job.
McDermott is another inexperienced doctor who wants to take over Olympia. (Remember what happened the last time we let an inexperienced doctor take over Olympia?)

McDermott is the question.
Spellman is the answer.

This ad ran in the Spokane papers. The same ad, minus the word "Seattle," ran in the Seattle papers.

state?" [italics ours] The politics of polarization had been shrink-wrapped and customized for both sides of the Cascades. The copy below the headline said, "We have nothing against psychiatrists or Jim McDermott. He means well. But good intentions aren't enough. ... We *know* John Spellman can do the job. McDermott is another inexperienced doctor who wants to take over Olympia. (Remember what happened the last time we let an inexperienced doctor take over Olympia?) McDermott is the question. Spellman is the answer." [13] Other ads with the same arresting design said, "Vote for Jim McDermott if you want to pay state income taxes." [14]

John Brown was a genius.

"Negative campaigning was not a tested science in 1980," Excell says. "Everyone says they hate it, but it moves the needle. We now have three decades of irrefutable evidence. You'd better make sure everyone knows who your opponent is because it's a lead-pipe cinch your opponent is going to make sure everybody knows who you are. Brown created one of the most controversial ads in Washington state political history. But all we did was tell the truth about who McDermott was. If John Spellman had been a liberal Seattle psychiatrist, I guarantee you Blair Butterworth would have been all over it." [15]

The waffle seemed like a good idea, too.

It was an Eggo. Excell popped it in the toaster before they left for the second debate at Pacific Lutheran University in suburban Tacoma. When they got to the auditorium, he handed it to Spellman, who placed it in a pocket of a handsome new blue suit, even though it was already getting greasy.

Spellman whipped out the prop at the 30-minute mark to declare that McDermott was a big spender who "waffles on the issues." One day, he tells you "we're going to have to raise taxes," only to back-track the next.

McDermott, oozing disgust, brandished the "liberal psychiatrist" ads. Their message was "innuendo and half truths," he said. It was a "scurrilous" maneuver to "divide people—the east against the west, the rural against the city"—and the ads that ran in Spokane didn't tell people "he lives in Seattle, too!" Moreover, "he has supported an income tax as often as I have." [16]

"The difference is that I'm not supporting one now," Spellman said. "I'm telling you I don't think a tax increase is the best solution. ... I think there are many ways to increase revenues without a tax increase," including wiser investment of funds in the pension system.[17] "Jim drew a pie chart last time and then asked how we'd pay for all those services. I said that I wouldn't bake such a big pie." [18]

They didn't disagree on everything. Both called for creation of a housing finance commission and agreed on the need for alternative energy sources. Spellman advocated a $100 million revenue-bond program to encourage development of new hydro power and a "conservation tax credit" as an incentive for consumers to take energy-saving measures. McDermott advocated a conservation program, coupled with development of cleaner energy sources such as wind turbines. With the state under a federal court order to alleviate prison overcrowding—one inmate was killed and 27 others injured in a riot at Monroe that caused nearly a million dollars' damage—they agreed that the state should acquire the McNeil Island Federal Penitentiary as a stopgap. But Spellman charged that McDermott's early-release plan for nonviolent criminals was inferior to his own plan using half-way houses. When Spellman asserted that he "had a great deal of experience with prisons," he had to join in the laughter. It was one of the few light moments.[19] Who won was debatable. The *Post-Intelligencer* said Spellman seemed "ill at ease" being so aggressive.[20] *The Times* said "the waffle swung both ways," and Spellman had failed to "skewer" the front-runner.[21] Excell knew better. "We could see the needle move every day. Everything was working." [22] When Bill Perry, a resourceful former King County GOP chairman, passed the collection plate, it now came back brimming. Howard Wright's donations included the use of a twin-engine plane and two pilots. The Spellman campaign would raise a record $1.2 million.

With 10 days left, Spellman's people announced the race was dead even. McDermott said he didn't believe it. The polls had been wrong down the stretch in September, he said. Reporters noted the spring in Spellman's step.

Spellman and his retinue arrived at *The Daily World* in Aberdeen precisely on time for a noon brown-bag editorial board meeting. At 12:15, a receptionist sent word that Senator McDermott, whose interview was set for 1, was waiting in the lobby. The editor turned to Spellman. "We have an extra sack lunch. Do you mind if we make this an impromptu debate?" "Fine with me," Spellman said with a shrug. The editor greeted McDermott, who loomed tall and tired. He'd had the flu and too many 18-hour days. "You're early. Spellman's here. Why don't you join us for lunch?" "I'll be back at 1," the senator said frostily. He glared at an aide, turned on his heel and left, taking care to ensure Spellman was gone before he returned. Polls indicated the race was close even in Grays Harbor County, a Democratic stronghold.

After McDermott released a letter from a dozen mental-health professionals, the Spellman campaign withdrew a radio spot featuring a woman who declared she was suspicious of psychiatrists. "It's taken us a long time to bring mental illness out in the open," McDermott said, calling the ads a slur on all mental-health workers. Some Spellman supporters found the ads out of character for a man whose integrity was, in the phrase most commonly uttered by his associates, "above reproach." [23] Spellman brushed aside the criticism. "McDermott's record is relevant. That's what the campaign is about. My job is to give people a clear choice." [24]

THE FINAL DEBATE, "Meet the Press"-style, in Richland with five days remaining, was puttering along anticlimactically until Adele Ferguson, the *Bremerton Sun's* cheeky columnist, asked McDermott about assurances he'd

Jim McDermott eyes his opponent as they appear before the State Building and Construction Trades Council in Seattle a month before the 1980 election.

made to a gay-rights group that if he became governor he wouldn't tolerate discrimination against gays and lesbians in hiring for state jobs: "Are you planning to turn the Evergreen State into the San Francisco of the north?" McDermott seemed sad and indignant all at once. He recalled the "no Irish need apply" signs his ancestors—and Spellman's—encountered when they arrived in America during the potato famine. "In a democracy, there's no place for discrimination and prejudice. ... I intend to make this a state free from prejudice during my administration." [25] Ferguson turned to Spellman, who simply said, "I have a record of 12 years in office with no discrimination." [26] Afterward, he regretted not being as forceful as McDermott.

Two days later, a frustrated McDermott over-reached. Decrying anti-Semitic acts by a fundamentalist church group in Spokane, he said he wasn't saying Spellman encouraged "that sort of thing," but the Republican's campaign ads were "all part of the same thing—when you start playing one group of people off against another group of people..." [27] Spellman called it "hate tactics." [28]

Ted Kennedy arrived in Seattle on the 30th to boost the endangered M&M's. The "peanuts" part of the confection was hailed with less enthusiasm. When Kennedy mentioned Carter, one crowd began to chant, "We want Ted!" [29]

Dan Evans, now president of The Evergreen State College, appeared on TV as the narrator of a sophisticated half-hour campaign documentary by filmmaker John Robert Strachan that amounted to "This is Your Life John Spellman," complete with an across-the-fence interview with Spellman's longtime neighbor. It ran three times at a total cost of $18,000. McDermott was outspent and out of time.

Spellman was on hand for a Magnuson photo-op that featured Maggie handing over a giant-size $110 million check for the long-awaited West Seattle Bridge. "As Magnuson began to speak, the sun came out briefly on a cold and blustery day. ..." [30]

JIMMY CARTER'S last hurrah as president played out an hour before midnight on election eve in a hangar at drizzly Boeing Field. He had barnstormed 6,600 miles across America to a swing state he thought he could carry. Arrayed behind him were Magnuson, McDermott and Jackson, Tom Foley, Mike Lowry and Norm Dicks. The throng of loyal Democrats below them cheered loudest for Maggie as Carter clasped his hand and poked the air with a fist. Scoop knew they were whistling past a graveyard. He'd been told of a Carter tracking poll that portended disaster for Democrats.

On November 4, 1980, "even before the cover of darkness had fallen over the West, a curtain of gloom descended on Democrats..." [31] In campaign headquarters and living rooms from San Diego to Seattle, they booed and cursed John Chancellor and Tom Brokaw. It was 5:15 p.m. West Coast time—two hours and 45 minutes before the polls closed—and NBC was predicting victory for Ronald Reagan based on exit polls. Carter called Reagan to concede 46 minutes later and addressed the American people within an hour. Party officials had urged him to delay his speech until the polls closed out West, but he was "worried the public, knowing that Reagan was projected to win by a wide margin, would think he was sulking in the White House and did not want to appear to be a bad loser." [32]

"It just burns my ass that we knew at 5 o'clock that it wasn't worth getting more Democrats out," said Seattle Mayor Charles Royer, a former newscaster. [33] "Why doesn't he think?" a McDermott volunteer shouted at Carter's sad-faced image on a TV. [34]

Did NBC's scoop and Carter's petulance change any outcomes in Washington State? Unlikely, given the sweep and magnitude of the margins. Spellman captured nearly 57 percent of the vote and carried 32 of the state's 39 counties.* He outpolled Reagan by 116,000. Gorton also won going away. Warren G. Magnuson's storied career in Congress had come to an end. Reagan carried 44 states, including Washington. They called it the "Reagan Revolution."

Republicans seized control of the Washington State House of Representatives for the first time in eight years, 56-42, while the Democrats' hold on the Senate was a tenuous 25-24. Senator Walgren, hobbled by "Gamscam," was swamped by Ellen Craswell, a fervent member of the Christian Right. "Big Daddy" Day went down too, together with fellow Democrat Al Henry, who'd been in the Legislature since 1941.

At the Edgewater Inn bestride Elliott Bay, all eight Spellmans basked in the roar of the crowd. John lit his pipe. Waldo and Excell had bugged him not to smoke it so much because it made him appear too mild-mannered. Now he could go back to being himself. The governor-reject called to congratulate the governor-elect. "She was cordial," Spellman said, and promised a smooth transition. He ducked out of the celebration and went down the hall to meet with Dick Schrock, who was holed up in a room by himself, watching the election returns. Spellman, ever the Jesuit, had reached out to his old friend. They'd talked often down the stretch. "I'm going to need your help," Spellman said.

Tonight they could celebrate, remembering the disappointment of Election Night four years earlier. Tomorrow he would be the governor-elect of a state facing a revenue shortfall estimated at a billion dollars. County Councilman Bob Greive, the canny former Senate majority leader, told reporters Spellman was tougher than they realized—a competent administrator and a reasonable man. However, "he's going to find his present job and the governor's job are vastly different. The job of governor is much more complicated, and it's different working with a 149-member Legislature and a nine-member commission." [35]

---

*McDermott carried the other seven by a combined total of 2,262 votes, Grays Harbor by only 127.

CHAPTER TWENTY-EIGHT

Transitions

For a few fleeting moments as he began his exacting review of the state of the state, file folders stacked high, Spellman felt a bit like the dog that chased the car and wondered what to do when it caught it. He smiled to himself, filled his pipe and set to work, figuring "I'll be as ready as any governor has ever been."

He asked Joe McGavick to begin assembling a transition team and headed for Washington, D.C., for a short working vacation. He met with Jackson, Magnuson, Gorton and Pritchard, as well as Sid Morrison, the new Republican congressman from Eastern Washington's 4th District. He talked with Caspar Weinberger and William Casey from Reagan's transition team. He had two key immediate goals: congressional authorization of a Northwest Power Planning Act and a short-term lease to use McNeil Island in Puget Sound to reduce prison overcrowding.

After three years of hard bargaining and adroit maneuvering by Washington Congressman Al Swift, a member of the Energy and Commerce Committee, the power bill was at the threshold of approval. Don Bonker of Vancouver, Swift's fellow Democrat, had championed creation of a Power Council as part of the act to ensure consumers had input. Spellman saw the act as the best long-range hope of ensuring adequate electricity to meet growing demands at reasonable rates while protecting the environment. "As things stand now, we're flirting with chaos." The Bonneville Power Administration had boosted wholesale power rates 88 percent, much of that to cover its obligations on three of the five nuclear-power plants being constructed by WPPSS. The program was billions over budget and years behind schedule, the bond market saturated.[1] Irate ratepayers would pay the pied piper of nuclear power, once predicted to be "too cheap to meter." The private utilities, public utility districts and BPA were jockeying for cots in their own fallout shelters. Swift worried that Oregon would create one giant PUD and siphon off the lion's share of federal power from the Columbia

River system.[2] Environmentalists and the tribes were leery of everyone, yet the act codified the importance of conservation and renewable resources. Washington, Oregon, Idaho and Montana were to have two seats apiece on the power council. Spellman relished the chance to make the appointments. It was power he planned to use wisely to protect Washington's preferential stake in the energy grid.

Spellman headed home confident. The Power Planning Act was signed by President Carter on December 5, 1980, and the General Services Administration agreed to lease McNeil to the state. Spellman would negotiate a three-year contract at $350,000 per year, with the possibility of two one-year extensions.[3]

Governor Ray made a landmark, lame-duck decision of which Spellman heartily approved. Charles T. Wright, a 69-year-old justice on the State Supreme Court, had died the day after the election. Dixy appointed a widely respected King County Superior Court judge, Carolyn Dimmick, as the first woman on the high court. Dimmick had been a pioneer at practically every stage of her career. She was smart, tough-minded and witty. John and Lois had known and admired her for years. "Dixy didn't ask my opinion, but she couldn't have made a better or more timely choice."

WITH REVENUES declining daily and "stagflation—unemployment plus inflation—escalating, Spellman asked Weyerhaeuser executive Walt Howe, a budget director during the Evans administration, to set up a fiscal committee. Spellman was intent on mastering the state budget. He wanted expert advice on the plan he was drafting for the final six months of the 1979-81 biennium. The group included Warren Bishop, who'd been Rosellini's budget manager, and Orin Smith, Dixy's director of the Office of Financial Management for three years. "Besides being one of the brightest guys around," the future Starbucks chairman "knew where all the bodies were buried," says Steve Excell, who assisted McGavick on the transition team. "Orin was a huge help to us."[4]

In all, Spellman's team was composed of three-dozen people arrayed in advisory groups. It included old friends and longtime allies, former aides and assorted experts. Dick Schrock and Norm Maleng offered advice, as did Chuck Collins, Bernice Stern and Lois North. Arnie Weinmeister of the Teamsters, who had broken with other unions to endorse Spellman, joined in the planning. Other members were Miner Baker, the longtime Seafirst economist, and Mel Tonasket of the Colville Tribe.

"John was very hands-on, very particular in terms of what traits he wanted to see in people for key jobs in his administration," Schrock recalls.

He had several people in mind but carefully weighed names presented by the Personnel Task Force headed by Hunter Simpson of Physio-Control. The talent scouts included Jim Waldo, Shani Taha, Rusty Rathfelder, a Boeing personnel expert, and Chris Smith, the versatile former Bellevue councilwoman who co-managed the Spellman campaign. "I told them I wanted the best possible people, regardless of ideology," Spellman says. Several searches went nationwide.

Duane Berentson was offered the job of legislative liaison. "After his disappointing loss, he'd worked hard for my campaign, but it wasn't a consolation prize—more like 'Team of Rivals.' His integrity and 17½ years of experience in the Legislature were important to our ability to work with lawmakers at such a stressful time. I was pleased when he accepted and sorry to lose him in the spring of my first year as governor, but he became an outstanding secretary of transportation."

Spellman's choice to head OFM was State Representative Joe Taller, Boeing's capable industrial-relations manager. Taller had backed Berentson's bid for governor, having worked with the former co-speaker as a member of the House Appropriations Committee during his two terms in the Legislature.

Ed Devine, Spellman's dear friend since the 1960s, was the slam dunk. Within 72 hours of his victory, Spellman asked the former deputy mayor to stay on in the same role he had performed so well during Spellman's years as county executive—federal skid greaser. Some hard-shell conservatives were annoyed that Spellman had picked a Democrat as the face of his administration in Washington, D.C., but he paid no heed. Divine was an astute bipartisan operator. Anyone with half a mind for politics as an art form admired his moxie. Asked which of his tentative new titles he preferred—Federal Liaison or Counselor to the Governor—Divine said he fancied "Philosopher Prince."[5]

McGavick was Spellman's first choice to manage the labyrinthine Department of Social and Health Services. "It was probably the most challenging job in state government, and I love snake pits," McGavick says, "but I was a consulting partner in Deloitte Haskins Sells, the top accounting firm in the U.S."[6] As good as McGavick likely would have been—especially given Spellman's plan to make DSHS more manageable by spinning off Corrections—his second choice proved stellar. A nationwide search produced Alan J. Gibbs, an assistant secretary of the Army with a background in both budgets and human services. Before arriving at the Pentagon in 1977 to oversee a $40 billion budget, Gibbs had been a deputy commissioner for New Jersey's Department of Human Services and, before that, Equal

Opportunity director for Alabama and Tennessee. Gibbs lived up to his advance billing as "a man with compassion who is an excellent manager."[7] He was "the first to get control of DSHS, masterfully absorbing Reagan budget shrinkages" without igniting firestorms among advocacy groups.[8]

Another catch was Amos Reed, at 65 one of the most experienced, respected corrections officials in America. Reed had spent 15 years as a prison administrator in Oregon before taking charge of North Carolina's troubled prisons in 1977. Tough-minded, sometimes abrasive but nevertheless humane, Reed didn't believe in "just warehousing" criminals. Most inmates are going to end up back in society sooner or later, he said, so job training and substance-abuse counseling were important. On his watch, however, the tail did not wag the dog. (Reed was stunned to discover the big-house biker bund at Walla Walla busy manufacturing shivs.) Excell called the governor of North Carolina, Jim Hunt, to see if reality matched Reed's resume. "Ah did not reappoint Amos," the governor drawled. "Son, I gotta tell ya something about North Carolina: Around here when you get elected governor everyone expects their brothers, sisters, cousins, uncles and aunts are all gonna get a job. And if they're in business they're gonna get contracts. Now, I'm trying to change all that, but it takes time. Amos, he just went in there and cleaned house. PO'd people. Got rid of all the cronyism and favoritism. So I had to let him go. But if you want the world's best corrections system, Amos is your guy."[9] Amos flew in to meet the governor-elect. Spellman was mightily impressed.

Keith Angier, Spellman's pick to manage the Department of General Administration, had directed the agency during Evans' third term. "This is one of those rare instances where you get a chance to go back and do something over again, and do it better," Angier said.[10] Hector Torres, a handsome 32-year-old Tacoma lawyer who'd been wounded in action twice as a Marine in Vietnam, was named to head the Office of Veterans Affairs. This did not turn out well. Within a year, the freewheeling Torres had shot himself in the foot several times. Another Hispanic, John Gonzalez, was picked to oversee the Department of Licensing. His deputy, Jesus Sanchez, turned out to be the real find. Likewise, Sanchez's wife, Naomi, a Japanese-American who worked on affirmative action issues in the governor's office.

In an edition of *the Weekly* largely devoted to the new administration, David Brewster saw an emerging Spellman. It was easy to predict he would be a good governor, "particularly compared" to the disaster Dixy had wrought. "But can he be an outstanding one? Will he be a true leader rather than a fine reactor? One reason for the mystery is that Spellman is not a stable political entity these days. He is over the boredom of being

King County executive ... He is less shy, less dependent on the bright ideas of other people in order to shine himself, more enmeshed in details of government, more adventurous in staffing, more of a leader and less mere referee. ..." The new cabinet promised some creative stress. (And did not fail to deliver). "An example is in the revenue side," Brewster observed, "where a cautious Joe Taller is heading the budget office, while a supercharged, idea-a-minute Mensa type, Glenn Pascall, is boss of the revenue department. They are expected to tangle, stimulating each other to better performance and keeping lots

ILLUSTRATION BY FRED HILLIARD

The cover of *the Weekly* as Spellman took office as governor in 1981.

of options in front of Spellman. The same could be predicted for the executive staff, where a solve-it technician like Steve Excell will be complimented by an imaginative Irish dreamer like Ed Devine."[11] There was a lot to like about Spellman's little "c" catholicity, Brewster concluded. He was a skilled consensus builder, and "blandness in politics can be a formidable political weapon."[12] Blandness, however, was not what Spellman wanted on his team. As things turned out, a little more of it, here and there, might have helped.

FOR CHIEF OF STAFF, Spellman chose, with a niggle of doubt, 41-year-old Richard Allison, a former Harvard history professor and top aide to Vice President Nelson Rockefeller. Suggested by Schrock, Allison was tall and trim, analytical in horn-rim glasses and button-down collar. His management style had been honed by a tour of duty in Vietnam as an Army captain. Though some found him too Teutonic, Allison had capably managed the King County Prosecutor's Office for Chris Bayley, a college friend. Spellman knew Allison only vaguely, but Maleng endorsed him as well. Allison was vacationing in South Africa when they tracked him down and asked him to meet with Spellman. "He has this uncanny ability to listen to you ramble on for half an hour, and then to extract, in two seconds, the essence of what you were trying to say all along," one of his new teammates said.[13] Sometimes, however, the way he said it rankled.

Spellman hedged his bets by naming Excell as Allison's deputy. Only 31, Excell had been in the mainstream Republican political trenches since high school in Seattle. From the UW he went on to receive a law degree from Georgetown, Spellman's alma mater, and served as Joel Pritchard's top aide in D.C. Excell was a walking, talking encyclopedia of Washington state politics. He gave up a job making real money in the construction industry to follow his first love.

Four other appointees were also people Spellman knew well and trusted implicitly from their days together at the King County Courthouse: Bob Bratton was appointed to the Utilities and Transportation Commission. Norwood Brooks, the county elections director, would head Employment Security. He was affable, efficient and a data-processing expert. That he was black was a bonus. Spellman was striving for diversity. Karen Rahm, King County's 36-year-old director of planning, filled the bill as a bright young woman with economic development expertise. Rahm was picked to head the Planning and Community Affairs Agency, with Pat Dunn as assistant director. Dunn would work closely with the counties, cities and port districts to promote job creation through Spellman's industrial revenue-bond program. A Housing Finance Commission was an outgrowth of what morphed into the Department of Community Development.

Don Moos, a charter member of the "Evans bloc" that propelled young Republicans to power in the 1960s, was Spellman's choice to direct the Department of Ecology. The former EPA regional administrator had served Evans as director of two departments—Agriculture and Fisheries. Sam Kinville, the labor representative on the Board of Industrial Insurance Appeals, was named to head the Department of Labor and Industries. He had been a miner in Montana, a school teacher, social worker and Labor Council lobbyist.

With a nod to his important agrarian constituency in Eastern Washington, Spellman appointed Keith Ellis, a self-made man with a Harvard MBA, to direct the Department of Agriculture. The Tri-Cities resident was an executive with a large agribusiness company.

Spellman's choice to oversee the Fisheries Department was Rolland "Rollie" Schmitten, a respected Republican legislator from Cashmere. Though Schmitten looked younger than 36, he'd seen combat as a Marine in Vietnam, was a graduate forester and owned a lumber company. He was a perfect fit at Fisheries, having led bipartisan legislative efforts to enhance the resource. In the fall of 1982, Spellman asked him to become his legislative liaison and natural resources adviser. Schmitten persevered through some of the hardest bargaining the Capitol had ever seen. Bill Wilkerson, a young lawyer with a fighter pilot's mustache and first-rate diplomatic skills, took over at Fisheries and set out to consummate the "co-management" plan he and Schmitten had recommended to Spellman to avoid further litigation by treaty tribes.

Ed Sheets, one of Magnuson's brightest young aides, was picked to "re-energize" the state Energy Office and work with the Regional Power Council. Hugh Fowler, a former official with the Federal Emergency Management Agency, was selected to head Emergency Management, which had its hands full with the Mount St. Helens recovery effort. As the new year began, scientists were warning that the volcano was still volatile.

Marilyn Showalter, Spellman's choice for house attorney, had been one of Maleng's top aides. Spellman did not know her well, but he was impressed by her disposition—upbeat, forthright—and credentials—Harvard Law. It was an excellent relationship.

Spellman told reporters he wanted "an open administration that tells the truth," even when it hurt. "We won't treat the media like the enemy." For press secretary he chose 33-year-old Paul O'Connor, a classic Irish-Catholic newshound from Chicago. O'Connor had apprenticed as a leg man for Mike Royko before landing in Seattle as a reporter and restaurant reviewer for the *P-I*, Dixy Lee Ray's least favorite newspaper. Skeptics had no quarrel with O'Connor's bona fides as a newsman. They saw him as bright, brash and intense and wondered if he had "the deference and peace-making tendencies he'll need as a PR man."[14] They were correct on every count.

Finally, Barbara Schmidt, gatekeeper and brewer of *Irish* breakfast tea, would be moving to Olympia too. "She was thoughtful, loyal and funny," Spellman says, "everything an executive secretary should be."

Spellman installed an interim director at the Department of Commerce and Economic Development. Come February, in a move that raised eyebrows, he gave the job to Dick Schrock. "Spellman explains hiring of friend," one headline said; another story called him a "crony." In times like these, Spellman said, "I think we need someone who is a marketer, a sales person," to promote industrial development, foreign trade and tourism.[15]

WHEN DAN EVANS exited the governor's office in 1977 he left on his successor's desk a bottle of champagne on ice in a silver bucket from the captain's mess on the USS *Olympia*, together with a personal note of best wishes. Nancy Evans was annoyed that pieces of the historic silver service entrusted to the mansion had left the premises. And they were both peeved when they heard not a word of thanks from Dixy.[16]

Spellman deserved at least a magnum of Pepto-Bismol, Dick Larsen wrote. Yet on January 14, 1981, there was not so much as a best-wishes Post-it note for Washington's 18th governor, who inherited a state government "entering the greatest fiscal crisis since the Depression."[17] A riot at the state prison at Shelton had caused damages estimated at $1.3 million. Inmates at Walla Walla were on strike, vowing not to go to their jobs or vocational training classes until their superintendent was replaced.[18] Taller and Pascall, like grinches in lockstep, had informed Spellman on Christmas Eve that revenue estimates for the current biennium, which would end on June 30, 1981, appeared "severely overstated." Earlier pegged at $600 million, the actual shortfall could be more than a billion dollars. Spellman and the Legislature would be struggling with both a supplemental budget and a plan for the two years beginning July 1.[19]

McDermott, as chairman of the Ways and Means Committee in the State Senate, had met with Excell and Taller in December. He groused that he had yet to be consulted, leaned forward with his considerable bulk and said, "Tell your boss the knife is on the table."[20] But when they got together a few days before the inauguration for their first face to face since the final debate, McDermott saw that Spellman's budget agenda was dramatically more moderate than what the hardcore conservatives in the governor-elect's party were intent on. He was of mixed emotions. Little did he know that his tenure as committee chairman was in jeopardy.

The Spellmans had a priest say Mass at their home before leaving for Olympia. "For better days to come, Lord hear our prayer."

CHAPTER TWENTY-NINE

Gray and Lonely

When John and Lois Spellman ascended the 19 marble steps to the soaring rotunda of the state Capitol, they were momentarily blinded by TV lights. Motorized Nikons whirred as applause enveloped them. It echoed down from the dome and around the vast landing with its roped-off golden state seal. School kids hopped up and down to catch a glimpse of the next governor. It was 11:50 a.m. Wednesday, January 14, 1981.

At the doorway leading to the House chamber, where the entire Legislature awaited, friends stepped forward to greet the Spellmans with broad smiles. "Hello, John," said a blond woman wearing a black suit and white blouse. ... Spellman whooped happily: "Well, would you believe this? Harriet!" They kissed. Harriet ... was one of the other students in the tiny class he attended at Bay Elementary School at Hunts Point. ... "I'm sorry it's so crowded in there," Spellman said, motioning toward the overflow crowd in the galleries. "It's OK," she replied. "We just wanted to be here." [1]

"There were four of us in the sixth grade," Harriet Tremper Culliton of Bellevue told Dick Larsen. John was a good student, she said, playful but charming. "I adored him." Another boy "bet John a nickel he wouldn't kiss me behind the Hunts Point grocery. And he did it!" [2]

The Legislature and galleries stood to applaud as the Spellmans made their way down the aisle. It was the first time a governor-elect's wife had accompanied her spouse to the dais. After the oath-taking, Spellman delivered an address he and Paul O'Connor, his press secretary, had been polishing as late as that morning. As oratory goes, it was nothing for the ages, "but I meant every word," Spellman says.

"When a new governor stands before the people and the Legislature for the first time," he began, "there is a moment when we can enjoy a sense of anticipation—a possibility that an era of candor and cooperation between the executive and the legislative branches will begin. ... Let us have a fresh start, a new relationship, not alone for you and me, but for the state and the people of Washington. Let us work together with mutual respect. ... I urge you to share my conviction that 105 days from today we will face the people of the state and tell them that we have served them well. That we have maintained vital services. That we have cut back the cost of ongoing programs. That we have provided with compassion for those of urgent need. I call for this optimism fully aware of the financial situation that faces us immediately and of the sacrifices that each citizen must share. Tomorrow I will propose a program to meet financial needs. That program will not require a tax increase."

While the decisions they faced would be difficult, sometimes agonizing, "we must not be parties to balancing our budget on the shoulders of the poor. The need for food and medical care for children and the aged does not decrease in tough times. The needs of the mentally ill and developmentally disabled do not diminish in times of tight budgets. We must not turn our backs on those who must turn to this government when all else fails."

ANN YARROW © THE SEATTLE TIMES 1981; REPRINTED WITH PERMISSION

Bob McGrath, who often sang the national anthem at Seattle sports events, joins the governor and new first lady on "When Irish Eyes Are Smiling" at Spellman's inauguration in 1981. House Speaker Bill Polk looks on at left.

Their constitutional duty was to ensure strong public schools, Spellman said. He believed the duty extended from "kindergarten to graduate school" and decried the cuts that in recent years had jeopardized "our future cultural and economic growth."

Next came a catechism that was vintage Spellman: "What is needed is a reaffirmation of traditional values. Families are the basic units of society. Work is good. Those who provide jobs are not the enemies of society. Education is essential. Government should regulate only to the extent necessary to protect the public. Society cannot provide everything people want, but it must be able to provide what they need. We can achieve more by working together than by fighting one another. We need to put aside the rhetoric that divides us. Let us emphasize those principles on which we agree—accentuate the positive. ...Working together, with God's help, we will enter a new era of progress—one which will satisfy the demands of the great stewardship that has been entrusted to us." [3]

Lieutenant Governor Cherberg, who'd heard Spellman sing "Tomorrow" from the hit musical *Annie* at a banquet hosted by the restaurant industry a few nights earlier, urged him to sing it again. Spellman obliged with lilting gusto:

> *When I'm stuck with a day*
> *that's gray and lonely,*
> *I just stick out my chin*
> *and grin and say, Oh!*
>
> *The sun'll come out tomorrow,*
> *so ya gotta hang on 'til tomorrow,*
> *come what may!*
> *Tomorrow! Tomorrow!*
> *I love ya tomorrow!*
> *You're always a day away!*

It brought the house down. Then he asked the new First Lady and Bob McGrath, who for years had sung the national anthem at Seattle sports events, thrilling crowds with his operatic tenor, to join him on "When Irish Eyes Are Smiling." It was pitch perfect. For a day at least, the gloom was gone from the Capitol. Legislators on both sides of the aisle found his speech "refreshing," especially compared to the lectures "we used to get from a former college professor," said Ted Bottiger, the Senate majority leader. [4]

Max Pillar's Orchestra and Red Kelly's Roadhouse Band provided the music at the Capitol Pavilion as they danced the night away. The First Lady was stunning in an emerald-green silk satin gown. Reality was only a day away. The next 105 days—the next 12 months, in fact, and much of the year after that—would be among the most tumultuous and trying in the history of Washington State government.

SPELLMAN ORDERED a hiring freeze and proposed "humane and realistic" budgets that made major cutbacks in state services. His cuts, however, were significantly less drastic than what Dixy had proposed in her final pro forma budget message. Spellman advocated spending $30 million more over the next six months and $300 million more during the 1981-83 biennium that would begin on July 1—a general-fund operating budget of $7.1 billion. The gap between that number and the cost of continuing all present programs into the next biennium was $950 million.[5]

How the state found itself in a billion-dollar hole is a cautionary tale that conservatives say keeps being forgotten. Liberals, and many moderates as well, maintain that the state's revenue stream—sales, B & O and property taxes, but no individual or corporate income taxes—is patently regressive. During downturns, when consumer spending dries up, it leaves the state "with less money at just the time it needs it most."[6] Yet wary voters had repeatedly rejected an income tax, despite Dan Evans' best entreaties. It was a non-starter, Spellman said.

Only 19 months earlier there was a $410 million surplus. "Washington was expected to whistle its way through the looming national recession," Ross Anderson wrote in a compelling analysis for *The Seattle Times* on the eve of the 1981 legislative session.[7] What happened? The number-crunchers underestimated inflation as lawmakers added programs and cut taxes:

> Orin Smith and other budgeteers admit they were guilty of some short-sightedness, but they point out they had more than a little help from the courts and the voters, all caught up in the "tax revolt" spirit of the times. State spending on schools, social services and government services has increased dramatically ... Welfare rolls are higher. Teacher salaries are higher. ... But most observers agree that the hardest crunch is on the income side of the ledger. In a few short years, the state tax base has been eroded by an accumulation of tax cuts. The revolt arrived here in the form of a 1977 initiative to remove the sales tax from food and drugs. Everybody agreed that it was a bad tax, but state officials warned that it should not be eliminated until it could be replaced with a

more progressive tax. The voters dumped the tax anyway. Two years later the same voters overwhelming approved Initiative 62, which put a lid on state spending. Meanwhile along came a court decision requiring state government to fully fund basic education. ...

Still, in 1979, Smith was optimistic that the state could afford the tax cuts. With Boeing's help, Washington would "outperform" the rest of the nation, he predicted. What Smith and the other experts failed to anticipate was interest rates. In an election-year effort to curb inflation, the Carter administration decided to attack consumption with double-digit interest rates. That hit Washington right where it hurt worst—in the housing industry. People stopped buying houses. Builders stopped building them. No housing sales, no lumber sales, no 1 percent real-estate excise tax, no new property taxes and no sales taxes on the new drapes and carpets for those unbuilt or unbought houses. The recession had arrived.[8]

And it would get worse, a lot worse, before it got better. As Spellman and Reagan took office, inflation was at 14 percent. The Fed chief, Paul Volcker, had prescribed a cure so drastic some said it might kill the pa-tient. He boosted the benchmark lending rate for federal funds from 11.2 to 20 percent. The prime rate followed suit. The 30-year home mortgage rate zoomed to 18.5 percent. U.S. unemployment soon topped 10 percent. In Washington State it was two percent higher than that—and 10 percent higher in timber counties.

While tighter money attacked inflation, the Reagan administration applied three more jumper cables to the U.S. economy: income and capital gains taxes were cut, government regulations reduced and spending slashed, especially on social-welfare programs. Defense, where Reagan said "you spend whatever you need," was the exception.

To Bill Polk, the speaker of the Washington State House of Represen-tatives, "Reaganomics" was just what the doctor ordered. The 45-year-old architect from affluent Mercer Island was a Reagan Republican who looked the part in wingtips and Windsor knot, driving a Datsun 280Z sports car. Polk was an agile parliamentarian with piercing eyes and a quick wit that could descend into withering sarcasm, even theatrics, when he was on a roll. He once brandished a hatchet while exhorting the House to cut the Democrats' budget. "I think Ronald Reagan is as close to being a mirror of the inner image of the populace than any politician we've ever seen," Polk said as the session got under way. "Reagan's ability is to articulate what people feel inside and are afraid to say, because it hasn't been popular." [9]

Polkanomics called for slashing welfare programs, most assuredly state-paid abortions, raising the state's 12 percent interest ceiling, weakening environmental regulations and reducing the product-liability onus on business. The speaker was also intent on finally breaking the state's monopoly on workmen's compensation policies. Private insurance companies had long sought a piece of the lucrative action. The state had collected $470 million in premiums during the previous fiscal year. Since 1971, some "well-qualified" employers—260 in all, including Boeing and Weyerhaeuser—had been allowed the option of self-insuring. Giving businesses the chance to buy coverage from a private carrier would be a third option—the so-called "three-way" plan that was anathema to organized labor. A lobbyist for the Pulp and Paper Workers pointed to Oregon where private companies handled workmen's compensation. "Those companies had little or no regard for the injured workers and wanted to settle claims in a way that would return the best profit," she said.[10]

Improving prisons was not high on Polk's list of priorities. This was preeminently a time for "cold, hard decisions," the speaker said. "I can see why people would come to the conclusion I'm not out of the mold of a populist."[11] Vowing there'd be no new taxes, Polk and his troops had gained seven seats in the last election and now enjoyed a 56-42 majority. He conceded they might not have made the pledge "if we had known the situation we'd be in," but swore he would oppose a tax increase to the bitter end, even if one was needed. "The Legislature must keep its faith with the public. One of the biggest challenges for the next two years is trying to instill some confidence in leaders. It's perhaps a bigger challenge than trying to get the issues done."[12]

Spellman would have to contend not only with "Railroad Bill," an ideologue, but with the House Republicans' chief clerk, Vito Chiechi, who had once achieved the feat of keeping Harley Hoppe from jumping the tracks.

"Most speakers are frustrated governors," Steve Excell observed. "And most governors wish they had as much leadership clout as the speaker of the House."[13] And most Senate leaders clinging to one-vote majorities wish they were back in Kansas. Some saw Bottiger, a 48-year-old Tacoma attorney with a comb-over and an engaging grin, as a "consummate politician," but managing his caucus was like herding cats. Jim McDermott and Pete von Reichbauer, a maverick Democrat from Vashon Island, were driving one another up the wall. "I like John Spellman," von Reichbauer said pointedly. "I've known him for a long time."[14]

If Polk "really wants to raise the interest rates, there's going to have to be some votes on Senate proposals," Bottiger said bravely. "Home builders are saying if we could raise interest rates they could sell more houses. I think that's a crock." The housing finance commission Spellman and Mc-Dermott favored—blocked by Republicans for the past two sessions—held the promise of actually boosting home construction, Bottiger said.[15]

Across the aisle sat Jeannette Hayner of Walla Walla, one of the most respected legislators in Washington State history. The Senate minority leader was "assertive, bright, diplomatic, quite conservative and decidedly feminine." She was Margaret Thatcher and Elizabeth Dole rolled into one, a crafty but collegial operator who seemed younger than 61. Her formula for success was "Think like a man, work like a dog and act like a lady."[16]

SPELLMAN'S PLAN to balance the budget called for an array of higher taxes and fees and cuts that would cause pain but "avoid marrow." Flanked by budget director Joe Taller and Glenn Pascall, the new revenue director, the governor tried to make a case that they weren't proposing tax increases "in the strict sense of the word" because the rates wouldn't rise. "We're not talking about a general tax increase." Tinkering with the business inventory tax and repealing the law that limited overall growth in state property tax collections to 6 percent a year would raise an additional $106 million, Spellman said. While "fairer in the long run," the tax shift would nick homeowners, largely in King County, some $178 million.[17] "It's a whopping tax increase," snorted Harley Hoppe, still King County assessor after a failed bid to get himself appointed as Spellman's successor.[18]

Spellman also advocated a 33 percent increase in tuition and fees at all state colleges, universities and vocational-technical schools. That was "far preferable to a continued decline in quality." Renewing drivers' licenses every four years instead of two was a painless expedient that would save $3 million, Spellman said. He called for higher license and user fees. Fishing licenses and camping at state parks would cost more, as would truck inspections. He said they should create a "rainy day" fund to cushion the impact of future downturns.[19]

Spellman's budget continued the chore-service program for the elderly and handicapped. He urged the Legislature to restore dental care and other health services for children in low-income families, saying it would save money in the long run. He agreed with Dixy's assertion that the state should eliminate welfare for able-bodied adults, but urged the lawmakers to reinstitute up to two months of emergency assistance for those seeking work. He wanted $26 million more than Dixy to pay for substitute teachers and maintain programs for disadvantaged students. He proposed deferring payments into the retirement systems for police officers, firefighters and teachers and advocated siphoning $22 million from the timber reserve account. His plan called for collecting insurance-premium taxes quarterly instead of annually. Critics called it "light-bulb snatching." [20]

Polk was leery of the cornerstone of Spellman's job-creation program—an industrial-development bond plan package that would allow counties, cities and port districts to expedite public-works projects. The hurdle was the state Constitution's prohibition against lending of the state's credit.

Some legislators, even old-hand Republicans, said it would be easier to justify an increase in the 4.5 percent sales tax than higher property taxes. When the Legislature placed a tenth-of-a-percent surcharge on the sales tax in the 1970s, "nobody noticed when you put it in; nobody noticed when you took it off," said Representative Sid Flanagan, a wizened old Republican wheat farmer with nicotine-stained fingers.[21] The Will Rogers-like observation produced smiles on both sides of the aisle, temporarily puncturing the tension. "Usually Sid just tolerated and ignored the rest of us, the way an old hound ignores the puppies climbing all over him," says Dan Grimm, who in 1981 was the Democrats' young caucus chairman.[22]

There were few defections from the Polk fold when the House passed a supplemental budget—critics called it a "package of tears"—that whacked $2 million from chore services and $22 million from medical care for needy kids and the low-income elderly. "I think it's wrong," Spellman said before meeting with leaders of both houses to appeal for a compromise.[23] Skirmishing gave way to full-scale partisan warfare on February 9 when Senate Democrats passed a "crisis budget" to forestall a March 1 cutoff of social-welfare programs.[24]

AS THE GOVERNOR and the lawmakers fastened their seat belts, Spellman made it clear he was reserving judgment on an issue that would become one of the defining moments of his political career: Northern Tier's proposed oil port at Port Angeles and pipeline beneath Puget Sound. From there the pipeline was to snake its way along the Snoqualmie, cross the Cascades and push east to Minnesota, 1,500 miles in all. Eight tribes maintained the pipeline could damage fish runs in violation of the treaty rights upheld in 1974 by federal Judge George Boldt. The Army Corps of Engineers and the Environmental Protection Agency would have their say as well. When all was said and done, the state Energy Facility Site Evaluation Council would forward its recommendations to Spellman. The Reagan administration was already telling him that energy independence was a national security issue.[25]

Spellman and a growing number of legislators believed energy independence was what the Washington Public Power Supply System had too much of. Yet WPPSS leaders, clearly in over their heads, came to the Capitol, hats in hand, seeking more "flexibility." They wanted the ability to negotiate bond sales to secure lower interest rates and the chance to bypass competitive bidding on some work at their beleaguered nuclear-power plants.[26]

At least he was off to a solid start with the Olympia press corps, which had been stonewalled and ridiculed by Governor Ray. She gave the pigs on her Fox Island farm the names of her least favorite scribes. As Spellman welcomed the reporters to seats at the long conference table in his new office, Gordy Schultz, the burly, quick-witted bureau chief for United Press International, intoned, "We should point out that this is a historic occasion because it is the first time that this room has been used by the governor for a full-fledged press conference since October of 1979." Spellman proceeded to say the main reason he'd called them together was to introduce Amos Reed and explain that Taller, brain bouncing from long hours on the budget, had misspoken when he said they were committed to building a new prison at Monroe. There'd be no decision until an environmental-impact statement was complete and Reed was up to speed. As the reporters filed out, Shultz said, "Not only did he hold a news conference, but he called a news conference to admit a mistake!"[27]

THE FIRST LADY was also candid and accessible—but protective, too. Her family came first. During the 1976 campaign she told Joanne Berentson that if John won "I'm not really convinced yet I'm going to go down there [to Olympia]. I'm a mom. I've got a bigger job, and I don't know that I would like that at all." The kids were now four years older and that made things easier, though she still worried that her life in Olympia "would be like moving into the Smithsonian and living over the store and trying to adhere to all the rules of the mansion ladies. I'm not one to take orders very gently."[28]

Lois Spellman's view of her paramount duty hadn't changed: She was the mom and wife. The kids had their chores, but she did the shopping and cooking, packed school lunches, prodded teens to clean their rooms, fed the pets and worried about her spouse's stress. When everyone was out the door in the morning or doing their homework after dinner, she was a hostess-ambassador in a house that wasn't just a home. Daughters Katherine ("Kat") and Teresa remember arriving home from school to find Mom fogging up the windows in the Mansion ballroom with aerobics classes for legislative wives. Lois saw early on that the mansion needed more help—a chef for the luncheons and banquets in addition to the people who vacuumed the rugs

WASHINGTON STATE ARCHIVES

The governor and first lady at the mansion in 1981.

and polished the floors in the public rooms. Her college major was labor relations. She insisted that the Legislature make the mansion workers regular state employees with health-care and pension benefits.

Three months after they'd settled in and grown accustomed to having strangers wandering around the house squinting at the silver and chandeliers, Lois was summoned to the Governor's Office. "I was told that the Mansion Foundation had filed a formal complaint because I was introducing Northwest art into the mansion." Kenneth Callahan and Jacob Lawrence, whom the Spellmans revered, were artists of international renown. However, some of the people who guarded the mansion's aura—volunteers all and well intended—felt modernist works were out of place. The Rembrandt Peale school of portraiture and classic landscapes of snow-capped peaks were what "fit." Nonsense, the First Lady said. The Governor's Mansion wasn't Monticello or Mount Vernon. She and John loved all sorts of art. A print of Hans Holbein's portrait of Thomas More, "The Man for All Seasons," hangs above their fireplace mantel in Seattle. "I told them classic art was fine, but it wasn't true to the architecture and style of the mansion." She met with John's legal counsel, Marilyn Showalter, and Keith Angier, the director of General Administration. "This went back and forth. It was pretty bad. But I won. Finally it was determined that I could hang Northwest art in the galleries and in the family rooms." [29] The Spellmans hosted a reception for Lawrence, an African-American whose narrative paintings of the black experience were being hailed for their brilliance. Soon there were more such soirees, featuring Callahan, Fay Jones, Elton Bennett and other Northwest artists. The First Lady also spotlighted programs she had championed when John was county executive, food banks in particular. There had been thousands of hungry people in King County during the Boeing Bust. This new recession, the worst since the 1930s, was being felt everywhere around the state. She lobbied the U.S. secretary of Agriculture for surplus commodities and worked with the Restaurant Association to collect leftovers to distribute to food banks.* The Help the Hungry program she inspired mobilized volunteers statewide.

---

* "What is wonderful is that the concern for feeding the hungry continues today in this terrible recession," Mrs. Spellman said in the summer of 2012. "I can go to a grocery store and see food-bank trucks pulling up to the rear of the store to pick up the past-dated merchandise."

CHAPTER THIRTY

Fear and Loathing at the Capitol

t rained heavily all day on February 12, 1981, and Friday the 13th dawned drizzly. There would be two earthquakes that day. One measured 5.5 on the Richter scale. It rolled and rippled for eight minutes from Centralia to Seattle, but did remarkably little damage. In Olympia, the tectonic plates of politics—grinding for weeks—buckled at 9:50 a.m. when Senator Peter von Reichbauer told a packed press conference, "I herewith resign as a member of the Democratic caucus." [1] As he crossed the aisle, Republicans controlled—on paper at least—both chambers of the Legislature and the Governor's Office for the first time in 28 years. In fact, nothing like this—a mid-session switch that altered the balance of power—had happened before in the 92-year history of the institution. "I think I've got 24 new friends," von Reichbauer said with a thin smile. [2]

And countless enemies, new and old. "Where is the little son of a bitch?" Senator Don Talley, a Democrat from Kelso, demanded when he arrived at his office and heard the news. Stronger message to follow. Others called von Reichbauer a turncoat and traitor—an unctuous, devious, petty, self-aggrandizing snake in the grass. Blair Butterworth, Jim McDermott's administrative aide, abandoned circumspection to suggest that whoever presided over von Reichbauer's circumcision "threw the wrong part away." [3]

Clearly the feeling was mutual, since a certain liberal Seattle psychiatrist, no longer chairman of Ways and Means, was at the epicenter of von Reichbauer's angst. "I am firmly convinced that Senator McDermott is a Pied Piper of taxation," von Reichbauer said. "He is still running against John Spellman and not trying to deal with the fiscal problems of the state. He's determined to prove that he was right last fall when he said we needed a tax increase. I am absolutely convinced that state government must set an example and cut its overhead, no matter how hard it hurts, so we can get by this critical period. ... I'm afraid the Democratic Party has gone astray from where it was when I joined it eight years ago." [4]

"We're glad he's gone," McDermott sneered. "From this point onward the total responsibility for what's happening in this state will be on the Republicans. ...When the timber companies get a tax break, it's the Republicans who did it at a time when they're taking food away from children."[5] McDermott now saw that Spellman was squarely in league with moderates in both parties who believed cuts alone would be unconscionable. He didn't say that, of course, because Spellman couldn't be the answer. He must atone for waving that waffle.

THE BANNER HEADLINE defection that gave the Republicans a 25-24 Senate majority had been the hottest rumor in town long before the session began. Spellman and von Reichbauer were erroneously perceived to be close friends. The senator, accompanied by Seahawk quarterback Jim Zorn and his star receiver, Steve Largent, was conspicuous at a 1980 Spellman fundraiser at the Kingdome. Von Reichbauer had told friends he wouldn't support McDermott "if he were the last Democrat on Earth."[6]

Jeannette Hayner and two other Senate Republican leaders, John Jones and George Clarke, had called the governor-elect on January 8 to urge him to persuade von Reichbauer to defect. Spellman balked. "Lots of negatives in my mind," he told his diary. "Demos would immediately hate me, press would smell collusion, von Reichbauer would be jeopardized & GOP Senate plus conservative House would go right over top of me. Doubtful I could get enough concessions from GOP Senate on my program before decision is made & accomplished ..." Spellman was ambivalent about his relationship with the squirrely senator. Von Reichbauer was a longtime friend of Booth Gardner, another wealthy, ambitious, enigmatic young man. Gardner was busy running for Pierce County executive as a Democrat. He made no bones about his ultimate goal: He wanted to be governor.

It wasn't clear what von Reichbauer wanted to be. His worst enemies conceded he was no political dilettante. By defying Senate Majority Leader August Mardesich and Governor Ray at a time when neither was someone "with whom

WASHINGTON STATE ARCHIVES

Peter von Reichbauer after his defection to the Republicans.

one trifled lightly," von Reichbauer earlier had made declarations of independence that either "bordered on the suicidal" or demonstrated prescient political genius: Mardesich and Ray were headed for a fall, together with Bagnariol and Walgren.[7] "Peter does not have any strong party convictions or alliances. ...[He] has always moved with the political tide," said Senator Marcus Gaspard, a Democrat from Puyallup considered one of von Reichbauer's closest friends in the Legislature.[8]

Von Reichbauer had visited Spellman on February 12. He said he felt ostracized in the Democratic caucus and had had it up to here with McDermott. "I told him to follow his own best interests & not do it because of me," Spellman wrote. "Not at all sure it would help me. (He is perceived by all to be my follower, which contributes to his problems.)"

Many said von Reichbauer's defection was rooted in redistricting. The 1980 Census indicated Washington was entitled to an eighth seat in Congress, likely representing central Puget Sound. His defection put the Republicans in the catbird seat to draw new lines. Even if von Reichbauer opted to stay put, the prediction was that by 1982 his redrawn 30th Legislative District would trend Republican. In any case, the boyish, clean-cut von Reichbauer was terrific on the stump, hugging his way through nursing homes and VFW halls. "He's more popular with the senior citizens ...than with the sophisticated Democrats," said Bob Stead, a 30th District Democrat. "The son of a gun usually manages to land on his feet." [9]

"Your betrayal of the Democratic Party and the voters in your district is unspeakable," Joe Murphy, president of the State Democratic Central Committee, told von Reichbauer. "If there is a shred of decency in you, you will tender your resignation immediately." [10] Von Reichbauer scoffed: He hadn't deserted the party, the party had deserted him. Democrats huddled with lawyers that afternoon to explore a recall movement. The State Patrol assigned von Reichbauer a bodyguard.

HAYNER'S LEADERSHIP team seized control of the Senate, appointed new committee chairmen, warned that the "bloated" Democratic staff would be cut and fired the longtime sergeant at arms. On Day One, they called a night session to pass a supplemental budget of their own.* They beat back salvos of Democratic attempts to add money for schools and social welfare programs. Finally, after 3½ hours of exhausting debate, Hayner, "in cold

---

*That Senate Secretary Sid Snyder kept his job was a testament to the bipartisan popularity of the grocer from Long Beach, who began his career at the Capitol in 1949 as an elevator operator. When the Evans Republicans formed a coalition in the 1960s to seize control of the House, Slade Gorton made sure Snyder wouldn't be fired.

fury, announced that the Senate was adjourning until tomorrow and that all committee meetings were postponed until further notice."[11] The first female majority leader in the history of the Washington State Senate was up early Saturday morning, regrouping the troops. Her caucus chairman, Jack Jones, had hardly been to bed. Acting on a tip, Jones entered the mail room in the bowels of the Capitol at 2:30 a.m. on St. Valentine's Day "and confiscated a mailing Democrats were doing at state expense to trigger a reaction to the upset," George W. Scott, the new chairman of the Ways and Means Committee, wrote in his legislative memoir, adding:

> They called it a "break in," and said we were out to "annihilate free speech." The new majority was sued when it tried to fire 51 of the nearly 300 Senate patronage employees for incompetence or partisan allegiances strong enough to make them potential moles. Federal Judge Jack Tanner intervened; we were forced to back off by half, and "patronage" was redefined.[12]

For all the *Sturm und Drang* surrounding Friday the 13th and Olympia's "Saint Valentine's Day Massacre," a mistaken impression lingers that von Reichbauer's defection changed everything. It didn't. When the smoke cleared, Jeannette Hayner developed a fuller understanding of how Ted Bottiger felt before the quake, for as majorities go, 25-24 is like babysitting a bear cub who might bite you in the derriere the minute you turn your back. Speaker Polk and the gung-ho conservatives in the other chamber found this hard to grasp. Though von Reichbauer's vote ostensibly made for a majority, the reality was that three other Republicans were wild cards. They were Ellen Craswell, the arch-conservative Christian (she had Jerry Falwell eyes) who defeated hapless Gordon Walgren; Bob McCaslin, the happy warrior from the Spokane Valley who ousted "Big Daddy" Day and never met a tax he liked, and Kent Pullen, a Boeing engineer who played politics the way he played chess—elusively.

When it came time to practice the politics of the possible as the budget crisis grew steadily worse, the Senate Republicans were a caucus without consensus. "This left us at the mercy of the outraged Democrats, none of whom had ever served in the minority ...," says Scott, a former Marine Corps captain with a Ph.D. in history.[13] Being "a compulsive moderate" in 1981 was character-building. Scott and Rod Chandler, the appropriations chairman in the House, worried about the practical and political consequences of a draconian budget and "vainly searched for any middle ground" for their caucuses.[14] Spellman, also dog-paddling against the choppy current, felt their pain. No one at the Capitol could recall a winter with more discontent. One day in the heat of battle over a second supplemental budget, John Jones was so frustrated with von Reichbauer that he half-jokingly asked Democratic leaders if they would take him back.[15]

"NO WAY ON THREE-WAY!" a crowd of 7,000 blue-collar workers chanted outside the Legislative Building. Spellman shared many of their concerns about the workmen's compensation plan being fast-tracked by Speaker Polk, particularly the experimental "wage-loss" system that would replace lump-sum disability payments. "If House Democrats had been railroad workers, they'd have deserved large benefits after being run over by the GOP-engineered train," *The Seattle Times*, not exactly a labor paper, editorialized.[16]

Spellman was booed and heckled as he stood on the Capitol steps to address the angry throng. "Veto it!" they shouted. "If you do your job and I do mine," Spellman promised, "there will not be a bill passed which deserves a veto. I will not support any system that lessens the benefits to the workers."[17] Backers said he was parroting labor's argument. They maintained that a competitive market and private-sector efficiencies would profit all sides.

There were troubled waters, too. Ferry workers who feared the loss of their collective bargaining rights staged a wildcat strike that stranded thousands. Whidbey Island commuters, unhappy over plans to raise fares, staged a "walk-on" boycott, leaving their cars behind to dramatize losses they said the state could sustain if car fares were unaffordable. The Transportation Commission, meantime, took three expensive new ferries out of service until safety questions about their electronic-control systems could be resolved. The contract for six more boats was in doubt.

The tenuous GOP majority in the Senate was backing a bill that would put ferry workers under Civil Service and remove wages from the bargaining table. The House version featured a salary schedule and outlawed strikes. Conservatives estimated that their plan would save the state $39 million over the next six years by placing ferry worker wages on par with other state employees. Spellman met with a delegation of labor leaders, including his friend Arnie Weinmeister, who had delivered the Teamsters' endorsement in the 1980 governor's race. The governor's middle-ground solution maintained collective bargaining but included a no-strike clause, with binding arbitration as a tie-breaking mechanism. House Republicans paid him no heed.[18]

One of the few respites from the tension came on March 19, which

Spellman had designated "Magnuson Appreciation Day." The governor led a joint session of the Legislature in the National Anthem. Then Lieutenant Governor Cherberg, Magnuson's old UW teammate, declared, "And now, here's Maggie!" They rose as one, whistling and cheering, to salute a man whose career in politics had begun in that very chamber in 1933. Magnuson, enjoying himself immensely, pointed to the place he sat when he introduced the first unemployment compensation bill in the nation. "And that was 48 years ago ... So there's a flood of memories—good memories. ... Legislators are the true keepers of the flame. If you have the votes, you don't need a speech. You must gauge your decisions on all legislation by asking what is in the best overall interests of the state, not just what might please some single-issue group ... Do not give in to the tyranny of single-issue politics." [19] The Spellmans hosted a luncheon at the mansion for the Magnusons and former members of the senator's staff. That night at Longacres, the Renton horse-racing track, a thousand people attended a fund-raiser to help retire Maggie's $300,000 debt from his race against Gorton. Spellman was there, together with Gorton, Jackson and many other members of Congress.

A DISCONCERTING thing happened that week. Spellman filed it in the back of his brain because "given the financial mess we were in, I was focused on the here and now."

One of his visitors was a former Republican legislator from Tacoma. Larry Faulk was a lively, good-looking fellow who loved politics. He'd been deputy director of the 1964 Evans gubernatorial campaign in Pierce County. Then, in a textbook campaign that featured hundreds of clean-cut doorbellers, Faulk upset a two-term Democrat to become at 30 the young-est member of the State Senate. In 1970, however, his bid for re-election collided with Booth Gardner. "Remember the name," Adele Ferguson would admonish readers of her popular column, for Gardner was little known outside Pierce County. In addition to his boyish charisma, Gardner had money, lots of money, and access to even more if he needed it. His stepfather, Weyerhaeuser heir Norton Clapp, was "born atop a mound of wealth, which he then turned into a mountain." [20] Clapp gave generously to Republican candidates, including John Spellman.

"I was a devout Republican by birth," Gardner told a biographer, "but I had a huge social-justice conscience." [21] He'd been working with underprivi-leged kids since his freshman year at the University of Washington. Clapp was at first incredulous when Gardner told him he had decided to become a Democrat. Then, thinking it over, he came to admire his stepson's inde-pendence. Out came the checkbook and down went Faulk, though it wasn't just money. Gardner campaigned tirelessly—and Faulk had taught him how. He'd written a field manual on how to run a race for the Legislature—everything from coffee hours to bumper strips. Gardner memorized it and went him one better.

Now, in 1981, Gardner and Faulk were rematched for a newly created job, Pierce County executive. Spellman and Gorton campaigned for Faulk. Scoop Jackson, relishing the thought of Clapp and his well-heeled friends giving money to a Democrat with cross-over appeal, declared that Gardner was "manna from heaven" and hit the stump for Booth.[22] Gardner had a half-dozen paid campaign staffers, money for polls, billboards, multiple mailers and full-page ads.

Faulk arrived at the Governor's Office to plead for more help down the stretch. "Spellman is sitting there, calmly smoking his pipe, and Steve Excell is standing right next to him, smoking a pipe, too. They looked like the Dad and his No. 1 son. I'm walking around waving my hands because I'm a Slav and I can't talk without my hands, and I said, 'Governor, *we can win this thing*. We need help, and we need it now.' Spellman said he'd make some calls. Finally I said, 'Well, governor, let me tell you something: If he gets me, he's gonna get you next!' "[23]

Spellman made some calls, but most big-buck Republican donors sat this one out, several because of their respect for Clapp. On March 10, 1981, with 53 percent of the vote, Booth Gardner became Pierce County's first county executive. "Given another week and more money we could have beat him," Faulk maintains. "We had momentum. I could feel it from the streets. But we didn't have more money. And, of course, the rest is history."[24]

So was Faulk's warning to Spellman. Less of a prophet was Gardner's friend von Reichbauer, who declared that if Gardner didn't take on Pierce County's Democratic machine in his first six months of office he would fail. The "narrowness of his victory" over Faulk was not only surprising, von Reichbauer said, it "will eliminate him as a contender against Governor Spellman in 1984."[25]

Spellman, the state's first "home rule" county executive, congratulated the second. Although he'd backed Faulk, the governor said he believed Gardner would do well. His advice was to be assertive. "I suspect that he already knows that. I would just underline it."[26]

Spellman was invited to von Reichbauer's wedding. He was chagrined to discover Booth was one of the ushers.

Spellman also antagonized one of Gardner's influential friends.

House Bill 166 squeaked through the Senate and arrived on the governor's desk. "School districts," it said, "shall not grant pay increases in excess of amounts or percentages granted by the Legislature." The limitations also applied to health benefits. The Washington Education Association's "primary argument against the bill was that by removing salary and benefits from the bargaining table, the Legislature was taking away the one ingredient—money—that made bargaining work. WEA's aggressive bargaining posture would be dealt a blow that would have devastating effects for years to come." [27] Union leaders urged Spellman to veto the bill. When he signed it, "that ended our relationship with him," said Carol Coe, a WEA leader. Before the Reagan Revolution of 1980, the teachers' union had been at the peak of its power. "The bill number '166' would live in the WEA vocabulary for decades to come." [28]

Reese Lindquist, the WEA's new president, was a personal friend and college classmate of Booth Gardner.

CHAPTER THIRTY-ONE

Choices

Having said "these may be the most important appointments I will make as governor," Spellman on April 6, 1981, chose Dan Evans and Chuck Collins, King County's former chief administrative officer, as Washington's representatives on the new four-state Northwest Power Planning Council. To a large extent, Spellman said, they would be "substitutes for the governor" in deliberations fraught with consequences for every citizen of the Northwest.[1]

The governor and his lobbyists had quashed two onerous amendments to the legislation creating the council. One would have forbidden naming to the council two persons from the same party—"as if party politics should have anything to do with the job," Spellman said.[2] (Collins, in any case, leaned Democrat.) The other, clearly aimed at Evans, now president of The Evergreen State College, would have barred council members from holding other jobs. Most of the detail work would be done by staff, Spellman said. What was needed was the gravitas and moxie to protect the state's interests. The three-term governor and Collins, who headed Metro's transit operations before becoming a business executive, admirably filled the bill, the governor said.

The State Senate quickly confirmed the appointments. Before the month was out, the eight-member council, with Spellman and Oregon Governor Vic Atiyeh looking on, met for the first time and unanimously elected Evans as chairman. The council's headquarters would be in Portland, which pleased Atiyeh. Spellman's prize was far bigger than a building: Washington's hegemony was sealed when Ed Sheets, the ex-Magnuson aide Spellman had appointed to oversee the state Energy Office, became executive director of the Power Council. "How you perform will tell the nation a great deal," Spellman said. "Many skeptics believe the states can't come together and solve problems." The task ahead was "a staggering thing," Collins said.[3] Within two years they must produce a comprehensive energy plan, including a 20-year load forecast, a resource assessment and a scheme to protect wildlife and enhance fish runs.

In 10 intense council meetings over the next six months, the WPPSS debacle loomed large. Evans and Collins "characterized the WPPSS Board as inept and unable to deal with the task of financing and managing construction of nuclear plants. They suggested that the Legislature should name a new, much smaller board to run the system ... and lambasted traditional utility practices in forecasting and planning new power resources."[4] Evans candidly rued the day as governor when he signed off on the Energy Facility Site Evaluation Council permits for the simultaneous construction of five nuclear-power plants. The Power Council early on gave credence to the principle that energy conservation is a resource, just as valuable and a lot cheaper than building new generating capacity. "People have got to realize the future lies in using less," said Collins, but "this is not Armageddon."[5] WPPSS bondholders and ratepayers around the region would soon beg to differ.

WHETHER THE State Patrol needed a new chief was a decision Spellman had been weighing since December. The reviews were mixed on Dixy's appointee, Robert Landon. Legislators from both parties believed the patrol's Organized Crime Unit had overreached in the "Gamscam" probe of Bagnariol and Walgren. After meeting with Will Bachofner, the respected former longtime chief, Spellman asked Fred Fiedler, a UW psychology professor and management specialist, to conduct a survey of the patrol's field commanders. The feedback was conclusive: It was time for a change. For the first time in 32 years, a chief was selected from outside the patrol. Spellman's choice was Neil Moloney, who headed the Port of Seattle's police force. Moloney had risen from beat cop to assistant chief before retiring from the Seattle Police Department. He was a spit-shined Marine Corps veteran—just the man, Spellman believed, to modernize a force "permeated by politics."[6] Personalities and prerogatives made things trickier yet. He and Moloney were in for a rough ride.

Moloney's mandate from the governor was to centralize command and expand the patrol's mission to drug enforcement and organized crime—this time "without any politics." Spellman also wanted troopers to get tougher on drunken drivers. The new chief promptly slashed the number of top-ranking officers and "tightened the reins on the traditionally independent troopers," asking them to do more with less.[7] He clashed repeatedly with Grant Sherman, the equally strong-willed but more politically savvy leader of the Troopers' Association. A new bumper sticker soon appeared: "If you can't find your trooper, he's at roll call." Nor did the chief get much sup-port from sheriffs and police chiefs, who saw the patrol's new initiatives as infringing on their turf. The conflicts between the patrol's top brass and troopers had been simmering for years. They boiled over as the budget crisis deepened and troopers prodded the Legislature to grant them union status. Moloney's by-the-book attitude made them even more intent on changing an "autocratic system where the chief is all-powerful." Less than a year after his arrival, the association overwhelmingly voted no confidence in the chief. Spellman said he had the vote that counted, and expressed "complete confidence" in Moloney. But the battle was now completely joined. It continued for three more years and played out along the 1984 campaign trail.[8]

AS THE LEGISLATURE trudged toward its adjournment deadline, Duane Berentson, the governor's legislative liaison, was blurry-eyed from lobby-ing for the gas-tax increase. Spellman's staunchest supporters in the Sen-ate, Dick Hemstad, Sue Gould and Bill Kiskaddon, often could be found plopped on the sofa in the governor's office, talking strategy. Hemstad, with his perky bow-ties, boyish smile and first-rate brain, had the knack of making everyone feel more optimistic yet never sugar-coated the facts. A diverse cast of characters—Berentson, Excell, budget director Joe Taller and revenue director Glenn Pascall—drifted in and out from early morning 'til late night. When Spellman and Taller holed up with George Scott and Rod Chandler, the Ways and Means chairmen, they sat around a long mahogany table, binders and spreadsheets at hand, "agonizing over who to take from or tax."[9] Spellman came up with several constructive alternatives, Scott recalled, "only to have them shoved back in his lap by Speaker Polk." Still, he avoided confrontations. The governor was interested in accomplish-ment, not rhetoric. "I believe profoundly that what you don't say is more important than what you say," Spellman told them.[10] The way you say what you say takes on added importance, however, when notepads and recorders are omnipresent. Spellman just wasn't a suave, sound-bite guy like Polk or curt combatant like McDermott. During the Kennedy era, *Esquire* magazine ran a memorable cartoon that depicted a waiter asking a ballroom full of presidents what they'd like to drink. Ike's answer was, "To the best of my knowledge I prefer Coke." When a reporter asked Spellman if he'd veto an anti-school busing bill many considered racist, this is what he said:

> I again would not predict. I have not spoken against school busing
> in the past. I don't expect to speak against school busing now. I think

> I would wait to see the outcome of the legislation and listen to the
> rationale and know a lot more about it before I would telegraph what
> I would do on it. ... My style, if you haven't noticed, is to work with the
> Legislative leadership on a one-to-one basis and try to influence them
> ... Rather than to trot out my proposal and get into confrontations, I
> have always been able to get more by meeting with people, suggesting
> amendments, suggesting compliance ... suggesting a plan.[11]

Spellman's not-to-trot style and distinctive features—silver hair,
ski-jump nose, ever-present pipe—were heaven sent for the state's prize-
winning political cartoonists. The *P-I's* David Horsey and *The Times'* Brian
Basset had a field day with the dramas being played out under the Capitol
dome. Jeannette Hayner was the Thatcheresque iron lady; "Railroad
Bill" Polk was the engineer, and Spellman, alas, the man in the caboose.
One day he was "The Amazing Waffleman." On another, a 98-pound
weakling, cowering before mean Republicans in black leather jackets and
motorcycle boots. Spellman, who had amused his junior high schoolmates
with cartoons of his own, framed some of Horsey's. "If you can't laugh
at yourself you shouldn't be in politics," he said. At some point, however,
the laughter has to die down or you shouldn't be in politics. Not a prideful
man, Spellman was nevertheless not without his pride. And he was tired of
the milquetoast bit. Paul O'Connor, Spellman's press secretary, had a belly
full of the boss being portrayed as "some sort of a weak nerd." Puffing a
cigarette and cursing Spellman's enemies, he told reporters that Polk's budget was "repugnant" to the governor. He was cautioned to cool it, though
he'd only told the truth, as usual.[12] O'Connor struck some reporters as "a
manifestation of Spellman's Irish soul." The governor "allowed Paul to do
things he never would have allowed himself to do," one reporter said. "We
had an ability to communicate almost by osmosis," Spellman recalls.[13] The
governor winced, however, when informed that O'Connor, outraged over
a column in the *Bremerton Sun*, had declared to a House communications
staffer, "Where is that bitch Adele Ferguson!?" Juicy news travels fast at the
Capitol. When Adele encountered Steve Excell, she said, "Tell O'Connor
that the bitch is still here."[14]

DESPITE SOME hard-wrought compromises, shortly before midnight on
the 105th day, Speaker Polk's locomotive and Senator Hayner's baling-wire
boxcar ran off the rails. "Dozens of bills were still volleying between the
House and Senate, including some measures needed to make the 1981-83
budget legal. By 2:15 a.m., the Senate Democrats had caucused and decided

they'd cooperate. They'd agree to vote for a quickie special session ... to clean up the unfinished business."[15] House Democrats, angered by Polk's tactics, were less compliant. "By 2:30 a.m.," Dick Larsen observed, "a few Republicans lounged in their chairs around the floor of the House, waiting. On each legislator's desk was a bouquet of bright tulips, which, like the lawmakers, had been wilting though the long day."[16]

House Democrats charged that the Republican budgets—dubbed "Jaws" and "Jaws II"—were balanced on the backs of the poor. House Republicans insisted they'd kept their promise that there'd be no "general" tax increase. The boost in the gas tax—1½ cents a gallon to a total of 13½ cents, with annual increases allowed—was a change from a flat-rate tax to a variable one, they said. And the auto-registration assessment, which would double to $19, was a fee. Dan Grimm, the Democrats' caucus chairman, was fluent in math and semantics. Let's not kid one another, he said. "It *is* a tax increase."[17] Soon, Senate Democrats appeared on the House floor, prodding their brethren to go along with a special session. House Democrats held out for something in writing on what bills would and wouldn't be considered.[18] Spellman brokered a deal. "Looking far fresher than the legislators," the governor emerged from his office at 4:20 a.m. to say he would formally call a special two-day session before noon.

As dawn broke over Budd Inlet on April 27, 1981, Representative Nita Rinehart, a Seattle Democrat, asked Polk, "Does this mean you didn't finish in 105 days?" Polk said it all depended "on what you mean by finish."

"I feel finished," she sighed.[19]

It took the weary lawmakers less than a day to wrap up their work. When they adjourned at 8:19 p.m., Spellman led the Senate in "Auld Lang Syne," told members of the House their hard work was deeply appreciated and announced there'd be cups o'kindness in his office. Legislators, lobbyists and reporters consumed 200 bottles of champagne in the next two hours before heading to their keyboards or bed.[20] What lay ahead was more like another tequila sunrise.

President Reagan, making his first public appearance since surviving an assassin's bullet, told Congress he was doing fine but the economy was "still sick." Delaying the "cure"—his spending and tax cuts—would just prolong the pain, he warned.[21] Washington State's pain seemed intractable for 20 months.

WHILE EVERYONE WAITED to see how the new governor would wield the prodigious power of the line-item veto, there was time to take stock of what had been done in those 106 days:

"Three-Way," allowing private insurance companies a share of the workmen's comp business, died when Senator Kent Pullen, the Republican from Kent who enjoyed good relations with the Federation of State Employees, said no way. Pullen told his caucus he couldn't support even a watered-down version of the bill that had sailed through the House because it "could be bad for both the injured worker and small business."[22] Spellman would have vetoed the plan had it reached his desk.

Spellman's request to give the hard-pressed cities and counties the option of raising the sales tax by a half-cent died in the Senate. But he won strong majorities for a constitutional amendment that would allow the cities, port districts and other municipalities to issue tax-free revenue bonds to spur job-creating projects. The decision was ratified by 56 percent of the voters that fall.

After some late-night lobbying by Dick Schrock and Steve Excell, the Legislature also agreed to not immediately eliminate a program that allowed new or expanding companies to defer sales taxes for up to eight years. "Somewhere we have to quit using the taxpayers' money to subsidize big business," said Senator A.N. "Bud" Shinpoch, a tough-minded liberal from Renton. Excell told him every other state, including Oregon, had a similar program. "At least we'll be on an equal footing with our neighbors."[23] Shinpoch just shook his head.

Spellman reluctantly signed off on legislation boosting college tuition and fees by more than 70 percent over the next two years to generate $90 million in new revenue. The legislation included an automatic escalator clause to ensure that students would pay a set proportion of the actual cost of their education.*

The tuition hike was Scott's bill, and he was not winning any campus popularity polls. More of the increase would be returned to the institutions for programs and salaries than ever before, he said. Concurrently, the state's student loan program would be boosted to help low-income students. And if Reagan slashed federal matching money for loans and grants, the senator from Seattle vowed to support more money for loans. Tuition, in any case, paid only 33 percent of the cost of a college education, Scott said. McDermott called him an "elitist," but Senator Ted Haley, a Tacoma Republican, declared, "I hope no one tells people in my district I voted for a bill that will require students to pay only 33 percent of the cost of their education. Some want it to be 50 percent, and I know some want them to have to pay all the cost." The philosophical battle lines in the Senate couldn't have been more clearly delineated.[24]

Cigarette taxes were boosted 4 cents a pack, liquor by 25 cents a fifth and beer by $1.60 a barrel. All told, higher taxes and fees would generate $400 million. Conservatives failed in a last-minute move to delete money for abortions for women on welfare. They succeeded at long last, however, in lifting the ceiling on consumer-loan interest rates. With inflation rampant, "marketplace interest rates had climbed so high that statutory limits were impeding all kinds of consumer financing." [25] A new death penalty law was enacted—one that would pass constitutional muster. And the Legislature appropriated $1.5 million for a study on whether two of the WPPSS nuclear plants should be completed. The study was a precondition for granting the Supply System more flexibility in negotiating variable interest rates on bond sales.

Spellman happily signed his executive-request bill creating a new Department of Corrections. The Legislature also appropriated $28 million for a new 500-bed maximum-security prison at Monroe. Amos Reed, the new corrections director, had begun moving state prisoners to McNeil Island in March. Some prisoners were living three to a cell at Walla Walla, and on any given night about 30 were sleeping on the floor at Shelton. The old Monroe prison was at capacity. The State Supreme Court had ordered Reed to accept the 284 state prisoners being housed in county jails, while

---

* Tuition and fees for in-state students at the University of Washington and Washington State University would jump from $687 per year to $1,041, then $1,158 in 1982. At the regional four-year schools, the increases were from $618 to $849, then $924. At community colleges, students who had paid $306 would now pay $459 and $507 in 1982.

the federal court was demanding a plan to reduce the inmate population at Walla Walla.

THE POLITICAL PRIZE for the new Republican majority, as Evans and Gorton had adroitly demonstrated during the 1960s, should have been redistricting—the opportunity to redraw legislative and congressional districts to enhance their chances of gaining more control, especially of the Legislature. The eighth congressional seat was a new plum. The legislative plan would prove counterproductive, and the congressional plan produced bipartisan astonishment. It penalized Joel Pritchard of Seattle and Sid Morrison of the Yakima Valley, the only Republicans in the delegation, while Norm Dicks of Bremerton and Don Bonker of Olympia would have smoother sailing. Spokane had been blatantly bisected to the detriment of Tom Foley. Spellman could barely believe his eyes. "He called me over just after he saw the details of the bill," says Ralph Munro, who was then Secretary of State across the hall from the Governor's Office. "He was very angry. 'Don't those guys realize what Tom has done for our state?' " [26]

Al Swift's new Second District sprawled from Whatcom County, bordering on Canada, to Grays Harbor on the coast where Aberdeen and Hoquiam, joined at the hip for a century, had been split apart. Everett, meantime, was mad as hell at being appended to North Seattle. The redrawn district was demographically more Democratic, but Swift would need a new set of tires every six months. He couldn't fathom what the Republicans were thinking: "I think it is flat dumb." [27] Senator Gorton, an acknowledged redistricting master, seconded the motion. Von Reichbauer, facing a recall election in September, said that if Spellman vetoed the congressional plan the Democrats probably would pour even more money into his district, but something had to be done about "a terrible, terrible process." [28] Munro, Spellman, Gorton, Common Cause and an array of other good-government groups said the state shouldn't wait another nine years for the next Census to set up an independent redistricting commission. Soon, the entire congressional delegation was urging Spellman to veto the bill.

And he did—the congressional portion, that is. There were also "glitches" in the legislative boundaries, Spellman said, but those could be easily repaired during the next legislative session. And if the lawmakers were diligent they should have time to produce a revised congressional plan before the 1982 elections.

Spellman struck a blow for open government by vetoing a bill backed by the Boeing Company. The bill would have short-circuited the "appearance of fairness" doctrine," which held that once a planning or land-use decision was under consideration all discussions would have to be conducted in public. Boeing argued that the doctrine restricted its lobbying rights by allowing courts to reverse land-use decisions simply because a closed-door meeting was held.

SPELLMAN FACED his first major crisis as governor on May 19, 1981. Some of the ferry-worker unions were offering him a deal: If he would veto the Republican bill placing them under Civil Service, they would promise not to strike—or engage in any "slowdowns, sickouts or any other disruptions"— during the remaining two years of their contracts. Republicans called it blackmail. Spellman called it a "very tender situation." [29] That was true in more ways than one. The governor had a bad backache from too much sitting and a headache from too much politics. If the ferry workers struck, the Longshoremen and other maritime unions might follow suit in solidarity or handicap his efforts to boost trade with the Pacific Rim. There was another tedious quid pro quo: In return for passage of the gas-tax increase, the governor had agreed not to block the Civil Service bill the conservatives wanted. They'd made it less punitive. And he didn't expect it to pass. It did. Now he couldn't break his word. He held his nose, attempted to maintain a measure of neutrality, appealed for calm and let the bill become law without his signature. That night, marine engineers called in sick or walked off the job. The next morning, 40,000 Puget Sound commuters were either stranded or taking the long way around for the second time in less than two months. It was Berentson's first day as secretary of the Department of Transportation. He and the governor commiserated over the task at hand, bringing "sanity out of chaos," as Spellman put it.[30] Then they learned that Harley Hoppe was in the Secretary of State's office filing an initiative to roll back their hard-won revenue package, which would generate $15 million to subsidize the ferry system and $59 million for the highways.

Spellman told the ferry workers that if they'd stay the course, work with him, a collective-bargaining bill with a binding arbitration clause would be a priority executive request to the Legislature in January 1982.[31] Some union leaders said Spellman seemed sincere. They blamed the "union-busting" Republicans in the Legislature. Others were livid with Spellman. "The governor himself said it was a bad bill," said one. "I don't see how he possibly could let it become law. Not if he wants to be governor for a second term." [32] Spellman appealed for a cooling off period. He talked with Jimmy Herman, the powerful president of the 60,000-member International Longshoremen's & Warehouseman's Union, who suggested a blue-ribbon commission to study the ferry system's problems. Spellman liked the idea.

He said he would chair it himself. It remained for Herman, a tough-talking old pro who had gone to sea at 17, to sell the idea to the rank and file. On the third day of the walkout, he went down to the docks and excoriated politicians "too stupid to know what the hell they are doing" for using ferry workers as scapegoats. "You're in good company," he told a ferry worker wearing a "Waterfront Thugs" T-shirt, a reference to a remark by a legislator. Then he urged them to go back to work. The cheering stopped. "We've been double-crossed before!" someone shouted. Herman promised there would be full amnesty. They ought to give the governor a chance. Unless the commission made real progress, "We'll shut everything down." They went back to work.[33]

Spellman's 14-member commission included Berentson, Herman, Arnie Weinmeister and Marvin Williams, president of the State Labor Council, as well as four lawmakers and two ferry riders. The plan it recommended embraced Spellman's call for restoration of collective bargaining, with binding arbitration and a ban on strikes. It ran aground in the 1982 legislative sessions. Spellman wouldn't get a bill to sign until the Democrats regained control the next year.

ANOTHER CLOSELY watched but ultimately easier decision was whether to sign the Republican anti-school busing bill. It would have cut off transportation funding for Seattle schools if the district persisted in busing students past the nearest or next nearest school to their homes to achieve desegregation. The program involved nearly 40 percent of the children in the district. An anti-school busing initiative approved by 66 percent of the voters in 1978 was on appeal to the U.S. Supreme Court. Spellman, who had brought civil rights cases as an attorney, let the bill become law without his signature. He believed that would hasten "an ultimate, binding decision" from the courts on its constitutionality. "This way of doing it might be more beneficial to the cause than just vetoing it," said Senator George Fleming, one of two African-Americans in the Legislature. Seattle School Superintendent David Moberly agreed. "We're always going to have this hanging over us unless we get a federal interpretation one way or the other."[34] Moberly had assured the governor the district would file suit as soon as he announced his decision.*

---

*The U.S. Supreme Court declared the initiative unconstitutional in 1982, but the divisive issue was far from settled. "The initial opposition to race-based busing came primarily from white parents living in racially homogeneous neighborhoods. By the late 1980s, the voices of dissent were coming from all sides, including some of the same white liberals and African-Americans who had originally endorsed busing. Critics complained that the Seattle Plan unfairly burdened children of color and contributed to a widening achievement gap between white and minority students. ..."[35] In the late 1990s, mandatory busing came to a quiet end.

Taking stock of his first six character-building months as governor, Spellman told a Rotary Club he felt "just like the guy who told himself, 'Cheer up, things could get worse!' So I cheered up and sure enough, things got worse."

CHAPTER THIRTY-TWO

What Next?

How much worse? To the brink of bankruptcy. Revenues tanked all summer. The week before Labor Day found State Treasurer Robert S. O'Brien, hat in hand, borrowing $400 million from Citibank of New York to meet the state's payroll and other obligations for the remainder of 1981. Spellman ordered an across-the-board, 10.1 percent cut that also applied to state funding for public schools. Thirty-two districts immediately appealed to the State Supreme Court, arguing "irreparable harm." The court, as divided as everyone else over the state of affairs, ruled 5-to-4 that the schools weren't exempt. "Some tax increase is a foregone conclusion," said Rod Chandler, the House appropriations chairman. Speaker Polk and Majority Leader Hayner disagreed.[1]

For higher education, the high court decision was actually what passed for good news in this climate. Had the K-through-12 schools been exempted, the rest of state government could have faced 20 percent reductions—cold comfort to UW President William Gerberding. Spellman's plan to close the budget gap also postponed the new student-loan program, boosted tuition for graduate students and reduced tuition waivers for teaching and research assistants.

Gerberding castigated the governor for discriminating against higher ed and ordered a full court press by faculty, regents and alumni. A nuclear-engineering professor said that if Spellman had his way a great research university would be transformed into "what we might call Montlake Community College."[2]

Newspapers spotlighted the plight of a 65-year-old Army vet who as a young GI had "splashed into the chill waves off the French coast and waded ashore ... into the hellfire of the Normandy landing." Now he lay helpless on a special bed in his Lynnwood home, both legs amputated. "He has suffered two strokes. He is a total invalid. And there's no public help available to him. ...The state Department of Veterans Affairs has denied him admission to the state soldiers' home at Orting in Pierce County. The reason: state budget cuts."[3]

Cost overruns, investor jitters, strikes and mishaps had brought work at two WPPSS nuclear projects to a near standstill. In September, a blue-ribbon panel appointed by Spellman and Governor Atiyeh recommended mothballing Project 4 at Hanford and Project 5 at Satsop in Grays Harbor County. The 88 public utilities sponsoring the plants—in way over their heads—agreed. They teamed with private energy users and desperately negotiated to arrange temporary financing for the mothballing plan. "The alternative: Abandoning the two projects and perhaps causing chaos in the nation's municipal bond market."[4]

The environmental battle over Northern Tier's proposed oil port at Port Angeles and pipeline beneath Puget Sound was also heating up. The state Energy Facility Site Evaluation Council had tentatively recommended that Spellman reject the plan. Northern Tier executed a clever end-around: Company lawyers reminded the Army Corps of Engineers that it was legally obliged to not wait for the state's final recommendation before issuing its own. Corps regulations held "that if any federal, state or local-government agency rejects a project before the Corps acts on it, the Corps cannot approve permits for the project."[5] The state, in other words, had veto power. Pipeline opponents were caught off guard when the Corps, confronted with this Catch 22, did an about-face and announced it was prepared to grant the permits. "Any engineering and safety problems aren't of sufficient magnitude to warrant denial."[6] Ecology Director Don Moos and the federal Fish & Wildlife Service protested, to no avail. The Reagan administration amped up its pressure on Spellman. America needed oil.

The forest-products industry was hemorrhaging jobs. Boeing retrenched as air travel declined and export markets stagnated. Then, on November 3, the voters resoundingly abolished the state inheritance tax, which would cost the treasury nearly $43 million. A thousand college students massed in front of the Capitol, chanting "No more cuts!"[7] The cities and counties pleaded for an additional half-cent sales tax.

What next—locusts? Many Democrats were celebrating their great good fortune in not being in the majority.

Von Reichbauer, for the record, easily survived the recall election, though the campaign was expensive and nasty.

SPELLMAN CALLED a special session, to begin on November 9. The lawmakers were unamused. McDermott hissed that the governor ought to "level with the people" about the need for taxes even higher than his proposal to

Spellman addresses the Seattle Rotary Club.

boost the state sales tax by seven-tenths of a cent. Gary Nelson, the House GOP floor leader, suggested Spellman terminate 4,000 more state employees "to bring the number down to what it was in 1977."[8] The House plan hammered the schools and the Department of Social & Health Services, where Alan Gibbs was doing extraordinarily deft work. He had created 250 "decision packages" that reduced spending by $70 million while driving "five tiers of bureaucracy to decisions with minimal friction."[9] Spellman declared, "Either we are going to meet the needs of the state or shut down."[10]

While the budget committees crunched numbers, the Republicans plowed ahead with hearings on a revised redistricting plan. Democrats called it a charade. Spellman and Ralph Munro renewed their call for a constitutional amendment to create a bipartisan, five-member redistricting board. Munro drafted a plan that gave priority to preserving "communities of interest" and stipulated that no district could be drawn to "purposely favor or disfavor any political party, incumbent legislator or other group or person."[11] Success would take two more years.

SPELLMAN THREATENED to veto the draconian House plan to balance the budget. Defiant conservatives in both chambers suggested closing The Evergreen State College and abbreviating the school year. Spellman said he would support raising the sales tax a penny to generate $531 million. Rounding up those 50 votes was the toughest thing he'd ever done, Polk said. But that left them only halfway to solving a billion-dollar problem. Spellman was willing to make cuts totaling $227 million but couldn't countenance laying off 5,000 more state employees. "It would have a profound effect on institutions. We've already cut 1,250 positions and this would be on top of that."[12]

On Thanksgiving eve, Spellman's hopes hinged on the Senate. "There's every reason to be hopeful," he told reporters after meeting with legislative leaders. In reality, the House budget was dead on arrival. An intransigent quartet of conservatives opposed any tax increase and McDermott was offering 50 amendments. Hope evaporated in less than two hours. They kicked sand in the governor's face. Dick Larsen wrote a stinging review in *The Times*: "It was, for the umpteenth time, an indication that Spellman, the former King County Executive, who'd assured voters he could deal with the legislative branch of government, was badly out of touch with the Legislature."[13] Wayne Ehlers, the new House minority leader from Pierce County, said Dan Evans knew how to get things done because he'd been in the trenches as a legislator. Democrats and Republicans clucked their tongues and said things went south for Spellman when he lost Berentson to the Department of Transportation. He'd better learn the ropes, they said. Excell and O'Connor saw that the "waffleman" stuff was really getting under Spellman's skin. They knew Lois hated it.

On December 2, the 24th day of the special session, came a grudging compromise: The sales tax increase would be "temporary," and they jettisoned the demand that Spellman make 5,000 layoffs. Instead, he agreed to order agency managers to reduce their payrolls by about 4 percent, or 2,500 layoffs, and impose travel restrictions. Redistricting wasn't resolved, a good thing under the circumstances, Spellman said. The proposal to help the cities and counties failed in the House, consigned to committee during the dying hours despite furious arm-twisting by lobbyists—a bad thing, said Spellman, a county man. He would try again next year.

Though they'd cut spending by another $300 million, no one, least of all Spellman, believed deeper trouble wasn't ahead when the Legislature reconvened in January. Each new revenue forecast was gloomier than the last. It was shortfall upon shortfall, and "no new taxes" was like the ghost of Christmas past. "The state is not facing one crisis," said Budget Director Joe Taller, "it is facing six crises at once": a cash-flow shortage, revenue shortfalls linked to low consumer confidence, declining timber-sale income, higher interest rates, huge cutbacks in federal aid and a declining bond rating. The loss of inheritance taxes made it seven. And then there was the $400 million loan that would come due October 1, 1982. That would be eight.[14] Rod Chandler had suggested deferring a $114 million payment into the police and firefighter pension fund and borrowing $90 million outside the general fund. "That goes right back to credit-card financing, funny money and bookkeeping shifts," the state treasurer warned. The state cannot spend what it doesn't have."[15]

JUST BEFORE CHRISTMAS, Spellman made his first appointment to the State Supreme Court. Former congressman Floyd V. Hicks of Tacoma, a

Democrat who had served on the court since 1977, was suffering from cata-
racts. To lighten his reading load and shorten his commute, Hicks asked
the governor to appoint him to the Pierce County Superior Court bench.
Spellman chose as Hicks' successor 58-year-old Vernon R. Pearson of Tacoma, a Republican who had served on the Court of Appeals since its inception in 1969. Pearson was "unassuming, soft-spoken, hesitantly thoughtful,
gregarious yet shy ... with a sharp, competitive, but open legal mind." [16] In
other words, precisely the sort of person Spellman wanted on the court.
Pearson proved to be a wise moderate, "a voice of reason and calm" at a
time when the court was divided by internal battles. [17]

The runner-up was James A. "Jimmy" Andersen, whose time came in
1984 when Justice Charles Stafford died. Andersen was a popular politician
and a prodigious worker with a first-rate mind. Together with Joel Pritchard
and Slade Gorton, Andersen was a charter member of the young Republican
coalition that propelled Dan Evans to power in the early 1960s. Andersen
had been coal miner as a youth, Spellman noted, and a front-line soldier
during World War II, suffering severe wounds in the Battle of the Bulge.
"He has been a prosecutor, a legislative leader and an appellate court
judge. His integrity is unquestioned." There was another reason Andersen got the job: Like Justice Carolyn Dimmick, with whom he worked in
the King County Prosecutor's office in the 1950s, Andersen was strong
on law and order. Andersen said his experience as a deputy prosecutor
gave him an understanding of "what crime really is and what it does to
people." [18] Seattle Times editors wrote, "Never has Governor Spellman made
a better appointment ... ." [19] Andersen served with distinction for 11 years.

Spellman had an opportunity during his last weeks as governor to appoint his third state Supreme Court justice when Dimmick resigned pending a Reagan appointment to the federal bench. Spellman jumped at the
chance and elevated Barbara Durham from the Court of Appeals. The brainy
42-year-old conservative had been on his short list when he appointed Andersen. Durham's appointment also allowed him to name his Georgetown
Law School classmate, Walter E. Webster Jr., to succeed Durham on the
appellate bench. Yet another vacancy on the Court of Appeals went to
Ken Grosse, who had served Spellman as personal legal counsel and chief
of staff.

IT WAS AN UNHAPPY NEW YEAR, Spellman acknowledged in a sobering
televised "Report to the People" on January 7, 1982. They'd need another
$309 million to hobble through the next 18 months. His economic advisers
expected no improvement until summer. (They were off by a year.) And

when the turnaround finally arrived, as surely it must, Spellman said, the
recovery would be sluggish. (Correct on that score.) More Americans, 9.5
million, to be precise, and more Washingtonians, 192,000, were jobless
than at any time since 1940. "And it's absolutely predictable that in February
we will have more than 213,000 unemployed," Spellman said. "We're still
in deep trouble. We're still losing ground." Grim-faced, he looked straight
into the KING-TV camera and acknowledged he had promised that if they
elected him their governor he wouldn't raise taxes. "That was a mistake,
and I was wrong." Now his whole political future might be at stake. "I
didn't run to get re-elected, but to do a job. ... We've gone as far as we can
go with cuts." [20]

What should be done? Extend the state sales tax to gasoline purchases,
which would generate $176 million, Spellman said; boost higher-education
fees; adopt an ability-to-pay fee schedule for the parents of handicapped
children in state institutions; tax private planes; accelerate tax collections
from big business; expedite the sale of public-works bonds to create new
jobs. If they did all that, they could end the shell game of borrowing against
expected income. They'd even have a modest cash umbrella to handle the
next rainy day. But if the Legislature rejected his plan, "a radical change" in
the state's tax structure might be necessary. Doubtless, some would once
again advocate an income tax, Spellman said, but he was opposed to that. [21]

Senator Hayner, still clinging to a 25-24 majority, said the governor
might be too pessimistic about revenues. In any case, a new gas tax was
dead on arrival. Senator McDermott agreed, but prodded Spellman to
"show backbone." [22] Then when he did, they were shocked and dismayed.
They said he had cut off his nose to spite his face.

THE EVENTS of January 18-20 were so astounding "it was as though, in the
middle of the night, someone had dumped a hallucinogenic into the Olympia water supply." [23] Republicans were talking about raising taxes; 16,000
blue-collar workers—loggers, hard hats, ferry workers, women wearing
black armbands to symbolize their anger over workplace discrimination and
cutbacks in child care—massed outside the state Capitol. And the "bland,
mild-mannered" governor abruptly canned his revenue director, Glenn
Pascall, a man hailed by Democrats and Republicans alike as brilliant.

On the 20th, the governor had opened the *Post-Intelligencer* over his
oatmeal to discover that Pascall had generated an unpalatable headline:
"Spellman now weighing a state income tax." The news was also on the
radio. Lois looked up and their eyes blazed together. To Spellman, the headline was untrue, politically incorrect and the last straw. He listened to a tape

recording of Pascall telling the House Revenue Committee that he and the governor had discussed an income tax, "and I think the consensus view is that the income tax is no longer an idea which is doomed to fail." [24] Spellman weighed his next move for about 60 seconds. Pascall was addressing the Seattle Chamber of Commerce's legislative steering committee when he received the call telling him he'd been fired. O'Connor rounded up the press. "I have not considered an income tax. I am not considering an income tax, and I do not expect to consider an income tax," Spellman said, jaw set. "Mr. Pascall has resigned." Not quite the unvarnished truth. He had *considered* an income tax—but rejected it as an exercise in futility. And Mr. Pascall hadn't resigned. Dick Larsen identified the root cause of the problem between the governor and his revenue director: Pascall was "open, articulate and communicative. Perhaps too communicative. Apparently, in the view of the governor's office, Pascall, while ceremonially speaking for the governor, sometimes spoke the views of Pascall." [25] One of Spellman's diary entries weeks earlier cut to the chase: "Big mouth." He had told Excell and Richard Allison, his chief of staff, that Pascall had to go. The First Lady, who had a keen eye for body language, had long thought Pascall presumptuous. (Some said the wrong Spellman was governor.) Lois emphatically agreed with John's decision. Representative Helen Sommers, a Seattle Democrat who admired Pascall, didn't. "It is so *unlike* John Spellman. He's usually a reflective, contemplative person." [26]

When he dithered before firing the fast-and-loose Hector Torres as director of Veterans Affairs they called him indifferent, insulated and indecisive. Now he was accused of impulsiveness.

Pascall was quickly hired by the Senate Republican Caucus as a researcher. "That was supposed to teach me a lesson," Spellman says.

Don Burrows, Pascall's deputy, succeeded him. Burrows was slight of build and unassuming, yet encyclopedic in his knowledge of the state's tax structure. "Don was what I was looking for all along," Spellman says. "He knew all about the job. He'd been with the Department of Revenue for 25 years. ... He could give me answers."

Spellman appointed a new Tax Advisory Council, and said it should consider all alternatives. Including an income tax? "I'm not going in there at the beginning or end and say you shall consider this or you shall not consider that," Spellman told reporters. "The same applies to the director of revenue. I do expect the director of revenue to come to me with his ideas instead of going elsewhere, and I'm sure he will." [27] Everyone laughed, including Burrows and his boss.

THE LEGISLATURE quickly stalemated over taxes and cuts, cuts and taxes, with Democrats and moderate Republicans outvoted by intransigent anti-tax conservatives. In late January, Speaker Polk "dropped a bombshell proposal for a 1 percent across-the-board cut, a state lottery, deferral of $221 million in pension payments, a $34 million hiring freeze, 'productivity increases' ... and state employees taking a day off without pay, which was as doomed as Spellman's mostly-taxes approach."[28] George Scott, the Ways and Means chairman in the Senate, observed that Polk, having "strong-armed his fellow conservatives into a half-billion-dollar sales tax increase in November, had shot his 'wad.'"[29]

They accomplished one major thing early on: a congressional redistricting plan that no one absolutely hated except a determined group of Everett residents who threatened a court challenge. Spellman signed the bill. When a three-judge federal panel threw out the plan later that year, it was back to the drawing board. The dispute hastened the birth of an independent redistricting commission, which was approved resoundingly by the voters in 1983.

The governor won praise from the cultural community for establishing a Task Force on the Arts. Washington ranked 48th in state funding of the arts, Spellman said, adding that art was "not some frill" to be ignored during difficult times. "The arts in Washington State and nationwide face a funding crisis of unprecedented proportions," he said, and "traditional funding sources can only partially address this crisis."[30] They must get creative.

Desperate creativity was being embraced by the Washington Public Power Supply System, which was trying to sell bonds to pay off bonds. The WPPSS board approved "controlled termination" for two of its five plants—one at Satsop, one at Hanford—after a mothballing plan collapsed. That left WPPSS with a debt load of $2.25 billion, three more plants hanging fire and a staggering cash-flow problem. A thousand workers were laid off, helping push the state's unemployment rate to 11.4 percent. If the process spiraled into uncontrolled termination, Spellman warned, every ratepayer and industrial-energy consumer would feel the squeeze. Washington's credit rating had been downgraded twice in the past year. If WPPSS defaulted on its bond obligations, he said the fallout would also hit counties, cities, ports, PUD's and school districts, to say nothing of individual investors.[31]

Spellman signed a bill allowing WPPSS to pay higher interest rates—15 percent—on loans from its member utilities to finance termination. In Hoquiam, 3,000 "Irate Ratepayers" staged a rally to excoriate their PUD commissioners. WPPSS would occupy a great deal of the governor's time for the next three years. His immediate problem was an unbalanced budget, and a Legislature to match. "I was very disappointed and very frustrated. They said I lacked backbone. The feeling was mutual."

CHAPTER THIRTY-THREE

The Ides of March

Act One, Scene Seven: March 11, 1982. The Governor's Conference Room on the 60th and last day of the tortuous regular session of the 47th Washington State Legislature. Barring a miracle, a special session will be necessary to break the logjam over a budget to bridge the next 15 months. Twenty-four hardcore conservative Republicans in the House and three stubborn senators say that even if Hell freezes over they won't vote for new taxes. Spellman says the "childishness" is unbecoming. Speaker Polk and Senator McDermott say the governor's statements are making things worse. "Baloney," says Spellman. Reporters, much stimulated by the drama, are arrayed around the long, lion's-paw table where governors have met the press since 1928.[1]

Governor Spellman (with modulated exasperation): Yesterday I sent to each member of the Legislature a memo attached to an analysis by the Department of Revenue regarding the lead time necessary to implement any new tax program. ... All of the revenue proposals by the Senate, by the conference Committee of Eight and by the governor assume an April 1 implementation date for a revenue package or a tax cut. ... Unless the Legislature acts by the 16th of March, it is perilous whether such a program could be put together in a timely way. Close to a million dollars a day is lost if that is not done. ... With each day of inaction, the problem for the state becomes deeper. The necessity for higher revenue or deeper cuts becomes more imperative.

Reporter: Governor, yesterday 24 members of the House Republican Caucus, that's *your* party caucus, signed a petition indicating that they believed this entire problem can be solved without new taxes. They said they went to the well for you in November with a higher tax package and what is needed now is better management of state government to be thrown into the equation. And that's the kind of message they want to

Spellman mulls a
question during a
press conference.

get across to you. What is your response to the action of those members
of the Republican caucus?

Governor: First, I do not think most of them went to the well for me
or for the public in November, nor have they in the full time I have
been governor. I think a group of troglodytes would have got together
and drafted that kind of proposal. It would decimate education both
at the primary and the secondary and the higher education levels. It is
predicated upon raiding the pension funds, which are already in serious
trouble. ... It cannot be taken seriously if you believe that government
is to preserve peace and promote the general welfare. It is a totally
unrealistic proposal. ...

Reporter: Are you a little disappointed in your own party's performance
in the Legislature?

Governor: I am, and I am very disappointed in the Democratic Party's,
too. It does no good for them to point fingers at one another. This is a
peoples' problem. If the Democrats say they are only going to give three
votes in the Senate, that is unacceptable to solve the peoples' problem.
If the Republicans fight among one another, that is unacceptable. We
simply must get together. A majority of the people in each house are
responsible legislators and they need to have the chance to vote on
something that is a responsible package.

Reporter: Governor, what should be done by you, by Speaker Polk, about
the sizable minority in his majority?

Governor: *By me?* Well, I certainly am frustrated with the group and
disapprove of the group. I am not talking about 24 people. I see a lot of

people on there who I think signed something because it was in support of the Speaker. But there are a few people in that group who I have very little hope for. I do not think they have contributed one thing to the welfare of the State of Washington. I guess that I would have a very hard time recommending that the electorate return people to this body who are stumbling blocks rather than builders.

Reporter: Are you suggesting that those legislators who you think are not contributing might find themselves in the next election with Governor John Spellman opposing them?

Governor: I would have a very hard time supporting them. This is too early to get involved in that. There is always hope for redemption.

Reporter: Governor, some of these conservatives in both houses who have refused to vote, who have opposed the budget cuts and have opposed increased taxes say that they actually almost welcome a challenge from you because they feel that you have not been the leader that they were expecting.

Governor: I am sure that is true. If they expected me to be a troglodyte they are wrong.

Reporter: They cite a public opinion survey ... by the State Republican Central Committee showing 57 percent of the folks said they did not want new taxes and to go back and try and solve...

Governor: (interrupting): *I do not want new taxes.* Nobody wants new taxes.

Reporter: Governor, do you see yourself drifting away from the mainstream conservative Republican Party?

Governor: No, I do not. I recall at a time like this Senator Norris Cotton's old story, and it applies exactly to me. He talked about the husband and wife who were riding along in a Model-T Ford. They were old farmers. And she said, "Don't you remember we used to always sit real close together before we were married?" And he sat there behind the wheel and said, "Well, I ain't moved." I have not moved. My position is the same as always. It is these people who have gone farther and farther out in the fringe.[2]

"Troglodyte" was a word Paul O'Connor had used in the briefing before the press conference. "I was venting about the conservatives in the House. But when the governor used it, I was surprised. I think my body temperature changed because I knew it might cause trouble."[3] Spellman didn't seem to care. He ordered the Legislature into immediate special session, urging them to get the job done in "10 consecutive days." Even 30, it turned out, wouldn't be enough.

THE 24 REBELS reported for duty on March 12 wearing "Join the Troglodytes" buttons. Alley Oop, the comic-strip caveman, was depicted placing a crown in the shape of the Capitol dome on Spellman's head. "This has united our caucus more than anything else this session," declared Representative Dick Bond, the die-hard conservative from Spokane who had led a petition drive telling Polk to stand fast. At noon, sympathetic senators informed the House, "Cave No. 1 is organized and ready to do business."[4] Olympia soon seemed to have gone to the Trogs. A "Troglodyte Joke Book" appeared. Sample:

> Q: Why do Troglodytes always vote no?
> A: Because they don't know three-letter words like "yes" and "tax."
> Q: How many Troglodytes does it take to screw in a light bulb?
> A: None, because Troglodytes don't use light bulbs. But it takes only 24 hours to screw up a budget.[5]

Another button said, "Cheer up. This is John Spellman's last term." Spellman shrugged. "There are some whose opposition I'm honored by. I feel those buttons are medals. ... If the anarchist, anti-government group doesn't like me, that doesn't upset me. I didn't get elected to see valid state programs, people programs, schools, social programs, go out of business." To those who said he wasn't being a leader, "My answer is that we have had four sessions and I got what I asked for in the first three and I expect to win this one."[6] His sense was that the Trogs "and other obstructionists" were more out of touch with the electorate than he was. Speaker Polk, meantime, "had lost control of his right wing ... ."[7]

In the immortal words of satirist Ring Lardner, "The curtain is lowered for seven days to denote the lapse of a week" in which nothing happened. Spellman blasted the House Ways and Means Committee for deep-sixing a Senate-passed budget. The House bill proposed spending cuts totaling $226 million—more than twice what the Senate had agreed to; cuts that would decimate education at every level, Spellman said. House Republicans also wanted to transfer programs for the developmentally disabled, alcoholics, addicts and juvenile delinquents to their communities. Spellman said it was a shell game that would just shift the need for higher taxes to the local level while subverting state standards for social services. As an alternative to the higher gas tax, Spellman suggested a 10 percent surcharge on all existing taxes except the property tax. A Senate Republican bill advocated an 8 percent surcharge and a 2.75 percent sales tax on food, which Democrats rejected. The House passed a lottery bill. The Senate pigeon-holed it.

As a condition for providing any votes, Senate Democrats demanded passage of a bill extending unemployment benefits from 39 weeks to 52 weeks. The House finally assented. And on the 30th day, April 10, most of the Troglodytes also caved on higher taxes. Sixteen of the 24 voted to reimpose the sales tax on food until June 30, 1983, the end of the biennium, to raise $273 million.* Spellman said a tax on food hurt those least able to pay. He flayed the duplicity of House Democrats, "who said the food tax was the best they could do and then circulated an initiative to repeal it the same night." [8] Seattle Mayor Charles Royer said the session was the "worst and meanest in anyone's memory." [9] Spending was cut by another $142 million.

It still wasn't enough. They'd all be back in June. But after November some wouldn't be back at all.

---

*Voting for the food tax were: Reps. Harold Clayton, Lyle Dickie, Emilio Cantu, Helen Fancher, Ray Isaacson, Dick Nickell, Curt Smith, Walt Sprague, Scott Barr, Sim Wilson, Joan Houchen, Bob Chamberlain, Noel Bickham, Pat Fiske, Dick Barrett and Mike McGinnis. The eight Trogs who stuck to their clubs were: Jeanette Berleen, Harry James, Bob Eberle, Karen Schmidt, Paul Sanders, Dick Bond, Mike Padden and Margaret Leonard.[9]

An Epic Process
of Due Process

"N
o outraged Chinese governor could stop the Emperor from building the Great Wall. Nor did a Roman senator thwart the Appian Way, nor a Russian prince prevent the Trans-Siberian Railroad. But today one of the nation's mightiest public-works projects, the $2.7 billion, 1,490-mile Northern Tier Pipeline designed to carry Alaskan crude oil from Puget Sound to Midwestern refineries, is being blocked by a single man, Governor John Spellman of Washington. ..."[1]

That was the opening paragraph of *People* magazine's profile of the little-known Western politician who was "bucking president and party to turn an oil pipeline into a pipe dream."

After 5½ years of hearings that produced 40,000 pages of testimony, the state Energy Facility Site Evaluation Council on January 27, 1982, voted decisively to deny permits for an oil port at Port Angeles and a pipeline beneath the Sound. The final decision would be Spellman's alone. Over the next 71 days, he was subjected to unrelenting pressure—from the corridors of the White House to union halls in Bellingham, Boise and Bismarck; from farmers and fishermen, iron workers and environmentalists; from fellow governors, party leaders and legislators, senators and congressmen, school children and senior citizens. The Governor's Office received 7,500 letters he would not read. Nor would he meet with placard-waving Greenpeace members or the pipeline supporters who staged a sit-in. When the Port Angeles High School Roughriders traveled to Bainbridge Island for a baseball game, Northern Tier sponsored the radio broadcast. It also paid for a poll that said 66 percent of the state supported the pipeline. All told, it was "perhaps the most imposing array of public and private interests ever to try to twist the arm of a Washington governor."[2]

The Site Evaluation Council's decision boiled down to two major concerns. The first was the stability of 22 miles of pipeline below Puget Sound between the Olympic Peninsula and Skagit County. Northern Tier's studies of the underwater terrain at depths up to 380 feet were deemed inadequate. The second concern was the risk of a disastrous tanker fire or explosion in Port Angeles harbor. Northern Tier and its supporters said the council was ignoring recent information from the Army Corps of Engineers and the U.S. Coast Guard.

Informed earlier that his consultants had missed key areas of the seabed along the proposed route when they drilled for core samples, Cortlandt Dietler, the chairman of Northern Tier's board, had been adamant that no additional core samples were necessary. Smoking a Churchillian cigar, the Denver oilman showed up at the Governor's Office and demanded a meeting with Spellman. Dietler poked a finger in the governor's chest and declared he wasn't going to drill another damn inch. "As miscalculations go, it was breathtaking," says Steve Excell, who had looked on with astonishment. Dietler's parting shot was "We're going to put the squeeze on you!"[3]

And they did. Proponents unleashed the political equivalent of a Duke full-court press. Spellman was set to attend a meeting of the National Governors' Conference in Washington, D.C., in February. U.S. Energy Secretary James Edwards urged the governor to meet with him, as well as Defense Secretary Caspar Weinberger and Secretary of State Alexander Haig, to discuss the "national-defense" implications of the pipeline. Commerce Secretary Malcolm Baldrige wanted to see him, too. Recent turmoil in Latin America raised concerns about the security of oil shipments through the Panama Canal to Gulf Coast ports, Edwards said. The proposed pipeline was the safest, most expeditious way to move large quantities of crude to the interior of the country, he said, noting that even President Carter had underscored the importance of the pipeline to America's long-term energy independence when he endorsed the project in 1980. Cecil Andrus, Carter's Interior Secretary, came to Seattle at Northern Tier's request to lobby the environmental community. If the pipeline was approved, there was the potential for a hookup with the state's four biggest refineries, Andrus said, and that "might eliminate much of the tanker traffic on Puget Sound." Though smaller than super, those tankers were still sizable, Andrus said, and they represented a greater environmental risk than the pipeline.[4] Spellman said he respected Andrus, a former Idaho governor, and certainly shared Edwards' commitment to national defense. However, he would not meet with members of the president's cabinet or, for that matter, with any other proponents or opponents. If he were to hear the administration's views he would be required to reopen the entire site-review process, and "nothing has been presented to me" that would justify such an action.[5]

IN A ROOM adjacent to the governor's office, staffers were sorting
mounds of mail. "I am among
many voters who have supported
you—but can also call for your
impeachment," wrote a man in
Auburn. An Olympia couple getting by on $600 a month said, "No
matter how tough times get, we'll
make it without the Northern Tier
Pipeline." A man in Bellevue said,
"A spill of biodegradable crude
oil isn't nearly as big a problem

as unemployed people." The Deep Sea Fishermen's Union of the Pacific
disagreed: "As ones who rely solely upon the Pacific Northwest region's
marine resources for our livelihood, we strongly and adamantly request
that the governor deny permits for the Northern Tier pipeline, for his sake
and ours." Marilyn Showalter, the governor's legal adviser, said the mail
was running 2 to 1 against Northern Tier. Each writer received a form letter
saying the governor valued input from concerned citizens but would base
his decision solely on the record compiled by the Site Evaluation Council.
"He's a lawyer himself," Showalter said, "and this was his position even
before he was elected. ...What does it say about that process if the governor
can talk to anyone he wants at the last minute?"[6]

Everyone in the office knew he'd been studying the report because he
packed it back to the mansion every night, no matter how late it was, and
could be seen marking passages with a yellow pen. "The other day he asked
for another copy of page 208," Showalter said.[7] He'd even flown over the
proposed pipeline route.

Scoop Jackson said Spellman was wise to go by the book and resist
pressure. "The Reagan administration would be in a very difficult position
to try to use unnecessary pressure. After all, the administration takes a very
strong stand in favor of state's rights."[8]

Speaker Polk and Majority Leader Hayner joined the fray, sending
Secretary Edwards a letter saying they would be pleased to meet with
him. Spellman was incensed. "It just occurs to me that the one person
who is operating according to the law and is not being influenced by
outside lobbyists for either side is the governor at this point in time."[9]
Editorial writers condemned the "end run" as unseemly and commended
Spellman for his integrity.[10]

Edwards abandoned all subtlety. Reporters around the state received a departmental news release noting that Washington was due to receive $2 billion from the Department of Energy in 1983, more than any other state. The former South Carolina governor followed up with a letter saying Spellman needed to "correct a number of fundamental deficiencies in the record" of the Site Evaluation Council. "Nothing in my experience in state government taught me that a governor can claim to be responsible when he closes his eyes to the consequences of his decision when they affect neighboring states and the security of the entire nation. Surely nothing in state law compels such deliberate blindness." Spellman shot back: "He presupposes what is and what is not in the record. I'll be the expert on the record by the time it's over. He won't. ... The secretary has the process backward. The EFSEC hearings were an opportunity for all of the parties that had an interest to make their cases, to present their briefs, to make their arguments. All the federal agencies had that opportunity." [11]

With unemployment nearing 12 percent—20 percent at Port Angeles, where the issue pitted neighbor against neighbor—labor was out in force, demanding that Spellman not "turn his back" on 4,000 new jobs for Washington and 8,000 to 10,000 in all from Clallam County to Minnesota. The jobs figures were hotly debated. Peak employment from the projects would be more like 2,300, the Bureau of Land Management said in the federal environmental impact statement. It also estimated that more than 40 percent of people working on the pipeline would come from out of state. State Representative Andy Nisbet, a Republican from the Olympic Peninsula, said that once construction was over there'd be only 125 jobs. "There's more permanent jobs for Clallam County at the new Safeway in Sequim." [12]

Northern Tier charged that the "Muskoxen," a "semi-secret" group of relatively low-level state and federal bureaucrats concerned about environmental issues, may have plotted to defeat the pipeline. Paul O'Connor, the governor's press secretary, dismissed the allegation as a "straw man." [13]

Although Lois Spellman wrote in her diary, "John seems terribly fatigued. I became greatly concerned he's not watching his diet or getting any exercise, which troubles me," John was having no second thoughts about his role as the decider.[14] To Steve Excell he seemed "even calmer than usual. He was serene while they were haranguing him from all sides." [15]

ON APRIL 8, Spellman announced his decision. Countless words had been printed and uttered telling him what he ought to do, he said, but he would need only a few to sum up his feelings: "It should be no surprise to anyone that I am rejecting the application of Northern Tier Pipeline." He had read and considered the council's findings—"an epic process of due process." Northern Tier had a year to present its final case, yet only "begrudgingly" gave evidence. The record was replete with its failure to support the feasibility of the project. An underwater pipeline capable of carrying nearly a million barrels of oil a day through an area with a history of earthquakes that could liquefy soils in seconds would be a "very real threat to Puget Sound, which in my mind is a national treasure." As for Port Angeles, an explosion or fire could place thousands in harm's way. Only 110 permanent jobs would be created by the project, while tens of thousands of people depended on the Sound for their livelihoods. He hoped to create many more jobs by promoting Washington ports as the hub of American trade with the Pacific Rim. He wanted to make it clear that he was not banning all pipelines, just this one. "It is the governor's duty to protect the state's environment, its natural resources and, above all, the interests of its people. ... I am satisfied that the findings of fact, conclusions of law and recommendations of the council are supported by the record. I concur therein." With that, he signed the order. Asked how he would react to a federal attempt to override his decision, he said, "I would view it as illegal and probably immoral."[16] Northern Tier's chairman said he couldn't help thinking that if Dixy Lee Ray had been re-elected, they'd be ordering pipe. "She would have been less legalistic."[17]

"It is a sad day when a major energy project from which all Americans would benefit is denied to them," said Secretary Edwards. Minnesota Governor Albert Quie, a Republican, denounced Spellman's decision as "parochial and short-sighted." A North Dakota official declared, "We've got to stop letting the Tom Haydens and the Jane Fondas make our energy policy for us. I really think Governor Spellman is afraid of a few little environmentalists pounding the table."[18] Congressman Al Swift, the Democrat whose district was in the pipeline's path, called Spellman's decision "wise and courageous." He warned that Northern Tier wouldn't give up. "We've already heard mice in the walls in Washington, D.C. I can't tell you what they're doing ... but I'm sure they're moving around," regrouping to advance the national defense argument. "We'll have to make clear what a preposterous argument that is."[19]

Spellman ordered the state Department of Ecology to file suit in federal court in Seattle to overturn the pipeline permits the Corps of Engineers had issued prior to his decision. "This is a state's-rights case," said Don Moos, the department's director. "If you could put this suit to music, you'd probably use the Washington State (University) fight song."[20]

Spellman had stood his ground. And Ronald Reagan, a former Western governor who maintained that "the nine most terrifying words in the English language are 'I'm from the government and I'm here to help,' " apparently wasn't inclined to give him the full "Gipper" treatment when saber-rattling by the Energy secretary and other officials had failed to shake Spellman's resolve. When the governor and the president met in the Oval Office later that month, Spellman stuck to anecdotes to illustrate his state's problems. (Reagan's aides had told him the last governor who came in with a wish list was poorly received.) Spellman told the president he'd been through the Boeing Bust of the 1970s and felt the pain of people who wanted work, not welfare. Recently, he'd met a logger in Raymond, a timber town hit hard by the recession. The sturdy fellow had been reduced to gathering ferns. The president shook his head sadly. They agreed that if they could jump-start home-building that would be a boon to the timber industry. Spellman pitched the federal Export-Import Bank program that helped Boeing sell jetliners. He lobbied, too, for military use of the 747 airframe. They commiserated over their mutual budget problems and travails with legislatures. Reagan's approval ratings were in the low 40's. Afterward, Spellman met with reporters on the White House lawn. They all wanted to know if he'd been "called on the carpet" over the pipeline. "It wasn't even mentioned," he said, and that was the truth. Edwards' point man on the project stood a few feet away, listening intently, saying not a word.[21] The Energy secretary, it turned out, had not been speaking for the Secretary of Defense. Cap Weinberger, a Reagan confidant, refused to participate in the Spellman arm-twisting because he worried that the pipeline "actually might not be in the best interests of national defense," multiple reliable sources told *Seattle Times* reporters Dean Katz and Eric Pryne. Defense strategists feared the pipeline would reduce the size of the U.S. oil-tanker fleet. "In the event of a war or national emergency, the Pentagon wants to have as many American tankers available as possible."[22]

A year later, after meeting with Spellman, Northern Tier officials threw in the towel. Getty Oil, which now owned two-thirds of the company, couldn't make the project pencil out.

Who killed Northern Tier? "I'd like to think we were responsible," said the director of the Washington Environmental Council, "but I suspect it was pure economics."[23] A disappointed Port Angeles businessman said, "Northern Tier was killed by time."[24] And Spellman had held fast against the tide—twice in the space of a month.

ON MARCH 8, 1982, the Legislature had sent Spellman a bill that amounted to a spot-zone circumvention of the Shoreline Management Act. It would have allowed Chicago Bridge & Iron to construct huge offshore drilling platforms for Alaskan oil fields on property it owned at Cherry Point just west of Ferndale in Whatcom County. Twenty acres of tidelands—part of a shoreline of "statewide significance"—would be filled. Polk and other backers said the project would generate thousands of sorely needed family-wage jobs. Critics said the area to be filled was part of one of the finest herring spawning grounds in the state. "The herring fishery was a budding industry of its own, and herring were ... the staff of life for Chinook salmon and—by way of the salmon—for Puget Sound Orcas," recalls Bob Simmons, a TV reporter who covered the story.[25] The issue had united treaty tribes, commercial fishermen and sportsmen for the first time in years. But most opponents focused on the legislative jujitsu that had created a special "economic significance" exemption to the Shoreline Act for a single company. The Legislature, in its zeal to create jobs, had "set itself up as a kind of super 'zoning appeals board'—a role it has no business playing," one of several critical editorials said.[26]

Steve Excell was in the wing of the House chamber lobbying against the rezone when Speaker Polk strolled over. "Nothing personal, but I'm kicking you out," he said. "You're peeling off too many votes."[27]

Just not enough votes.

Spellman surprised environmentalists and angered developers and their legislative allies by vetoing the measure. It did "great violence" to the Shoreline Management Act by creating a precedent that would open the door to piecemeal development of shorelines, Spellman said.

On the day after the governor rejected Northern Tier's pipeline application, the Senate overrode his veto of the shorelines bill. But Polk didn't have the votes to give it a go in the House. Chicago Bridge & Iron looked elsewhere.

That summer, the Washington Environmental Council saluted Spellman as its Elected Official of the Year. The banquet crowd "rose as one, applauding the Republican governor loud and long." Spellman said it was pleasant to be honored but he'd only been doing what was right. What was good for the environment would be good for economic growth, he said. "I hope I will not let you down in the future."[28] The head of the council's political-action committee remarked afterward that she'd been so thrilled by the Northern Tier and CBI decisions that she was tempted to call Olympia just to say, "I am proud to have him be my governor." Another longtime environmental activist hedged her bets. While Spellman was talking, "I was trying to figure out whether he meant it."[29]

THAT SPELLMAN MEANT to put an end to the fisheries war that had been raging in courtrooms, on riverbanks, Puget Sound and the great gray Pacific since the landmark Boldt Decision of 1974 was beyond dispute.

Judge Boldt granted treaty tribes the right to catch up to 50 percent of the fish in their "usual and accustomed" places. In practice, setting equitable seasons—while simultaneously protecting the resource from over-fishing—was a taller order. It involved places far beyond Washington's borders that were accustomed to having their way. Alaska, with its powerful U.S. senator, Ted Stevens, jealously guarded its access to the fishery. So too the Canadians. Rollie Schmitten and Bill Wilkerson, his successor as Fisheries director, were of the same mind: Litigation was making things worse.

"When I took over as Fisheries director in 1981, we had 72 pending lawsuits against the department," Schmitten says. "Our win-loss record was dismal. In fact I can't remember winning a fisheries case involving the tribes during our first year in office. Bill and I had often discussed a better way of doing business and interacting with the tribes."[30]

"Spellman is an astute lawyer and an avid fisherman," Wilkerson says. "He absolutely loves fishing. I remember going into his office early on and telling him about our pathetic track record in the courtroom. 'I think we've got to put an end to it,' he said. 'Give me a plan.'"[31]

What brought things to a head, Schmitten says, was the admission by the department's fish management staff that they had made a major error in the calculation of the Puget Sound Chinook salmon catch. The imbalance was grossly in favor of the non-treaty fishermen. Schmitten and Wilkerson instantly agreed that the department needed to level with the recreational fishing community. Hundreds of anglers attended a meeting. They were angry, but they listened. Next, in an out-of-the-way restaurant, Schmitten and Wilkerson met with Billy Frank Jr., the charismatic chairman of the Northwest Indian Fisheries Commission. "Our approach was to level with Billy that they had it within their power to shut down sport fishing in Puget Sound, but the result likely would be open warfare that would just make the divide deeper," Schmitten says. "We offered a different approach: We needed to stop the constant fighting over the last salmon and approach all fisheries decisions through 'co-management.' Since we had a common interest in getting more fish for everyone, we resolved to reach our conservation decisions first, then focus on allocation."[32]

Frank sold his board on the plan. Spellman said it was not only the right thing to do, it was a century overdue. Still, they were taking a major risk. "You know what this means if it fails," Spellman said, with what Schmitten describes as "one of his famous smiles."[33]

Wilkerson credits another longtime Spellman ally, Jim Waldo, "as help-ing everyone understand what was at stake" as a mediator. "But the governor supported me a thousand percent the whole time we were negotiating, even when we were being hung in effigy. Spellman's instincts as a lawyer—and a fisherman—were what put us over the top in getting consensus on setting the seasons cooperatively. We brought together Washington and Oregon; the tribes; Trout Unlimited and the charter boat people. If Spellman hadn't stood by what we were doing, I don't think the breakthroughs we reached in 1983, 1984 and the years that followed would have never happened." *[34]

---

*Schmitten went on to serve as national director of Marine Fisheries, and in 2009 became a member of the state Fish and Wildlife Commission. Wilkerson headed both Fisheries and the Department of Revenue for Spellman's successor, Booth Gardner.

CHAPTER THIRTY-FIVE

Scratch and Match

Five million dollars a day—day after day, state revenues continued their grinding decline. After the springtime special session raised taxes by $278 million and cut spending by $241 million, Spellman was told the budget would be balanced by the end of the biennium with $100 million to spare. But by June of 1982 another $253 million hole had to be patched. His new Tax Advisory Council would be looking for new ways to more means, Spellman said, but things couldn't wait until who knows when. He summoned the legislators back to Olympia for the sixth legislative session of his first two years, "the most of any biennium since statehood."[1] Since January of 1981, they had raised taxes by $923 million and cut state spending by $469 million. The cuts were actually $850 million deeper if you subtracted the present budget from the amount it would have taken to continue state services at 1979 levels, Spellman said.

The leaders of all four caucuses—Polk, Ehlers, Hayner and Bottiger—agreed on one thing: Another session was a terrible idea. No one wanted to raise taxes a few months before the elections. Dick Bond, the Troglodyte-in-chief, told the governor his troops might not even show up. "Sipping a glass of iced tea in downtown Spokane on a 90-degree day," the stocky gas-company manager said a lot of Republicans who had grudgingly voted for taxes over the past six months weren't going to do it again. Spellman was now on his own. "A few blocks away, hundreds of Democrats gathered at the state convention to begin piecing together the party platform and perhaps to congratulate themselves for not being in power...."[2]

Representative Dan McDonald, R-Bellevue, a tall, amiable engineer with an orderly mind, asked Revenue Director Don Burrows why the revenue forecasts were so volatile. "No one seems to be able to predict what the consumers are going to do," Burrows said. One month they'd go shopping, only to sit on their hands the next. In the mid-1960s Burrows said he was able to forecast revenues within a fraction of 1 percent. "Then I was elected

Spellman with
a constituent.

head of the National Revenue Estimators Conference and things have been going downhill ever since!" The committee room erupted in laughter.[3] Levity, otherwise, was in short supply.

Faced with losing another 8.2 percent from their budgets absent other solutions, school superintendents and college administrators praised Spellman's decision to call back the lawmakers. It "took considerable courage and was against the odds," said the UW's William Gerberding, who had castigated the governor the previous fall when higher education funding was reduced. "We appreciate the opportunity to make our case and we are deeply grateful."[4]

Democrats wore Band-Aids to signify that the Republicans "really haven't done anything ... except apply Band-Aids."[5] All four caucuses applied a few more in the space of seven days, and they were back on the campaign trail before the Fourth of July. It was in this session that Dan Grimm, the intense 33-year-old House Democratic caucus chairman from

Puyallup, and Denny Heck of Vancouver, his younger, more abrasive but equally bright colleague, came into their own—Heck as assistant minority leader. During late-night negotiations with Republicans, both wore "No More Mr. Nice Guy" T-shirts presented to them by an admiring caucus. From now on there would be sharper elbows under the basket, but their coach always seemed to know when to call a time-out. In Wayne Ehlers, the next speaker of the House, Democrats had a savvy, old-shoe politician. "Wayne was impervious to intimidation," Grimm remembers. "He was also bright and mischievous but incapable of hypocrisy or holding grudges. He never expected anything of anyone he didn't demand of himself, which means he had very high expectations."[6] Spellman, who "would have loved to have had a split legislature" from the outset, found working with Ehlers refreshing.[7] Even when they disagreed, "there was never a hint of duplicity from Wayne."

George Scott, not seeking re-election, found his final outing as Senate Ways and Means chairman fraught with frustration and irony. "All else having failed," Jeannette Hayner was scrounging for the final pieces of the adjournment puzzle.[8] She asked him to hold his nose and move a lottery bill out of his committee. Both had opposed state-sponsored gambling, Scott having boasted earlier that lottery bills would be dead on arrival at Ways and Means. Other states had seen declining revenues once the novelty wore off, he said, so the estimated $20 million in annual revenue amounted to a shaky bet. The potential for corruption troubled him too, as did the need for additional law enforcement and the societal implications of institutionalizing gambling. Spellman had come of age as a politician as an opponent of "tolerance." However, he was not morally opposed to all gambling—just illegal gambling. His reservations revolved around the uncertain revenues. The governor's willingness to sign a lottery bill underscored his aversion to deeper cuts. Alan Gibbs, his DSHS administrator, said proposed cuts in welfare and other social-service programs would leave the state 36 percent below accepted standards.[9]

The lottery needed 60 percent majorities. "It got just that in the House on the fifth day, and in the Senate on the sixth day," legislative historian Don Brazier notes. The Legislature also agreed to delay phasing out the business inventory tax, cut spending by $100 million and imposed a temporary three percent surcharge on taxes. "As a safety valve, the governor was authorized to impose further selective cuts in spending up to $20 million if it became necessary" to balance the budget.[10] Spellman wasn't surprised when Senator Phil Talmadge, an astute attorney and ambitious politician, challenged that mandate as an unconstitutional delegation of legislative powers. "Which of course it was," Spellman says. "Giving a governor the absolute power to make cuts was setting up a dictator, and the Thurston County Superior court said so very rapidly. There were no grounds for appeal."

The State Supreme Court rejected a move by the Moral Majority to force a public vote on the lottery. Spellman had never expected to find himself entering the history books as the father of the State Lottery. Now he promised, "I'm going to get a very tough group to run it. It's going to be a clean-as-a-whistle lottery." [11] He appointed the FBI's former top man in the state, Paul Mack, to head a diverse, five-member Lottery Commission. He picked Robert A. Boyd, a retired vice president of the Frederick & Nelson department store, to be lottery director. There were startup skirmishes with license applicants—5,000 applied—and ticket vendors; a controversy over on-line games and revenue ups and downs, but no scandals on their watch.

The first "scratch and match" tickets for the Pot O'Gold Instant Lottery Game went on sale at 12:01 a.m. on November 15, 1982. "By the tens of thousands Washington residents laid down their dollars to inaugurate the nation's 16th state lottery." [12] Instant payoffs ranged from $2 to $5,000. Hundred-dollar winners and up were entered in a drawing for $1 million. Forty percent of the gross revenue was earmarked for the General Fund. The take exceeded everyone's wildest expectations—$60 million in the first year—though the proletariat, plunking down their dollars at 7-Elevens, got the mistaken impression from overblown marketing that the lottery would be a panacea for the public schools. Nevertheless, as of 2012—30 years on—the lottery had generated $3.08 billion for the treasury.

CHAPTER THIRTY-SIX

China

Spellman stood on the Great Wall of China, braced his gimpy knee on a steep incline and tried to imagine how much brute labor it had taken to construct something so astounding. He craned his neck to see it snake into the distance, up, down and around rolling hills, 4,000 miles in all, the handiwork of 20 dynasties.

It was October 5, 1982. Nearby stood Boeing and Weyerhaeuser executives, bankers and university presidents, port managers, stevedore leaders, orchardists and wheat growers. For Washington State, struggling to shake the worst downturn since the Depression, China was the land of opportunity.

Four months earlier, the red and gold flag of the People's Republic of China had flown at the state Capitol for the first time as Spellman welcomed a high-level Chinese delegation. On recent visits to Japan and Hong Kong to promote Washington trade, the governor had met with bankers, businessmen and Boeing overseas operatives. Boeing had sold 10 of its 707-320's to the People's Republic a few months after Nixon's landmark journey to Beijing in 1972. The Chinese proceeded to build an overweight knock-off before abandoning the effort. The high-quality 707's "proved to be the best ambassadors imaginable in welding the Chinese into the Boeing family." [1] The country had been "woefully unprepared" for modern commercial aviation. [2] But the pace of change was now rapidly accelerating. The Chinese wanted more airplanes, trucks and tractors, lumber and wheat—Coca-Cola, too. Richard Allison, Spellman's chief of staff, and Dick Schrock, his director of Commerce and Economic Development, moved quickly to capitalize on the opportunities. The tricky part, Spellman recalls, was risking the state's significant trade with Taiwan. "We had to walk a tightrope." [3] But the potential for establishing close economic ties with the world's most populous nation was well worth the risk. Spellman compartmentalized a personal misgiving: The loss of his brother 31 years earlier when thousands of Chinese soldiers clashed with the 187th Airborne Infantry in Korea. The world had changed. It was time to move on.

The ice had really broken in 1979 "during the 11th meeting of the Communist Party's Central Committee, when Mao's successor, Deng Xiaoping, convinced his comrades that an opening to the West would help everybody." Deng was fond of metaphors: "Black cat, white cat? What does it matter as long as it catches mice?"[4] Soon thereafter he visited Seattle, having signed an agreement with Jimmy Carter to normalize relations.

The visitors from Sichuan—Deng's home province—invited Spellman to bring a delegation of his own to their country. Schrock assembled a diverse 25-member group. It included Jerry Grinstein and Stan Barer, two former Magnuson aides who well understood the enormous potential for China trade. Magnuson had advocated trade and diplomatic ties with China since the 1930s, to his electoral peril during the Red Scare of the 1950s. "The truth was, Maggie thought trying to ignore a nation of a billion people was political and economic folly," wrote Shelby Scates, the well-traveled reporter for the *Seattle Post-Intelligencer* who covered the Spellman delegation on its eventful two-week tour of China.[5] Scoop had come around, too, concluding that the Chinese were less of a threat than the Soviet Union, and more open to capitalizing on capitalism. Jackson had hosted Deng's trip to Seattle.

Microsoft, which had doubled its workforce to 220 in the past year, was making its initial forays into Europe, intent upon becoming the first global computer software company. It wanted a detailed report from the delegation.

The trade trip was of more urgency for Eastern Washington. "From the Waterville plateau to the channeled scablands of Lincoln County, from the deep-soiled richness of the Palouse to the dry central plain," Washington State's wheat farmers were bracing for what looked like another rough year," Stephen H. Dunphy, business editor for *The Seattle Times*, wrote that October. Crop prices were "falling dizzyingly short of high production costs."[6] Credit lines were stretched thin. They were getting about $3.80 a bushel for grain that cost $4.50 to grow.

Washington grew more than half of the soft white winter wheat produced in America. It had exported 85 percent of it to China where it was used to produce noodles, a staple of Chinese life. In 1979, China had purchased 26 million bushels of Washington wheat. The Chinese heat-treated the grain, fearing that spores from a smut-disease common to Washington State might contaminate domestic crops. Unfortunately, the process tainted the taste of the ground kernels, and imports were halted. The Chinese sent two scientists to Oregon State University to work with a renowned

Spellman on the
Great Wall of China
in 1982.

plant pathologist. Happily, after two years of studies they concluded that "their country offered almost impossible conditions for the smut to exist."[7] The door was open again. Spellman intended to keep it that way. The governor's trade mission would prove to be "the snowflake that causes the avalanche" in ending the Chinese embargo, said Scott Hanson, administrator of the Washington Wheat Commission.[8]

The tradition-steeped ceremony that saw Spellman sign a document establishing a sister-state relationship between Washington and Sichuan Province was the highlight of the two-week trip. They exchanged toasts with a local concoction that Scates pronounced "powerful enough to fuel a tractor engine," then dined on roast duck at a lavish banquet.[9] The alcohol took the edge off a *faux pas* or two. The Washington delegation had brought along hundreds of green baseball caps to hand out as mementoes. The Chinese laughed uproariously when handed their hats but refused to put them on. "It turned out that a green hat was a symbol that the wearer had been cuckolded," Grinstein says. The hats went back in the bags. Then, at a full State Dinner in the Great Hall, their Chinese hosts offered a panoply of entertainment—singers, dancers, acrobats. One member of the Washington delegation suggested they should respond with some good-old American songs, and, Mitch Miller-style, led a chorus of "I've Been Working on the Railroad." Bill Gerberding, the UW president, paled. Imported Chinese laborers had built much of the transcontinental railroad, working from sunup to sundown six days a week for a pittance. But no slight seemed to register.[10]

The delegation visited Chinese farmers. "Most had only two or three acres," Grinstein remembers, "and few as many as 10. They were blown away when a Ritzville wheat farmer in our delegation told them that he and his son, and on rare occasions a single hired hand, planted, maintained and harvested 17,000 acres. It was then that our Chinese hosts realized that technology provided scale, efficient production and low cost."[11]

"We couldn't anticipate what would happen," said Stan Barer, who in due course ushered COSCO, the Chinese shipping line, into Puget Sound.[12] "We'd been told negotiations would be very difficult," Spellman recalled. "That didn't pan out. And, recall, there was more at stake than trade business. There was a peace dividend."[13]

The governor was nearly moved to tears when, accompanied by Schrock, Paul O'Connor and Ted and Darleen Bottiger, he attended 6:30 a.m. Mass in a beleaguered, low-ceilinged Catholic Church at the end of a narrow street. "The bishop, a tiny old man, said Mass in Latin. There were a hundred people in all in the congregation. Their piety was moving."

"We unlocked the door to a significant population of the world," Spellman told reporters when he arrived back home. "But this isn't something like pulling a rabbit out of the hat. This is something that will take 50 to 100 years to develop." While the Chinese had agreed to purchase winter wheat from Eastern Washington, "I wouldn't start putting it on the boxcars yet. It's going to take some time." He was particularly pleased with the progress they'd made in promoting exports of timber and aircraft from the Northwest. In return, he said Washington importers could expect to receive textile products and "some very sophisticated machinery at a very reasonable price."[14] He was greatly impressed by the Chinese work ethic and ingenuity and predicted they would quickly adapt to Western manufacturing methods and produce high-quality goods. "We knew the country was big to begin with, but it's big beyond belief. Also, the standard of living is improving every day." Americans who visited China often told him the pace of change was amazing. "If you went there next year it would be different from what we saw this year."[15]

A quarter-century later, in 2006, Scates summed up how very different things were:

> "Be careful what you wish for," one might be tempted to say, with a sigh these days, of our booming, if one-sided, trade with the People's Republic of China (aka "Red" China) and its murky attendant, the prospect of economic challenge from another world superpower.... [W]e see modern vessels flying Chinese flags sailing past Port Townsend into Puget Sound. That's the look of prosperity-Pacifica.

We wished for it, we got it. The upshot? Here in Washington State, we got it to such a degree that Puget Sound is running short of dock space. Vessels from Shanghai, bearing huge cranes that stab Seattle's waterfront skyline, lift more and more Chinese goods from ship to shore. Our ports and their critical facilities—the cranes and the Burlington Northern freight trains—are swamped. ...

What price this surge of seaborne prosperity?

Never mind the threat of an economic rival. The U.S. trade deficit with China was at $202 billion as of 2005—the difference in our purchase of Chinese goods and the sum of U.S. goods purchased by China. It drives politicians in Washington, D.C., nuts—and it is not to be confused with China's balance of trade with the Northwest. They buy a lot of our coffee, wheat, computers and Boeing airplanes. So when Chinese officials come calling, Seattle responds with open arms and red carpets. After all, the Asian giant is our state's fastest-growing trade partner. Nevertheless, the Northwest provides a vivid illustration of the trade disparity. Forget for a moment our Boeing aircraft. We also export alder logs-cut from forests in southwestern Washington and Oregon to China, where they are manufactured into furniture for export to—guess where?—the United States. In the shadows of our towering Douglas fir and cedar, foresters once regarded alder as weeds. In trade terms, China pays pennies for the "weeds," then makes dollars from their conversion into chairs and tables—another spike in the overall trade imbalance.[16]

Moreover, what Microsoft hadn't seen coming in 1982 was the loss of billions upon billions of dollars to China through intellectual property theft in the years to come.

"We didn't invent the China trade," said Schrock, but given the depth of the recession the Spellman administration faced, they jumped at the opportunity and never looked back.[17] "It was the most important thing accomplished by our administration," Spellman says.[18]

CHAPTER THIRTY-SEVEN

Checks and Imbalances

I t was a house of cards from the outset, replete with jokers and two-dozen clubs, a king and queen with unruly subjects and nary an ace. The Republican new deal in Olympia lasted only 20 months. "We were bled to death by dissenters more than opponents or the recession," ex-Senator George Scott wrote in his legislative memoir. Between the Troglodytes in the House and three recalcitrant senators, it was "the worst of all political worlds: responsibility without authority."[1] The Republicans had also failed to capitalize—botched, in fact—their opportunity to mastermind redistricting.

Two weeks after Spellman arrived home from China, Democrats recaptured control of the Legislature, winning a 54-44 majority in the House and a 26-23 edge in the Senate. Spellman was neither surprised nor especially disappointed. Confronted by brutal fiscal realities and right-wing ideologues, he had renounced his dodgy no-new-taxes pledge and proceeded to walk, talk and act like a moderate Democrat. Now, in his final two years as governor, he strategically donned his Republican hat to keep the pendulum from swinging too far to the left. And if that also improved his chances for re-election, so much the better. "He's like a willow reed," an exasperated Democratic staffer said. "The slightest breeze and he blows parallel to the earth."[2] Spellman, in fact, was just being Spellman, a checks-and-balances executive, more pragmatist than politician. "I have not changed since I became governor. My style of administration relies more on love than fear."[3] If love is all you need, you couldn't prove it with the governor's midterm approval ratings. He was mired in the 40's.

What the election demonstrated was that the electorate was restless. Voters had soundly rejected a Labor Council initiative to limit consumer interest rates; said they would rather put up with the sales tax on groceries for eight more months than enact the corporate profits income tax proposed by Senator McDermott and trounced an Oregon-style "bottle bill" requiring a nickel deposit on beverage containers. Further, many of the legislative races were close. "This was no tidal wave that crashed over the political beachhead," said Dan Grimm, the new chairman of the House Ways and Means Committee. "We took over because they didn't do the job of running the state and people knew it. But anyone who assumes this is a Democratic mandate is somewhat off base."[4] Speaker-elect Wayne Ehlers and the new majority leader, 31-year-old Denny Heck, had 44 freshmen to herd. Scott observed that "coping with the ideologues, flakes and solipsists who comprise up to a third of any caucus takes two-thirds of leaders' energy."[5] Ehlers went him one better. When reporters asked how he'd cope, he deadpanned, "I used to teach junior high."[6]

Ted Bottiger was re-elected Senate majority leader, fending off a challenge from McDermott, who was critical of Bottiger's conciliatory style and spoiling for a rematch with Spellman. Unemployment still topped 12 percent. The deficit for the 1983-85 biennium was estimated at $1.3 billion. The Seattle School District had taken the state to court once again—and it would win once again—charging that the Legislature was still shirking its constitutional duty to make "ample provision" for basic education.

ON NOVEMBER 22, 1982, Spellman's Tax Advisory Council strongly recommended "the most comprehensive overhaul of the state tax system since 1935."[7] It called for a flat-rate personal income tax, concurrent with the elimination of the sales tax on food, and a flat-rate net corporate-income tax. The tax on gross business receipts would be reduced. The plan was less regressive, fairer for all, said Graham Fernald, the Seattle lawyer who headed the broad-based commission. It included Marvin Williams, president of the State Labor Council; Philip Cartwright, a UW economics professor; Charles Hodde, a former state revenue director; Hal Haynes, Boeing's chief financial officer; Denny Heck and Ray Moore, the plain-talking old senator from Seattle. The state Grange master, Jack Silvers, and two Eastern Washington Republicans, Richard "Doc" Hastings and George Sellar, cast the dissenting votes. They were only three of 15 but their constituencies were potentially formidable.[8]

Ehlers, who admired an income tax bill proposed by Grimm and Heck, predicted by means of understatement that it and all others faced an "uphill" battle in the Legislature, where a constitutional amendment would require two-thirds majorities in both chambers. An apostle of "leadership by finesse"—and a terrific poker player—the 44-year-old librarian from Pierce County admired Lyndon B. Johnson's legendary ability to count noses. (Ehlers also understood the importance of image, having turned in

Bill Polk's red Datsun 280Z for a lease on a beige, no-frills Dodge sedan.) Spellman said he would support putting an income tax on the ballot if the Legislature came up with guarantees so persuasive that there was a fighting chance to convince the voters it wasn't just a game of bait-and-switch. To those who chided him for not leading the crusade, Spellman said he had watched Dan Evans at the top of his game go all-out for an income tax in 1970 and 1973 only to see the proposals thrashed at the ballot box—by 77 percent the second time. "It doesn't do one bit of good" to propose something that doesn't have a prayer of passing, Spellman said. "If that's leadership, I'll eat my hat."[9] Ehlers agreed. At the same time, however, he counseled Spellman to try channeling LBJ and twist some arms. "If he tried it, he might like it. He'd find he could affect policy."[10] Regardless, they could work together. "He's a good guy. ... I tell my people, 'I don't want to hear any talk of getting even. Even isn't good enough.'"[11]

In Rollie Schmitten as his legislative lobbyist, liaison to the business community and natural resources expert, Spellman had an adroit arm-twister. It would be the most productive session of his tenure as governor.

SPELLMAN'S $8.1 BILLION budget called for restoring many of the recent cuts and making a new "investment in infrastructure—people programs as well as bricks and mortar."[12] He wanted more dollars for public schools, higher education, social services and the corrections system, as well as economic development, tourism and highways. He said they needed to lower deductibles for Medicaid patients, provide additional funds for vocational-rehabilitation and fully fund programs for children with learning disabilities and other handicaps. At the colleges and universities, the governor's priority was the restoration of funds for science and engineering programs. To reinforce the progress Amos Reed had made in Corrections, Spellman sought an appropriation to start building a prison at Clallam Bay, finish the new prison at Monroe and add 600 beds at Shelton.

The governor plows through his in-basket.

The deficit for the biennium

ending June 30, 1983, was estimated at $145.7 million. Spellman's solution was to boost the sales tax by a penny for four months, then permanently from 5.4 to 5.6 percent and extend it to practically all services, including lawyer's fees, accounting and architectural services, entertainment, beauty parlors and barber shops. Conservatives gasped; hairdressers and CPA's blanched.[13] Grimm huffed that it would "likely be accidental" if the tax package adopted by the Legislature bore any resemblance to the governor's.[14] We'll see, said Spellman.

For all the angst over higher taxes, some comparisons were illuminating, especially to liberals like McDermott and moderates like Ehlers and Spellman. "In 1971, the average Washington taxpayer paid $122.83 in state and local taxes for every $1,000 of personal income. That had dropped to $100.45 per thousand in 1981."[15] Even with the billion-dollar increases of the past two years the tax rate was still back up to only about $108 per thousand—"only" being in the eye of the beholder.

While state spending had tripled in a decade, inflation accounted for most of it. Factoring in population growth, "real" growth in spending was 12.6 percent, and "most of that went to schools, prisons and pensions. Welfare accounted for just 1.4 percent of the overall increase."[16] Conservatives countered that in 1965 there were 10 state employees for every thousand residents. Now there were 15.* And even with the previous year's cuts, state spending was up 16.8 percent over the previous biennium.

THE LEGISLATURE would be in session for 137 tedious days in 1983. On the 44th, *The Seattle Times* ran a banner headline:

Lest One Should Forget, Gov. Spellman Is a Republican

"Spellman's veto of more than $550 million in new business taxes stunned Democratic leaders in the Legislature who, just a few days before, had been congratulating themselves for digging the state out of its financial hole with a record $1.9 billion in new taxes. But after four days of intensive lobbying by business leaders and Republican lawmakers, Spellman decided to slice the business taxes from the Democrat tax package and leave intact a 1.1 cent increase in the sales tax."[17] Now, however, the budget was badly out of balance and Spellman was insisting that further cuts in education and social-services were "unattainable in a real world."[18] The Democrats were livid that he hadn't warned them earlier—especially Ehlers. "He owed

---

* The comparable number for 2012 was 15.54 state employees per thousand residents. Both numbers included general government and higher education.

me the courtesy of a warning. It made my caucus, with all those freshmen, question my leadership." [19] John Jones, the Senate Republican Caucus Chairman, felt Spellman was just getting tougher. "They misjudged the man. They didn't see those vetoes coming. McDermott's psychiatric profile (of the governor) was bad." [20] Doug Underwood of *The Times* Olympia Bureau had seen it coming:

> Democrats became so accustomed, during the past two years of Republican control of the Legislature, to seeing Spellman out in front pushing for new taxes that they apparently forgot the political circumstances have changed. No longer is Spellman the moderate fighting the no-new taxes "Troglodytes" in his own party. Instead, it is Spellman faced with a Democratic Legislature and a business community whose Republican candidates were beaten at the polls, protecting business from taxes they felt were unreasonable. In fact, a close look at Spellman's record shows the veto of the business taxes is consistent with his past politics. While Spellman may have occasionally sided with environmentalists against the business community, he has almost never opposed large-business interests such as Boeing or the timber industry on bread-and-butter tax issues. ... Spellman's defense of his veto—that the Democrats' tax plan was "a real body blow to jobs"—is also consistent with his record. [21]

Restoring collective-bargaining rights to ferry workers was a bipartisan moment in an otherwise fractious session. Spellman strongly endorsed the bill Democrats supported. It banned strikes, with stiff fines, even jail sentences for violations, and mandated mediation and binding arbitration to resolve disputes. Those were the key recommendations of the commission he appointed in 1981 in the wake of the wildcat strike that paralyzed Puget Sound ferry traffic. Jimmy Herman, the Longshore Union leader who helped end the strike, attended the bill-signing ceremony, one of the year's best photo-ops for the governor.

As March ebbed into April, Grimm's heavily caffeinated committee worked from 5:30 p.m. to dawn crafting a budget that called for tax increases of $750 million and a $250 million reserve fund to eliminate the "25th month," an Evans-era, Boeing Bust bookkeeping gimmick. Revenues received in July were deposited to the previous month. The downside was that the state started each new fiscal year 30 days in the hole. Ehlers was intent on ending the practice. Then two Democrats voted with the 11 minority Republicans and the 13-13 tie sent the chairman back to his caucus to regroup. With an eye to the 1984 elections, "Republicans had rolled out dozens of amendments, demanding recorded votes."[22] Democrats were busy passing bills sought by the Washington Education Association and the other unions that had helped them regain control of the Legislature. The teachers had mobilized 15,000 campaign volunteers. In a move to undercut Commerce Director Dick Schrock, Spellman's lightning-rod former campaign strategist, Democrats moved to combine his department with the Planning and Community Affairs Agency and underfund the hybrid. Spellman warned he would veto the move, and was as good as his word. Soon, they were embroiled in overtime—a 30-day special session. Some legislators wore buttons declaring, "Home by Mother's Day."

SPELLMAN'S 14-HOUR days grew longer yet as he took the lead in a scramble to forestall the mother of all municipal bond defaults. A year earlier, the Washington Public Power Supply System had terminated two of its five nuclear power projects. Now, in the spring of 1983, it was poised to mothball Project 3 at Satsop and lay off another 1,200 workers. Worse, WPPSS was teetering at the precipice of default on the $2.25 billion in bonds it had sold to finance the terminated plants. Chemical Bank, the New York-based bond trustee, warned of litigation, while the public utilities that had sponsored construction asserted they had been bamboozled by the Bonneville Power Administration's "dire predictions of energy shortages."[23] The PUDs wanted the debt spread to all BPA customers, an idea going nowhere in a hurry. Default would be "a blow to the solar plexus" of the Northwest economy, the governor said, releasing a sobering report on the potential fallout.[24] A congressional study requested by Mike Lowry said any potential solution to the WPPSS mess would be costly. It also suggested that Northwest ratepayers had scant sympathy from the rest of the country, unwilling as they were to "recognize that electric rates in the region are well below the national average, even with the WPPSS debt."[25]

Spellman hosted a closed-door "WPPSS Summit" with the star-crossed stakeholders, including the CEOs of private utilities and aluminum industry representatives. Gorton and Foley sat in on one marathon session and emerged shaking their heads at the logjam. "Each time we'd get close to a deal, one of the stakeholders would get cold feet," Spellman recalls. "Then they'd all say the others were unwilling to appreciate what they were up against—irate ratepayers, long-term interest, BPA duplicity—you name it."

On May 4, Spellman made an eleventh-hour appeal "not only to lawmakers but to all parties in the ongoing dispute."[26] He asked for a law that might forestall full-scale bankruptcy by allowing individual projects to fail. But 25 of the Senate's 26 Democrats said that would treat "only a symptom

...while disregarding the larger consequences." And Speaker Ehlers was leery of doing anything that might leave the state on the hook. "John was doing his best to broker some sort of solution, but there was none. We wanted to keep WPPSS at arm's length." [27]

Reluctantly, Spellman threw in the towel, concluding that "the problems facing plants 4 and 5 are out of control." There was nothing the state could do to shield ratepayers. It was up to the Power Planning Council to make sure the lessons of the mess would be long remembered. [28]

A month later, Chemical Bank took its case to the Washington Supreme Court, which held that the PUDs lacked the legal authority to enter into the construction contracts and were off the hook. On July 22, 1983, WPPSS defaulted on the bonds. The bondholders, more than half of whom were small-time, individual investors looking to shore up their retirements, were the ones who took it in the solar plexus. [29] The dire predictions that the default would haunt the state on Wall Street never came true.

STILL RECOILING from the WPPSS meltdown, the Legislature was shaken by a banking crisis. Seafirst was Washington's oldest, largest bank; its name a household word, its founder Dexter Horton an icon. Now it was in a fix of its own making, yet deemed too big to fail. Dropping oil prices had decimated Seafirst's billion-dollar portfolio of energy-exploration loans. After losing $91 million in 1982, the publicly traded corporation hemorrhaged another $131 million in the first quarter of 1983. The U.S. Comptroller of the Currency warned that a run on the bank's deposits was imminent unless the Legislature took action on a bill allowing Seafirst to consummate a $400 million merger with BankAmerica.

In the final hours of the 1983 regular session, amidst a lobbying blitz, the Legislature approved the measure. Many Democrats with long memories swallowed hard and voted "yes." Seafirst had bankrolled a lot of Republicans and participated in redlining. The chairman of the rival Rainier Bancorporation, G. Robert Truex Jr., who struck many as supercilious, took his case to the governor. Allowing out-of-state banking companies to purchase ailing banks was patently unfair to healthy banks, Truex said. What was needed was a law that would allow Washington banks to be acquired by outsiders regardless of their financial condition. The bill on Spellman's desk amounted to a bailout for Seafirst shareholders rather than a move to protect depositors, Truex argued. Seafirst had $9.6 billion in assets it could sell off to stay afloat, and Rainier was prepared to buy $1 billion worth. "I think they've dramatized their case to the point where they put a terrible fear into everybody that they're going to fail. I find that hard to believe." [30]

Spellman didn't. "Losing Seafirst would have been catastrophic to the state," he says. For better or worse, his signature on that bill "opened the door, four years later, to full interstate banking in Washington, leading in turn to widespread consolidation in the state's banking industry and the disappearance, via acquisition by out-of-staters, of such venerable names as Rainier, Puget Sound and Peoples."[31]

Mike Edwards, Washington State's banking supervisor at the time of the merger, was opposed to interstate banking, "fearing the concentration of financial resources that would result from consolidation." But the alternative of letting the bank fail was even less palatable, he said in a 2008 interview. "Most of our banks in the state had a clearing account with Seafirst. Those deposits would have been forgone. ... It was truly a turning point. It proved you could do a transaction without the world falling down on us."[32]

IN ONE FELL SWOOP on what Democrats would call "Bloody Tuesday," Spellman pre-empted a conservative challenge to his re-election campaign but put a union-label target on his chest. He vetoed a raft of labor-backed bills, including a move to repeal the Civil Service reforms Republicans had pushed through when they were in power. Performance-based raises and layoffs that disregarded seniority were anathema to labor. Spellman also rejected collective bargaining for university professors; denied employees access to their personnel files and balked at allowing teachers and state workers to buy back into retirement programs if they had cashed out previously. Earlier in the session, the governor vetoed collective bargaining for State Patrol troopers. They were mad before; now they swore they'd take him down. Spellman said he wrestled longest with the higher-education collective bargaining bill, but concluded the timing was terrible. "Why now, when we're having such severe financial problems? ... I wonder if some of those bills would have passed with a Democratic governor."[33] Some Democrats privately agreed. Spellman noted he had steadfastly opposed more cuts in state programs; strongly supported additional funding for public schools and higher education and signed into law expanded benefits for injured workers and widows. "But I don't think governors are supposed to make everybody happy."[34]

It was a banner year for unhappiness. Spellman now supported $415 million in new business taxes, which angered the conservatives he had pleased with his vetoes 60 days earlier. The Democrats, meantime, had hiked the sales tax $1.2 billion; business taxes by $476 million and the gas tax by $175 million for a total of $1.85 billion. It was the fourth longest session in state history and the most taxing to date.

The $8 billion 1983-85 budget that won approval just before midnight May 25 during a final, frantic one-day session was "remarkably close to what Spellman had proposed in January." The governor had also outlasted and outmaneuvered Bottiger to win final authorization for the $90 million State Convention Center that would straddle Interstate-5 in Seattle. (Republicans charged that the Pierce County clique was out to protect the new Tacoma Dome.) Spellman, Jim Ellis and Rod Chandler had pushed hard for the freeway-topping convention center destined to win national awards. Another victory was the approval, at long last, of an independent redistricting commission. Spellman was no longer "Governor Dullman," one editorial concluded.[35] Lobbyists, legislative staffers and other railbirds disagreed. To them, Spellman was "the ultimate consensus politician," unwilling "to articulate any kind of vision for the state except his promises of good management."[36] Yet no one in leadership got high marks from the peanut gallery, which yearned for the days when strong leaders like Augie Mardesich, Martin Durkan, Bob Greive, Dan Evans and Slade Gorton "got things done and no one asked too many questions about how." Speaker Ehlers was pronounced too easy going. He ought to have cracked the whip on his freshmen, critics told Doug Underwood—not for attribution, of course. "The House has given virginity a bad name," a Senate staffer groused. Heck was "too intense and too abrasive." Grimm "too brash and too inexperienced." Bottiger "too willing to let the old bulls run the show." McDermott too much the "game-player ... with the ego and ambition of someone still longing to be governor."[37]

Those allegedly halcyon days of yesteryear were pronounced "totally mythical" by both Spellman and Democrats who knew the real score. The old bulls always did exactly what they wanted to do. Mardesich, Evans et al either had enough votes to do what they wanted without them or the old bulls wanted to vote the same way for reasons of their own.

Undeniably true was that McDermott was sore-vexed right and left. When Spellman vetoed his plan for big permanent business tax increases, he never really recovered any momentum. Defying the legislative tradition that the House should defer to its elders in the Senate, Ehlers' team "came out the winner when it came time to settle differences."[38] McDermott loyalists were left to grumble about "Pierce County leadership"—Ehlers, Grimm, Bottiger and their friend Booth Gardner, the Pierce County executive gearing up to run for governor.

The complicated battle lines for the 1984 elections were drawn a summer early. What Spellman did next was taken as a sign that he was getting his house in order.

THE DOOR POPPED OPEN, then slammed shut. Steve Excell's jaw dropped when Richard Allison, the governor's chief of staff, face beet red, declared, "He fired me!" It was July 8, 1983. Whenever Spellman did something out of character—bouncing Revenue Director Glenn Pascall 18 months earlier, for instance—it was "Stop the presses!" This one was a cause célèbre all out of proportion to its importance, but the headlines were nearly as big: "Spellman stuns top aide with abrupt firing," the *P-I* reported.[39]

While Allison was summoning reporters to an impromptu press conference in the lobby of the Governor's Office, Spellman had a plane to catch for a meeting in Spokane. "You're in charge," he told Excell, who with that had just received a battlefield promotion to captain. Rarely at a loss for words, the governor's policy aide summed it up with one: "unbelievable." It wasn't so much that Allison was out. Excell had seen that coming for months. "It was the way Dick took it. He always counseled us that 'You take a bullet for the boss.'"[40] Mr. Cool, the Harvard history professor who had done a tour in Vietnam as an Army officer, was now in high dudgeon. Every document that came into the office had passed through his hands. He was a brilliant bureaucrat and a chilly boss, said Barbara Schmidt, Spellman's longtime personal secretary. Paul O'Connor, the press secretary, also bristled at Allison's brusque demeanor. The governor's State Patrol executive protection detail didn't like him either. Spellman's decision amounted to a personnel matter, as opposed to the sudden dismissal of an agency director. Yet Allison blew a fuse, telling reporters he was "stunned and astonished" by the governor's decision. They were discussing other matters, when "all of a sudden he said, 'I think we'd better part company at the end of the summer.'" Staff members had threatened to quit if he stayed on, he said the governor said. "It hit me with no warning. I said, 'In that case, I'd better leave now.... If the staff people can't live with me and they haven't got the guts to come and talk out their problems with me, then I don't want to be around them, whoever they are.'"[41] With that, Allison cleaned out his desk, sold another staffer his 1969 Oldsmobile and caught the next plane for L.A. where his mother lived.

Writing for the Bellevue *Journal-American*, Walter Hatch came closest to identifying a nuance missing from all the other stories: "Spellman had hoped to push Allison gradually and gently out the door."[42] And he wasn't inventing excuses. "I did not fire him," Spellman says. "What I said was, 'I think we ought to put you in a new role by the end of the summer'—not 'part company.' It was clear that Dick's style wasn't working as chief of staff. I was thinking of making him director of a board or commission. But as soon as I got the words out of my mouth, he became angry and quit on the spot. Which I regretted then and still do. He is a very talented man and I still consider him a friend."

Spellman acknowledged that his "Sounding Board" of business people was frustrated that Allison had set up a palace guard where nothing got to the governor without first going through him. He flatly denied, however, that the decision to reassign Allison was motivated by re-election politics. His personal secretary's opinion—and she had seen it all during 14 years of faithful service, from the Courthouse to the Capitol—carried more weight than a corporate vice president's.[43] Still, as the smoke cleared, Hunter Simpson, president of Physio-Control Corporation and a charter member of Spellman's kitchen cabinet, said, "I'm not a big Allison fan. He just doesn't have my kind of style. My style is open. I like to delegate to others. He has this Teutonic kind of militaristic method." The governor's office "doesn't have to be a command post in Vietnam."[44]

Commerce Director Dick Schrock, a strong personality who had his own set of detractors, regretted the departure of his friend—especially the way it played out. Being chief of staff was "a tough, thankless job during a rolling fiscal crisis," Schrock says. "Richard was a superb taskmaster, not a politician or a salesman, and his own popularity was never his priority."[45]

CHAPTER THIRTY-EIGHT

A Sad Plum

Spellman smiled when he saw the wirephoto from Peking in the Sunday papers. Scoop Jackson and Deng Xiaoping were hugging cheek to cheek in the Great Hall of the People. The accompanying story made the governor even happier. Taiwan, the island redoubt of the stubborn nationalists, remained an obstacle, the Chinese leader told reporters; otherwise, Sino-American relations were much improved. Deng said he looked forward to expanded cooperation and trade with the United States.

Spellman had been to Sichuan, the chairman's home province, the year before. Now Jackson, with Reagan's blessings, was opening the door even farther.

It was August 28, 1983.

That night, Jackson returned from his grueling two-week tour of China. The senator was an old hand at international travel. He'd been to China four times before. He seemed years younger than 71 and usually had more stamina than jet-lagged young aides and reporters. If they boarded the bus looking bedraggled he'd give them a ribbing. This time, however, Jackson had come down with a chest cold and hacking cough. But three days of rest and antibiotics had him on the mend from what he dismissed as the "Oriental crud."[1]

Jackson called Slade Gorton on the 31st to brief him on the trip. He said he'd be back to work in his Seattle office the next morning. Daybreak brought news that shook the world. Jackson, the ranking Democrat on the Armed Services Committee, awoke to a call from the State Department. The Soviets had shot down Korean Air Flight 007, a 747 that strayed into their airspace. All 269 people aboard the Boeing jetliner en route to Seoul from Anchorage perished, including a U.S. congressman and 29 other Americans. It was a "dastardly, barbaric act against humanity," Jackson told a press conference, shaking a fist. Afterward, Ron Dotzauer, who headed the senator's state office, told Jackson he'd never sounded better. Scoop smiled.

"You know, I was pretty good, wasn't I?"[2] Still coughing, Jackson went back to the doctor, then home to bed in Everett. He died that night of a ruptured aorta. "It was an enormous shock," Spellman remembers. "For nearly 40 years it had been 'Scoop and Maggie,' and no one—least of all Maggie—expected Scoop to go first. He seemed indestructible."

As practically half the U.S. Senate, Vice President Bush, Henry Kissinger and Chief Justice Burger made plans to fly to Everett for the funeral, the political rumor mill was "grinding out the names of potential successors."[3] The choice, a rare political plum for both appointer and appointee, would be Spellman's. Though Karen Marchioro, the Democrats' rambunctious state chairwoman, declared that the governor should fill the seat with a Democrat—Scoop having won re-election in a landslide just a year earlier—state law imposed no such obligation on the governor. (If it had, he would have happily appointed Tom Foley.) Washington State last had two Republicans in the U.S. Senate in 1923, and the White House was anxious to build on its GOP majority there.

Senator Jackson receives a farewell embrace from Deng Xiaoping on August 27, 1983.

Spellman tasked Steve Excell, Rollie Schmitten and other staffers with vetting his possible choices. Dan Evans and Joel Pritchard headed every list. Others mentioned were William Ruckelshaus, on his second tour of duty as head of the federal Environmental Protection Agency, and Congressmen Sid Morrison and Rod Chandler. A dark horse was former chief justice Robert F. Utter, a liberal Republican. Number One on Mrs. Spellman's list was John Dennis Spellman, who said, "Thank you, dear, but that would be a terrible mistake." Not that he wouldn't have loved to be a senator. "I had visited the Senate often while I was in law school and found it fascinating. After Slade won Maggie's seat in 1981, he took me onto Senate floor—Governors have that privilege—and introduced me to his colleagues. It felt very comfortable. But it's not in my character to do something like appointing myself to a prestigious job. Besides being wrong, there was no way I could have been elected if I had made such a decision."

His first choice, deep down, was Pritchard. "Joel had the talent and temperament to be a great senator. He was a team player—a genial, collegial guy, but also a man of principle. Add in the fact that he was a shrewd campaigner and you had quite a package," Spellman says. "I admired Evans. He was an activist governor who had run and won three times statewide. He was doing a great job as chairman of the Power Planning Council. The Goldwater-Reagan wing of the party hated him, and the King County branch didn't much care for me either, so pleasing the conservatives wasn't part of the equation. Sid Morrison was also a very capable guy and a moderate. It came down to those three."

ATTORNEY GENERAL Ken Eikenberry, his lieutenants having parsed state law, declared on September 6 that whoever Spellman appointed would have to stand for election that November. There would be no primary. Bipartisan consternation erupted. In a free-for-all like that someone could win five years in the U.S. Senate with nothing remotely approaching a majority. Marchioro and Jennifer Dunn, the polished state GOP chairwoman, were equally aghast. The Democrats, with support from the GOP, took their case for a primary to the State Supreme Court. To hedge their bets, they lobbied Spellman to call a special session to let lawmakers create a primary.

Spellman, meantime, had heard from Pritchard, Morrison and Utter. They'd all be honored to serve. Ruckelshaus wasn't interested. He was for Evans. Pritchard had been uncharacteristically low-key. His brother Frank and others believe his emotions were mixed because he and Dan had been such good friends for so many years—that and the fact that Evans, in Joel's assessment, stood a better chance of winning. The week before Jackson's stunningly unexpected death, Evans had made an appointment to meet with the chairwoman of The Evergreen State College trustees. He was going to tell her he would stay on as president for 10 more months. He wanted to finish the autobiography he'd been working on for years, then do something else. He wasn't sure what. Gorton prodded him to seek the Senate appointment. They'd be a great team all over again, he said.

Spellman was annoyed. "Slade came to me said I should appoint Dan. But I hadn't heard from Dan. I'd heard from everyone else. I told Slade I wouldn't appoint Dan unless he really wanted it. That's the best job in the United States, I said, and he's got to want it—he's got to be committed to it. And he's got to want it so much that he'll run hard to keep it. It's not going to be a hobby for someone or a trophy. I said I admired independence— Slade had stood up to Reagan on principle over deficits—but the president deserved a fair shake from his party, not some maverick Republican." There was also an undercurrent of rivalry between Spellman and Evans. It had existed since 1975 when Spellman made it clear he planned to run for governor regardless of Dan's decision on whether to seek an unprecedented fourth term. And in the spring of 1983, when a raft of possible challengers—Jim McDermott, Booth Gardner, Charles Royer, Lands Commissioner Brian Boyle, Harley Hoppe and Bill Polk among them—were either testing the gubernatorial waters or being wooed, Evans had said, "I don't flatly rule anything out." [4]

Ralph Munro, Evans' former aide and good friend, told him he'd better get off his duff and call Spellman about the Senate vacancy. Even if he was conflicted, it was discourteous not to do so, Munro said. "You're probably right," Evans said.[5] On the morning of Jackson's funeral, as Evans drove from The Evergreen State College campus on Cooper Point to the Governor's Mansion to have breakfast with Spellman, he listened to radio reports on the tension over the Korean Air tragedy. "Good God," he remembers thinking, "with this many problems and the challenges that we're facing ... how can you *not* want to really get involved?"[6] He told Spellman that if chosen he'd been honored to serve. (Spellman didn't hear the story about Evans' NPR epiphany until 28 years later. "I have been a Dan Evans fan for more than 50 years, and count him as a friend, but I'm convinced that deep down he had made up his mind before he turned on the radio. He wanted it.")

That night it was down to Pritchard, Evans and Morrison—and electability. Who could win a 60-day sprint? Steve Excell was holed up in the library at the Mansion waiting for the results of a GOP Senatorial Campaign Committee poll while Spellman talked with Republicans from around the state. Jennifer Dunn, a charter member of the Ronald Reagan Fan Club, made it clear she didn't want Evans, who had supported Ford in 1976 and Bush in 1980.

At 10:30 the results came in. "It was overwhelmingly Evans," Excell says. "I wrote down the numbers and showed them to the governor. Neither Joel nor Sid had ever run outside their districts. Dan was a three-term governor. He could run with the cachet of an incumbent."[7]

On September 8, Spellman appointed Evans to the U.S. Senate, saying, "I think the last thing that Scoop Jackson would have wanted is for this state to be divided up into warring factions. Dan Evans has the experience, the integrity and the ability to unite our state."[8] Dunn was conciliatory, saying Spellman had chosen the most electable candidate, "someone whose reputation of honesty and integrity is reminiscent of the late Senator Jackson." However, the Republican chairman in King County, which had been at war with "that liberal Evans crowd" since the 1960s, said Spellman had just driven "a wedge into the party." [9] As if it wasn't already there.

The State Supreme Court rejected the parties' pleas for a primary. Spellman called a one-day special session that in less than two hours approved an October 11 primary, with only five dissenting votes.

Excell took a leave of absence to join Jim Waldo in steering the Evans campaign. Evans handily outpolled conservative broadcaster Lloyd Cooney in the primary, then took 55 percent of the vote against Mike Lowry. They had deftly contrasted Lowry's bearded rumpledness and tub-thumping liberal rhetoric with Evans' senatorial mien.

THE REST of the story proved disappointing to Spellman—and Evans, who found the United States Senate tedious. In the fall of 1987, he announced he would not seek re-election, explaining why in a compelling essay for *The New York Times Magazine*:

> I came to Washington (D.C.) with a slightly romantic notion of the Senate—perhaps natural for a former governor and civil engineer whose hobby is the study of history—and I looked forward to the duel of debate, the exchange of ideas. What I found was a legislative body that had lost its focus and was in danger of losing its soul. In the United State Senate, debate has come to consist of set speeches read before a largely empty chamber; and in committees, quorums are rarely achieved. I have lived though five years of bickering and protracted paralysis. Five years is enough. I just can't face another six years of frustrating gridlock. ...[10]

Gorton, who had lost to Brock Adams in 1986, defeated Lowry in 1988 to return to the Senate. "I respected Dan's decision," Spellman says, "and, thanks to Slade, we kept the seat. But I'll always regret not appointing Joel. I think he would have loved the Senate and that we would have held both seats for a long, long time." Frank Pritchard, also close to Evans, agrees that the Senate would have been a better fit for his brother: "Joel was basically a legislator and Dan was basically an administrator." [11]

CHAPTER THIRTY-NINE

Affordable Housing

Kent Pullen, the King County senator who already suspected Spellman was a closet Democrat, wondered what they had done to him over there in China. Pullen was so appalled by the governor's push for a state Housing Finance Commission that he introduced an amendment to give the measure a new title: "The Socialized Housing Act of 1983"—because "that's what it is: socialism. It's a monstrosity … a bureaucrat's paradise, like the Soviet Union!"[1]

Washington in 1983 was the only state in the nation without an agency to promote affordable housing, a cause Spellman had championed since 1964 when he campaigned for mayor of Seattle as an opponent of racial redlining. As county executive, he had taken a keen interest in the King County Housing Authority. And as he moved through the leadership chairs in the National Governors' Association and heard the housing commission success stories from other states it struck him as folly that Washington was passing up the opportunity to prime the mortgage pump. Federal law allowed housing commissions to sell tax-exempt bonds and funnel the funds to private lenders to grant mortgages to first-time home buyers. Housing activists and sympathetic legislators, notably State Senator George Fleming, the charismatic former UW football star, had been pushing a state housing agency since the 1960s. They ran afoul of people like Pullen and Senator A.L. "Slim" Rasmussen, the flinty Democrat from Tacoma, as well as turf-conscious bankers. There was a legal hurdle, too—the State Constitution's prohibition on the lending of the state's credit "except for the necessary support of the poor and infirm."[2]

Adversity was the mother of invention. When interest rates topped 20 percent and unemployment 12 percent, thousands of Washingtonians "deferred their dream of buying a home, while others struggled to simply find decent housing of any kind."[3] Loggers stopped logging. Mills that produced 2-by-4's, shakes and shingles fell silent. Homebuilders laid off their crews. Lenders weren't lending, and Realtors weren't selling houses. "In a slow-motion one-two punch, the economy was hammering both those who needed housing and those who profited from it. ... Spellman saw in this bleak picture an opportunity to recast a housing finance commission as a much-needed stimulus for the state's economy, as well as a means of addressing the housing crisis," Kevin Jones and Katia Blackburn wrote in their history of the commission. [4]

At a press conference before the 1983 session, Spellman assembled a supporting cast of bankers, builders, real estate agents and developers. He said their shared goal was to create a new agency that would make below market-rate home loans available to first-time home buyers and help finance affordable multi-family developments. Spellman's allies were now:

> ... the very interests that had blocked past attempts to create a housing finance commission. This time, these groups would ensure the commission's creation and largely determine its shape. They'd help Spellman launch a new kind of state agency, one that was the very definition of "public-private partnership": a self-sustaining entrepreneurial agency that would help create affordable housing for hundreds of thousands of people, finance millions of dollars in community-based capital projects, and pump billions into the state economy—all without spending a cent of public funding. [5]

Two of Spellman's favorite people from his days at the King County Courthouse, Karen Rahm and Pat Dunn, were the go-betweens with the business community. Rahm headed the Planning and Community Affairs Agency; Dunn was assistant director. "We showed the bankers that this was their meal ticket," Rahm recalled 20 years on. "And builders and companies like Weyerhaeuser were all for it." At one meeting an executive with the timber giant nearly jumped out of his seat to shake her hand, saying, "It's about time." [6] Spellman says Rahm and Dunn were well aware of the speed bumps a commission had encountered in the past. "They didn't go to the bankers or to labor with a plan. They went there asking what the problem was, and 'How can we solve it?'" [7] That strategy cleared away many of the old obstacles long before the bill hit the hopper at the Capitol. The administration's successful earlier effort to win legislative and voter approval for industrial revenue bonds had built trust among the stakeholders.

The housing commission bill differed from its previous incarnations in key areas: Income limits were lifted. It was no longer just a low-income measure. The commission would be only a "conduit" between bond sales and private lenders. Pat Dunn became a frequent flier. He visited housing finance agencies all over America, compiling a portfolio of best practices. "He knew Washington would have to create a leaner, more nimble agency to appease the business community and conservatives in the Legislature."[8] Dunn and Rahm "spent much of the fall of 1982 traveling the state, explaining the intricacies of the bill to chambers of commerce, affordable housing advocates and other groups, 'road-testing' the measure and their arguments for it. ..."[9]

The bill was submitted as executive request legislation in both the House and Senate. "Time is of the essence," Spellman warned.[10] Brian Ebersole, a freshman from Tacoma destined to become speaker, sponsored the legislation in the House. Fleming, the majority caucus chairman, went to work on the Senate, aided by his staff director, Ron Sims, who went on to become King County executive and deputy secretary of the U.S. Department of Housing and Urban Development. "George was already well regarded," Sims recalled. "But when you're African-American there's always a double standard. I think in many respects he knew that if this passed, here was another ceiling broken through. It wasn't civil rights. It wasn't human services. It wasn't education. It was housing. He was very driven."[11]

Spellman signed the landmark legislation into law on May 11, 1983. "Two hurdles remained. To take advantage of hundreds of millions of dollars in bond authority available for that budget year, the commission ... would have to go about the complex business of issuing its first bonds by the end of 1983. And before investors would even consider purchasing bonds, the commission had to file a test case in the State Supreme Court to prove its own constitutionality—a process that could take far longer than the seven months remaining in the year."[12]

"We always knew the Supreme Court would be a tough hurdle," Dunn recalls. "But you know the old story goes that even members of the Supreme Court read the newspaper, so that's why we were intent on passing the measure with broad support from the Legislature."[13]

Working with Marilyn Showalter, Spellman's legal counselor, Rahm and Dunn had already retained a legal team to file a test case. The strategy it developed called for State Treasurer Robert O'Brien, the Housing Commission's newly designated secretary, to sue himself. "Since O'Brien was a constitutional officer, the case skipped the gantlet of the lower courts" and landed at the Supreme Court.[14] The commission's lawyers, Jay Reich and Larry Carter, argued that "since the lower interest rates made available to homebuyers and developers through the commission would be derived from federal tax law rather than state funds, Washington's prohibition against the lending of the state's credit was not relevant." [15] Crucially, there were no income limits on prospective borrowers.

"You mean to tell me," one justice asked Carter, "that you don't have to be poor to buy a house under this program?"

"John Beresford Tipton could qualify for a house, and it wouldn't be a constitutional issue," Carter responded, invoking the mystery benefactor who bestowed millions on needy strangers on *The Millionaire*, a huge hit on TV in the 1950s. [16]

On October 28, in a 5-4 ruling, the high court found that the commission was "consistent with the state's legitimate function and that the risk to the state's taxpayers and effectuation of the public purpose remains under public control." [17] In short, the Housing Finance Commission did not violate the State Constitution. It was a watershed decision in another way as well: The precedent "allowed the court over the next few years to reverse some of its earlier, restrictive interpretations of the 'poor and infirm' clause." [18] The public-private partnerships that led to the construction of new stadiums for the Seahawks and Mariners were an offshoot of the decision. In other words, John Spellman, as father of the Washington State Housing Finance Commission, also inadvertently paved the way for the implosion 17 years later of the signature achievement of his 11 years as King County executive, the Kingdome. That, of course, never entered his mind at the time. "Giving people an opportunity to have a decent place to live has more to do with the Golden Rule than socialism," Spellman says. "The state's job is to promote the public good." Fleming and Spellman would also work together to create an office promoting Minority and Women's Business Enterprises, denounced by foes as social engineering.

"On December 1, 1983, with a month to spare before the Congressional deadline, the Washington state Housing Finance Commission issued more than $193 million in mortgage revenue bonds. The following year, 3,040 first-time homebuyers from communities across Washington took advantage of 30-year loans financed by the commission and made through bankers around the state. ... The Commission's work had finally begun." [19]

In the spring of 1984, Spellman met with officials of the Federal National Mortgage Association—"Fannie Mae"—and secured the go-ahead for Washington to become the first state to issue bonds to build multifamily housing through a new program. "Here we were, the newest, smallest, least experienced housing finance agency in the nation and we wanted to use Fannie Mae's payment guarantee to meet pent-up demand for new rental housing in Washington after the 1982 recession," Kim Herman, executive director of the Housing Commission since its inception, recalls.

"Our chairman and finance team briefed Governor Spellman on why we felt the program would be a success, and he made our case in a trip to D.C. Fannie Mae officials later told me that our governor was so convincing in his presentation that he overcame their doubts. We issued more bonds and developed more affordable multifamily housing under the program than any other state." [20]

Since 1983, the Washington State Housing Finance Commission has financed mortgage loans for nearly 44,000 single-family homes and 89,000 apartment units. As of 2011, the programs had contributed $42.5 billion in wages and material purchases to the economy of the state. [21]

CHAPTER FORTY

Strong, Ill-defined Negatives

B ooth Gardner dropped by the Governor's Office and asked to see Steve Excell. "I like your boss," he said, "but our polls say he's likely to lose, and if someone else is going to be governor it might as well be me." [1]

By Thanksgiving 1983, Spellman and Gardner had hired live-wire campaign consultants. Spellman's new strategist was former New Yorker Paul Newman, not the movie star but a political junkie with a growing national reputation. One day he'd be in South Dakota working with George McGovern's challenger; the next in Seattle overseeing the "Let's Give Maggie a Gold Watch" campaign that propelled Slade Gorton to the U.S. Senate.

Spellman's polls disagreed with Gardner's. They found him well ahead of McDermott, with Gardner a distant third, virtually unknown beyond Pierce County. Spellman, Newman and Excell knew, however, that Gardner could and would spend whatever it took to change that. Norton Clapp, the heretofore reliably Republican, bigger-than-life Weyerhaeuser heir, was Booth's stepfather. Equally worrisome, Spellman's support was shallow and tepid, pollsters found, with "strong, ill-defined negatives." [2] The undecideds were huge. Though the economy was on the rebound, the governor wasn't perceived as the catalyst. Enter Paul Newman.

RON DOTZAUER, Gardner's campaign manager, was at loose ends when Booth invited him to dinner and turned on his famous boyish charm. Dotzauer had been a political prodigy. He was elected Clark County auditor just two years out of college. Then his upward mobility collided with the Reagan Revolution. He lost a close race for secretary of state to affable Ralph Munro, a Dan Evans' protégé. Two years later, Scoop Jackson, Dotzauer's boyhood hometown hero, asked him to manage his re-election campaign. It was a landslide victory, albeit against an underdog, Doug Jewett, yet still a text-book outing. Afterward, Dotzauer joined the senator's staff. He was crushed by Jackson's death. Scoop had wanted Booth to be the next governor, so Dotzauer signed up.[3] He ordered thousands of "Booth Who?" buttons and mobilized an army of volunteers to blanket the state with 27,000 signs. He arrived at campaign headquarters one day to discover the parking lot piled with 10-foot stacks of lovely Weyerhaeuser plywood. "Holy shit!" Dotzauer cackled. "We have enough wood to build half of downtown Seattle."[4] Spellman had been the state's first "million-dollar governor." Gardner would spend $1.3 million just to win the primary.

Running for re-election.

The good news for Spellman was that he'd won points with his party for appointing Evans to Jackson's Senate seat—even some conservatives conceded the former governor was the strongest candidate—and by vetoing McDermott's anti-business bills. The trade mission to China, the industrial-revenue bonds, the new housing commission and lower unemployment also gave Spellman's stock a boost. "The party is more unified behind John Spellman than it has been at any time since 1981," said John Carlson, spokesman for the State Republican Central Committee.[5] McDermott was off to a slow start, and had lost twice before; Seattle Mayor Charles Royer was damaged goods after his crushing defeat by Mike Lowry in the special senatorial primary, and Gardner, at this stage of the game, was seen by many "as a kind of Spellman clone ... a competent but unexciting administrator" who would have a hard time overcoming McDermott's liberal base.[6] "Spellman is stronger than most people think he is," Newman said.[7] Dotzauer said everyone was underestimating his guy, too. He and Newman were at the top of their game, and if at times too self-celebratory for sufferance, what great salesman isn't?

Republicans from around the state assembled at the Tacoma Dome in December to hear Vice President Bush pass the hat for his "old friend" Spellman, who led a rousing rendition of "God Bless America" and took home $70,000. That was pocket change for Team Gardner.[8]

Booth was promising to be "The Education Governor" who would spend at least one day a month in a public-school classroom. He emphasized his experience as assistant to the dean of the Harvard Business School and director of the School of Business Administration at the University of

Puget Sound in Tacoma. He and Spellman, in fact, were on parallel tracks in promoting high-tech partnerships between the state's research universities and business. And both had joined the nationwide push for standards-based education. On his overseas trips, Spellman had visited many schools. Even in developing countries where books, let alone computers, were in short supply, he saw rigorous math and science being taught. In 1982, he created a committee to study the structure of public-school education in Washington State. The outgrowth was the "Education for Excellence Act" that Spellman asked the 1984 Legislature to approve. Its hot button was a call for mandatory competency tests for students and new teachers. "There are those who say we cannot mandate excellence in education," Spellman told the Washington State School Directors' Association. "I say we have to try to mandate it through the establishment of demanding standards for students, teachers and administrators." Mere "pass-fail sufficiency" was relegating American schools to second-class status in a global economy, Spellman said. Under his plan, high school students by 1990 would be required to pass a minimum-competency examination. "It will make the high school diploma what it should be—a certificate of measurable achievement."

Spellman also asked the state Board of Education to establish a "Teacher of the Year" program to recognize and reward excellence.[9] Gardner's friend, Reese Lindquist, president of the state's largest teachers' union, and state school Superintendent Frank "Buster" Brouillet were skeptical that a graduation competency test represented a good investment. "We believe you take care of the problem before they get to the 12th grade," Brouillet said.[10] Spellman said they weren't listening: That was exactly what he had in mind. The emphasis on excellence had to begin in the earliest grades, setting the stage for more rigor in high school, including three years of math and science and two years of foreign language for college-bound students.

Spellman saw a direct correlation between school dropouts, delinquency and the road to serious crime. Amos Reed, his Corrections director, was winning bipartisan praise for gaining control of the state's volatile, bulging prisons and instituting new job-training programs. A commission Spellman appointed to study the system warned, however, that the prisons were still at 135 percent of capacity. "We're in the red zone now and things are likely to get worse before they get better," Reed said.[11] He and the governor advocated new community-based corrections programs, including an early-release program with intensified parole. They said there was scant evidence that long-term incarceration in large and isolated prisons rehabilitated inmates to become productive members of society. Spellman urged the Legislature to authorize $61 million in general obligation bonds for Corrections improvements and additional beds.

The governor also wanted $6 million more to promote tourism and trade and $2 million to launch Education for Excellence, but the bulk of the $41.2 million supplemental budget he proposed for 1984 was to deal with enrollment increases in public schools. Revenues generated by the rebounding economy could fund his entire wish list and still leave a $33.5 million surplus at the end of the 1983-85 biennium, Spellman said.

IT WAS THE WEEK before Christmas. Notably missing from beneath Spellman's tree was a program wrapped in the initials AFDC-E. Aid to Families with Dependent Children provided short-term welfare assistance for two-parent families that had exhausted jobless benefits. Its funding, some $32 million, was set to expire in June. With the economy on the rebound, Spellman said the program needed to be re-evaluated. McDermott said the governor was acting "like Ebenezer Scrooge." [12] The program prevented the breakup of families and kept 16,000 children from going to bed hungry, the Ways and Means chairman said, burnishing his status as the liberal front-runner for governor. Speaker Ehlers, Gardner's leading surrogate, said Spellman was underestimating tax revenues for political purposes, trying to make the Democrats look like big spenders. Ehlers proposed an $80 million supplemental budget. Everything he wanted, including AFDC-E and more health benefits for state workers in the second year of the budget, could be funded without new taxes and still produce a $30 million surplus, Ehlers said.

Spellman's present from Uncle Sam by way of the Reagan administration and Senator Evans was McNeil Island, a $50 million parcel of prime real estate. Flanked by Evans, Gorton, Congressmen Norm Dicks and Sid Morrison, Spellman signed papers deeding the 4,400-acre island to the state. The old federal penitentiary was now housing 950 state inmates. The rest of the island would become a wildlife preserve. Rent had been set to escalate from $400,000 a year to $1 million. Spellman and the feds had negotiated an outright sale for about $9 million, "but Evans, in his first Senate victory, was able to push through legislation turning it over to the state for free." [13]

There was a changing of the guard at the Department of Social and Health Services. Spellman appointed Karen Rahm to succeed Alan Gibbs, who departed to become director of Seattle Metro. Gibbs had won high marks for keeping legislators and special-interest groups in the loop, taking extra care to seek guidance when he was forced to make cuts. His moxie defused critics and created a new level of trust between the super-agency and its easily riled constituents. Rahm, a willowy 39-year-old, came to the Capitol with Spellman after serving as King County's planning director. The former Federal Reserve Bank economist had managed the Planning and Community Affairs Agency with élan and efficiency on a tight budget. Now she took on the toughest job in state government. Spellman was certain Rahm had the management chops to head the 12,000-employee department. And he was right. "She's smart as hell, but she's tough as nails," said one senior bureaucrat.[14] Pat Dunn, Rahm's deputy, who knew everyone in Olympia and every county commissioner from Montesano to Pomeroy, succeeded her as director of Planning and Community Affairs.

THE LEGISLATURE had been in session for a total of 364 days over the previous three years. Now, with the economy on the rebound—unemployment was under 10 percent for first time in 27 months—and 98 members of the House and 25 senators facing re-election, everyone was eager to go home. For the first time in 27 years, the Legislature wrapped up its business in 60 days. Not that it was easy. The fighting focused on the welfare program liberals wanted and a tax break timber companies said they desperately needed to recover from the recession. Gardner, moving shrewdly to co-opt the center, favored both proposals. He said he alone among the candidates understood the needs of the needy and the realities of big business. His work with underprivileged and special-needs kids and his experience as a corporate manager and board member gave him "a unique perspective." Moreover, he said he was "electable," a not-so-subtle dig at McDermott, the two-time loser. "People want a winner," Dotzauer said.[15] While McDermott was busy in Olympia as chairman of Ways and Means, Gardner was on the hustings. When they appeared together in January before the State Democratic Central Committee, McDermott finally got some licks in, suggesting that Gardner was a Democrat in name only: "We won't beat incumbent Republicans with cardboard cut-out look-alikes."[16]

Gardner made his candidacy official in February, barnstorming the state in a private plane. A standing-room-only crowd of 500 in Fife chanted "Booth! Booth! Booth!"[17] He criticized Spellman for breaking his no-new-taxes pledge, but emphasized that if new taxes were necessary to provide important services, such as higher pay for teachers, "I will be the first to step up and lead that charge." In Seattle, he said he would promote "coalition building," emphasizing that labor and industry, loggers and environmentalists, Indians and non-Indians, needed to be brought together to solve the state's problems. In Spokane and the Tri-Cities, he said Spellman had done little to promote economic growth.[18]

That wasn't so. At the Department of Commerce and Economic De-velopment, Dick Schrock's astringent self-confidence, coupled with his baggage as Spellman's longtime political brain, had generated detractors in the business community. (Now that Allison was gone, they were telling Spellman, Schrock should be next.) By any objective measure, however, Schrock's department was achieving results—not even counting the divi-dends to come from the overseas trade missions. Washington State, which had been lagging at the back of the pack before Spellman took office, was now a significant player. It ranked ninth among the states in the push for high-tech jobs. At the same time, some $20 million had been funneled to local governments to help create industrial jobs through the Community Economic Revitalization Board—CERB grants. In all, 33 prospective inves-tors had announced plans for new plants or expansions, while industrial revenue-bond financing for another 90 companies was in the pipeline. Mil-lions more had been allocated to promote the growth of small business. Spellman early on had established a committee to promote high-tech train-ing. Some $3.5 million had been appropriated for the 1983-85 biennium to help community colleges and vocational schools work with the private sector on job-skill development.[19] At the university level, Spellman had proposed and secured funding for new biotechnology and engineering programs. The Washington Technology Center was an outgrowth of those initiatives.

Still, "we had some of the best political people in the county tell us, 'We've never seen an incumbent governor with such a high negative rat-ing.' They were just amazed," Dotzauer recalled.[20]

ON MARCH 7, 1984, the session's 59th day, the divisive timber tax bill finally arrived on Spellman's desk. The arm-twisting by timber company lobbyists had been intense. Republicans mustered a majority by forging an alliance with business-oriented Democrats. The existing 6.5 percent tax on har-vested timber would be phased down to 5 percent over the next five years. The 12.5 percent excise tax on reforested lands would be phased out over the next 10 years. The legislation was estimated to cost the state $176 mil-lion over the next eight years. The counties and other local taxing districts were to be insulated from revenue losses. Without that provision, Spellman would have vetoed the legislation. As passed, he said the bill represented not "a rip-off," as Democrats claimed, but tax-burden equity for one of the state's most vital industries. Property tax rates had been reduced 40 percent during the time the timber tax had been in place, while the legislation he was signing cut the harvest tax by 23 percent.[21]

Adjournment at 2:05 a.m. a day later had hinged on passage of a supplemental budget that included money to continue Aid to Families with Dependent Children. It passed, and Spellman said he would sign it.

The salvo of vetoes that followed incensed organized labor.

Spellman vetoed part of a "right-to-know" bill whose backers asserted it would offer more protection to workers handling toxic substances and other hazardous materials. He believed the bill would create a "monstrous paper burden" on the Department of Labor and Industries, small business and agriculture.[22] Next, he "virtually gutted the complicated hospital cost-containment bill over which the Legislature had agonized for weeks."[23] Spellman said he had talked with hospital managers and board members all around the state. "Many, particularly the smaller ones, feared they would not be able to continue offering service if they had to meet the charity care standard" mandated in the legislation.[24] Then he killed a bill requiring food-service workers' tips to be counted as wages when they were seeking unemployment benefits. Finally, for the second time in two years, he spiked legislation allowing collective bargaining by community college faculty. The "welfare grant for the shareholders of large timber companies," was bad enough, said Marvin Williams, president of the Washington State Labor Council. Now Spellman had shown his true colors as a "tool and patsy for big business and the industrial community."[25] "We realize this is an election year for Governor Spellman ... but his vetoes have shown he has little concern for the citizens, the workers or the union members of our state."[26] Senator Phil Talmadge, the Seattle Democrat who sponsored the "right-to-know" bill and was running for attorney general, called the veto "an atrocious act." McDermott charged that Spellman's "callous attitude toward workers couldn't be more clearly stated...."[27]

Spellman also vetoed a bill requiring governors to fill U.S. Senate vacancies with someone from the same party as the former senator. Democrats, still mourning the loss of Jackson and ruing the return of Evans, didn't like that either.*

A few weeks later, when the State Supreme Court expanded the veto power of Washington governors and validated Spellman's 1982 line-item veto of a measure unions wanted, the Washington Federation of State Employees and other labor groups that had joined the lawsuit were thwarted again.

---

*In 1975, in a preemptive strike against Governor Evans, Democrats pushed onto the ballot a referendum on whether governors should be required to fill Senate vacancies with a person from the same party as the former incumbent. Fifty-four percent of the voters rejected the restriction.

The man who began his career as an attorney representing unions was now squarely in labor's cross-hairs as he sought re-election for governor. Only the Teamsters, his longtime ally, did not join the withering chorus of criticism over the vetoes. In the bruising seven months ahead, he lost them too.

CHAPTER FORTY-ONE

Booth Whew

"We have met the enemy and he is us."
—Pogo the possum

B y of the summer of '84, thanks to signs that sprouted like dandelions and a barrage of commercials, hundreds of thousands knew who Booth was and what he was promising to do. "Booth Gardner's management expertise turned red ink into black. He did it in Pierce County and he can do it for the state. That was our mantra," Ron Dotzauer said.[1] Gardner's campaign manager believed beating McDermott would be harder than evicting Spellman, while McDermott early on said, "My campaign is directed at the present governor of this state. I think he's the opponent."[2] When McDermott changed course, he was rowing against a tide. Spellman fully expected a rematch with McDermott. The one opponent he couldn't shake was his own image—those strong, ill-defined negatives.

It was unprecedented for an incumbent governor with only token primary opposition to be running campaign commercials in the spring. Spellman's team felt it had no choice after Gardner hit the airwaves early and often—$117,000 worth of commercials in April alone. President Reagan, who began 1983 with an approval rating of 35 percent, far lower than Spellman's, was now cruising into the high 50's, with the resurgent economy as a tailwind. But John D. Spellman was not Ronald Reagan, the best retail-politics salesman since FDR. The recession and broken no-new-taxes promise trailed Spellman like a strip of toilet paper stuck to a shoe.

Gardner had his own wake-up call. Dotzauer had warned him that McDermott, having lost twice, would come out swinging. They must spend hours studying the issues and rehearsing for the debates. Gardner instead coached his girls' soccer team. Dotzauer couldn't bear to watch what happened next.

Tall, handsome, forceful, McDermott was fast on his feet; always well prepared. The ring-wise Blair Butterworth was back in his corner. They sized up Gardner as a political dilettante. His nasally voice—which one wag described as "Elmer Fudd on helium"—grew more pipsqueaky when he was tense.[3] Dotzauer's worst fears came true. McDermott mopped the floor with his candidate in front of the Seattle Rotary Club, ostensibly Booth's kind of audience. Visibly nervous, Gardner mumbled management jargon and offered lame comebacks when McDermott flailed him as a double-talker. Gardner claimed to have resuscitated Pierce County without raising taxes. The truth, McDermott said, was that the sales tax had been raised. Gardner claimed to have the common touch, to be a champion of government transparency, yet he had shielded the scope and sources of his wealth in a blind trust. Gardner and Spellman were peas in a pod, McDermott said, two county executives who maintained that "if you've found the right manager, the problems of the state will go away."[4]

Chagrinned practically to tears, Gardner apologized to Dotzauer for letting him down. "OK, I'm ready," he said. "I don't want that to happen again." Dotzauer was amazed by the transformation. "Here was this diminutive kind of guy. Never would you think for a minute that he had this fiery, competitive piece to him."[5] They holed up in a hotel room and did debate prep—intense debate prep, complete with podiums. Denny Heck, the self-assured young legislative leader from Vancouver, hyper-played McDermott as a pit bull. Booth grew so frustrated that he threw down his pen. But he held his own in the next debate. From that day on his confidence grew. Dotzauer had been told Gardner had a "near-photographic" memory. When he saw him absorbing briefing books and mounds of newspaper clippings, he was astounded not only by his memory but his ability to distill the most important details.

Momentum was Gardner's when the State, County & Municipal Employees issued a dual endorsement and the State Labor Council and Washington Education Association opted to stay neutral. He already had a lock on the State Patrol Troopers' Association, which loathed Spellman. Dotzauer ordered a batch of T-shirts that said "No more Hill Street Blues for the WSP."[6] The Spellman campaign riled the troopers even more when it ran a TV spot showing the governor and a trooper approaching a traffic violator. It was meant to dramatize the governor's successful push for legislation cracking down on drunken drivers. Grant Sherman, the politically astute leader of the Troopers' Association, charged that using a uniformed trooper in a political commercial violated State Patrol policy and probably state law as well. The trooper, a member of the governor's executive protection detail, took part in the commercial on his own time. The patrol had been duly reimbursed for use of the car. When Spellman and Chief

Moloney were fined $75 apiece by the Public Disclosure Commission, the headlines cost the campaign infinitely more than that. Gardner was intent on chipping holes in Spellman's reputation for integrity. They had given him another opportunity.[7]

Steve Excell took a leave of absence to re-boot the Spellman campaign. Like the Luftwaffe general who saw a thousand B-17's heading his way and exclaimed, "What I would give to have such power!" he and Butterworth could but envy the resources at Dotzauer's disposal. The 1984 campaign for governor turned on TV commercials, at $500 per half-minute.

DAN EVANS WAS STUNNED and disgusted when the 60-day campaign to retain the Senate seat he had won by appointment cost $1.8 million in 1983. Dixy Lee Ray had spent $96,000 in 1976 to win the hotly contested Democratic nomination for governor. Common Cause and other critics called the new levels of campaign spending across America "outrageous" and "obscene." Paul Newman observed, however, that "in the coming year United Airlines will spend more than $120 million to persuade us to fly the friendly skies. Underarm deodorant firms will spend almost as much."[8]

Money was practically no object for the Gardner campaign. By August, it was flying high and closing in on McDermott. Dotzauer charted a course with day-to-day tracking polls. He deployed an army of volunteers to doorbell 200,000 homes and mailed 650,000 brochures to areas targeted by computer analysis. "When one reporter grumbled that a press release wasn't legible, the campaign quickly bought a sophisticated new copy machine—a little few-thousand-dollar item."[9]

Gardner surged from 14 points behind in August to a six-point lead in September. Leaving nothing to chance, Dotzauer summoned the ghost of Scoop Jackson. A letter signed by Sterling Munro and other influential former Jackson aides was sent to 90,000 former Jackson boosters. "Last summer," the letter said, "Scoop encouraged Booth Gardner to run for governor ...Scoop knew that Booth shared his views about the purposes of government ...that its worth should be measured by how well it meets the needs of those who can't help themselves, how it educates the young and gives dignity to the lives of the elderly."[10]

"A masterstroke," said Excell. Butterworth's groan seconded the motion: "It sounds like Scoop Jackson, with his last breath, said that Booth should be governor. ... We've never before seen the impact of this kind of money in a primary in this state." The McDermott campaign had just spent its last $135,000, hoping a new round of TV spots might reverse Gardner's gains. "If we lose this election," Butterworth said, "it would be the only campaign I remember losing where I didn't think we could have done anything differently."[11]

On September 18, 1984, Gardner crushed McDermott, two-to-one, and bested the second-place Spellman by nearly 182,000 votes. The Democrats outpolled Spellman and a perennial also-ran Republican by 403,000. An Elway poll on the general-election finalists now had Gardner with a nine-point lead, with 23 percent still undecided.[12] Spellman and Excell said they weren't worried (they were) and observed that Republican crossovers and stay-at-homes accounted for Gardner's impressive showing. There was truth to that. Twenty-two percent of the Republicans polled by Stuart Elway said they had voted for Gardner. A follow-up poll found that Gardner could win 24 percent of those who self-identified as Republicans. But only 4 percent of the Gardner voters intended to switch to Spellman come November. Spellman had to win over the undecideds as well as wayward Republicans. And there was no future in harping on Gardner's ability "to buy an election." For all the talk about his wealth—he had spent $1.3 million to defeat McDermott—more than half of those surveyed by Elway said Gardner's money was not an issue for them. "And many of the ones who said it was an issue indicated it was a plus for Gardner."[13] A retired social worker said, "I thought the fact he would spend his own monies for his campaign spoke very well for him. It indicates he is sincere." Others said that since he was rich he was less likely to be a captive of special interests.[14] Gardner voters also said they were impressed by his ads, which emphasized his management expertise and humanitarian activities. McDermott was a deeply disappointed but gracious loser. He told Booth to not waste time celebrating. When it came to campaigning, Spellman could get down and dirty, he warned. They'd better not be overconfident.

Spellman's campaign had spent virtually all of the nearly $900,000 it had raised to date. There was no way it could match Gardner's bankroll—$1 million from his own pocket and the numerous Clapps. Brian McCauley, Spellman's finance director, nevertheless kept them competitive—despite cash-flow problems—until late in the game. Hunter Simpson of Physio-Control and most of Spellman's other longtime supporters from the business community stuck with him. But Spellman would be outspent by nearly a million dollars. By October 1, Gardner's lead had surged to as high as 22 points in some polls. Paul O'Connor, Spellman's pugnacious press secretary, said Spellman was coming out "duking," just as he had four years earlier to defeat McDermott. They were going to dispel the notion that Gardner was not a tax-and-spend liberal. "There is a presumption that because he's rich, he's a conservative," O'Connor said, adding that Gardner's knowledge of

state issues was "candy-coat, shell thin. All he is is a trained dog on the issues." [15] That was just "desperate" duplicity from "the same John Spellman
who said 'no new taxes in 1980,' " Gardner spokesman Jim Kneeland shot
back. "John Spellman and Paul O'Connor better put on their crash helmets
if they're going to try to run on their record." [16]

"WHY GAMBLE ON GARDNER?" Spellman's ads asked, zeroing in on the
Democrat's amorphous platform. Gardner was promising to "run this state
in the businesslike manner it requires." He was disarmed by his own candor, however, admitting to newspaper editorial boards that he hadn't "spent
a lot of time worrying about state government." [17] Once in office, he and
his team would analyze what needed fixing and just do it, like he'd done in
Pierce County.

Spellman had a hard time laying a glove on the guy. He said Gardner
had voted for an income tax when he was in the Legislature. But he was
vulnerable to the same charge, having backed Evans' attempts to enact an
income tax. That was then; this is now, Spellman said, promising to oppose an income tax under any circumstances. Gardner countered that he
wouldn't support an income tax unless it came with "hefty cuts in other
taxes" and business supported it. The issue fizzled. [18]

Spellman's team—Excell, Newman, McCauley, O'Connor, Chris Smith
and Helen Rasmussen—went to work on his image. This was no time for
modesty. "I am convinced," Spellman said, "that no governor in the history of the state has ever made as many decisions in as brief a period of
time on as many important issues as I have." [19] He pointed to a reorganized
Corrections Department; a Department of Social and Health Services that
had maintained, even improved, vital services while absorbing huge budget
cuts; a more accurate system to forecast revenues and a 10 percent reduc-
tion in the growth of government spending, even with the tax increases that
had been necessary to balance the budget during the worst of the recession.
Moreover, Spellman said he had protected Puget Sound from oil spills and
preserved the integrity of the Shoreline Management Act. He and William Ruckelshaus, administrator of the federal Environmental Protection
Agency, had established a new state-federal office to expedite the cleanup of
Puget Sound.

If all that had the added advantage of being true, Gardner was still
winning the beauty contest hands down. He kissed babies, paused to offer
Little Leaguers batting tips, hugged cheerleaders, mugged with the Seafair
pirates, mingled with mill workers, had coffee and pie with truck drivers
and took senior-citizen centers by storm. He loved to be loved and had a

gift for connecting. Spellman came off as a ribbon-cutting governor, never mind that he could burst into song at the drop of a hat and liked a pint of Guinness. It didn't register. He was "bland."

When Dotzauer played hard to get on debates, citing "scheduling conflicts," it underscored a reversal of traditional roles: The incumbent was now the underdog. (And by far the better debater.)[20] They finally agreed on three televised appearances, starting in mid-October. Spellman groused that the campaign would be half over before their first face-to-face. He said he felt "like a Ghostbuster fighting a phantom. ... Inside that Brooks Brothers suit is a carbon copy of Jim McDermott."[21] At a campaign breakfast in Kitsap County, Spellman declared, "You name me a program [Gardner has accomplished] and I'll give you a cigar!"[22] His hands "trembling with anger," the governor startled a press conference when he chewed out two reporters for not printing his statements about Gardner.[23]

WITH SPELLMAN TRAILING Gardner 40 to 27, the consensus was that they had little choice but to start duking for the 32 percent of undecideds. They seized on a fulsome letter Gardner had sent to labor leaders before the primary. His promises came across as the latter-day equivalent of FDR's famous standing order to "Clear everything with Sidney," a powerful labor leader.* The Spellman campaign, in quick succession, ran three increasingly tough "Big Labor Boss" commercials. In the first, a Hoffaesque character is sitting at a humongous desk, fat cigar in a crystal ashtray. Voice over in a disgusted tone: "This June Booth Gardner made the big union bosses some pretty big promises." Camera focuses on a paragraph in a letter signed by Booth. The union boss reads it aloud: "If I'm elected I will support the goals and programs which organized labor has fought for. I will appoint representatives of organized labor to state boards and commissions. And my record clearly shows I am a strong supporter of organized labor's legislative agenda."

A still from the "Big Labor Boss" commercials the Spellman campaign ran against Gardner.

*Gardner would repudiate the letter as an over-the-top overture authored by a campaign staffer. He said all he was promising was an open door.

The union boss chuckles: "Nice!" He picks up his cigar and takes a satisfied drag. Voice over: "Why gamble on Gardner's ties to the big unions. Re-elect Governor John Spellman." In the second commercial, the boss is briefing a roomful of pals. They're all smoking cigars. "Listen to what this Booth Gardner guy is promising us. ... You know I think we got him *just where we want him!*" The third commercial ranks as a tour de force even by today's production values. First we see a puppet that's a perfect caricature of Gardner. Who's pulling the strings? A big labor boss. The Booth puppet dances. Finally, the boss slackens the strings and the puppet collapses on his desk. Voice over: "The truth about Booth Gardner is he'd be a puppet governor... So if you don't want union bosses running our state, vote for a governor with no strings attached. ..." [24]

Dotzauer ordered several thousand buttons that rank-and-file union members soon wore proudly. "Hi!" the buttons said, "I'm a 'Big Labor Boss.'" Arnie Weinmeister, president of the Joint Council of Teamsters in Seattle, had been Spellman's friend even before the beginning of his political career in the 1960s. When Weinmeister hand-delivered a letter saying the union was withdrawing its endorsement, "it was a terrible shock," Spellman recalls. The letter said:

> During your tenure as King County Executive, our Local Unions negotiated many favorable contracts with you, including the Kingdome operation. Four years ago we endorsed your candidacy for Governor because of your labor history and record in King County. During the past four years your record was one-hundred percent on Teamsters' issues and concerns. ... Your office door and your staff were always open to our concerns and new ideas. For these reasons, we wholeheartedly endorsed your re-election and reaffirmed our support, in writing, to our 60,000 Teamster families in this state after the Primary election. However, in the past month you have chosen to viciously attack labor unions, their members and their duly elected officials. ... Your attacks on your opponent's labor endorsements and snide slurs on elected union officials is a gross insult to all working men and women of this state ...[25]

The campaign made things worse by trying to spin it that Spellman wasn't upset, just disappointed, particularly because the Teamsters "were one of the few union groups who stood up to the big union bosses and made an endorsement based on the facts." The real union bosses knew "they've already got Booth Gardner in their pocket ... contrary to the overall interests of Washington workers." [26]

Gardner called Spellman a hypocrite and handed out copies of Spellman's 1980 campaign speech to the State Labor Council. It began with a salutation to his "Brothers and sisters in the labor movement" and ended with a promise that labor would get its "fair share" of appointments to boards and commissions. [27]

"It was stupid to run that ad because I'd had very good relationships with labor over the years," Spellman says, shaking his head. "But Paul Newman read the polls and believed that if we didn't establish that Booth was in the pocket of labor I was going to lose. That was bad advice. I should have known better. At the same time as we were antagonizing labor, we allowed the Gardner people to say we had no interest in the environment. Hell, we had vetoed the Northern Tier pipeline and the Chicago Bridge & Iron rezone. They said Booth would work to promote peace between the tribes and white fishermen. With Bill Wilkerson at Fisheries, we were already doing precisely that. They said I didn't do anything on international trade, when I'd been to China and Japan, multiple times, and forged important agreements—landmark agreements. Nobody had done more. They even attacked us on tourism, when our 'See America's Other Washington' campaign was very successful."

Newman says he advised the campaign team that Gardner was vulnerable for giving labor carte blanche. "But advocating a strategy without controlling the tactics will always get you burned if it goes wrong, and let someone else take the glory if it works." [28]

The labor boss ads were conceived by John Brown, the Seattle ad man whose agency produced the hard-hitting "McDermott is the question" ads that carried Spellman to victory in 1980. Excell recalls Spellman "sitting very silently, obviously conflicted," when the ads were pitched. "I had my own misgivings, but I thought it was a gamble worth taking. We were way behind." [29] Spellman even defended the commercials at the time. He told the P-I's Joel Connelly they had to "puncture the atmosphere" created by homespun TV spots showing Gardner sitting at his kitchen table or talking with a man in a wheelchair. "We have to get to the gut issues and get there fast." [30] Dick Schrock—not a Newman fan—says that if he had been part of the 1984 campaign team he would have argued passionately against airing the ads: "Labor was where Spellman came from as a young lawyer. As county executive he would go to the Catholic Seamen's Club, Teamsters'

meetings and the Longshoremen's hall. It was contrary to the persona
and image of John D. Spellman to be attacking labor, and it was not good
politics."[31]

SPELLMAN WAS FORCEFUL in their first debate; far more knowledgeable
on the issues. Yet Gardner surprised many with his poise. He accused
Spellman of being a "fumbling" governor who had signed more than 80 tax
hikes in the space of four years. Spellman countered that Gardner's vaunted
management expertise was a sham. He had "ripped off the road fund"
to balance the Pierce County budget and "left the county in a shambles."
In the second debate a week later, the first words out of Gardner's mouth
were "John, I think you've run one of the dirtiest campaigns we've seen in
Washington in a long time."[32] New polls showed Spellman gaining. The
final face-off came on Halloween in Spokane. Spellman twice referred to
Gardner as "Mr. Governor"—a Freudian slip? That was as scary as it got.
Spellman said he was proud to stand on his record. He'd made tough decisions to help the state weather the toughest economy in a half century. The
recession was almost over. "I think the State of Washington is on a real
high." Gardner said the voters knew better: "Basically, in the last four years,
the governor has done nothing."[33]

Evans and Gorton barnstormed with Spellman. Gardner made one
last lap of the state on *Spud One*, the plane placed at his disposal by Pete
Taggares, the potato mogul. Spellman was a half-million-dollars behind in
the money race. When Excell, O'Connor and other top staffers offered to

Spellman assails Gardner during their debate in Spokane.

On election eve 1984, Spellman's campaign team is hoping for a miracle. From left, Chris Smith, deputy campaign manager; Paul Newman, consultant; Steve Excell, campaign manager; Brian McCauley, finance director; Helen Rasmussen, field coordinator; Paul O'Connor, press secretary.

contribute a week's salary to help finance last-minute ads, Spellman reluctantly accepted.

After firing up volunteers to ring 600,000 more doorbells, Dotzauer thought, "What else can we do?" He called Helen Jackson, Scoop's widow, who immediately agreed to write a "Dear Friend" letter endorsing Booth. It went to 250,000 likely voters age 55 and older who had supported Jackson.[34]

ON NOVEMBER 6, 1984, Booth Gardner was elected Washington's 19th governor. He captured 53.3 percent of the vote and carried 23 of the state's 39 counties—even Lewis, ordinarily reliably Republican. Gallingly, Spellman lost King County by 30,000 votes. Reagan clobbered Mondale in Washington State en route to a 49-state landslide. Nationwide, Spellman was one of the few major Republican office holders to lose. All the incumbent statewide officeholders in Washington State, including three other Republicans, were easy winners.

Kat Spellman, the governor's youngest, forlornly snuggled her father. He kissed her head. Teresa, Kat's sister, fought back tears and locked him in a hug. The other five Spellmans gathered around. "My faith remains strong in this state and my faith remains strong in God," Spellman said with warmth and sincerity. "I am convinced this evening that God has another purpose for me."[35] He said he had no regrets about the hardball campaign. It was their only chance. That was a lie. He had a lot of regrets. And he was angry with himself.

Teresa Spellman hugs her father as he concedes to Booth Gardner on election night 1984.

Excell, red-eyed and exhausted, said Gardner was "much harder to define than McDermott. But things were closing so rapidly that with another couple of weeks we might have pulled it off. ... Who knows?" As for the labor boss commercials, "Defeat is always an orphan."[36]

"I've seen it happen over and over again," Dan Evans said. "He raised taxes when he had to, and people remember that. If asked, those people might admit that it was absolutely necessary, but they remember all the same."[37]

With all due respect to God, Paul O'Connor was an Irishman in no mood for gallant benedictions. The governor's devastated press secretary had a meltdown at an impromptu press conference, railing against the reporters and columnists who'd written "so many stupid, unfair, bullshit" things about his boss. Many others, including Glenn Pascall, the revenue director with the "big mouth," had also let a good man down, O'Connor fumed.*[38]

During an editorial-board interview at *The Seattle Times* earlier in the campaign, Spellman was asked why someone with a strong track record as

---

*O'Connor, who spent the next year searching his soul and drawing unemployment, was still fuming as he departed for Chicago to become assistant director of the Illinois Department of Public Health. The capitol press corps was a sad example of the "tyranny of pack journalism," he said. "Throw them a piece of meat and they'll run with it." He also blamed himself for not creating "emotional bonding" with the press. O'Connor said he was "purged" from strategy sessions during the 1984 campaign when he objected to turning "a nice guy into a mean and nasty gutter-fighter."[40]

an administrator often came across to the public as indecisive. "I think I'm a good manager," he said. Then, with a shrug and a sigh, "I guess maybe I'm not a very good salesman." [39]

Stuart Elway's final poll, conducted in the last four days of the campaign, found that Spellman was the question and Gardner was the voters' answer. "In the primary, people voted for Gardner because he was not McDermott," the pollster observed. "In the general, people voted for Gardner because he was not Spellman." [41] The labor boss commercials cut two ways, Elway said. They won back a sizable number of Republicans who had voted for Gardner in the primary, but "started to backfire" when they didn't let up. [42]

TWO DAYS AFTER the election, Spellman held a press conference in his office. It was a classic November day in the Northwest, with a gray drizzle enveloping the marble columns of the Capitol. The reporters were surprised to find an upbeat governor. He was smoking his pipe, leaning back in his big leather chair embossed with the state seal. He was relaxed and engaging. At peace with himself.

"What are you going to do next?" someone said. "Are any companies calling you?"

"Lots of them," Spellman said with a laugh. "Unfortunately, they're the gas company, the electric company and the phone company!"

Everyone cracked up.

"Will you ever run for office again?"

"There may come a day when people will be standing on my doorstep with torches and signs and it will be hard to turn them down." [43]

Bob Partlow, the capitol correspondent for *The Olympian* and other Gannett Papers, jotted it all down in his notebook and thought to himself, "If *that* John Spellman—the warm, jocular Irish pol—had shown up on the campaign trail, all of Booth's money couldn't have beat him." [44]

Judge Not

Spellman was 58 years old, about to be unemployed and $100,000 in debt. When he made public his income tax returns during the campaign, many were surprised to discover that his only source of income was the $63,000 a year Washingtonians paid their governor. For 18 years, in fact, he had passed up a far more lucrative career as a lawyer to serve the public. In this respect, losing turned out to be a smart career move. He accepted an offer to join the Seattle law firm of Carney, Stephenson, Badley, Smith & Mueller as a partner. His niche would be international business.

Friends and admirers organized a $100-a-plate "Bipartisan Appreciation Dinner" at Longacres to help him retire his campaign debt. Senator Magnuson, turning 80 the next day, was a special guest. With 500 on hand and the witty Bill Ruckelshaus as master of ceremonies, the two old friends had a warm and nostalgic double date. It was a toast, roast and birthday party rolled into one. Magnuson and Slade Gorton sat side by side at the head table. "It took me 80 years to get invited to a Republican event," Maggie quipped. "I'm touched by your warm welcome. However, not half as touched as you'll be. No one asked me for $100!"[1] Ruckelshaus, the former federal EPA administrator, assured Spellman, "All of these people are your friends, John. You can't hurt them anymore, so why shouldn't they be?"[2] Maggie recalled how John's father had taken him under his wing 60 years earlier when he was a walk-on with the University of Washington football team. Magnuson said he was only a "scrub," which amounted to being a human tackling dummy for the varsity. But Bart Spellman was a coach who admired grit, and Maggie made the team. Bart would have been proud of what his son accomplished as county executive and governor, he said. "John Spellman exemplified public service."[3] Spellman said Maggie had been one of his role models since childhood. Being governor was "a singular honor," and he had "nothing but the highest optimism for the future of this state."[4]

Neither mentioned that Spellman had hosted Magnuson Appreciation Day at the Capitol four years earlier and helped him retire his debt from the loss to Gorton. It was payback time. Perhaps only Warren Magnuson fully understood how much it hurt to lose.

Spellman absorbed another loss a month later—the death of his plucky mother, who had instilled in him his abiding faith.

BOOTH GARDNER, to be sure, now fully understood the significance of something Spellman said on election night: "In terms of the Legislature, it was a lot worse than I thought it would be." [5] The new governor early on faced a series of frustrating setbacks and stinging criticism. When he warned that salary increases for public employees, teachers and college faculty were unlikely in 1985 because the reserves for the current biennium were practically gone, the unions said he was a Democrat in name only. "The Education Governor" was asking $117 million less than Spellman for public schools. "Any talk of education excellence a cruel joke," the teachers' union said. [6]

To the Republicans' delight, the majority Democrats "degenerated into an inter-house, inter-generational, self-destructive feud" and went home without passing a budget. The governor seemed clueless. Larsen wrote that "Waffleman" had been succeeded by "Prince Faintheart," a governor who would rather schmooze through photo-ops with school kids than play hardball with the Legislature. A lawmaker dubbed Gardner "The Cabbage Patch Governor." Whenever he was feeling low, Booth would shake his State Patrol bodyguards and sneak out the back door for a hamburger. Under the eaves of Eagan's Drive-in or the Frisko Freeze, there were "real people" who loved him.

Spellman was pleased when Gardner retained Bill Wilkerson as Fisheries director and Amos Reed at Corrections (Reed for the time being at least), and unsurprised when the governor's new State Patrol chief collided head-on with the Troopers' Association. With his keen eye for talent, Gardner in due course named Wilkerson to head the Department of Revenue. The governor and the engaging young lawyer became the two amigos of tax reform, touring the state to promote consensus for a "revenue-neutral" plan. Without dramatic changes, "you're dreaming—absolutely dreaming," to think that the business-and-occupation taxes won't keep soaring, Wilkerson warned the Association of Washington Business. [7] When Gardner said his personal preference was for an income tax, his stepfather scowled. The Legislature likewise was underwhelmed. Like Spellman and Evans before him, Gardner came to realize he was flogging a lame horse. Spellman stayed out of the fray. He believed old governors should be seen and not heard, at least during their successors' first terms. He was also busy drumming up business in China, Korea and Japan, and teaching night classes on constitutional law at Seattle University. His interaction with the students was a source of particular pleasure.

In the 1988 race for governor, Spellman lent his support to his friend Norm Maleng, the widely respected King County prosecutor. Maleng's moderate Republican base underestimated the evangelical "Family values" conservatives. They turned out in droves for State Representative Bobby Williams, a crusading accountant from Longview who hadn't a prayer against the Gardner. Booth won a second term with 62.2 percent of the vote.

SPELLMAN MADE a controversial return to politics in 1990. He entered the race for the Supreme Court seat to which Richard Guy, a large, affable Spokane attorney, had been appointed by Gardner a year earlier. From his earliest days at law school, Spellman could see himself on the bench someday. He had taken great care and pride in his judicial appointments. Many who knew him well believed he was temperamentally better suited to the robe than retail politics. Washington's courts were suffocating under a soaring caseload. "Solutions must first come from the State Supreme Court," Spellman said.[8] A number of judges from around the state had urged him to run, and he believed he could make an important difference. Now, however, he was wading into the piranha-filled pond of Bar Association politics. He'd spent the last five years immersed in immigration law and international business. During the 18 years before that he'd been out of the loop as a whole new generation of attorneys came of age. He also made a major mistake in not announcing his candidacy until late July. He'd done no fundraising either. The biggest issue of all, however, was whether a former governor belonged on the high court—never mind that "Mr. Dooley," the legendary Irish bartender, famously observed that even the Supreme Court "follows th' iliction returns."[9]

They turned their cannons and canons on him.

"Bringing a career politician into the Supreme Court could set a dangerous precedent," some lawyers said, warning of "the day when courts are composed of judges elected on the basis of demagoguery and political gimmickry."[10] Nonsense, Spellman said, pointing to Earl Warren's three terms as governor of California and vice-presidential candidacy before he became one of the greatest chief justices in the history of the United States. Justice Jim Dolliver, a shrewd politician, had been Dan Evans' top aide, Spellman said, while one of his own appointees, Justice Andersen, had been an influential legislator. Spellman said his political experience and skill as a mediator would be a plus on the court during fractious times. He knew how government worked. He'd seen law and justice issues from the administrative side as governor and as the statutory chief law enforcement officer of the state's largest county. He knew civil and criminal law, he said. He understood jail and prison management and the challenges law enforcement officers face daily. "I'm not running against Rich Guy," Spellman said. "He's never been elected to the Supreme Court. ... I'm running for the unexpired term of Vern Pearson, his predecessor." [11]

Rich Guy was running against John Spellman. "It never occurred to me that a former governor would run against me. The disciplines are different. ... There are a lot of people, a lot of public officials around, who are also lawyers, who are very competent as public officials but wouldn't be (competent) here. I think it's a dangerous precedent." [12] Thirty-seven of the state's 39 county prosecutors—even Maleng—endorsed the former Superior Court judge. "I know one thing," said Spokane County Prosecutor Don Brockett, Guy's good friend, "Governor John Spellman would never have appointed attorney John Spellman to the Supreme Court." [13]

Others fretted about name familiarity and "personal popularity" playing too big a role in the election of judges. Some said all judges should be appointed. Guy and Spellman disagreed, as did Charles Sheldon, a Supreme Court historian. "You need public accountability, more so today than ever before," Sheldon said. "The Supreme Court justices are affirming or rejecting or redefining public policy. ..." [14] Later, Sheldon would write: "State judges are political creatures. ...They behave like politicians while on the bench and, on occasion, make political decisions. They reflect the politics of their age, and also practice and define those politics. That judges are politicians should not denigrate the judiciary nor tarnish the judges. As officials involved in making public policy decisions, judges, like other policy-makers, ought to be part of the state's politics." [15]

The Olympia rumor mill ginned up a story that Spellman was just out to sweeten his state pension. Spellman said he stood to earn a lot more than the $86,700 a year justices were paid if he remained in private practice. Guy supporters said Spellman was out to shed his loser image. Spellman laughed at that one, too. "It never dawned on me that anyone would think I had a different agenda than what I was doing, as though I were going to use this as either a psychological or political building block. ...I think I can make a contribution as a Supreme Court justice and I want to do it." [16]

The Seattle-King County Bar Association rated Guy exceptionally well qualified and Spellman "adequate." [17] Gardner signed a fundraising letter for Guy and asked his fans around the state to help with the campaign.

The handwringing over judicial politics reached an ironic conclusion down the stretch. Guy, once of counsel to legendary House Speaker William "Big Daddy" Day, outraised and outspent Spellman 5-to-1. He was "a judge—not a politician," his billboards declared. [18]

Guy captured 56 percent of the vote in a low-turnout primary and was elected on the spot. "He ran a very good campaign for a non-politician," Spellman said, laughing. [19] It was his last bid for public office. He was 63. "Politics had still never broken my heart, but the things people in my own profession said and did during that campaign were very disappointing."

He Couldn't Watch

T he Kingdome was on borrowed time for eight years before it collapsed in 16.8 seconds. Frank Ruano, its most dogged foe, was as
frustrated as Spellman by the string of events that sealed its fate.

Spellman's hard-won domed stadium made Seattle a big-league city in
the 1970s. By the 1990s, however, Seattle was leading a league of its own.
Microsoft opened new Windows to the world, and King County became a
leading player in the dot.com revolution. Its utilitarian stadium, though still
big enough, was now judged not nearly good enough. The owners of the
Seahawks, Mariners and Sonics groused that joint occupancy compromised
scheduling and stunted the growth of their franchises. The Kingdome's
"amenities" were also lacking. The fans who painted their faces Seahawk
blue and raised the ear-numbing din that rattled opposing quarterbacks
were content with beer and nachos. The owners and league brass said it
would take sushi, brie and mimosas to attract the corporate VIPs and high
rollers who populate plush skyboxes.

Barry Ackerley, who owned the Sonics, said his team had to have its
own new arena to stay super. When the financing didn't pan out, he moved
the NBA club back to the Seattle Center Coliseum. The city, happy to re-
claim a major tenant, issued bonds for a major renovation of the arena.

Baseball purists complained that the Kingdome was a world without
sunshine or real grass. Baseball, an old timer famously observed, shouldn't
be played on anything a horse wouldn't eat. When the Mariners were sold
in 1992 to an ownership group anchored by Nintendo's Hiroshi Yamauchi,
the push for a new ballpark—and a winning team—accelerated.

A year later, when the Kingdome's roof was pressure-washed, prepa-
ratory to a new seal-coat, water seeped into the acoustical tiles lining its
ribs. Shortly before the gates were opened for a Mariners' game on July 19,
1994, two 26-pound tiles plummeted to the seating area. Had it happened
30 minutes later someone might have been killed. The repairs, the merits

of investing in a new roof and the very future of the stadium became a hot potato for the County Council. Spellman told the council the problems were the result of poor maintenance, not a design flaw. If they maintained it correctly, he said, the stadium would be there long after they were all long gone.

THE KINGDOME REOPENED that November. A task force to study its suitability for big-league baseball was appointed by Gary Locke, the new King County executive. "As the panel reached the predictable conclusion in 1995 that a new, baseball-only stadium was the best solution," Seahawks owner Ken Behring "went into me-too mode."[1] The beefy land developer had tried to move the team to Southern California, winning only the enmity of Seahawk fans. If he couldn't have a new stadium of his own, Behring demanded $150 million in improvements to the Kingdome. The county was already on the hook for a $70 million repair job and annual debt payments of $11.4 million. Without improvements, "I do not understand how the NFL can be expected to have a positive view of the Seahawks' future prospects in Seattle," NFL commissioner Paul Tagliabue said in a letter to Locke and the County Council.[2]

The Mariners' Kingdome lease was set to expire after the 1996 season. Absent the promise of a new stadium, the owners told the county they would sell the team rather than continue to lose money. The conflicted council asked King County voters if they would authorize raising the sales tax to build a new ballpark for the Mariners and remodel the Kingdome for the Seahawks. Frank Ruano, using a walker, arrived at the Courthouse to call it folly. It had been 30 years since he first challenged public financing of a domed stadium. Spellman's old sparring partner was slower of foot at 74 but as feisty as ever. Having failed to persuade a judge to halt the election, he appealed to the council to stand up for the taxpayers. "If they want to leave, fine," Ruano said of the Mariners. "I'll give them a dollar to help them on their way."[3]

On September 19, 1995, the stadium-financing plan fell 1,082 votes short. Mariners chairman John Ellis gave the council until October 30 to come up with a new plan. His ball club, meantime, was playing like there was no tomorrow. At the beginning of August the M's were 13 games behind the California Angels. On October 1 they were tied. The next day, the franchise reached the postseason for the first time in its 19-year history by shelling California, 9-1. The team departed for New York that night for a best-of-five series with the Yankees to determine who would play for the American League pennant. They returned home four days later, trailing

2-0, with every game do or die. In the 11th inning of game five, with Ken Griffey Jr. on first and Joey Cora on third, Edgar Martinez ripped a double down the left field line to tie the game. All 57,000 eyes swiveled to Griffey. Arms pumping as he rounded third, Junior sprinted home, crossing the plate in an emphatic slide as the Kingdome exploded. Afterward, George Steinbrenner, the Yankees mercurial owner, "trudged solemnly out of the Kingdome's visitor dugout," glanced around and declared, "This building killed us."[4] Though they went on to lose the American League Championship to Cleveland in six games, the "refuse to lose" Mariners had saved baseball for Seattle. The Kingdome, however, was one step closer to oblivion.

GOVERNOR MIKE LOWRY had called a special session of the Legislature to pick up the pieces from the failed bond issue. Opponents of public financing warned the lawmakers not to ignore the public will, while the Chamber of Commerce pleaded for assistance and baseball fans at the dome hung out a banner that said "If you build it we will re-elect you!"[5] The lawmakers authorized the county to enact an admissions tax and surcharges on food, drinks and car rentals to help finance a $320 million ball park. The state's contribution included profits from a new lottery game with a sports theme. As for the Kingdome, "the state told the county and the Seahawks to drop dead."[6]

In 1997, with Microsoft billionaire Paul Allen holding an option to buy the Seahawks, contingent on a successful ballot measure to help fund a new football stadium, voters statewide narrowly approved a $300 million package of taxes and lottery revenues to tear down the Kingdome and pay for a new stadium and adjacent exhibition center. Dan Evans, who had campaigned for the Kingdome when he was governor, supported the ballot measure. He said big-league sports deserved credit for raising Seattle's profile over the past 20 years. The city shouldn't turn its back on those franchises now just because it thinks it has "arrived," Evans said. "Would we dry up and blow away if the Seahawks left? Of course not. We would be poorer for it, though—a less vibrant community."[7]

That it had come to this saddened Spellman. "We live in a very disposable society. We throw things away awfully fast. It was built with the best advice available. I don't know if that sense has gone away, but times have changed. The facility is still what it was in the beginning. It has not deteriorated. It's not dilapidated. Nothing's wrong with the Kingdome."[8] Jack Christiansen, the lead architect on the Kingdome, said, "I feel terrible. Sick. Mad as hell, actually."[9]

On Sunday, June 27, 1999, Spellman threw out a ceremonial pitch as the Mariners played their last game in the Kingdome. Then he was a melancholy face in the crowd of 56,530—the 40th and last sellout in 22½ baseball seasons, 32 million spectators in all—as the Mariners beat Texas 5-2. Griffey, fittingly, hit the final homer in the Kingdome, a three-run shot in the first inning. Then in the fourth inning, Junior robbed the Rangers of a three-run homer by climbing the wall in left-center field. The Kingdome was the only home the future Hall of Famer had ever known in the big leagues. "Gray Lady shows true colors," *The Seattle Times* headline said. Dave Niehaus, the broadcasting voice of the Mariners, offered the final benediction: "Ladies and gentlemen, this place has been called an ugly duckling by a lot of people. She's always been beautiful to me." [10]

THE ATTORNEYS and staff in the offices of Carney Badley Spellman on the 36th floor of the sleek Columbia Center skyscraper were gathered around the windows at 8:32 a.m. on March 26, 2000. They had a perfect vantage point from which to marvel at the handiwork of the demolition experts. Like clockwork, a sequence of explosions rippled along the ribs of the Kingdome's roof, fractured the supporting columns and collapsed the tension ring circling the stadium. In another heartbeat, the rebar crumpled inward and the world's largest concrete dome was reduced to rubble. The remains vanished in a billowing cloud of dense gray smoke.

One of the law firm's partners was notable by his absence. Spellman couldn't bear to watch.

The walls of his office feature many mementoes: a photo of his brother

The Kingdome crumbles in 16.8 seconds on March 26, 2000.

bivouacked in Korea; a snapshot from a meeting with Nixon; another from
the day Queen Elizabeth came to town; awards, proclamations and an Irish
blessing. Just to the right of his leather swivel chair is a framed photo of
the Kingdome, together with a copy of a column Peter Callaghan wrote
for the *Tacoma News Tribune* in 1999. Lois Spellman was often critical of
the things reporters and columnists (she called them "the newsies") wrote
about her husband. But she liked Callaghan—and not just because he was
a lanky Irish-Catholic guy with nice manners. She said he wasn't afraid to
say things that others wouldn't, "or didn't even recognize." This is what the
column says:

> Former Gov. John Spellman tossed out the ceremonial first pitch at
> Sunday's final Mariners game at the Kingdome. Giving him the last first
> pitch was a good choice by a team management that hasn't exactly been
> scoring public-relations points of late.
>
> Without John Spellman, there'd be no Kingdome.
>
> By extension, without John Spellman there'd be no Mariners.
>
> Does this one politician deserve so much of the credit? Only
> because a less-resilient (some would say stubborn) officeholder would
> have walked away from the political and legal battles that sought to
> block construction of the dome. ...Being the father of the Kingdome
> helped elect Spellman governor in 1980. It was a visible—and then
> quite popular—example of his skills as King County executive. ...
>
> It is easy now to belittle the Kingdome. State voters decided two
> years ago to implode the homely dome and replace it with an outdoor
> football stadium. State of the art, we're told.
>
> What is hard, however, is to remember what the times were like
> when the Kingdome was built. There was no major league baseball or
> football in the Northwest. It took three tries to win voter approval for a
> domed stadium that would attract both.
>
> All the designers had to do was create a technology to build a
> massive domed stadium that could seat around 60,000 and house every
> sport and event imaginable. They had a relatively limited budget that
> grew tighter with every legal and political delay.
>
> Once built ... the building met every one of its expectations. It
> brought the Mariners and the Seahawks. Later, professional soccer and
> basketball teams moved in. It hosted post-season games for all four.
>
> Sixty-six million people have attended events there. The NCAA
> Final Four. Baseball and basketball's all-star games. Football's Pro-Bowl.
> High school's Kingbowl. Rodeos. Motocross.

It wasn't just sports. Billy Graham. Paul McCartney. The Rolling Stones. Evel Knievel. Paper airplane designers. Home shows. Boat shows. Jehovah's Witnesses, Madonna, Boy Scouts. ...

It isn't the fault of designers that the economics of professional sports changed. It's not their fault that other cities met the ever-escalating ultimatums by team owners.

Spellman now calls it the most honest building in Seattle.

Sounds right. Solid, unadorned and hardworking. It was just fine for a region built by loggers and longshoremen and machinists. When it was built, they shared the same seats with lawyers and bankers and managers.

We don't sit together anymore. The Kingdome is no longer good enough for a region of white-collar wealth, for people who attend sporting events to be entertained, not to watch a game.

By today's standards, the Kingdome is ugly and dysfunctional. But that says more about today's standards than about the building.

The Kingdome kept its promises.[11]

The Old Guvs' Club

Former governors, like former presidents, comprise an exclusive club of strange bedfellows. Who would have guessed that Harry Truman and Herbert Hoover or Dan Evans and Al Rosellini—"Danny Boy" and the "Godfather"—would become, if not friends, genuinely friendly? "As you get older, old wounds disappear," Booth Gardner said in 2007. "This is a unique job."[1] "Yes," Spellman said with a wink, "and I'm sorry I sang 'If I Were a Rich Man' at the legislative reception before you took office."

Spellman rates his successors as "all high-caliber people," with special admiration for Mike Lowry, with whom he served at the King County Courthouse, and Chris Gregoire, who was an assistant attorney general he met with often during his term as governor. That she is a Roman Catholic, christened Christine O'Grady, has nothing to do with it, of course.

Empathy is the common denominator. When Lowry took office in 1993 and within weeks proposed Civil Service reforms that had eluded Spellman and Gardner, Democrats in the Legislature ran for cover and state workers called him a Judas. "What do we want?" they chanted on the steps of the Capitol. *"A new governor!* When do we want it? *Now!"*[2] Spellman wasn't surprised by Lowry's initiative or the reaction. "Mike is maybe the most liberal politician ever to serve as governor of Washington—but he's not a lockstep liberal. He studies issues exhaustively." In the end, Lowry succeeded by finessing the issue. "He linked something he wanted—more flexible work rules and increased privatization of state services—with something the unions wanted—the right to bargain for wages and benefits."[3]

As the years rolled by, the former governors got together annually and teamed up frequently in twos, threes or more to promote an array of causes. Rhetoric long since abandoned, their partnerships underscore the shades of gray in Washington State politics. Rosellini was a progressive, yet fiscally more conservative than Evans, the latter-day Bull Moose hardshell conservatives loathed; Spellman is a moderate who became an ad hoc liberal for two tumultuous years and raised taxes more than any governor before or since; Gardner, with his huge social conscience and Harvard MBA, personified "Republicrat," while Lowry wasn't always as liberal as his fan base wanted him to be.

In 1997, Gary Locke summoned his predecessors (Dixy had died in 1994) to the Governor's Mansion for a benefit luncheon and the first "Gathering of the Governors." They missed Booth, who was taking a new round of drugs his doctors hoped would arrest the acceleration of Parkinson's. It was nasty stuff, said Evans, whose brother was also afflicted by the cunning neurological disease. Rosellini, a vigorous 87, observed that his protégé was only 61. They should all count their blessings, he said. And they did. As they poked around their cavernous old office, Locke asked Spellman where Dixy had her private bar. It was right behind the governor's desk, he said, pointing to the place. "She never offered us a drink," Rosellini grumbled. "She kept it for herself." Evans said he was working on a memoir. Spellman said he had been assembling his papers and making notes for a book of his own, "but a lot of those people are still alive, and I don't dare write it." He was without his trademark pipe. They gave him a bad time about it. He said he had stopped smoking a year earlier because there were so many places

DICK BALDWIN PHOTO

Governor Spellman with three predecessors at a state reception. From left, Dixy Lee Ray, Al Rosellini and Dan Evans.

where you couldn't smoke anymore and there were grandchildren around the house. "I'm much more frank," he warned them. "The pipe gives you time to slow down." [4]

They focused on how to maintain the state's quality of life, particularly around fragile Puget Sound. "Growing with grace," was the way Spellman put it. [5] The consensus was that the gas tax needed to be increased to fund highway improvements. They were grateful their state was a hub of high-tech innovation, but said the wealth had to be dispersed beyond the I-5 corridor via better roads and the information superhighway. Otherwise, the divide between the "two Washingtons" would only grow wider. Education was everyone's top priority.

SPELLMAN WAS an active attorney well into his 70s, representing a wide range of international clients on immigration issues and business invest-ments. He represented everyone from PEMCO insurance to the hard rock band Rage Against the Machine. The county sheriff tried to stop their con-cert at The Gorge at George, Washington, citing the potential for trouble. The show went on, and the band opened with an admonition to "Fuck the police!" [6] Spellman winced, but observed, "Free speech is free speech."

He has been chairman of the board of the Evergreen Safety Council since the 1990s, and helped resuscitate the nonprofit organization after a fundraising scandal. He's proud of its programs promoting industrial safety—from forklift operator training to hazardous materials handling. He served on the TVW board and was president of the Serra Club, a group promoting Roman Catholic vocations and religious life. He is a booster of Camp Brotherhood, the interfaith program founded by his longtime friends, the Reverend William Treacy of Saint Thomas More Parish and the late Rabbi Raphael Levine.

In 2001, Spellman and Gardner—rejuvenated by deep-brain surgery—called for free ridership on buses, van pooling and improvements to carpool lanes as alternatives to Sound Transit's light rail proposal, which was $1 billion over budget and three years behind schedule.

Spellman commiserated with Locke later that year when the economy tanked after 16 years of expansion. Chang Mook Sohn, the state's chief economist, was the bearer of bad news: State revenues were down $800 million. The state and national economies began faltering even before the September 11 terrorist attacks. Consumer confidence was in rapid decline. Airlines and other companies around the state were downsizing. The only good thing about "Dr. Doom's" sobering report—and the ones to follow—was that it was unquestionably accurate. Before Spellman and the majority Democrats in the Legislature reached a resolve to create a bipartisan Revenue Forecast Council, the governor's office and the House and Senate caucuses devised dueling forecasts often shaded for political ends. It seemed at times to be the equivalent of Ouija board economics. The six voting members of the Revenue Council are now the state's budget and revenue directors and a senior member from each legislative caucus. Chang, a brilliant Korean immigrant with a wry sense of humor, was thus insulated from pressures to cook the books.

At the dawn of 2003, Governor Locke told lawmakers they were facing "the largest budget deficit in the state's history"—$2.4 billion, or about 10 percent of the biennial budget. Spellman and Chang set the record straight. What Spellman faced when he took office in 1981 was worse—22 percent of a $6.8 billion budget. "Compared to 20 years ago," the economist said, "it is really a mild headache."[7] Spellman agreed, however, that if you were in the trenches, like Locke and the Legislature, it felt like a migraine.

That same year, with the deficit now $2.6 billion, Evans, Rosellini, Spellman, Gardner and Lowry teamed up with King County Prosecutor Norm Maleng to block the spread of electronic slot machine gambling. They also won legislative approval of a construction budget that gave a major boost to projects on college campuses.

In 2004, Spellman—recovering from a broken leg that forced him to reluctantly end his part-time job as a college professor—hobbled against a populist headwind. Together with Locke and Lowry, he opposed the "Top Two" primary election initiative subsequently upheld by the U.S. Supreme Court. "I have a personal stake in this," Spellman acknowledged, emphasizing that the broader issue was whether limiting choices disenfranchised voters.[8] In the 1976 primary, Spellman had finished third behind Dixy Lee Ray and Wes Uhlman. Under the Top Two system, the two Democrats would have advanced to the general election. In 1980, Spellman finished way behind Jim McDermott and Ray. A number of editorialists agreed with Spellman's contention that a Top Two primary would be a blow to the two-party system as well as third parties. The Vancouver *Columbian* observed:

> An argument for the top-two system is that it weeds out extremists, with, say, two moderate candidates from one party advancing to the finals while the top finisher in the other party, who might be a wild-eyed nut, falls by the wayside. But one person's "radical" is another person's "creative, innovative breath of fresh air who can prompt voters to start thinking about things from a new perspective," even if it takes a few years for some ideas to really catch on. But the top-two system also

weeds out more than just extremists. ...Under the top-two system, which I-872 would create, Spellman, who was arguably the most moderate of the top three would not even have been on the general-election ballot [in 1980], let alone been elected governor.[9]

In 2007, Spellman joined Gregoire and the teachers' union to endorse a constitutional amendment allowing for simple-majority passage of school levies. "As long as I've been a voter, we've had our priorities mixed up," Spellman told reporters. "It is very shortsighted to make schools jump over a higher hurdle than anybody in getting the money to do the job that's necessary."[10] The amendment was approved by the voters.

That year, at a TVW forum, moderator Denny Heck asked each former governor, "What would you have done differently if you knew then what you know now?" Spellman said, "I guess I would have acted earlier on the ferry strike, which was a disaster. And if I could have manufactured a good economy, I would have loved that!" Booth leaned in to quip, "Thank God it didn't!" Turning serious, he said, "There were three years where I couldn't be by myself; couldn't be alone. I'd work my butt off to make sure seniors could stay in their homes and some way get funds to them." Next, Heck asked, "Is there an issue today that you think deserves to be higher on the public agenda?" Spellman said, "Education is terribly neglected. ...It's too darn bad we have to have levies. The state's paramount duty is to support education. I passed more taxes than anybody here and I'm the Republican! But you have to keep government running, especially in hard times. You gotta provide for kids in schools and you gotta provide for social services."[11]

Spellman with Pat Dunn, left, and King County Executive Dow Constantine in 2011.

Asked what she had learned from her six living predecessors, Gregoire said, "There's a life after politics."[12]

For the first time since leaving office, Spellman publicly took issue with his successor. He was deeply troubled by Gardner's "Death with Dignity" initiative to allow terminally ill people to obtain lethal prescriptions. It wasn't just his Christian faith that compelled his opposition, Spellman said. "I've had experience with clients and friends who were darn near talked into doing away with themselves for the benefit of their friends and relatives, and that's a very serious thing. ...I worry about undue influence on an otherwise rational person."[13]

When Evans added his voice to the campaign for Initiative 1000, Spellman wrote a guest editorial that appeared in the *Seattle Post-Intelligencer* and other papers around the state:

> Both frame the issue as one of strictly personal choice. But what's at stake is actually much broader. Derek Humphrey, co-founder of the Hemlock Society, has asserted repeatedly that euthanasia and assisted suicide will inevitably prevail in our society because they make economic sense. Think about that for a second. What on Earth is he saying? Obviously it's cheaper to have people with serious illnesses die sooner rather than later. But when economics enters the picture, it's no longer a matter of strictly personal choice. ... When Gardner says I-1000 is a good "first step," I think we have to take that claim very seriously.[14]

Nearly 58 percent of the voters sided with Gardner in 2008.

HONORS AND AWARDS also came Spellman's way. There seemed to be a growing sense that he had been neglected. King County created a John D. Spellman Award for Achievement in Historic Preservation in recognition of the Landmarks and Heritage Program he launched as county executive and promoted as governor. On his 80th birthday, Adele Ferguson, the habitually crusty columnist for the *Bremerton Sun*, offered this backhanded yet sincere salute: "Happy birthday, John. You may not have been the greatest governor we ever had, but you sure weren't the worst. You didn't do anything to make us ashamed of you."[15] He was tempted to frame that one, too.

The Metropolitan King County Council hosted a party and proclaimed him the "father of modern King County government." Lois, his children, grandchildren and many old friends looked on as he grew particularly nostalgic in surroundings so familiar for so many years. "I was sworn in to the bar in 1953 on the ninth floor of this building. I practiced law here for 14 years ...and I started to get ulcers here as a county commissioner in 1966. ... The difference between Olympia and this courthouse is that you can get things done here. You don't have a lot of delays. Party designation wasn't decisive here. People would come in and talk and we'd get a lot done. Ed Heavey, Mike Lowry and Bob Greive were Democrats, but I didn't think of them as the enemy. I enjoyed every minute here. People ask me which job I preferred. Obviously it was being county executive." [16] "And Lois always gave you the best advice," said County Councilman Pete von Reichbauer—kinder and gentler 26 years after he shook the Legislature by switching parties. Spellman choked up for a moment, then said, "She has been the difference in my life, and I can't thank her enough." [17] Maleng led the applause. "The most exciting time in my life ...was being the prime lawyer for John Spellman during eight years ... Building the stadium, laying the framework for our land-use and environmental laws. What a transformation there was of county government, with the bright and energetic young people John recruited working around the clock." At 80, Spellman was still committed to community service and mentoring, Maleng said. "And we've got so many days ahead of us." [18] Four months later, the energetic prosecutor was suddenly, shockingly dead at 68 of cardiac arrest.

Mortality is the common thread that binds us all together. If you live a long life you attend a lot of funerals—checking the obituaries daily "to make sure you're not in there," Spellman jokes. He said goodbye in 1998 to Alan Gibbs, his superb director of Social and Health Services. He lost his brother-in-law, Gerald Murphy, a world-renowned cancer researcher, in 2000. Helen Rasmussen, who in her day marshaled panzer divisions of campaign volunteers, died in 2001. Justice Barbara Durham, only 60, succumbed to a neuro-degenerative illness in 2002. Chuck Carroll departed at 96 in 2003. Bygones had been bygones long before. The inimitable Frank Ruano checked out at 84 in 2005, mind feisty to the end. Mary Tedesco, the beloved receptionist in the County Executive's Office, died in 2006, Al Rosellini, at 101 in 2011. Spellman's friend Sid Snyder, everyone's Mr. Olympia, died in 2012. They were born the same year—1926.

IN 2008, when the worst downturn since the 1930s actually was at hand—with a deficit twice as large as he faced in 1981—Spellman and Governor Gregoire began to talk often. She cut, pasted and persevered, yet there seemed no end to the pain. Her dreams of being a governor who made giant strides became a relentless nightmare. In December of 2010, with Marty Brown, the savvy old pro who headed the Office of Financial Management, at her side, Gregoire presented a balanced budget for the next biennium.

It addressed a $4.6 billion shortfall. "We've had to cut the unthinkable to prevent the unbearable," she said, voice brittle with emotion. "But let me be clear: This budget does not represent my values. And I don't think it represents the values of anybody in Washington State. ... When you cut K4 class size, you lose 1,500 teachers. ...*I hate my budget.* I hate it because in some places I don't even think it's moral. Who'd ever thought that I would be doing this? It's just beyond me." [19]

Spellman hated it too. The notion of cutting teachers and poking huge holes in the social-services safety net was appalling to him. Not only did he endorse her push for a half-cent increase in the state sales tax to head off more cuts, he said, "The only question in my mind is, Should it be more? ... You don't get elected to get re-elected. You get elected to do the job." [20]

"He gave me more insight than anybody," Gregoire says, "because he says exactly what every economist has said in this country, which is, 'You can't do just one thing. You can't just cut. You have to raise revenue *and* cut. ... Do one or the other and you'll put yourself in a greater crisis economically.' ... John Spellman was a man ahead of his times. My heart goes out to him because I've always believed good policy is good politics, and there's a man who did what his head and his heart told him to do, for which he was not re-elected. But I steadfastly believe history should show him to be one of the tallest of our governors for standing on what was the right thing to do irrespective of party, irrespective of pressure." [21]

A PLAQUE on Spellman's office wall features a quotation from the works of Andrew Oliver (1731-1799), a jurist, scientist, lawyer, mathematician and philosopher. Dick Gordon, Spellman's old moot court partner at Georgetown Law School, had it done up handsomely by a calligrapher. This is what it says:

> Politics is the most hazardous of all professions. There is no other in which a man can hope to do so much good to his fellow creatures— and neither is there any in which by a mere loss of nerve he may do as widespread harm. There is not another in which he may so easily lose his own soul, nor is there another in which a positive and strict veracity is so difficult. But danger is the inseparable companion of honor. With all its temptations and degradations that beset it, politics is still the noblest career a man can choose.

While politics has never broken his heart or sapped his soul, Spellman still has a monkey on his back. On November 6, 2012, Rob McKenna—the student body president at the University of Washington when Spellman was governor—lost the governor's race to Democrat Jay Inslee. McKenna was the sixth consecutive Republican challenger to end up singing the King County blues. The former county councilman carried 31 of the state's 39 counties, but couldn't muster the 40 percent share of King County Republicans now need to have a fighting chance. The Republican gubernatorial loss string in Washington State is the nation's longest. So for at least another four years they'll still be writing, "John Spellman, Washington's last Republican governor ..."

AUTHOR'S NOTE
AND ACKNOWLEDGEMENTS

Every biographer hopes for a subject who tells the truth, even when it hurts. John Spellman—Lois, too—personified candor. I thank them for sharing intensely personal memories, including diary entries—the sorts of detail biographers thrive on. This is a good place for an important disclaimer: While friends and admirers of John Spellman raised the money for this printed version of his biography (the online version is free and unabridged), it is in no way an "official" biography. No one outside the Office of the Secretary of State asked for or received any editorial oversight. Neither I nor Secretary of State Sam Reed would have it any other way.

John Spellman's life story is the tenth biography/oral history of my first four years with The Legacy Project. The 42 years I spent as a newspaper reporter and editor taught me how to write quickly, but I brought a twofold sense of urgency to my new job in 2008. While fighting colon cancer, I learned to make the most of every day and how important it is to keep your I-Love-You's up to date. The second sense of urgency revolves around my Uncle Marvin's favorite saying: "We're burnin' daylight!" I think of Lillian Walker, the 96-year-old civil rights pioneer from Bremerton whose inspiring life story would have gone untold had we not discovered her 18 months before she died. It was remarkable, too, how many people in Kitsap County wanted to share their stories about her. And what stories they were! Every school library in Kitsap County now has a copy of Mrs. Walker's biography. Daily, inexorably, Tom Brokaw observed, we're losing thousands of Lillians, members of what he called "The Greatest Generation." Ken Burns, the award-winning filmmaker, told me that oral histories have proven crucial to his storytelling. A good digital tape recorder can be purchased for less than $50. Start interviewing your own Uncle Marvin.

We're losing another priceless resource: Newspapers—"the first rough draft of history." I know—*spoken by an old newspaperman.* But I'm not the only one. I routinely encounter historians, scholars, librarians, archivists, genealogists and students who share my sense of loss. In the acknowledgements for my biographies of Booth Gardner and Slade Gorton, I noted that my job was made so much easier by the State Library's clipping files. They're brimming with stories written by some of the most talented journalists our state has ever known. Now, having once again tapped the library's powerful search engines and trove of microfilm to trace Spellman's long, eventful political career, my anxiety about the future only grows. When Spellman was King County executive, *The Seattle Times, Post-Intelligencer,* Bellevue *Journal-American,* Everett *Herald* and several other papers closely covered the Courthouse. As a young reporter covering the State Legislature in the 1960's, I had colleagues from all over the state. Even the smallest daily newspapers sent someone to Olympia for at least part of the session. Today there are only a handful of capitol reporters. God bless Brad Shannon, Peter Callaghan, Jerry Cornfield, Andrew Garber, Rachel La Corte and Austin Jenkins. It's lonely amidst the marble. And sometimes you don't know what you've got until it's gone. History unquestionably is the poorer for fewer sources. Mine for this project have been indispensable. Thank you David Brewster, Richard W. Larsen, Shelby Scates, Walter Hatch, David Ammons, Rebecca Boren, Bob Partlow, Dean Katz, Eric Pryne, Bob Simmons, Ed Donohoe, Adele Ferguson, John White, Gordon Schultz, Doug Underwood and Alex MacLeod, to name a few. Walt Crowley's legacy, HistoryLink.org, is indispensable. Fortunately, historians for years to come also will have the benefit of Sam Reed's material legacy. He saved the State Library, created the nation's preeminent (and free) digital archives and broadened the scope of the oral history program. After 12 years as secretary of state and 45 years in public life, he retires to further his love of history and promote civility.

I can't say enough about my teammates—Trova Heffernan, Lori Larson, Carleen Jackson and Laura Mott. They are amazing. A special thank-you to Frank Blethen of *The Seattle Times,* David Zeeck of *The Tacoma News Tribune* and Doug Barker of *The Daily World* at Aberdeen for generous access to their photo files.

Large portions of this book were written at the historic Hoquiam Timberland Library, my home away from home for 40 years. Many thanks to Mary Thornton and her staff. I am indebted to many others as well for their help on the Spellman project, including:

Dick Albrecht, Rick Anderson, Dick Baldwin, Chris Bayley, Katia Blackburn, Bob Bratton, Don Brazier, John Brown, Marty Brown, Tim Burgess, Jeff Burlingame, Blair Butterworth, Ritajean Butterworth, William J. Chambliss, Bruce Chapman, Frank Chesley, Joel Connelly, Ron Dotzauer, Pat Dunn, Wayne Ehlers, Jim Ellis, Stu Elway, Dan Evans, Steve Excell, Larry Faulk, Adele Ferguson, George Fleming, Teresa Spellman Gamble, Booth Gardner, Tommi Gatlin, Howard Giske, John Gordon, Slade Gorton, Chris Gregoire, Dan Grimm, Jerry Grinstein, Lou Guzzo, Jerry Handfield, Allen Hayward, Ed Heavey, Denny Heck, Ben Helle, Harley Hoppe, David Horsey, Lem Howell, Claude Iosso, Kevin Jones, David Kingma, Mike

Lowry, Mary Ellen McCaffree, the Rev. Tom McCarthy, Dan McDonald, Joe McGavick, Barbara McKenzie, Katherine "Kat" Spellman Miner, Ralph Munro, the Rev. John Navone, Scott North, Paul O'Connor, Frank Pritchard, Bob Santos, Jerry Schlatter, Rollie Schmitten, Dick Schrock, George W. Scott, Charles Z. Smith, Payton Smith, Sid Snyder, Bart Spellman, David Spellman, Jeff Spellman, Margo Spellman, Mary Spellman Tully, Barry Sweet, Al Swift, Art Thiel, Robert F. Utter, Jim Waldo, Gordon Walgren, Scott Wallace, Bill Wilkerson and Matt Winters.

And goodnight, Frank Ruano, wherever you are.

JOHN C. HUGHES

Spellman and Magnuson at a party for both.

DONORS

With gratitude to the following donors whose admiration for Governor John Spellman and generous gifts to the Washington State Heritage Center Trust made possible the publication of this book.

Justice James Andersen
Keith and Joan Angier
Ray and Edith Aspiri
Association of Washington Business
Basil Badley
Christopher and Cynthia Bayley
Duane and Joanne Berentson
Mike Bernard
Ted and Marilyn Bowsfield
Robert and Aileen Bratton
Jim Bricker
Norward and Violet Brooks
Don and Jeri Brunell
Carney Badley Spellman, P.S.
Gary and Deborah Chandler
Derwin Christensen
Tim Clancy
Lynn Claudon
Chuck and Nancy Collins
Cynthia Curreri
John and Karen Donohue
Katherine Dunn
Mike and Ginna Dunn
Patrick and Susan Dunn
James R. Ellis
Dan and Nancy Evans
Steve Excell
William H. Gates Sr.
John Giese
Slade and Sally Gorton
Lloyd Hara

The Spellmans in 1980 after John was elected governor.

Jerry and Patricia Harper
Kim Herman
Jim and Jerri Honeyford
Lem Howell
Catherine Hyslop
William and Deborah Hyslop
Justice Faith Ireland
Clair and Carol Jones
Bruce and Brigid Laing
Peggy Lykins
Robert E. Mack
Jim and Louise Madden
Mary Ellen and Kenneth McCaffree

Jane McCurdy
Dan and Norah McDonald
Patrick McDonald
Hugh and Teel McGough
Mike McKay
Stan and Kathy McNaughton
W. Howarth Meadowcroft
Alan Merry
Louise and Stafford Miller
Roman Miller
Mike Murphy
Della Newman
Bud and Marcia Norris
Lois North
PEMCO Foundation
Adele Ferguson Philipsen
Paul Razore
Caroline Rimbach
Phil and Anita Rockefeller
John and Patricia Rose
William and Jill Ruckelshaus
Dan Satterberg

SPELLMAN FAMILY ALBUM

A happy fisherman.

The Seattle Mariners
Marilyn Showalter
Chris Smith-Towne
Bart Spellman
David Spellman
Jeffrey and Lisa Spellman
Kat Spellman Miner
Margo Spellman and Bryan Tagas
Teresa Spellman Gamble
    and Tim Gamble
Paula Rinta Stewart
Doug Sutherland
Joe Taller
Gregory and JoAnn Tripp
Mary and Eugene Tully
Peter von Reichbauer
Jim and Shirley Whiteside
Shirley Winsley
Van Youngquist
Washington Association of Counties

SPELLMAN FAMILY ALBUM

Spellman with his former law partner,
Joe Kane, and Kane's wife June.

SOURCE NOTES

ABBREVIATIONS

Seattle Post-Intelligencer, P-I
Seattle Times, Times
Tacoma News Tribune, TNT
Olympian, Oly
Oregonian, Org
the (Seattle) Weekly, Weekly
The Columbian, Columbian
New York Times, NYT

Associated Press, AP
United Press International, UPI
Wall Street Journal, WSJ
Bellevue American, American
The Daily World, Aberdeen, World
Spokesman-Review, S-R
Spokane Chronicle, Chronicle

PREFACE: A PARADOXICAL POLITICIAN

1. Bancroft to author, 10-17-12
2. Constantine to author, 11-5-12
3. Grimm to author, 10-22-12
4. Constantine to author, 11-5-12
5. Heck to author, June 2012
6. Weekly, 1-14/20-81, p. 15
7. Scott, *A Majority of One*, p. 95
8. Times, 5-23-83, p. C-1
9. Quoted in Scott, *A Majority of One*, p. 111
10. Grimm to author, 9-20-12
11. Times, 1-9-83
12. Times, 1-9-83, p. C-2
13. Weekly, 10-24-84

CHAPTER ONE: MATTERS OF THE HEART

1. Bartlett, *Ireland, A History*, pp. 281-285
2. Emmons, *Beyond the American Pale, The Irish in the West 1845-1910*, p. 6, p. 35
3. Ibid., p. 247 (original spelling, capitalization and punctuation)
4. *Seattle and Environs, Vol. II*, pp. 561-562
5. Org, 9-3-16, *Varsity's football prospects bright*; 10-15-16, *Bezdek's men busy*
6. Org, 12-31-16, *Football men to end season New Year's Day*
7. Org 1-2-17, *Penn Crushed by Oregon's Heroes*
8. Ibid.

9. Ibid.
10. Org, 10-9-17, *Ex-Oregon and Ex-Aggie Men at Camp Lewis;* 9-12-19,
    Spellman Boosts Oregon, Return of Big Guard Sends Football Stock Up
11. Org, 12-16-20, p. 8
12. Susan van Dyke, *Joseph Gottstein, Sportsman and capitalist,*
    Washington Racing Hall of Fame Web site
13. Org, 12-28-21, p. 12; 1-15-22
14. Times, 3-1-25, p. 21
15. Times, 2-12-25, p. 19; GoHuskies.com, UW Football Coaching
    History; UW Tyee Yearbook 1925; University of Oregon Libraries,
    Alumni magazine, October 1941, p. 3; goducks.com, 1917 Rose
    Bowl; NationChamps.net, Oregon Football History database
16. David Wilma, HistoryLink.org Essay 4216, 2003,
    Charles O. Carroll
17. Ibid.
18. Scates, *Warren G. Magnuson,* p. 13
19. Ibid., p. 25; Watson, *My Life in Print,* p. 100
20. Magnuson Papers, University of Washington, quoted in Scates,
    Warren G. Magnuson, p. 26
21. Times, 1-4-27, p. 2

CHAPTER TWO: GROWING UP

1. Crowley, *Seattle & King County Timeline,* pp. 49-54;
   Victor A. Meyers, HistoryLink.org Essay 8392
2. Crowley, *Seattle & King County Timeline,* pp. 49-54
3. Keane, *Irish Seattle,* p. 78
4. Eastside Heritage Center, *Lake Washington/The East Side*
5. Weekly, 10-13/19-76, *John Spellman, The man behind the mask*
6. Times, 8-6-44, p. 14
7. Times, 10-24-76, p. G-1
8. Ibid.

CHAPTER THREE: THE GRADUATE AND THE NOVICE

1. Crowley, *Seattle University, A Century of Jesuit Education;*
   Seattle University Web site, *A History of Excellence*
2. Lois Spellman to author, 7-24-12
3. Ibid.
4. Ibid.
5. Quoted in HistoryLink.org Essay 7296, *Lemieux, Reverend A.A*
6. Crowley, *Seattle University,* p. 59
7. P-I, 6-4-49, p. 3; Times, 6-4-49, p. 2
8. Times, 5-22-49, *Seattle University to Graduate Record Class;*
   P-I, 6-4-49, p. 3

9.   Burns, *The Jesuits and the Indian Wars of the Northwest*, p. 36
10. Bischoff, *The Jesuits in Old Oregon*, p. 36; Crowley, *Seattle University*, p. 19; Raymond A. Schroth, *The American Jesuits: A history*
11. Beman, *Collegiate and Theological Education in the West*, New York, 1847
12. Norwich, *Absolute Monarchs*, p. 362
13. *Jesuits of the New Orleans Province, Characteristics of Jesuit Spirituality*, http://www.norprov.org/spirituality/

CHAPTER FOUR: HEARTBREAK

Interviews with Mary Spellman Tully

1.   Dolan, *America in the Korean War*, pp. 21-24
2.   187th Infantry Regiment Web site
3.   C.J. Magro, *Paratroopers of the 50's*, Korean War Series Web site
4.   Halberstam, *The Coldest Winter*, p. 516; Michael J. Dator, *Battles at Wonju proved critical*, Eighth Army Web site
5.   Waterhouse, *The Rakkasans Airborne, 187th 'The Steel Berets,'* p. 65
6.   H.W. Brands, *American Dreams*, p. 58
7.   Quoted in Scott Farris's *Almost President*, pp. 124-126
8.   Quoted in Connor Mullin's *Edward Bennett Williams for the Petitioner*, Journal of Supreme Court History, p. 212, published on-line 6-15-09
9.   Ibid.
10. Ibid., p.204
11. WSJ, *Edward Bennett Williams profile*, 11-8-66
12. Quoted in *Edward Bennett Williams for the Petitioner*, p. 204

CHAPTER FIVE: KANE & SPELLMAN

1.   Crowley, *Seattle University*, p. 57
2.   Weekly, 10-13/19-76, *John Spellman, The man behind the mask*; Times, 1-28-01, *Joseph Kane dies, Democratic activist*
3.   Times, 3-5-55, *Bart Spellman killed in Mexico crash; wife hurt*; P-I, 3-6-55, p. 22
4.   Times, 6-20-57, p. 19
5.   Times, 2-20-60, p. 19
6.   Times, 6-3-56, p. 18
7.   Times, 6-3-58, p. 18
8.   Hughes, *Charles Z. Smith, an oral history*, p. 56
9.   Corr, *KING*, pp. 157-158
10. Nelson, *Seattle*, p. 77
11. Times, 3-18-55, p. 14; 3-19-55, p. 2
12. Times, 3-20-55, p.1, 14
13. Dennett, *Agitprop*, p. 182, 257
14. Ibid., p. 189

15. Ibid., p. 190; Times, 11-1-56, p. 22; P-I, 11-2-56, p. 21
16. Bridgman, *Samuel J. Smith, an oral history*, p. 24
17. Ibid., p. 30
18. Ibid
19. Ibid., p. 32
20. Times, 8-5-58, p. B-25
21. 52 Wn.2d 745, Mabel R. DeFilipis, Plaintiff, v. Leonard Russell et al.,
    Defendants and Relators, The Superior Court for King County,
    Honorable Hugh Todd, Judge, Respondent; No. 34850, Department Two,
    8-15-1958

CHAPTER SIX: THE SWAMP

1. Times, 2-6-56, *Why Seattle Needs A New Mayor*
2. Scott, *Turning Points*, p. 30
3. Ibid., p. 34
4. Quoted in Hughes, *Slade Gorton, A Half Century in Politics*, p. 35, 36, 98
5. Chambliss, *On The Take*, p. 47, 59
6. Times, 2-6-56, *Why Seattle Needs a New Mayor*
7. Scott, *Turning Points*, p. 38
8. Times, 12-8-61, p. 6
9. Times, 3-6-59, *Toward Lowering Color Bars in Housing*
10. P-I, 2-10-64, p. 15
11. Times, 1-15-64, p.7
12. Argus, 11-8-63, p. 1
13. Times, 1-16-64, p. 17; 1-22-64, p. 14
14. Times, 2-3-64, p. 10
15. Times, 1-22-64, p. 14
16. P-I, 2-5-64, p. 3
17. Times, 2-9-64, p. 38
18. Times, 11-26-61, *Sheriff Sees Danger In Crowded Old Jail*
19. Argus, 2-7-64, p. 1
20. P-I, 2-12-64, p.7
21. Argus, 3-13-64, p. 1
22. Anderson, *Seattle Vice*, p. 73
23. Weekly, 1-14/20-81, p. 17

CHAPTER SEVEN: FEAR AND LOATHING AT THE COURTHOUSE

1. Times, 7-8-65, *New Courthouse-Remodeling Plan Expected*
2. Times, 7-14-65, *Friendship—Not Politics—In Selection*
3. Ibid.
4. Times, 7-29-65, *Consultant Recommended on Courthouse*
5. North Central Outlook, 9-30-65, *John Birch 'hot' topic at GOP session*

6. P-I, 10-18-66, *Heading down the stretch*
7. Times, 11-6-58, *Chores greet Wallace on victory morn*
8. American, 8-29-63, p. 1; *Lake Washington Story*, p. 143
9. Wallace to author, 9-21-11
10. Times, 1-21-59, p. 45
11. P-I, 10-10-65, *GOP shoots for Wallace*
12. P-I, 2-24-66, p.1

CHAPTER EIGHT: PSYCHOLOGICAL WARFARE

1. Times, 3-17-66, *Waiver Dispute Causes Turmoil*
2. Times, 3-10-66, *Expert should have been hired—Wallace*
3. P-I-, 4-3-66, *King County laboring under a horse-and-buggy political structure*
4. P-I, 3-20-66, *"Flower Funds": Grand Jury Gets the Scent*
5. P-I, 3-11-66, *'Disloyalty' Charged In Firing*
6. P-I, 3-22-66, p.1
7. Times, 4-15-66, p.1
8. Times, 5-4-66, p. 1, 7
9. Times, 4-15-66, *Grand Jury Lauds Prosecutor, Staff*
10. Wallace to author, 9-21-11
11. Argus, 3-25-66, *Two-way Responsibility*
12. Argus, 2-25-66, p. 1
13. Times, 6-1-66, p. 14; 7-10-66, *Candidate Blasts Commissioners*;
    7-27-66, p. 42
14. Times, 9-21-66, *Wallace Is Down But Not Out*
15. Seattle magazine, September 1966
16. Times, 10-13-66, p. 24
17. Times, 10-16-66, *400 Turn Out For Spellman Dinner*
18. Times, 10-24-66, p. 50
19. Times, 11-166, *Grand-Jury Head Criticizes Wallace*
20. Washington Teamster, 11-4-66
21. Times, 11-9-66, p. 1
22. Ibid.; 11-11-66, *Rogstad Confident*; UPI, 11-9-66, *Election Results Exceed
    Republican Expectations*
23. Times, 12-11-66, *Ken Rogstad Had Broad Support*
24. P-I, 8-21-68, p. C-5
25. Ibid.
26. Times, 10-24-76, p. 1
27. Wallace to author, 9-21-11
28. P-I, 8-21-68, p. C-5
29. Wallace to author, 9-21-11

CHAPTER NINE: CHANGING TIMES

1. UPI, 1-11-67, *Selective Service Board Refuses to Reclassify Clay*
2. 1968, *The Year That Changed the World*, p. VI
3. Sell, *Wings of Power*, p. 26; HistoryLink.org books, *Seattle & King County Timeline*; Crowley, *Rites of Passage, The 60's Day by Day* appendix
4. Times, 11-2-60, *The Sporting Thing*
5. Tate, HistoryLink.org Essay 7833
6. Ibid.
7. James R. Ellis, *Survival Tips for Part-time Activists: Reflections on Lawyers and Reform*, the Condon-Falknor Lecture, University of Washington School of Law, 11-8-90
8. Seattle magazine, June 1969, p. 52
9. Tate, HistoryLink.org Essay 7833
10. Kilgannon, *Joel M. Pritchard, An Oral History*, Forward
11. Times, 11-3-65, p. 1; 11-4-65, p. 11
12. Quoted in *Washington, Blessed with Three World's Fairs*, Columbia magazine, Winter 2011/12, p. 20
13. Ellis to author, 2011
14. Seattle magazine, January 1968, p. 30
15. Times, 1-23-68, *Forward Thrust Is Socialistic*
16. Gorton biography, p. 78
17. HistoryLink.org Essay 2168

CHAPTER 10: THE CRISIS OF THE OLD ORDER

1. Wallace to author, 11-14-11
2. Times, 2-7-67, p. 1
3. Times, 2-11-67, *Munro Criticizes Plan*
4. Ibid.
5. Seattle magazine, November 1970, p. 44
6. Ibid.
7. Ibid.
8. Ibid., p 46
9. Wallace to author, 2011
10. Times, 10-27-60, *Teamsters' Ex-Lawyer Wins Verdict*
11. Albrecht to author, 11-16-11
12. Times, 11-2-52, *Issues of Voter Interest*
13. Ibid.
14. Times, 10-2-67, *Oddly Conceived Freeholder Slates*
15. Times, 11-2-52, p. 35
16. Times, 1-26-69, p. 47
17. Corr, *KING*, p. 158
18. Chambliss, p. 54

19. Ibid., pp. 52-55
20. Ibid., p. 217
21. Seattle magazine, September 1968, p. 23
22. P-I, 8-21-68, p. C-5
23. Ibid.
24. Ibid.
25. Ibid.
26. Seattle magazine, September 1968, p. 22
27. Ibid., p. 32
28. Utter to author, 12-8-11
29. Crowley, *Rites of Passage*, p. 43; Seattle magazine, *The Cops on Trial*, June 1968
30. Seattle magazine, September 1968, p. 22
31. P-I, 8-22-68, p. 1
32. Times, 9-4-68, p. 26; Anderson, *Seattle Vice*, p. 98
33. Evans to author, 1-9-2012
34. Times, 8-23-68, *Evans Talks Over Reports With Carroll*
35. Times, 9-4-68, p. 26
36. Washington Teamster, 9-6-68, *Badge 16*
37. Ibid., 9-13-68, p. 7
38. Joel Rindal to Chris Bayley, 7-19-2011
39. Chambliss, p. 65
40. Seattle magazine, September 1968, p. 26
41. Anderson, *Seattle Vice*, p. 99; Times, 5-31-69, *City Pinball Figure Drowns Near Home*; P-I, 5-31-69, *Pinball Figure Is Found Dead*
42. Bayley to author, 12-7-11
43. Chambliss, p. 130
44. Times, 10-30-68, *County Project Looks Like Work of Keystone Cops*
45. Times, 10-31-68, *Courthouse-Remodeling Is Just One Of O'Brien's Problems*
46. Times, 10-6-68, *A Topic of Much Discussion*; 10-31-68, *The Charter*
47. Times, 10-8-68, *Deputies' Local Opposes Charter*
48. Washington Teamster, 10-18-68, p. 1
49. Times, 11-1-68, *'Ballooning' costs of Charter Denied*

CHAPTER 11: MAKING AL OLD

1. Times, 12-7-68, p.1
2. Times 12-4-68, p. 60
3. Times, 12-4-68, *Rosellini Will Run*
4. Spellman campaign press release, Washington State Archives; Times, 12-10-68, p. 18
5. Times, 12-13-68, *County GOP Needs New Leadership*
6. Schrock to author, 11-22-11

7. Butterworth to author, 11-22-11
8. Times, 1-17-69, *Candidates Give Solutions*; 2-4-69, p. 2
9. Times & P-I, 2-10-69, *The Truth about John Spellman*
10. Pritchard to author, 12-1-11
11. P-I, 3-8-69, 3-10-69, *Elect John Spellman*
12. *Rosellini*, p. 214-216
13. Smith to author, 2011
14. McGavick to author, 5-23-11
15. *Rosellini*, p. 217; Times, 2-12-69, p. 41
16. Ibid.
17. Seattle magazine, February 1969, pp. 11-12
18. Teamster, 1-31-69, p. 6
19. Sears to author, 2-9-12
20. Times Sunday magazine, 6-19-77, *Crusader or crank?*; Times, 12-24-70, *Hylites*
21. Times, 2-18-69, p. 7; 3-1-69, p. 4; P-I, 3-1-69, p. A-1
22. Times, 3-2-69, p. 56
23. Ibid.
24. Ibid.
25. P-I, 3-2-69, p. 2
26. Times, 2-14-69, p. 12
27. P-I, 3-13-69, B-1
28. Times, 3-12-69, *End of Trail?*
29. Times, 3-12-69, p. 1

CHAPTER 12: THE POLITICAL JOB

1. Times, 3-13-69, p.1
2. Times, 4-6-69, p. 12
3. Ibid., 4-26-69, *Historic First County Council Meeting*
4. Times, 4-15-69, *Spellman Hints County Use of Warrants, Layoffs*
5. Times, 4-17-69, *Spellman Warns of Cutbacks*
6. Times, 4-28-69, *O'Brien, Spellman In Hassle With Carroll*
7. Times, 6-15-69, p. 126
8. Excell to author, 12-7-11
9. Ibid.
10. McGavick to author, 5-23-11, 12-7-11
11. Heavey to author, 1-4-12
12. Ibid.
13. McGavick to author, 5-23-11, 12-7-11
14. *Slade Gorton*, p. 88; Times, 4-30-69, p. 1, and *Gambling Opinion 'Soft' on Bingo*
15. Times, 7-14-69, *Spellman Unhappy*

CHAPTER 13: BREAKING BARRIERS

1. HistoryLink.org, Essay 1186
2. Seattle magazine, March 1969, *Inside the Kramer Report*
3. Crowley, pp. 136-137
4. Times, 5-23-69, *Central Area Problems Belong to All, Spellman Says*
5. McGavick to author, 12-13-11
6. Smith to author, 12-13-11
7. Times, 8-25-04, *Ex-Councilman Bob Dunn*
8. Times, 9-6-69, *Council Action Aims At Jobs For Blacks*
9. Heavey to author, 2012
10. Times, 7-3-69, *Spellman to Attend Federal Parley*
11. Times, 8-29-69, *Candidate Challenges Charter*
12. Seattle magazine, December 1969; HistoryLink.org Essay 8222
13. *Seattle in Black and White*, p. 94; HistoryLink.org File #1238
14. Sell, *Wings of Power*, p. 26
15. Sale, *Seattle Past to Present*, p. 232

CHAPTER 14: WAY OUT FRONT

1. Times, 10-8-69, p. 1
2. *Seattle in Black and White*, pp. 90-91
3. Times, 8-31-69, p. 35
4. Ibid.
5. Times, 1-26-70 *County to Act on Minority Jobs*
6. Times, 10-8-69, *Whites Present Demands*
7. Times, 9-5-69, *Ironworkers' Wives Talk to Spellman*
8. Times, 10-12-69, *Spellman's Statement*
9. Washington State Board Against Discrimination, quoted in
   Seattle in Black and White, pp. 92-93
10. Howell to author, 2012
11. Times, 10-8-69, p.1; 10-9-69, p.1; P-I, 10-9-69, p. 1
12. Times, 10-8-69, p. 1, 39; 10-9-69, p. 6; 10-12-69, *Spellman's Statement*
13. Times, 10-8-69, p. 1, 39; 10-9-69, p. 6
14. Roberta Byrd, *Face to Face*, 1-12-10, KCTS Archives
15. Ibid.; Times, 10-8-69, p-1, 10-9-69, p-1, 10-12-69, *Spellman's Statement*
16. Burgess to author, 2012
17. Times, 10-9-69, p. 8
18. Burgess to author, 2012
19. Times, 10-17-69, *Evans Firm On Minority Employment*; Crowley,
    Rites of Passage, p. 158
20. Times, 6-17-70, *Court Enjoins Unions From Bias Acts*
21. Howell to author, 2012; Tyree Scott, HistoryLink.org Essay 8222
22. Ibid.

23. P-I, 10-9-69, p. 1, multiple editions; Anderson, *Seattle Vice*, p. 97, 99; Corr, *KING*, pp. 166-167

24. P-I, 10-9-69, p. 1; 10-10-69, p.1; 10-11-69, B-5

25. P-I, 10-9-69, p. B-1

CHAPTER 15: MUDVILLE

1. Times, 4-1-70, C-2

2. Times, 2-6-70, C-1

3. Times, 2-27-70, p. 1

4. Hughes, *Slade Gorton*, p. 135

5. Thiel, *Out of Left Field*, p. 13

6. Bouton, *Ball Four*

7. Boswell and McConaghy, *100 Years of a Newspaper and Its Region*, p. 46

8. Times, 3-27-70, *Spellman Asks Support for Revenue Sharing*

9. Times, 3-21-70, *Group Works On U.S. Aid For Jobless*

10. Times, 2-17-70, p.1; P-I, 2-18-70, p. 1

11. Times, 7-29-70, p. 1

12. Scates, *Magnuson*, p. 212

13. Crowley, *Rites of Passage*, p. 180

14. Grinstein to author, 2012

15. Times, 3-4-70, p. E-5

16. HistoryLink.org Essay 3919, *Dorm Braman*

17. Times, 5-14-70, *'Thrust' Can Help*

18. Ibid.

19. Grinstein to author, 2012

20. Ibid.

21. Times, 3-24-70, *Pro-Football Rates Seattle High*

22. Times, 2-25-70, p. A-8

23. Times, 6-19-77, Sunday magazine, *Crusader or Crank?*

24. Ibid.

25. P-I, 4-24-05, *'First suburban rebel'*

26. Argus, 7-4-75, p. 1

27. Times, 3-14-70, *Group Seeks to Void Charter;* 4-1-70, p. 24

28. Ibid.

29. Times, 3-30-70, *Computer Expert Named Chief*

30. Times, 5-3-70, *Low-Key Politics in a Job With Clout;* Seattle magazine, September 1970, *You've Come a Long Way, Wes*

31. Times, 7-29-73, *Fired aide didn't 'watch his back'*

32. P-I, 7-28-76, p. A-6

33. Bayley to author, 12-7-11

34. Times, 10-11-69, *Dr. Ray To Advise President*

CHAPTER 16: THRUST BACKWARD

1. Times, 5-8-70, *The Multi-purpose Stadium*
2. Times, 5-17-70, *Bay Freeway, Parking Hinge on Election*
3. Ibid.
4. Ibid.
5. Times, 5-14-70, *Thrust Can Help*
6. Times, 5-20-70, *Thrust Defeat Laid to Economic Lag*
7. Hughes, *Slade Gorton*, p. 78
8. Times, 5-20-70, *Thrust Opponents Cite Distrust*
9. Times, 5-21-70, *Implement Bus Plan—Spellman*
10. HistoryLink.org Essay 3961
11. Times, 7-4-2000, *Arnie Weinmeister Dies*
12. Times, 6-19-70, *Vote on Any New Stadium Site Appears Certain*
13. Weekly, 10-13/19-76, *John Spellman, The man behind the mask*
14. Times, 5-29-70, *Spellman Tells Cole...*
15. McGavick to author, 3-5-12
16. Ibid.
17. Times, 8-19-70, *Gifts affected votes ...*
18. Times, 8-9-70, *County Delegates Ousted*
19. Times, 9-16-70, *Bayley defeats Carroll; Wise election decisions*
20. Times, 9-16-70, *'Publicity politics' hit by Heavey*
21. Times, 5-18-73, p. 1
22. Anderson, *Seattle Vice*, p. 110
23. Ibid.
24. Times, 9-21-70, A-10
25. Times, 11-9-70, A-14
26. Times, P-I, 11-11-70
27. Times, 5-19-71, *Ruano ends bid to recall*
28. Times, 12-3-70, p. 1
29. Scates, *Magnuson*, pp. 280-281
30. Duncan, *Washington, The First 100 Years*, p. 110
31. Boswell and McConaghy, *100 Years of a Newspaper and Its Region*, p. 46

CHAPTER 17: THE KINGDOME

1. Times, 12-15-70, p. D-2
2. Times, 12-21-70, *Stadium-site report adopted*
3. Times, 12-18-70, *All aboard for King St. Station stadium?*
4. Times, 12-24-70, *Hylites*
5. Times, 12-24-70, *Merry Christmas, regardless of site*
6. Times, 12-31-70, *Ross Cunningham*
7. Times, 12-24-71, *The petitions*
8. Times, 12-30-71, *Ruano gives clerk petitions*

9.   Times, 1-10-72, *New Council Council head*
10. Times, 3-24-72, *Initiative out; stadium gets go ahead*
11. Howell to author, 4-11-12
12. Times, 7-25-72, *Voice of Moderation*
13. Times, 1-18-73, p. 1
14. Belcher to author, 3-27-12
15. Times, 6-27-75, *Stadium has a name*
16. Kilgannon, *Joel M. Pritchard, An Oral History*, p. 185

CHAPTER 18: GROUNDBREAKING

1.   Times, 11-2-72, p. 1; P-I, 11-3-72, p. 1; Sanders, *Seattle & The Roots of Urban Sustainability*, pp. 164-167; Santos, *Hum Bows, Not Hot Dogs!*, pp. 78-81
2.   Ibid.
3.   Ibid.
4.   Ibid.
5.   P-I, 11-3-72, p.1
6.   Frank Chesley, HistoryLink.org Essay 8989, *Bob Santos*
7.   Santos, *Hum Bows, Not Hot Dogs!*, p. 90
8.   Ibid, p. 87
9.   Ibid, p. 88
10. Santos to author, 4-2-12
11. Chesley, HistoryLink.org Essay 8989, *Bob Santos*
12. Santos to author, 4-2-12
13. P-I, 11-16-72, *Spellman isn't sad Nixon hasn't called*
14. Times, 1-12-73, p. C-2
15. Times, P-I, 7-17-73, p. 1
16. Times, P-I, 9-17-73
17. Times, 10-24-73, *Lowry vs. Spellman*
18. Ibid.
19. Ibid.
20. Times, 11-4-73, p. C-6
21. P-I, 11-4-73, p. A-14

CHAPTER 19: SAND JACKS AND SMOKE SCREENS

1.   Times, 8-16-72, p. 1
2.   Schlatter to author, 4-25-12
3.   Times, 1-17-73, *Vibration possible cause*
4.   Times, 11-19-73, *County applies for stadium funds*
5.   View Northwest, March 1975, p.22
6.   Argus, 5-3-74, p. 1
7.   Ibid.
8.   Ibid.

9.　Times, 11-1-72, *New stadium could attract baseball*
10.　Times, 7-19-74, p.1; 7-20-74, p. 1
11.　Willamette Week, 2-3-78, *Drake Construction: Kingdome or doom?*
12.　Times, 12-4-74, p.1
13.　Ibid.
14.　Times 12-6-74, *Solitary rib ...*
15.　Times, 12-4-74, p. 1
16.　Times, 12-7-74, *Drake won't be allowed to bid*; P-I, 12-8-74, p. 1
17.　Schlatter to author, 4-25-12
18.　View Northwest, March 1976, p. 23
19.　Ibid, p. 20
20.　Ibid., p. 25

CHAPTER 20: OFF AND RUNNING

1.　Washington State Archives, Evans press conference, 10-28-75
2.　Weekly, 8-18/24-76, *Hoppe Days Are Here Again*; Argus, 7-4-75, p. 1
3.　Times, 11-17-75, p. A-6
4.　Times, 10-24-75. *Hoppe preparing to run for governor*
5.　Emily Lieb, HistoryLink.org Essay 7854, 2006
6.　Guzzo, *Is It True What They Say About Dixy?*, pp. 184-186
7.　Times, 11-30-75, p. D-4
8.　Times, 2-4-75, p. A-11
9.　Times, 10-19-75, p. C-1
10.　Ibid.
11.　Times, 2-28-76, p. B-1
12.　AP by Ammons in Oregonian, 3-26-76, p. 1
13.　P-I, 3-28-76, p.1
14.　HistoryLink.org, Essay 2527
15.　Times, 3-28-76, p. 1
16.　Times, 3-28-76, p. G-11
17.　Times Sunday Magazine, 6-19-77, cover story

CHAPTER 21: PRIMARY COLORS

1.　Spellman campaign opposition research file, Washington State Archives
2.　Excell to author, 4-3-2012
3.　Times, 2-23-76, p. 1
4.　Argus, 10-15-76, p. 1
5.　Butterworth to author, 5-14-12
6.　Argus, 10-15-76, p. 1
7.　Guzzo, *Is It True What They Say About Dixy?*, p. 212
8.　Ibid.
9.　Butterworth to author, 5-14-12

10. Schrock to author, 5-14-2012
11. Argus, 7-2-76, *Poll Watching*; Times, 7-15-76, *Spellman poll*
12. Weekly, 8-4/10-76, *Politics '76*
13. Times, 8-27-76, p. C-9
14. P-I, 7-21-76, p. A-4
15. Times, 4-22-76, p. E-3
16. Argus, 7-2-6, *The Voice of Sweet Inevitability*
17. Times, 8-27-76, p. C-9
18. Butterworth to author, 5-14-12
19. Weekly, 9-8/14-76, p. 5
20. Weekly, 9-29/10-5-1976, *Down-home in Dixyland*
21. Times, 9-22-76, p. 1
22. Times, 9-22-76, p. B-6
23. Times, 9-22-76, *Durkan hasn't decided...*

CHAPTER 22: DIXYLAND

1. Guzzo, *Is It True What They Say About Dixy?*, pp. 212-214
2. Butterworth to author, 5-14-12
3. Times, 9-15-76, p. B-5; Weekly, 9-29/10-5-76, *A stunning setback on supertankers*
4. S-R, 10-9-76, p. 1
5. Ibid.
6. Ibid.
7. Ibid.
8. Ibid; Times, 10-10-76, p. A-8
9. Ibid.
10. Times, 10-13-76, *Dr. Ray wrong on stadium—Spellman*
11. 10-15-76, p. A-10
12. Ibid.
13. Ibid.
14. Ibid.
15. Times, 10-15-76, *'John got a little fire in his belly'*
16. Times, 10-16-76, *Ray ignorant*
17. TNT, 10-10-76, *Dan did Dixy wrong*
18. Times, 10-17-76, *Ray blasts Evans*
19. Times, 10-17-76, *Gorton reprimands Ray*
20. Butterworth to author, 5-14-12
21. Times, 10-17-76, *'How to deal with woman opponent?'*
22. Times, 10-21-76, *Ray listens to women's issues*
23. Tri-City Herald, 10-27-76, p. 2; Times, 10-26-76, p. 1, A-14
24. Ibid.
25. Times, 10-28-76, *Ray country?*

26. Time, 10-8-76, *Some fresh faces for '76*
27. Times, 10-24-76, p. G-1
28. Weekly, 10-13/19-76, *John Spellman: The man behind the mask*
29. Weekly, 10-27/11-2/1976, *Election endorsements*
30. Butterworth to author 5-14-12
31. Times, P-I, TNT, 10-31-76
32. Butterworth to author, 5-14-12
33. Times, 11-3-76, p. B-4
34. Times, 3-14-77, p. A-18
35. Butterworth to author, 5-14-12
36. Times, 11-3-76, p. B-4
37. Ibid.

CHAPTER 23: SECOND THOUGHTS AND THIRD TERMS

1. HistoryLink.org File 8600, *Mike Lowry*
2. Times, 2-24-77, *Spellman to run again*
3. Times, 3-15-77, *Cuts add to problems of mentally ill*
4. Times, 4-6-77, p. D-1
5. Times, 8-7-77, p. A-15
6. Times, 7-21-77, p. B-1
7. Times, 7-30-77, *Hoppe to vie for county executive*
8. Times, 8-7-77, p. A-15
9. Times, 11-7-77, p. A-14
10. Times, 7-8-77, *McDermott won't run*
11. Times, 9-8-77, p. E-1
12. Times, 8-4-77, *Opponent hits Spellman, Hoppe*
13. Times, 7-13-77, *Why the county 'goofed'*
14. Ibid.
15. Times, 4-23-77, *County road outlay probed*
16. Weekly, 10-5-77, *Stalemated, as usual*
17. Times, 4-23-77, *County road outlay probed*
18. Times, 7-16-77, *County road fund sufficient, after all*
19. Times, 7-23-77, *Special road-fund probe 'unnecessary'*
20. Times, Pacific Northwest Magazine, 6-27-2003, *Aubrey Davis is in it for the long haul*; HistoryLink.org Essay 8179, *Aubrey Davis*
21. Times, 7-27-77, p. A-15; 9-2-77, *The race for county executive*; P-I, 11-4-77, p. A-6
22. Times, 9-8-77, p. E-1
23. Times, 7-30-77, p. D-2
24. Times, 10-7-77, p. A-18
25. Times, 9-14-77, *Candidates split on farm issue*; Argus, 9-30-77, p. 1
26. P-I, 11-4-77, p. A-6

27. P-I, 11-1-77, p. A-3; Argus, 9-30-77, p. 1
28. Times, 9-29-77, *An enlightened request*; 10-4-77, *County grants funds*
29. Times, 11-2-77, *Outsider fights for recognition; A push for Hoppe that backfired?*
30. Ibid.
31. Weekly, 10-26/11-1-77, *Alas, poor Aubrey*
32. Times, 11-3-77, *Davis beckons Hoppe supporters*; P-I, 10-28-77, p. A-12
33. Hoppe to author, 6-19-12
34. Times, 11-9-77, *An easy day for Spellman*; P-I, 11-9-77, p. A-5
35. Scates, *Magnuson*, p. 294
36. Times, 10-8-77, p. D-6; HistoryLink.org Essay 5620, *Magnuson's amendment*
37. Scates, *Magnuson*, p. 305
38. Times, 10-6-77, p. 1

CHAPTER 24: FULLY JUSTIFIED

1. Times, 12-22-77, *County spending*; Daily Journal of Commerce,7-10-78, p.1; Times, 12-22-77, *County spending twice Drake's*
2. Times, 11-28-77, p. A-14; 11-29-77, *Kingdome trial*
3. Times, 12-6-77, *Dome firm 'could have profited'*
4. Times, 12-22-77, *Drake engineer details problems*
5. Times, 2-9-78, *Drake threats recalled*
6. Ibid.
7. Times, 2-23-78, p. D-4
8. Times, 3-1-78, *Drake tells of county's contract 'breach'*
9. Times, 4-20-78, *Spellman reneged*
10. Times, 6-3-78, *Kingdome trial*
11. Washington State Archives, Transcript of Court's Oral Decision, King County vs. Donald M. Drake Company, et al, No. C74-568S, Honorable Morell E. Sharp, U.S. District Judge for the Western District of Washington, Seattle, 10-7-78
12. Ibid.
13. Ibid.
14. Daily Journal of Commerce, 7-10-78, p.1
15. P-I, 7-8-78, p. 1
16. P-I, 7-8-78, p. 1
17. Times, 7-2-78, *Spellman still has eye on governor's office*
18. Ibid.
19. Times, 6-17-80, *Dome settlement irks attorney*

CHAPTER 25: YOU WIN SOME, YOU LOSE SOME

1. Times, 3-28-78, A-14
2. Times, *100 Years of a Newspaper and Its Region*, p. 49
3. HistoryLink.org Essay 10057, *King County Conservation Futures Program*
4. Times, 7-18-78, *Economic benefits seen*
5. HistoryLink.org Essay 10057, *King County Conservation Futures*
6. Times, 11-2-79, Farmlands preservation letter to the editor
7. Times, 9-19-79, p. B-4
8. Times, 9-14-79, A-6
9. HistoryLink.org Essay 4112, *King County voters approve Farmland Preservation Bond*
10. Times, 11-7-79, A-16
11. Times, 2-5-77, *'Power play'*
12. HistoryLink.org Essay 10057, *King County Conservation Futures*
13. Times, 9-2-78, A-7
14. Times, 8-1-79, A-14
15. Times, 6-16-77, *Ray signs bill*
16. Times, 11-4-79, *Metro merger*
17. Times, 11-1-79, *Merger foes accused*
18. Times, 9-2-78, A-7
19. Times, 2-14-77, *County-Metro debate*
20. Times, 2-7-79, *Ray awaits results of study*
21. Ibid.
22. Cunningham v. Municipality of Metropolitan Seattle, 751 F.Supp. 885 (W.D. Wash. 1990); HistoryLink.org Essay 2705
23. Brazier, History of the Washington Legislature, 1965-1982, pp. 36-39

CHAPTER 26: A REAL GOVERNOR

1. Times, 11-18-79, p. 1
2. Ibid.
3. Ibid.
4. Ibid.; Seattle Sun, 3-12-80, *How new is the new Spellman?*
5. Schrock to author, 7-12-12
6. Times, 11-30-79
7. Times, 11-18-79, A-14
8. Times, 1-22-80, *Debate turns into sniping at Ray*
9. Boswell, *Ray Moore, an oral history*, p. 84
10. Scates, *Magnuson*, p. 306
11. Quoted in S-R, 9-21-80, p. G-1
12. Washington National Guard Web site, *Mount St. Helens eruption*
13. Hughes, *Slade Gorton*, p. 150
14. Times, 9-4-80, *Spellman misses forum but not jabs*

15. Grays Harbor Washingtonian, 4-23-36, p.1
16. Ibid.; World, 6-12-80, p. 1
17. Scates, *Magnuson*, pp. 306-307
18. Times, 6-15-80, p.1; World, 6-15-80, p.1
19. World, 6-15-80, p. 1; Times, 6-15-80, p.1
20. Ibid.
21. Excell to author, 6-27-12
22. Schrock to author, 7-16-12
23. Julian P. Kanter Political Commercial Archive, University of Oklahoma, Norman
24. Excell to author, 7-16-12
25. Argus, 4-4-80, *No more mashed potatoes*
26. Times, 9-14-80, D-6
27. Times, 8-17-80, p. A-14
28. Times, 9-14-80, D-6
29. Ibid.
30. Times, 9-28-80, p. 1
31. Doty, *Duane Berentson, Life as a Team Player*, pp. 43-44
32. Weekly, 1-14/20-81, p. 19
33. Waldo to author, 7-16-12
34. Weekly, 1-14/20-81, p. 19
35. Ibid.
36. S-R, 9-29-80, p. 6

CHAPTER 27: MCDERMOTT IS THE QUESTION

1. Times, 9-23-80, *Adviser leaves Spellman campaign*
2. Times, 9-23-80, *Chapman endorses Spellman's candidacy*
3. S-R, 10-12-89, p. A-10
4. Excell to author, 6-27-12
5. Ibid.
6. Ibid.
7. Brown to author, 7-23-12
8. Excell to author, 6-27-12
9. Weekly, 1-14/20-81, p. 28
10. S-R, 10-1-80, *Spellman unveils conservative approach*
11. Ibid.
12. S-R, 10-9-80, p. 6
13. Times, 10-12-80, p. C-6; S-R. 10-13-80, p. 9
14. S-R, 10-12-80, p. G-3
15. Excell to author, 6-27-12
16. Times, 10-16-80, p. 1; P-I, 10-16-80, p. A-5
17. Ibid.

18. P-I, 10-17-80, p. B-2
19. P-I, 10-16-80, p. A-5
20. P-I, 10-20-80, p. A-3
21. Times, 10-17-80, p. B-2
22. Excell to author, 8-1-12
23. P-I, 10-26-80, *How others view the candidates for governor*
24. P-I, 10-29-80, p. A-2
25. Times, 10-30-80, *Ethics questioned*
26. P-I, 10-30-80, p. A-6
27. P-I, 11-1-80, p. A-2
28. P-I, 11-2-80, p. 1
29. P-I, 10-31-80, p.1
30. P-I, 11-2-80, *A celebration for a bridge – and Maggie*
31. P-I, 11-5-80, p.1
32. Scott Farris, *Almost President*, p. 7
33. P-I, 11-5-80, p.1
34. Ibid.
35. P-I, 10-26-80, *How others view the candidates for governor*
36. P-I, 11-6-80, *She's Dunn ...*

CHAPTER 28: TRANSITIONS

1.   Times, 1-6-80, *Outlook '80*; P-I, 11-8-80, p. 1
2.   Swift to author, 8-8-12
3.   HistoryLink.org Essay 5238, *McNeil Island and the Federal Penitentiary 1841-1981*
4.   Excell to author, 8-7-12
5.   Weekly, 1-14-81, p. 17
6.   McGavick to author, 8-6-12
7.   Times, 1-19-81, p. C-1
8.   Scott, *A Majority of One*, p. 97
9.   Excell to author, 8-7-12
10. Weekly, 1-14-81, p. 17
11. Weekly, 1-14-81, p. 15
12. Ibid.
13. Weekly, 1-14-81, p. 17
14. Ibid.
15. Times, 2-28-81, p. A-9
16. Hughes, *Nancy Evans*, p. 163
17. Times, 1-11-81, *Bouquet of tough problems*
18. Times, 1-3-81, p. A-11; 1-7-81, p. A-3
19. World, 12-24-80, p. 1
20. Excell to author, 8-7-12

CHAPTER 29: GRAY AND LONELY

1. Times, 1-15-81, p. B-1
2. Ibid.
3. JDS Inaugural Address, 1-14-81, Washington State Archives
4. Times, 1-15-81, p. B-1
5. Times, 1-16-81, p.1
6. Times, 1-11-81, p. 1
7. Ibid., p. C-2
8. Ibid.
9. Times, 1-7-81, p. C-2
10. Times, 2-10-81, *Interim budget*
11. Times, 1-7-81, p. C-2
12. Ibid.
13. Scott, Excell Oral History, p. 35, Washington State Archives
14. Times, 1-18-81, p. A-17
15. Times, 1-4-81, p. A-24
16. Times, 1-4-81, *Minority leader is queen of the 'Men's Club'*
17. Times, 1-16-81, p.1, B-2; P-I, 2-12-81, p. A-16
18. Times, 1-16-81, *Spellman proposal*
19. Times, 1-16-81, p.1, B-2
20. Ibid.
21. P-I, 2-12-81, p. A-16
22. Grimm to author, 8-14-12
23. P-I, 2-8-81, p. A-9
24. P-I, 2-10-81, p. A-4
25. Times, 2-10-81, p. B-2
26. P-I, 2-10-81, p. 1
27. Times, 1-17-81, *Gracious governor*
28. Lois Spellman to author, 7-24-12

CHAPTER 30: FEAR AND LOATHING AT THE CAPITOL

1. Times, 2-14-81, p. 1
2. P-I, 2-14-81, p. 1
3. Ibid., p. A-12
4. P-I, 2-14-81, *Always an enigma*; 2-16-81, p.1; Oly, 2-15-81, p. 1
5. P-I, 2-14-81, p. A-1, A-12
6. Oly, 2-15-81, p. 1
7. P-I, 2-14-81, *Always an enigma*
8. Oly, 2-14-81, p.1
9. Times, 2-14-81, p. 7
10. P-I, 2-15-81, *Von Reichbauer vows to stay*
11. P-I, 2-15-81, p. B-4

12. Scott, *A Majority of One*, p. 144
13. Scott, *A Majority of One*, p. 100
14. Ibid., p. 101
15. *Ray Moore, An Oral History*, p. 85, SOS Legacy Project web site
16. Times, 3-18-81, *Questions about worker-comp bill*
17. Times, 3-19-81, p. 1
18. Times, 4-19-81, p. A-17
19. Times, 3-20-81, '*Maggie Day*'
20. Quoted in Hughes, *Booth Who?*, p. 33
21. Ibid. p. 77
22. TNT, 2-12-81, *Senators stump for executive candidates*
23. Faulk to author, 8-11-12
24. Ibid.
25. TNT, 3-13-81, *Gardner must control Demos or fail*
26. TNT, 3-12-81, *Be assertive, Spellman urges Gardner*
27. *Class Wars*, p. 127
28. Ibid.

CHAPTER 31: CHOICES

1. Times, 4-6-81, *Evans, Metro ex-chief...*
2. Times, 3-5-81, *Need for prompt action*
3. Times, 4-29-81, *Evans elected chairman*
4. Times, 9-21-81, p. A-10
5. Ibid.
6. S-R, 8-29-84, *Spellman firmly behind chief*
7. Times, 3-20-82, *State Patrol chief...*
8. Times, 4-7-83, *State troopers...*
9. Scott, *A Majority of One*, p. 101
10. Ibid.
11. Times, 4-19-81, p. A-17, *Image problems*
12. Ibid.
13. Times, 11-13-85, *Parting shots*
14. Excell to author, 9-10-12
15. Times, 4-27-81, *Drowsy lawmakers*
16. Ibid.
17. Times, 4-27-81, p. 1
18. Ibid.
19. Ibid.
20. Times, 4-29-81, p. 1, p. C-2
21. Times, 4-29-81, p. 1
22. Times, 4-7-81, p. C-1
23. Times, 4-27-81, p. C-2

24. Times, 4-16-81, p. C-2
25. Brazier, *History of the Washington Legislature, 1965-82*, p. 45
26. Munro to author, 9-11-12
27. Times, 5-13-81, *Pritchard, Morrison shaken*
28. Ibid.
29. Times, 5-20-81, p. C-2
30. Ibid.
31. Ibid.
32. Times, 5-20-81, *Ferry engineers*
33. Times, 5-22-81, p. 1; 5-23-81, *Peacemaker.*
34. Times, 5-20-81, p. 1
35. Cassandra Tate, HistoryLink.org Essay 3939, *Busing in Seattle: A Well-Intentioned Failure*

CHAPTER 32: WHAT NEXT?

1. Times, 10-6-81, *Schools to make cuts*
2. Times, 10-30-81, *UW president*
3. Times, 10-30-81, p. D-2
4. Times, 12-27-81, p. B-2
5. Times, 11-1-81, p. B-14
6. Ibid.
7. Times, 11-14-81, *Mass protest*
8. Times, 9-16-81, *Legislators don't welcome...*
9. Scott, *A Majority of One*, p. 160
10. Ibid., p. 162
11. Times, 11-4-81, p. A-18
12. Times, 11-24-81, p.1
13. Times, 12-6-81, *Spellman, Legislature not exactly close*
14. Times, 9-12-81, *State needs tax boost*
15. Times, 12-4-81, p.1
16. Sheldon, *The Washington High Bench*, p. 273
17. Utter to author, 8-15-12
18. Sheldon, *The Washington High Bench*, p. 75
19. Times, 7-11-84, p. A-10
20. Chronicle, Times, 1-8-82, p.1
21. Ibid.
22. Ibid.
23. Times, 1-21-82, p. B-2
24. Ibid.
25. Ibid.
26. Ibid.
27. Times, 6-13-82, *Revenue director named*

28. Scott, *A Majority of One*, p. 104
29. Ibid.
30. Times, 1-15-82, p. D-4
31. Times, 1-21-82, p. A-14

CHAPTER 33: THE IDES OF MARCH

1. P-I, 3-11-82, *Spellman and legislators trade barbs*
2. JDS press conference, 3-11-82, Washington State Archives
3. O'Connor to author, 8-29-12
4. P-I, 3-11-82, *'Troglodytes' unite*; Times, 3-12-82, p. 1
5. Times, 3-13-82, p.1
6. P-I, 3-14-82, p. A-13
7. Scott, *A Majority of One*, p. 106
8. Times, 4-15-82, p. E-1
9. Ibid.

CHAPTER 34: AN EPIC PROCESS OF DUE PROCESS

1. People, 4-26-82, p. 59
2. Times, 3-15-82, *End run*
3. Excell to author, 9-4-12
4. Times, 1-12-82, *Andrus stresses need*
5. Times, 2-22-82, p. C-1
6. Times, 3-28-82, p. C-4
7. Times, 3-28-82, p. 1
8. Times, 2-22-82, p. C-1
9. Times, 4-8-82, p. B-2
10. Times, 3-15-82, *End run*
11. Times, 3-17-82, p. 1
12. Times, 3-28-82, p. C-4
13. Times, 4-7-82, p. A-20
14. Lois Spellman to author, 7-24-12
15. Excell to author, 8-8-12
16. Times, 4-8-82, p. 1; P-I, 4-9-82, p. 1; JDS press conference, 4-8-82, State Archives
17. Times, 4-9-82, p. 1
18. Times, 4-9-82, *Northern Tier rejection*
19. Times, 4-8-82, *Pipeline supporters*
20. Times, 4-27-82, p. D-16
21. Times, 5-1-82, *2 cases of jet lag*
22. Times, 5-27-82, *Defense secretary rejected...*
23. Times, 4-21-83, *'Real reason'*
24. Ibid.

25. Crosscut.com, 10-19-11, *Cherry Point's coal debate*
26. Times, 3-15-82, p. A-10
27. Excell to author, 10-30-12
28. Times, 4-4-82, *Spellman vetoes*
29. Times, 7-4-82, *He's their honoree*
30. Schmitten to author, 10-29-12
31. Wilkerson to author, 10-23-12
32. Schmitten to author, 10-29-12
33. Ibid.
34. Wilkerson to author, 10-23-12

CHAPTER 35: SCRATCH AND MATCH

1.   Brazier, *History of the Washington Legislature, 1965-1982*, p. 50
2.   Times, 6-12-82, *Budget is Spellman's problem*
3.   Times, 6-22-82, *Legislators leery*
4.   Times, 6-12-82, *Education leaders*
5.   P-I, 6-19-82, *Demos' Band-Aids*
6.   Grimm to author, 9-6-12
7.   Scott, *A Majority of One*, p. 99
8.   Ibid., p. 106
9.   Times, 3-26-82, p. B-2
10. Brazier, *History of the Washington Legislature, 1965-1982*, p. 50
11. Times, 7-19-82, A-10
12. Times, 11-15-82, p. 1

CHAPTER 36: CHINA

1.   Bauer, *Boeing, The First Century*, p. 255
2.   Ibid., p. 251
3.   Washington Law & Politics, April 2006, *Port Whine*
4.   Ibid.
5.   Ibid.
6.   Times, 10-12-82, p. C-1
7.   Ibid.
8.   Ibid.
9.   Washington Law & Politics, April 2006, *Port Whine*
10. Grinstein to author, 9-18-12
11. Ibid.
12. Ibid
13. Ibid
14. Times, 10-19-82, *Trade channels*
15. Ibid.
16. Washington Law & Politics, April 2006, *Port Whine*

17. Ibid.
18. Ibid.

CHAPTER 37: CHECKS AND IMBALANCES

1. Scott, *A Majority of One*, p. 160
2. Times, 1-9-83, p. C-2
3. Ibid.
4. Times, 11-4-82, *Drift to Democrat*
5. Scott, *A Majority of One*, p. 160
6. Ehlers to author, 9-24-12
7. Times, 1-5-83, p. C-2
8. Times, 11-23-82, *Spellman advisory council*
9. Times, 12-21-82, p. B-1
10. Times, 1-9-83, p. C-2
11. World, 1-9-83, *House gavel changes hands*
12. Times, 12-21-82, *Spellman offers 'hard-times' plan*
13. Ibid.; Oregonian, 12-21-82, *Spellman tax increase package*
14. Ibid.
15. Oregonian, 12-21-82, *Spellman tax increase package*
16. Times, 1-5-83, *Conservatives wish you didn't know*
17. Times, 2-23-83, *Lest one should forget*
18. Ibid.
19. Ehlers to author, 9-24-12
20. Ibid.
21. Ibid.
22. Times, 4-7-83, *Budget bill too big to swallow*
23. Miller, *Energy Northwest*, p. 403
24. Times, 4-10-83, p. C-4
25. Times, 5-25-83, p. A-12
26. Miller, Energy Northwest, p. 403
27. Times, 5-25-83, *Senate demos say no*; Ehlers to author, 9-24-12
28. Miller, *Energy Northwest*, p. 404
29. Beckwith, *On the Harbor*, p. 162
30. Times, 4-25-83, *Legislature passes Seafirst bill*
31. P-I, 3-17-08, *Did Seafirst rescue set stage for current banking crisis?*
32. Ibid.
33. Times, 5-23-83, p. C-1
34. Ibid.
35. Times, 5-27-83, p. A-14
36. Times, 6-5-83, *What happened to leadership?*
37. Ibid.
38. Ibid.

39. P-I, 7-9-83, p. A-3
40. Excell to author, 9-19-12
41. Times, 7-9-83, p.1; P-I, 7-9-83, p. A-3; Journal-American, 7-17-83, p. A-5
42. Journal-American, 7-17-83, p. A-5
43. Ibid.
44. Ibid.
45. Schrock to author, 9-26-12

CHAPTER 38: A SAD PLUM

1. Times, 9-2-83, p. 1
2. Hughes, *Gorton*, p. 185
3. Times, 9-3-82, p. 3
4. Times, 4-17-83, *Who's Next?*
5. Hughes, *Nancy Evans*, pp. 242-243, Hughes, *Gorton*, pp. 185-186
6. Ibid.
7. Excell to author, 1-6-11
8. Times, 9-9-83, *Evans moving from campus calm*
9. Ibid.
10. NYT, 4-17-88, *Why I'm quitting the Senate*
11. Frank Pritchard to author, 9-5-12

CHAPTER 39: AFFORDABLE HOUSING

1. Times, 3-10-83, *Legislators OK housing finance agency*
2. Article 8, Section 7, Washington State Constitution
3. *A Catalyst for Community, WSHFC's first 20 years*, p. 6, Washington State Library, Tumwater
4. Ibid., p. 6-9
5. Ibid.
6. Ibid., p. 10
7. Ibid.
8. Ibid., p. 13
9. Ibid., p. 13-14
10. Ibid.
11. Ibid., p. 16
12. Ibid., p. 20
13. Dunn to author, 9-27-12
14. *A Catalyst for Community*, p. 20
15. Ibid., p. 21
16. Ibid.
17. Ibid.
18. Ibid.
19. Ibid. p. 23

20. Herman to author, 9-28-2012
21. Washington Center for Real Estate Research, WSU

CHAPTER 40: STRONG, ILL-DEFINED NEGATIVES

1. Excell to author, 9-26-12
2. Elway to author, 3-15-12
3. Hughes, *Booth Who?*, p. 116
4. Ibid., p. 117
5. Times, 12-4-83, *No opposition in sight*
6. Times, 4-17-83, p. D-2
7. Times, 9-1-83, p. A-26
8. Times, 12-4-83, *Pep talk*
9. Times, 12-11-83, *Spellman proposes exams*
10. Times, 12-20-83, p. C-4
11. Ibid.
12. Ibid.
13. Times 1-6-84, *It's official ...*
14. P-I, 12-18-83, *A working mom*
15. Times, 4-3-84, *Gardner has $100,000*
16. Times, 1-15-84, p. D-6
17. TNT, 2-13-84, *Gardner makes his race official*
18. *Booth Who?*, p. 119
19. Times, 3-4-84, p. C-2
20. Times, 11-11-84, p. A-21
21. Times, 3-22-84, p. D-16
22. Times, 3-30-84, *Hospital-cost bill*
23. Ibid.
24. Ibid.
25. Times, 4-3-84, *Labor chief*
26. Ibid.
27. Times, 4-4-84, *Spellman attacked*

CHAPTER 41: BOOTH WHEW

1. Hughes, *Booth Who?*, p. 117
2. Times, 4-4-84, *McDermott renews bid*
3. P-I, 1-11-08, *Gardner crusade*
4. *Booth Who?*, p. 123
5. Ibid., p. 124
6. Ibid., p. 126
7. Times, 5-25-84, *Patrol Association files complaint*
8. P-I, 9-8-84, *The high cost of politics*
9. Times, 9-23-84, *How did he do it?*

10. Ibid.

11. Ibid.

12. Times, 9-21-84, *Gardner riches*

13. Ibid.

14. Ibid,

15. *Booth Who?*, pp. 130-131

16. Ibid.

17. Times, 10-28-84, *Endorsements*

18. Times, 11-4-84, *The governor's race*

19. Times, 10-28-84, *Spellman record in hard times*

20. P-I, 9-26-8, *Spellman hoped for more debates*

21. Times, 10-4-84, *Spellman uses Gardner absence*

22. World, 10-5-84, p. A-3

23. World, 10-1-84, Ferguson column, p. A-4

24. Julian P. Kanter Political Commercial Archive, University of Oklahoma, Norman

25. Weinmeister to Spellman, on behalf of Joint Council of Teamsters No. 28, 10-24-84, Washington State Archives

26. Spellman for Governor press release, 10-24-84, Washington State Archives

27. Times, 10-16-84, *Candidates come out swinging*

28. Newman to author, 10-9-12

29. Excell to author, 10-9-12

30. P-I, 10-21-84, p. A-22

31. Schrock to author, 3-14-12

32. Oly, 10-22-84, *Punches get rougher*

33. Oly, 11-1-84, *Debate arms vote*

34. Times, 11-11-84, *What went wrong?*

35. Times, 11-7-84, *Spellman leaves the ring ...*

36. Ibid.

37. Ibid.

38. Times, 11-18-84, p. A-14

39. Times, 11-11-84, *What went wrong?*

40. Times, 11-13-85, *Parting shots*

41. Times, 11-11-84, *Gardner won race because...*

42. Times, 11-7-84, *Negative ads hurt Spellman*

43. Times, 111-11-84, *Real Spellman*; Partlow to author, 2011

44. Partlow to author, 2011

CHAPTER 42: JUDGE NOT

1.   Times, 4-12-85, p. C-2

2.   P-I, 4-12-85, p. A-6

3. Ibid.
4. Ibid.
5. Quoted in *Booth Who?*, p. 135
6. Ibid., p. 147
7. Ibid., p. 186
8. Times 7-26-90, *Spellman to seek high-court seat*
9. Quoted in Dunne, Peter Finley, *Mr. Dooley: In the Hearts of His Countrymen*
10. Times, 8-19-90, *Spellman's court bid raises issues*
11. Ibid.
12. Ibid.
13. Times, 9-16-90, *Spellman stirs up high-court debate*
14. Ibid.
15. Sheldon, *The Washington High Bench*, p. 27
16. Times, 9-16-90, *Spellman stirs up high-court debate*
17. Times, 8-23-90, *Bar rates Guy, Spellman...*
18. Times, 9-16-90, *Spellman stirs up high-court debate*
19. Times, 9-20-90, *Disappointed Spellman*

CHAPTER 43: HE COULDN'T WATCH

1. Thiel, *Out of Left Field*, p. 148-149
2. Times, 10-24-95, *Stadium gets OK*
3. Times, 8-26-95, *Judge rejects challenge*
4. P-I, 6-28-99, p. E-1
5. Thiel, *Out of Left Field*, p. 113
6. Ibid., p. 155
7. Times, 6-10-97, *Referendum 48*
8. Times, 5-18-97, *Kingdome stories*
9. Times, 8-18-97, *What they're saying*
10. P-I, 6-28-99, p. 1
11. TNT, 6-29-1999, *Ugly, perhaps, but Kingdome served us well*

CHAPTER 44: THE OLD GUVS' CLUB

1. P-I, 1-23-07, p. B-2
2. TNT, 3-28-93, p. F-1
3. TNT, 3-8-94, p. A-7
4. Times, 11-14-97, *Ex-governors recall good ol' days*
5. Columbian, 11-14-97, p. 1
6. Columbian, 9-26-97, p. 1
7. S-R, 1-16-03, p. B-3
8. Times, 10-12-04, *Three governors oppose top-two primary*
9. Columbian, 9-21-04, *In Our View*

10. P-I, 10-23-07, *Amendment would lower school levy threshold*
11. TVW, 10-19-07, *State Senior Citizens Foundation Fall Conference*
12. P-I, 1-23-07, p. B-2
13. TVW, 10-19-07, *State Senior Citizens Foundation Fall Conference*
14. P-I, 10-22-08, p. B-7
15. Kitsap Business Journal, 1-8-07, *Remembering our far-from-worst governor*
16. TVW, 1-22-07, *King County Council*
17. Ibid.
18. Ibid.
19. Gregoire Press Conference, 12-15-10, Washington State Archives
20. Q13fox.com, 12-8-11, *Former governor endorses sales tax hike*
21. Gregoire to author, 9-14-12

Spellman does a stint as a guest deejay on KPLU's jazz show in 1983.

BIBLIOGRAPHY

Anderson, Rick,
Seattle Vice,
Sasquatch Books, Seattle, 2010

Andrus, Cecil D., and
Connelly, Joel,
Cecil Andrus, Politics Western Style,
Sasquatch Books, Seattle, 1998

Bartlett, Thomas,
Ireland, A History,
Cambridge University Press,
Cambridge, Mass., 2010

Berentson, Duane,
Life as a Team Player,
self-published, 2008, Washington
State Library, Tumwater. Wash.

Berger, Knute,
Pugetopolis,
Sasquatch Books, Seattle, 2009

Billington, Ken,
People, Politics & Public Power,
Washington PUD Association,
Seattle, 1988

Bischoff, William N., S.J.,
The Jesuits in Old Oregon,
The Caxton Printers Ltd.,
Caldwell, Idaho, 1945

Boswell, Sharon, R.
Frank Atwood, An Oral History,
Washington State Oral
History Program, Office of the
Secretary of State, Olympia, 2003

Boswell, Sharon,
Frank B. Brouillet, An Oral History,
Washington State Oral History
Program, Office of the Secretary of
State, Olympia, 1999

Boswell, Sharon,
R.R. "Bob" Greive, An Oral History,
Washington State Oral History
Program, Office of the Secretary of
State, Olympia, 2001

Boswell, Sharon,
Jeannette Hayner, An Oral History,
Washington State Oral History
Program, Office of the Secretary of
State, Olympia, 2007

Boswell, Sharon,
Charles W. Hodde, An Oral History,
Washington State Oral History
Program, Office of the Secretary of
State, Olympia, 1997

Boswell, Sharon,
Ray Moore, An Oral History,
Washington State Oral History
Program, Office of the Secretary of
State, Olympia, 1999

Boswell, Sharon, and
McConaghy, Lorraine,
*100 Years of a Newspaper and
Its Region,*
The Seattle Times Centennial Project,
1996

Bouton, Jim,
Ball Four, The Final Pitch,
Bulldog Publishing,
North Egremont, Mass., 2000

Brands, H.W.,
American Dreams,
The Penguin Press,
New York, 2010

Brazier, Don,
*History of the Washington
Legislature, 1854–1963,*
Washington State Senate,
Olympia, 2000

Brazier, Don,
History of the Washington
Legislature, 1965-1982,
Washington State Senate,
Olympia, 2007

Bridgman, Dianne,
Richard O. Barnes, An Oral History, Washington State Oral History
Program, Office of the Secretary of
State, Olympia, 1994

Bridgman, Dianne,
Samuel J. Smith, An Oral History, Washington State Oral History
Program, Office of the Secretary of
State, Olympia, 2000

Burns, Robert Ignatius, S.J.,
*The Jesuits and the Indian
Wars of the Northwest,*
Yale University Press,
New Haven, Conn., 1966

Burton-Rose, Daniel, (editor), *Creating
a Movement With Teeth,
A Documentary History of the
George Jackson Brigade,*
PM Press, Oakland, Calif., 2010

Chambliss, William J.,
*On the Take, From Petty Crooks to
Presidents,* Second Edition,
Indiana University Press,
Bloomington, Ind., 1988

Clark, Robert Carlton,
*History of the Willamette Valley Oregon,
Vols. I, II and III,*
S.J. Clarke Publishing Co.,
Chicago, 1927

Clayton, Cornell W., and
Lovrich, Nicholas P., (editors), *Governing Washington,*
WSU Press, Pullman, Wash., 2011

Corr, O. Casey,
*KING, The Bullitts of Seattle and Their
Communications Empire,* University of
Washington Press, Seattle, 1996

Crowley, Walt, and
MacIntosh, Heather,
*The Story of Union Station
in Seattle,*
HistoryLink, Seattle, 1999

Crowley, Walt,
*Rites of Passage, A Memoir of the Sixties
in Seattle,*
University of Washington Press,
Seattle, 1995

Crowley, Walt,
*Seattle University, A Century
of Jesuit Education,*
Seattle University, 1991

Crowley, Walt,
Seattle & King County Timeline,
A HistoryLink Book, Seattle, 2001

Dennett, Eugene V.,
*Agitprop: The Life of An American
Working-Class Radical,*
State University of New York Press,
Albany, N.Y., 1990

Dolan, Edward F.,
America in the Korean War,
The Millbrook Press,
Brookfield, Conn., 1998

Dorpat, Paul,
Seattle Now & Then,
Tartu Publications, Seattle, 1984

Doty, Nancy Talbot,
Duane Berentson, Life as a
Team Player,
privately published, 2008

Dougherty, Phil,
Mudballs Fly at Groundbreaking
for Kingdome,
HistoryLink.org Essay 9359, 2010

Duncan, Don,
Washington, The First 100 Years,
1889-1989,
The Seattle Times, 1989

Emmons, David M.,
Beyond the American Pale,
The Irish in the West, 1845-1910,
University of Oklahoma Press,
Norman, 2010

Eastside Heritage Center,
Lake Washington/The East Side,
Images of America series,
Arcadia Publishing,
San Francisco, 2006

Farris, Scott,
Almost President,
Lyons Press, Guilford, Conn., 2012

Guzzo, Louis R.,
Is It True What They Say
About Dixy?,
The Writing Works,
Mercer Island, Wash., 1980

Halberstam, David,
The Coldest Winter, America and
the Korean War,
Hyperion, New York, 2007

Hughes, John C.,
The Inimitable Adele Ferguson,
A Biography and Oral History,
The Legacy Project, Office of the
Secretary of State,
Gorham Printing,
Centralia, Wash., 2011

Hughes, John C.,
Booth Who?,
Gorham Printing, Centralia, 2010

Hughes, John C.,
Nancy Evans, First Rate, First Lady,
Gorham Printing, Centralia, 2010

Hughes, John C.,
Slade Gorton, A Half Century
in Politics,
Thomson-Shore, 2011

Hughes, John C.,
Charles Z. Smith, An Oral History, The
Legacy Project Web site, 2009

Keane, John F.,
Irish Heritage Club,
Irish Seattle, Images of America, Arcadia
Publishing, Chicago, 2007

Kilgannon, Anne,
Thomas L. Copeland,
An Oral History,
Washington State Oral History
Program, Office of the Secretary of
State, Olympia, 2007

Kilgannon, Anne,
Don Eldridge, An Oral History, Wash-
ington State Oral History Program,
Office of the Secretary of State,
Olympia, 2005

Kilgannon, Anne,
Joel M. Pritchard, An Oral History,
Washington State Oral History
Program, Office of the Secretary of
State, Olympia, 2000

Kink, Steve, and Cahill, John,
Class Wars,
Washington Education
Association, Federal Way, Wash., 2004

MacIntosh, Heather,
*John Spellman, King County Politics
in the Sixties, Seventies and Beyond,*
HistoryLink.org Essay 2200, 2000

MacIntosh, Heather,
*Kingdome: The Controversial Birth
of a Seattle Icon,*
HistoryLink.org Essay 2164, 2000

McDonald, Lucile,
The Lake Washington Story,
Superior Publishing Co., Seattle, 1979

Miller, Gary K.,
*Energy Northwest, A History of the
Washington Public Power Supply System,*
Energy Northwest, 2001

Mitchell, Greg,
Tricky Dick and the Pink Lady, Random
House, New York, 1998

Morgan, Murray,
Skid Road, revised edition,
Comstock Editions,
Sausalito, Calif., 1978

Morgan, Murray,
*Century 21, The Story of the
Seattle World's Fair, 1962,*
Acme Press, Seattle, 1963

Morgan, Murray, and
Morgan, Lane, with Dorpat, Paul,
Seattle, A Pictorial History,
Donning Company,
Norfolk/Virigina Beach, Va., 1982

Nelson, Gerald B.,
*Seattle, The Life and Times
of an American City,*
Alfred A. Knopf, New York, 1977

Norwich, John Julius,
*Absolute Monarchs, A History
of the Papacy,*
Random House, New York, 2011

Oldham, Kit,
*King County Holds First Primary
Election Under New Charter,*
HistoryLink.org Essay 7945, 2006

Oldham, Kit,
*King County Farmland
Preservation Program,*
HistoryLink.org Essay 7691, 2006

Pioneer Historical Publishing Co.,
*Seattle and Chicago, Seattle and Its
Environs, 1852-1924, Vol. II,*
1924

Sale, Roger,
Seattle Past to Present,
University of Washington Press,
Seattle, 1976

Sanders, Jeffrey Craig,
*Seattle & the Roots of
Urban Sustainability,*
University of Pittsburgh Press,
Pittsburgh, Pa., 2010

Santos, Bob,
Hum Bows, Not Hot Dogs!,
International Examiner Press,
Seattle, 2002

Scates, Shelby,
Warren G. Magnuson,
University of Washington Press,
Seattle, 1997

Scott, George W.,
A Majority of One: Legislative Life,
Civitas Press, Seattle, 2002

Scott, George W., (editor),
*Turning Points in Washington's
Public Life,*
Civitas Press, Seattle, 2011

Seeberger, Edward D.,
Sine Die, 1997 Edition,
University of Washington Press,
Seattle, 1997

Sell, T.M,
Wings of Power,
University of Washington Press,
Seattle, 2001

Sheldon, Charles H.,
The Washington High Bench,
WSU Press, Pullman, Wash., 1992

Singler, Joan; Durning, Jean;
Valentine, Betty Lou; Adams, Maid,
Seattle in Black and White,
University of Washington Press,
Seattle, 2011

Smith, Payton,
Rosellini,
University of Washington Press,
Seattle, 1997

Steiner, Frederick R., and
Theilacker, John E., (editors)
Protecting Farmlands,
AVI Publishing Co.,
Westport, Conn., 1984

Stratton, Eugene Aubrey,
Plymouth Colony, Its History &
People 1620-1691,
Ancestry Publishing, 1986

Taylor, Quintard,
The Forging of a Black Community,
Seattle's Central District from 1870
through the Civil Rights Era, University
of Washington Press, Seattle, 1994

Tate, Cassandra,
James Reed Ellis,
HistoryLink.org Essay 7833, 2006

Thiel, Art,
Out of Left Field,
Sasquatch Books, Seattle, 2003

Time magazine,
1968, The Year That Changed the World,
Time Books, New York, 2008

Torrance, Roscoe C., with
Karolevitz, Bob,
Torchy!,
Dakota Homestead Publishers,
Mission Hill, S.D., 1988

Verhovek, Sam Howe,
Jet Age, The Comet, the 707 and the
race to shrink the world, Avery,
the Penguin Group, New York, 2010

Warren, James R.,
Seattle, 150 Years of Progress, Heritage
Media Corp., Carlsbad, Calif., 2001

Waterhouse, Fred J.,
The Rakkasans Airborne, 187th
'The Steel Berets,'
Turner Publishing Co.,
Paducah, Ky., 1997

Watson, Emmett,
Digressions of a Native Son,
The Pacific Institute,
Seattle, 1982

Watson, Emmett,
Once Upon a Time in Seattle,
Lesser Seattle Publishing, Seattle, 1992

Watson, Emmett,
My Life in Print,
Lesser Seattle Publishing, Seattle, 1993

Willison, George F.,
Saints and Strangers,
Reynal & Hitchcock, New York, 1945

Wright, Mary C., (editor),
More Voices, New Stories, King County,
Washington's first 150 years,
King County Landmarks & Heritage
Commission, Pacific Northwest
Historians Guild, Seattle, 2002

ABOUT THE AUTHOR

John C. Hughes joined the Office of the Secretary of State as chief oral historian in 2008 after a 42-year career in journalism, retiring as editor and publisher of *The Daily World* at Aberdeen. He is a former trustee of the Washington State Historical Society and an award-winning investigative reporter, columnist and historian. Hughes is the author of six other books: *On the Harbor, From Black Friday to Nirvana,* with Ryan Teague Beckwith; *Booth Who?,* a biography of Booth Gardner; *Nancy Evans, First-rate First Lady; Lillian Walker, Washington State Civil Rights Pioneer; The Inimitable Adele Ferguson,* and *Slade Gorton, A Half Century in Politics.*

John Hughes with his Washington State Heritage Center Legacy Project teammates, Lori Larson, left, and Trova Heffernan.

INDEX